Apache Spark Deep Learning Cookbook

Over 80 recipes that streamline deep learning in a distributed environment with Apache Spark

Ahmed Sherif
Amrith Ravindra

BIRMINGHAM - MUMBAI

Apache Spark Deep Learning Cookbook

Commissioning Editor: Amey Varangaonkar
Acquisition Editor: Tushar Gupta
Content Development Editor: Snehal Kolte
Technical Editor: Dharmendra Yadav
Copy Editors: Safis Editing, Vikrant Phadkay
Project Coordinator: Manthan Patel
Proofreader: Safis Editing
Indexer: Aishwarya Gangawane
Graphics: Jisha Chirayil
Production Coordinator: Nilesh Mohite

First published: July 2018

Production reference: 1090718

Published by Packt Publishing Ltd.
Livery Place
35 Livery Street
Birmingham
B3 2PB, UK.

ISBN 978-1-78847-422-1

www.packtpub.com

31. VNC Viewer may be downloaded using the following link:

    ```
    https://www.realvnc.com/en/connect/download/viewer/
    ```

32. Once installed, click to open VNC Viewer and in the search bar, type in `localhost::5901`, as shown in the following screenshot:

33. Next, click on **continue** when prompted with the following screen:

```
[Amriths-MacBook-Air:~ Chanti$ gcloud compute ssh \
[> ubuntuvm1 \
[> --zone us-east1-b \
[> --project arctic-column-189121 \
[> --ssh-flag "-L 5901:localhost:5901"
Warning: Permanently added 'compute.8215749887981449261' (ECDSA) to the list of
known hosts.
Welcome to Ubuntu 16.04.3 LTS (GNU/Linux 4.13.0-1002-gcp x86_64)

 * Documentation:  https://help.ubuntu.com
 * Management:     https://landscape.canonical.com
 * Support:        https://ubuntu.com/advantage

  Get cloud support with Ubuntu Advantage Cloud Guest:
    http://www.ubuntu.com/business/services/cloud

0 packages can be updated.
0 updates are security updates.


*** System restart required ***

The programs included with the Ubuntu system are free software;
the exact distribution terms for each program are described in the
individual files in /usr/share/doc/*/copyright.

Ubuntu comes with ABSOLUTELY NO WARRANTY, to the extent permitted by
applicable law.

WARNING! Your environment specifies an invalid locale.
 The unknown environment variables are:
   LC_CTYPE=UTF-8 LC_ALL=
 This can affect your user experience significantly, including the
 ability to manage packages. You may install the locales by running:

    sudo apt-get install language-pack-UTF-8
      or
    sudo locale-gen UTF-8

To see all available language packs, run:
    apt-cache search "^language-pack-[a-z][a-z]$"
To disable this message for all users, run:
    sudo touch /var/lib/cloud/instance/locale-check.skip

Chanti@ubuntuvm1:~$
```

30. Once you see the name of your instance followed by " : ~ $ ", it means that a connection has successfully been established between the local host/laptop and the Google Cloud instance. After successfully SSHing into the instance, we require software called **VNC Viewer** to view and interact with the Ubuntu Desktop that has now been successfully set up on the Google Cloud Compute engine. The following few steps will discuss how this is achieved.

`mapt.io`

Mapt is an online digital library that gives you full access to over 5,000 books and videos, as well as industry leading tools to help you plan your personal development and advance your career. For more information, please visit our website.

Why subscribe?

- Spend less time learning and more time coding with practical eBooks and Videos from over 4,000 industry professionals

- Improve your learning with Skill Plans built especially for you

- Get a free eBook or video every month

- Mapt is fully searchable

- Copy and paste, print, and bookmark content

PacktPub.com

Did you know that Packt offers eBook versions of every book published, with PDF and ePub files available? You can upgrade to the eBook version at `www.PacktPub.com` and as a print book customer, you are entitled to a discount on the eBook copy. Get in touch with us at `service@packtpub.com` for more details.

At `www.PacktPub.com`, you can also read a collection of free technical articles, sign up for a range of free newsletters, and receive exclusive discounts and offers on Packt books and eBooks.

Foreword

If you are reading that, it's safe to assume that you are well-aware of the tremendous impact of **Artificial Intelligence (AI)** and **Machine Learning (ML)**, and the uncanny effectiveness of deep neural networks. Matei Zaharia and his team started Spark, not as a competitor to Hadoop, but rather as an effort towards the democratization of AI and ML. As Zaharia has famously said, *The only focus in Spark is how you compute stuff, not where you store it*. Dubbed as unified analytics engine for large-scale data processing, Spark is optimized for resilience, speed, ease of use, generality, and run-everywhere features, and this book does a phenomenal job explaining it to you, converting you to a spark enthusiast.

As a reader, if you are excited about getting started with Spark's application in deep learning, this book can help. The authors begin by helping to set up Spark for Deep Learning development by providing clear and concisely written recipes. The initial setup is naturally followed by creating a neural network, elaborating on the pain points of convolutional neural networks, and recurrent neural networks. AI find new use cases every day, mostly starting with verticals. In the practitioner's spirit, authors provided practical (yet simplified) use cases of predicting fire department calls with SparkML, real estate value prediction using XGBoost, predicting the stock market cost of Apple with LSTM, and creating a movie recommendation engine with Keras.

The AI and ML landscape is nothing if not heterogeneous; the dizzying diversity of toolset and libraries can be intimidating. The authors do an excellent job mixing it up with different libraries, and incorporating relevant yet diverse technologies as the reader moves forward in the book. As deep learning frameworks start to converge and move up in abstraction, the scale of the exploratory data analysis inevitably grows. That's why instead of creating a proverbial one-trick pony (or YOLO model, pun intended), the book covers pertinent and highly relevant technologies such as LSTMs in Generative Networks, natural language processing with TF-IDF, face recognition using deep convolutional networks, creating and visualizing word vectors using Word2Vec and image classification with TensorFlow on Spark. Aside from crisp and focused writing, this wide array of highly relevant ML and deep learning topics give the book its core strength.

I have had a unique opportunity to see Spark in action, both in academia and in the industry. As a Stanford visiting scholar, I have attended various sessions by Matei Zaharia, the co-creator of Spark and enjoyed his vision concerning Databricks, the operationalization of algorithms at scale, and future of big data. At the same time as a practitioner and chief architect of AI and ML, I witness first-hand how world's largest retailer labs standardized their operational ML model deployments with Spark. As cloud enables new data application architectures, I see Spark as a key enabler and accelerator for new and unpreceded ML implementations across a variety of industry verticals. The rationale is quite simple; C-suite looks at cutting-edge modern technology to go beyond typical developer's hello world test or a science project. It needs to solve a real-world business problem at scale, have a thriving eco-system, and ability to provide enterprise-grade SLAs with around the clock support. Spark fulfill all these criteria; and goes beyond the basics with unprecedented speed, resilience, and community adaption. Spark is regularly used in advance analytics; use cases such as complex outlier analysis for system telemetry that observes and perceives meaningful patterns prior to these becoming unanticipated problems, or a missed opportunity as outliers can be both. Consider Spark as a tool that bridges the gap between traditional BI, and modern ML enabled services for delivering meaningful business outcomes. As data becomes the central competitive advantage, it is crucial to see disruptions before they occur, all while keeping account of seasonality, cyclicity, and ever-increasing temporal correlations. Ease of operationalization is the key to industry adaption, and that's where Spark shines like no other; data to insight, and insight to action.

This manuscript you are holding is another step towards democratization of AI, and ML by providing you the tools and techniques to apply in real-world problems. Consider it your head start on a journey of discovery, to become not a Spark superstar but rather a well-rounded ML engineer and evangelist. We hope this book will help you leverage Apache Spark to tackle business and technology-related issues easily, and efficiently.

Adnan Masood, PhD
Visiting Scholar, Dept. of Computer Engineering. Stanford University
Chief Architect AI & ML – Microsoft MVP
Gates Computer Science Building, Stanford.
June 12th, 2018

Contributors

About the authors

Ahmed Sherif is a data scientist who has been working with data in various roles since 2005. He started off with BI solutions and transitioned to data science in 2013. In 2016, he obtained a master's in Predictive Analytics from Northwestern University, where he studied the science and application of machine learning and predictive modeling using both Python and R. As a data scientist, he strives to architect predictive capabilities with big data solutions for companies to better leverage their data and make more informed decisions. Lately, he has been developing machine learning and deep learning solutions on the cloud using Azure. In 2016, he published his first book, Practical Business Intelligence. He currently works as a Technology Solution Profession in Data and AI for Microsoft.

> *I would like to begin by thanking my wife, Ameena, and my three lovely children, Safiya, Hamza, and Layla, for giving me the strength and support to complete this book. I could not have done it without their love and support. I would also like to thank my co-author, Amrith, for all of his hard work and determination to write this book with me.*

Amrith Ravindra is a machine learning enthusiast who holds degrees in electrical and industrial engineering. While pursuing his masters he dove deeper into the world of ML and developed love for data science. Graduate level courses in engineering gave him the mathematical background to launch himself into a career in ML. He met Ahmed Sherif at a local data science meetup in Tampa. They decided to put their brains together to write a book on their favorite ML algorithms. He hopes that this book will help him achieve his ultimate goal of becoming a data scientist and actively contributing to ML.

> *I would like to begin by thanking Ahmed for giving me this opportunity to work alongside him. Working on this book has been a better learning experience for me than college itself. Next, I would like to thank my mum dad and sister, who have continued to give me motivation and instilled in me the desire to succeed. Finally, I would like to thank my friends, without whose criticism I would have never grown so much as a human.*

About the reviewers

Michal Malohlava, the creator of Sparkling Water, is a geek and developer; as well as being a Java, Linux, programming languages enthusiast who has been developing software for over 10 years. He obtained his Ph.D. from Charles University in Prague in 2012 and post-doctorate from Purdue University. He participates in the development of the H2O platform for advanced big data math and computation, and its incorporation in into Spark engine published as a project called Sparkling Water.

Adnan Masood, Ph.D. is an AI and ML researcher, software architect, and Microsoft MVP for Data Platform. He currently works at UST Global as Chief Architect of AI and ML, where he collaborates with Stanford Artificial Intelligence Lab, and MIT AI Lab for building enterprise solutions. A Visiting Scholar at Stanford University and author of Amazon bestseller in programming languages, *Functional Programming with F#*, His recent talk at **Women in Technology Conference**, Denver highlighted the importance of diversity in STEM and technology areas and was featured by a variety of news outlets.

Packt is searching for authors like you

If you're interested in becoming an author for Packt, please visit authors.packtpub.com and apply today. We have worked with thousands of developers and tech professionals, just like you, to help them share their insight with the global tech community. You can make a general application, apply for a specific hot topic that we are recruiting an author for, or submit your own idea.

Table of Contents

Preface

With deep learning gaining rapid mainstream adoption in modern-day industries, organizations are looking for ways to unite popular big data tools with highly efficient deep learning libraries. This will help deep learning models train with higher efficiency and speed.

With the help of *Apache Spark Deep Learning Cookbook*, you'll work through specific recipes to generate outcomes for deep learning algorithms without getting bogged down in theory. From setting up Apache Spark for deep learning to implementing types of neural nets, this book tackles both common and not-so-common problems in order to perform deep learning on a distributed environment. In addition to this, you'll get access to deep learning code within Spark that can be reused to answer similar problems or tweaked to answer slightly different problems. You'll also learn how to stream and cluster your data with Spark. Once you have got to grips with the basics, you'll explore how to implement and deploy deep learning models such as CNN, RNN, and LSTMs in Spark using popular libraries such as TensorFlow and Keras. At the end of the day, this is a cookbook designed to teach how to practically apply models on Spark, so we will not dive into the theory and math behind the models used in this chapter, although we will reference where additional information on each model can be obtained.

By the end of the book, you'll have the expertise to train and deploy efficient deep learning models on Apache Spark.

Who this book is for

This book is for anyone with a basic understanding of machine learning and big data concepts and who is looking to expand their understanding through a top-down rather than a bottom-up approach. This book gives access to deep learning as well as machine learning algorithms in a plug-and-play fashion. Anyone without previous programming experience, especially with Python, can easily implement the algorithms in this book by following the recipes step by step as instructed. Most of the code in this book is self-explanatory. Each code block performs one particular function or executes on the action in mining, manipulating, transforming, and fitting data to deep learning models.

This book is intended to give the reader both hands-on experience through fun projects such as stock price prediction, as well as a more solid understanding of deep learning and machine learning concepts This is possible the numerous links provided to online resources, such as published papers, tutorials, and guides, throughout every chapter in the book.

What this book covers

Chapter 1, *Setting Up Spark For Deep Learning*, covers everything you need in order to get started developing on Spark within a virtual Ubuntu Desktop environment.

Chapter 2, *Creating a Neural Network with Spark*, explains the process of developing a neural network from scratch without using any deep learning libraries, such as TensorFlow or Keras.

Chapter 3, *Pain Points of Convolutional Neural Networks*, walks through some of the pain points associated with working on a convolutional neural network for image recognition, and how they can be overcome.

Chapter 4, *Pain Points of Recurrent Neural Networks*, covers an introduction to feedforward neural networks and recurrent neural network. We describe some of the pain points that arise with recurrent neural networks and also how to tackle them with the use of LSTMs.

Chapter 5, *Predicting Fire Department Calls with Spark ML*, walks through developing a classification model for predicting fire department calls from the city of San Francisco using Spark machine learning.

Chapter 6, *Using LSTMs in Generative Networks*, gives a hands-on approach to using novels or large text corpora as input data to define and train an LSTM model, while also using the trained model to generate its own output sequences.

Chapter 7, *Natural Language Processing with TF-IDF*, walks through the steps to classify chatbot conversation data for escalation.

Chapter 8, *Real Estate Value Prediction Using XGBoost*, focuses on using the Kings County House Sales dataset to train a simple linear model and uses it to predict house prices before diving into a slightly more complicated model to do the same and improve prediction accuracy.

Chapter 9, *Predicting AAPL Stock Market Price with LSTMs*, focuses on creating a deep learning model using LSTM on Keras to predict the stock market price of the AAPL stock.

Chapter 10, *Face Recognition Using Deep Convolutional Networks*, utilizes the MIT-CBCL dataset of facial images of 10 different subjects to train and test a deep convolutional neural network model.

Chapter 11, *Creating and Visualizing Word Vectors Using Word2Vec*, focuses on the importance of vectors in machine learning, and also walks users through how to utilize Google's Word2Vec model to train a different model and visualize word vectors generated from novels.

Chapter 12, *Creating a Movie Recommendation Engine with Keras*, focuses on building a movie recommendation engine for users using the deep learning library Keras.

Chapter 13, *Image Classification with TensorFlow on Spark*, focuses on leveraging transfer learning to recognize the top two football players in the world: Cristiano Ronaldo and Lionel Messi.

To get the most out of this book

1. Utilize all the links provided to gain a better understanding of some of the terms used in this book.
2. The Internet is the biggest university in today's world. Use websites such as YouTube, Udemy, edX, Lynda, and Coursera for their videos about various deep learning and machine learning concepts.
3. Don't just read the book and forget about it. Practically implement each step while reading the book. It is recommended that you have your Jupyter Notebook open while going through each recipe so that you can work through every recipe while reading the book and simultaneously check the outputs you obtain for each of the steps mentioned.

Download the example code files

You can download the example code files for this book from your account at www.packtpub.com. If you purchased this book elsewhere, you can visit www.packtpub.com/support and register to have the files emailed directly to you.

You can download the code files by following these steps:

1. Log in or register at www.packtpub.com.
2. Select the **SUPPORT** tab.
3. Click on **Code Downloads & Errata**.
4. Enter the name of the book in the **Search** box and follow the onscreen instructions.

Once the file is downloaded, please make sure that you unzip or extract the folder using the latest version of:

- WinRAR/7-Zip for Windows
- Zipeg/iZip/UnRarX for Mac
- 7-Zip/PeaZip for Linux

The code bundle for the book is also hosted on GitHub at https://github.com/ PacktPublishing/Apache-Spark-Deep-Learning-Cookbook. In case there's an update to the code, it will be updated on the existing GitHub repository.

We also have other code bundles from our rich catalog of books and videos available at https://github.com/PacktPublishing/. Check them out!

Conventions used

There are a number of text conventions used throughout this book.

CodeInText: Indicates code words in text, database table names, folder names, filenames, file extensions, pathnames, dummy URLs, user input, and Twitter handles. Here is an example: "Save under the trained folder inside the working directory."

A block of code is set as follows:

```
print('Total Rows')
df.count()
print('Rows without Null values')
df.dropna().count()
print('Row with Null Values')
df.count()-df.dropna().count()
```

Any command-line input or output is written as follows:

```
nltk.download("punkt")
nltk.download("stopwords")
```

Bold: Indicates a new term, an important word, or words that you see on screen. For example, words in menus or dialog boxes appear in the text like this. Here is an example: "Right-click on the page and click on **Save As...**"

Warnings or important notes appear like this.

Tips and tricks appear like this.

Sections

In this book, you will find several headings that appear frequently (*Getting ready, How to do it..., How it works..., There's more...,* and *See also*).

To give clear instructions on how to complete a recipe, use these sections as follows:

Getting ready

This section tells you what to expect in the recipe and describes how to set up any software or any preliminary settings required for the recipe.

How to do it...

This section contains the steps required to follow the recipe.

How it works...

This section usually consists of a detailed explanation of what happened in the previous section.

There's more...

This section consists of additional information about the recipe in order to make you more knowledgeable about the recipe.

See also

This section provides helpful links to other useful information for the recipe.

Get in touch

Feedback from our readers is always welcome.

General feedback: Email feedback@packtpub.com and mention the book title in the subject of your message. If you have questions about any aspect of this book, please email us at questions@packtpub.com.

Errata: Although we have taken every care to ensure the accuracy of our content, mistakes do happen. If you have found a mistake in this book, we would be grateful if you would report this to us. Please visit www.packtpub.com/submit-errata, selecting your book, clicking on the Errata Submission Form link, and entering the details.

Piracy: If you come across any illegal copies of our works in any form on the internet, we would be grateful if you would provide us with the location address or website name. Please contact us at copyright@packtpub.com with a link to the material.

If you are interested in becoming an author: If there is a topic that you have expertise in and you are interested in either writing or contributing to a book, please visit authors.packtpub.com.

Reviews

Please leave a review. Once you have read and used this book, why not leave a review on the site that you purchased it from? Potential readers can then see and use your unbiased opinion to make purchase decisions, we at Packt can understand what you think about our products, and our authors can see your feedback on their book. Thank you!

For more information about Packt, please visit packtpub.com.

Setting Up Spark for Deep Learning Development

1

In this chapter, the following recipes will be covered:

- Downloading an Ubuntu Desktop image
- Installing and configuring Ubuntu with VMWare Fusion on macOS
- Installing and configuring Ubuntu with Oracle VirtualBox on Windows
- Installing and configuring Ubuntu Desktop for Google Cloud Platform
- Installing and configuring Spark and prerequisites on Ubuntu Desktop
- Integrating Jupyter notebooks with Spark
- Starting and configuring a Spark cluster
- Stopping a Spark cluster

Introduction

Deep learning is the focused study of machine learning algorithms that deploy neural networks as their main method of learning. Deep learning has exploded onto the scene just within the last couple of years. Microsoft, Google, Facebook, Amazon, Apple, Tesla and many other companies are all utilizing deep learning models in their apps, websites, and products. At the same exact time, Spark, an in-memory compute engine running on top of big data sources, has made it easy to process volumes of information at record speeds and ease. In fact, Spark has now become the leading big data development tool for data engineers, machine learning engineers, and data scientists.

Since deep learning models perform better with more data, the synergy between Spark and deep learning allowed for a perfect marriage. Almost as important as the code used to execute deep learning algorithms is the work environment that enables optimal development. Many talented minds are eager to develop neural networks to help answer important questions in their research. Unfortunately, one of the greatest barriers to the development of deep learning models is access to the necessary technical resources required to learn on big data. The purpose of this chapter is to create an ideal virtual development environment for deep learning on Spark.

Downloading an Ubuntu Desktop image

Spark can be set up for all types of operating systems, whether they reside on-premise or in the cloud. For our purposes, Spark will be installed on a Linux-based virtual machine with Ubuntu as the operating system. There are several advantages to using Ubuntu as the go-to virtual machine, not least of which is cost. Since they are based on open source software, Ubuntu operating systems are free to use and do not require licensing. Cost is always a consideration and one of the main goals of this publication is to minimize the financial footprint required to get started with deep learning on top of a Spark framework.

Getting ready

There are some minimum recommendations required for downloading the image file:

- Minimum of 2 GHz dual-core processor
- Minimum of 2 GB system memory
- Minimum of 25 GB of free hard drive space

How to do it...

Follow the steps in the recipe to download an Ubuntu Desktop image:

1. In order to create a virtual machine of Ubuntu Desktop, it is necessary to first download the file from the official website: `https://www.ubuntu.com/download/desktop`.
2. As of this writing, Ubuntu Desktop 16.04.3 is the most recent available version for download.

3. Access the following file in a `.iso` format once the download is complete:

```
ubuntu-16.04.3-desktop-amd64.iso
```

How it works...

Virtual environments provide an optimal development workspace by isolating the relationship to the physical or host machine. Developers may be using all types of machines for their host environments such as a MacBook running macOS, a Microsoft Surface running Windows or even a virtual machine on the cloud with Microsoft Azure or AWS; however, to ensure consistency within the output of the code executed, a virtual environment within Ubuntu Desktop will be deployed that can be used and shared among a wide variety of host platforms.

There's more...

There are several options for desktop virtualization software, depending on whether the host environment is on a Windows or a macOS. There are two common software applications for virtualization when using macOS:

- VMWare Fusion
- Parallels

See also

To learn more about Ubuntu Desktop, you can visit `https://www.ubuntu.com/desktop`.

Installing and configuring Ubuntu with VMWare Fusion on macOS

This section will focus on building a virtual machine using an Ubuntu operating system with **VMWare Fusion**.

Getting ready

A previous installation of VMWare Fusion is required on your system. If you do not currently have this, you can download a trial version from the following website:

`https://www.vmware.com/products/fusion/fusion-evaluation.html`

How to do it...

Follow the steps in the recipe to configure Ubuntu with VMWare Fusion on macOS:

1. Once VMWare Fusion is up and running, click on the + button on the upper-left-hand side to begin the configuration process and select **New...**, as seen in the following screenshot:

2. Once the selection has been made, select the option to **Install from Disk or Image**, as seen in the following screenshot:

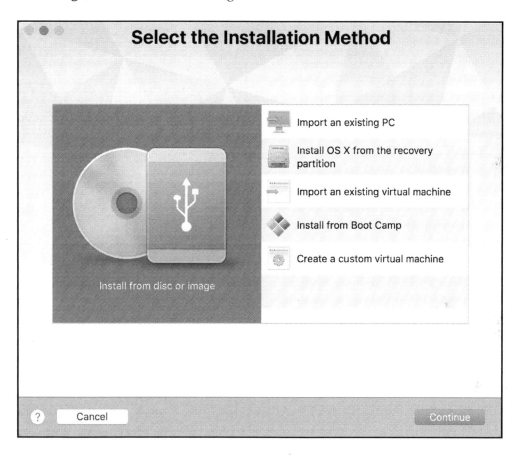

3. Select the operating system's `iso` file that was downloaded from the Ubuntu Desktop website, as seen in the following screenshot:

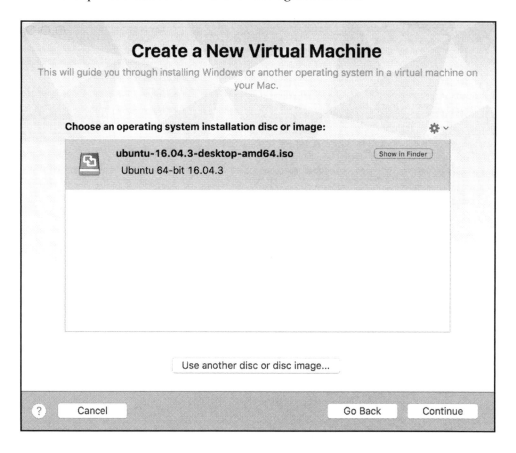

4. The next step will ask whether you want to choose **Linux Easy Install**. It is recommended to do so, as well as to incorporate a **Display Name/Password** combination for the Ubuntu environment, as seen in the following screenshot:

5. The configuration process is almost complete. A **Virtual Machine Summary** is displayed with the option to **Customize Settings** to increase the **Memory** and **Hard Disk,** as seen in the following screenshot:

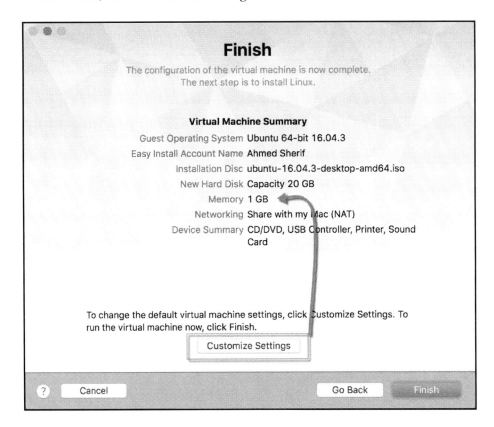

6. Anywhere from 20 to 40 GB hard disk space is sufficient for the virtual machine; however, bumping up the memory to either 2 GB or even 4 GB will assist with the performance of the virtual machine when executing Spark code in later chapters. Update the memory by selecting **Processors** and **Memory** under the **Settings** of the virtual machine and increasing the **Memory** to the desired amount, as seen in the following screenshot:

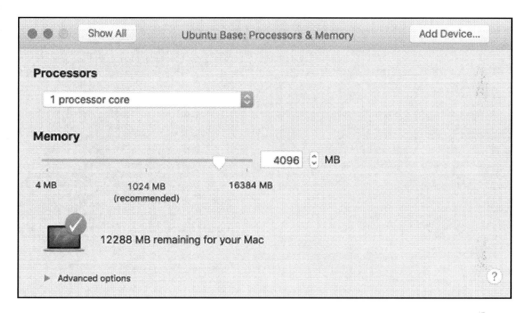

How it works...

The setup allows for manual configuration of the settings necessary to get Ubuntu Desktop up and running successfully on VMWare Fusion. The memory and hard drive storage can be increased or decreased based on the needs and availability of the host machine.

There's more...

All that is remaining is to fire up the virtual machine for the first time, which initiates the installation process of the system onto the virtual machine. Once all the setup is complete and the user has logged in, the Ubuntu virtual machine should be available for development, as seen in the following screenshot:

See also

Aside from VMWare Fusion, there is also another product that offers similar functionality on a Mac. It is called Parallels Desktop for Mac. To learn more about VMWare and Parallels, and decide which program is a better fit for your development, visit the following websites:

- `https://www.vmware.com/products/fusion.html` to download and install VMWare Fusion for Mac
- `https://parallels.com` to download and install the Parallels Desktop for Mac

Installing and configuring Ubuntu with Oracle VirtualBox on Windows

Unlike with macOS, there are several options to virtualize systems within Windows. This mainly has to do with the fact that virtualization on Windows is very common as most developers are using Windows as their host environment and need virtual environments for testing purposes without affecting any of the dependencies that rely on Windows.

Getting ready

VirtualBox from Oracle is a common virtualization product and is free to use. Oracle VirtualBox provides a straightforward process to get an Ubuntu Desktop virtual machine up and running on top of a Windows environment.

How to do it...

Follow the steps in this recipe to configure Ubuntu with **VirtualBox** on Windows:

1. Initiate an **Oracle VM VirtualBox Manager**. Next, create a new virtual machine by selecting the **New** icon and specify the **Name**, **Type**, and **Version** of the machine, as seen in the following screenshot:

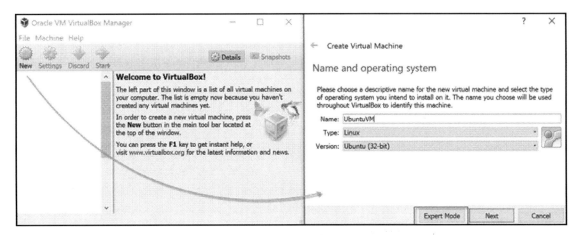

2. Select **Expert Mode** as several of the configuration steps will get consolidated, as seen in the following screenshot:

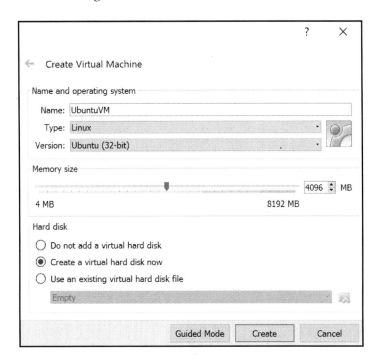

Ideal memory size should be set to at least 2048 MB, or preferably 4096 MB, depending on the resources available on the host machine.

3. Additionally, set an optimal hard disk size for an Ubuntu virtual machine performing deep learning algorithms to at least 20 GB, if not more, as seen in the following screenshot:

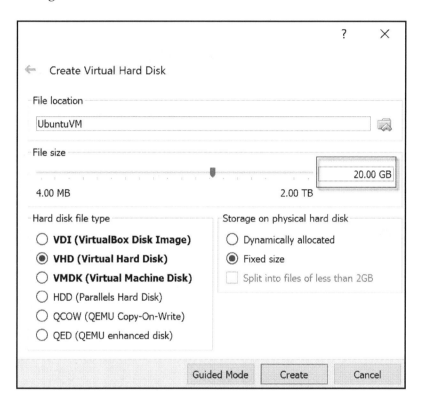

4. Point the virtual machine manager to the **start-up disk** location where the Ubuntu `iso` file was downloaded to and then **Start** the creation process, as seen in the following screenshot:

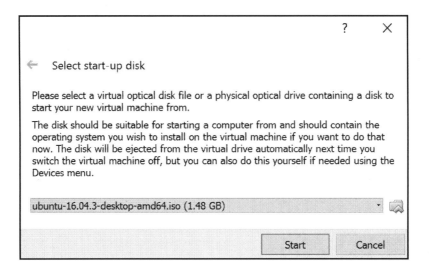

5. After allotting some time for the installation, select the Start icon to complete the virtual machine and get it ready for development as seen in the following screenshot:

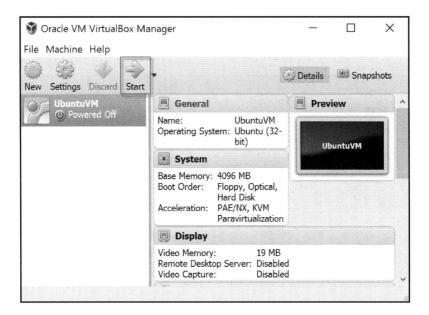

How it works...

The setup allows for manual configuration of the settings necessary to get Ubuntu Desktop up and running successfully on Oracle VirtualBox. As was the case with VMWare Fusion, the memory and hard drive storage can be increased or decreased based on the needs and availability of the host machine.

There's more...

Please note that some machines that run Microsoft Windows are not set up by default for virtualization and users may receive an initial error indicating the VT-x is not enabled. This can be reversed and virtualization may be enabled in the BIOS during a reboot.

See also

To learn more about Oracle VirtualBox and decide whether or not it is a good fit, visit the following website and select **Windows hosts** to begin the download process: `https://www.virtualbox.org/wiki/Downloads`.

Installing and configuring Ubuntu Desktop for Google Cloud Platform

Previously, we saw how Ubuntu Desktop could be set up locally using VMWare Fusion. In this section, we will learn how to do the same on **Google Cloud Platform**.

Getting ready

The only requirement is a Google account username. Begin by logging in to your Google Cloud Platform using your Google account. Google provides a free 12-month subscription with $300 credited to your account. The setup will ask for your bank details; however, Google will not charge you for anything without explicitly letting you know first. Go ahead and verify your bank account and you are good to go.

How to do it...

Follow the steps in the recipe to configure Ubuntu Desktop for Google Cloud Platform:

1. Once logged in to your **Google Cloud Platform**, access a dashboard that looks like the one in the following screenshot:

Google Cloud Platform Dashboard

2. First, click on the product services button in the top-left-hand corner of your screen. In the drop-down menu, under **Compute**, click on **VM instances,** as shown in the following screenshot:

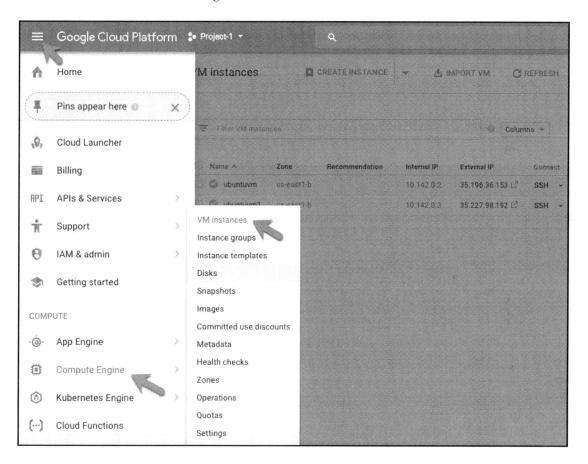

3. Create a new instance and name it. We are naming it ubuntuvm1 in our case. Google Cloud automatically creates a project while launching an instance and the instance will be launched under a project ID. The project may be renamed if required.

4. After clicking on **Create Instance**, select the zone/area you are located in.

5. Select **Ubuntu 16.04LTS** under the boot disk as this is the operating system that will be installed in the cloud. Please note that LTS stands for version, and will have **long-term support** from Ubuntu's developers.

6. Next, under the boot disk options, select **SSD persistent disk** and increase the size to 50 GB for some added storage space for the instance, as shown in the following screenshot:

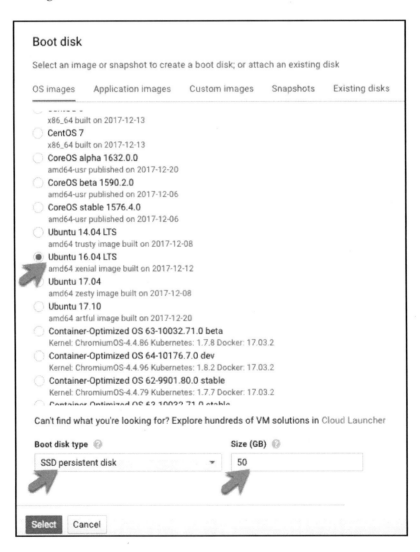

7. Next, set **Access scopes** to **Allow full access to all Cloud APIs**.
8. Under firewall, please check to **allow HTTP traffic** as well as **allow HTTPS traffic**, as shown in the following screenshot:

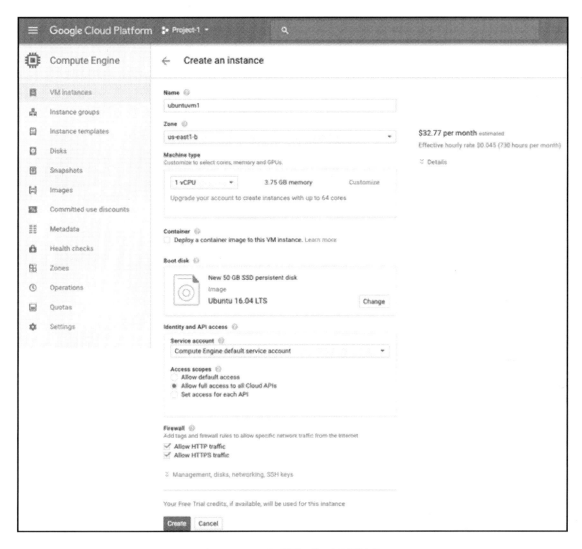

Selecting options Allow HTTP traffic and HTTPS Traffic

9. Once the instance is configured as shown in this section, go ahead and create the instance by clicking on the **Create** button.

After clicking on the **Create** button, you will notice that the instance gets created with a unique internal as well as external IP address. We will require this at a later stage. SSH refers to secure shell tunnel, which is basically an encrypted way of communicating in client-server architectures. Think of it as data going to and from your laptop, as well as going to and from Google's cloud servers, through an encrypted tunnel.

10. Click on the newly created instance. From the drop-down menu, click on **open in browser window**, as shown in the following screenshot:

11. You will see that Google opens up a shell/terminal in a new window, as shown in the following screenshot:

12. Once the shell is open, you should have a window that looks like the following screenshot:

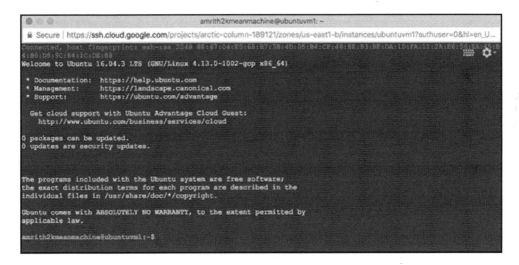

13. Type the following commands in the Google cloud shell:

```
$ sudo apt-get update
$ sudo apt-get upgrade
$ sudo apt-get install gnome-shell
$ sudo apt-get install ubuntu-gnome-desktop
$ sudo apt-get install autocutsel
$ sudo apt-get install gnome-core
$ sudo apt-get install gnome-panel
$ sudo apt-get install gnome-themes-standard
```

14. When presented with a prompt to continue or not, type `y` and select **ENTER**, as shown in the following screenshot:

```
After this operation, 869 MB of additional disk space will be used.
Do you want to continue? [Y/n] y
```

15. Once done with the preceding steps, type the following commands to set up the `vncserver` and allow connections to the local shell:

```
$ sudo apt-get install tightvncserver
$ touch ~/.Xresources
```

16. Next, launch the server by typing the following command:

```
$ tightvncserver
```

17. This will prompt you to enter a password, which will later be used to log in to the Ubuntu Desktop virtual machine. This password is limited to eight characters and needs to be set and verified, as shown in the following screenshot:

```
amrith2kmeanmachine@ubuntuvml:~$ vncserver

You will require a password to access your desktops.

Password:
Verify:
Would you like to enter a view-only password (y/n)? n
```

18. A startup script is automatically generated by the shell, as shown in the following screenshot. This startup script can be accessed and edited by copying and pasting its `PATH` in the following manner:

```
xauth:  file /home/amrith2kmeanmachine/.Xauthority does not exist

New 'X' desktop is ubuntuvml:1

Creating default startup script /home/amrith2kmeanmachine/.vnc/xstartup
Starting applications specified in /home/amrith2kmeanmachine/.vnc/xstartup
Log file is /home/amrith2kmeanmachine/.vnc/ubuntuvml:1.log

amrith2kmeanmachine@ubuntuvml:~$ vim /home/amrith2kmeanmachine/.vnc/xstartup
```

19. In our case, the command to view and edit the script is:

```
:~$ vim /home/amrith2kmeanmachine/.vnc/xstartup
```

This PATH may be different in each case. Ensure you set the right PATH. The vim command opens up the script in the text editor on a Mac.

 The local shell generated a startup script as well as a log file. The startup script needs to be opened and edited in a text editor, which will be discussed next.

20. After typing the vim command, the screen with the startup script should look something like this screenshot:

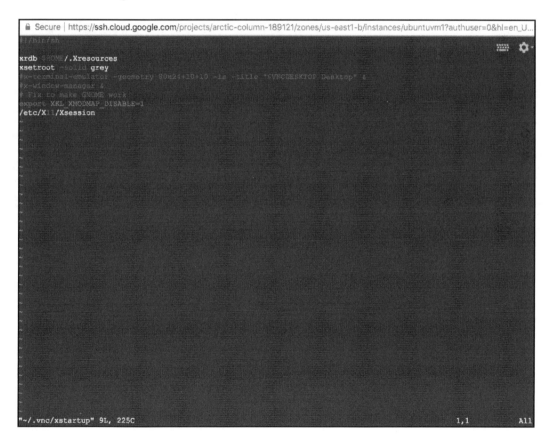

21. Type i to enter INSERT mode. Next, delete all the text in the startup script. It should then look like the following screenshot:

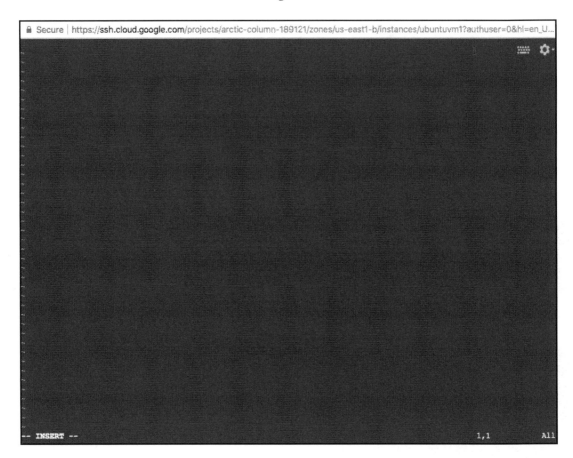

22. Copy paste the following code into the startup script:

```
#!/bin/sh
autocutsel -fork
xrdb $HOME/.Xresources
xsetroot -solid grey
export XKL_XMODMAP_DISABLE=1
export XDG_CURRENT_DESKTOP="GNOME-Flashback:Unity"
export XDG_MENU_PREFIX="gnome-flashback-"
unset DBUS_SESSION_BUS_ADDRESS
gnome-session --session=gnome-flashback-metacity --disable-
acceleration-check --debug &
```

23. The script should appear in the editor, as seen in the following screenshot:

24. Press **Esc** to exit out of INSERT mode and type :wq to write and quit the file.

25. Once the startup script has been configured, type the following command in the Google shell to kill the server and save the changes:

```
$ vncserver -kill :1
```

26. This command should produce a process ID that looks like the one in the following screenshot:

```
amrith2kmeanmachine@ubuntuvm1:~$ vncserver -kill :1
Killing Xtightvnc process ID 9831
amrith2kmeanmachine@ubuntuvm1:~$
```

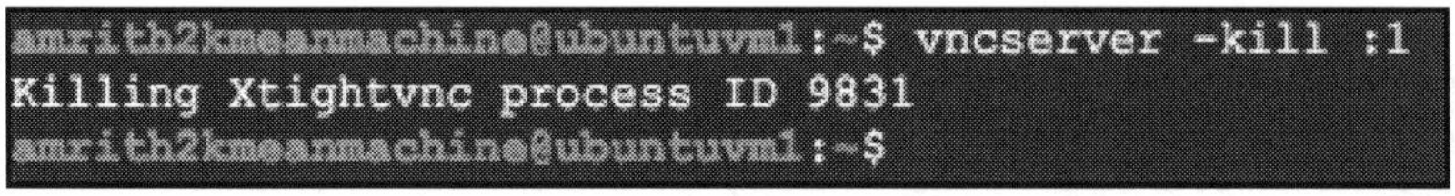

27. Start the server again by typing the following command:

```
$ vncserver –geometry 1024x640
```

The next series of steps will focus on securing the shell tunnel into the Google Cloud instance from the local host. Before typing anything on the local shell/terminal, ensure that Google Cloud is installed. If not already installed, do so by following the instructions in this quick-start guide located at the following website:

```
https://cloud.google.com/sdk/docs/quickstart-mac-os-x
```

28. Once Google Cloud is installed, open up the terminal on your machine and type the following commands to connect to the Google Cloud compute instance:

```
$ gcloud compute ssh \
YOUR INSTANCE NAME HERE \
--project YOUR PROJECT NAME HERE \
--zone YOUR TIMEZONE HERE \
--ssh-flag "-L 5901:localhost:5901"
```

29. Ensure that the instance name, project ID, and zone are specified correctly in the preceding commands. On pressing **ENTER**, the output on the local shell changes to what is shown in the following screenshot:

34. This will prompt you to enter your password for the virtual machine. Enter the password that you set earlier while launching the `tightvncserver` command for the first time, as shown in the following screenshot:

35. You will finally be taken into the desktop of your Ubuntu virtual machine on Google Cloud Compute. Your Ubuntu Desktop screen must now look something like the following screenshot when viewed on VNC Viewer:

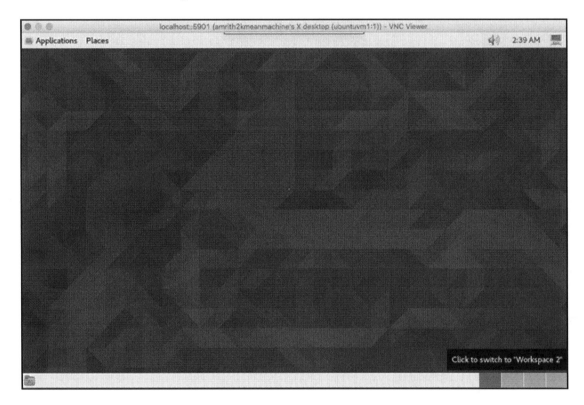

How it works...

You have now successfully set up VNC Viewer for interactions with the Ubuntu virtual machine/desktop. Anytime the Google Cloud instance is not in use, it is recommended to suspend or shut down the instance so that additional costs are not being incurred. The cloud approach is optimal for developers who may not have access to physical resources with high memory and storage.

There's more...

While we discussed Google Cloud as a cloud option for Spark, it is possible to leverage Spark on the following cloud platforms as well:

- Microsoft Azure
- Amazon Web Services

See also

In order to learn more about Google Cloud Platform and sign up for a free subscription, visit the following website:

```
https://cloud.google.com/
```

Installing and configuring Spark and prerequisites on Ubuntu Desktop

Before Spark can get up and running, there are some necessary prerequisites that need to be installed on a newly minted Ubuntu Desktop. This section will focus on installing and configuring the following on Ubuntu Desktop:

- Java 8 or higher
- Anaconda
- Spark

Getting ready

The only requirement for this section is having administrative rights to install applications onto the Ubuntu Desktop.

How to do it...

This section walks through the steps in the recipe to install Python 3, Anaconda, and Spark on Ubuntu Desktop:

1. Install Java on Ubuntu through the **terminal** application, which can be found by searching for the app and then locking it to the launcher on the left-hand side, as seen in the following screenshot:

2. Perform an initial test for Java on the virtual machine by executing the following command at the terminal:

```
java -version
```

3. Execute the following four commands at the terminal to install Java:

```
sudo apt-get install software-properties-common
$ sudo add-apt-repository ppa:webupd8team/java
$ sudo apt-get update
$ sudo apt-get install oracle-java8-installer
```

4. After accepting the necessary license agreements for Oracle, perform a secondary test of Java on the virtual machine by executing `java -version` once again in the terminal. A successful installation for Java will display the following outcome in the terminal:

```
$ java -version
java version "1.8.0_144"
Java(TM) SE Runtime Environment (build 1.8.0_144-b01)
Java HotSpot(TM) 64-Bit Server VM (build 25.144-b01, mixed mode)
```

5. Next, install the most recent version of Anaconda. Current versions of Ubuntu Desktop come preinstalled with Python. While it is convenient that Python comes preinstalled with Ubuntu, the installed version is for **Python 2.7**, as seen in the following output:

```
$ python --version
Python 2.7.12
```

6. The current version of Anaconda is v4.4 and the current version of Python 3 is v3.6. Once downloaded, view the Anaconda installation file by accessing the `Downloads` folder using the following command:

```
$ cd Downloads/
~/Downloads$ ls
Anaconda3-4.4.0-Linux-x86_64.sh
```

7. Once in the `Downloads` folder, initiate the installation for Anaconda by executing the following command:

```
~/Downloads$ bash Anaconda3-4.4.0-Linux-x86_64.sh
Welcome to Anaconda3 4.4.0 (by Continuum Analytics, Inc.)
In order to continue the installation process, please review the
license agreement.
Please, press ENTER to continue
```

 Please note that the version of Anaconda, as well as any other software installed, may differ as newer updates are released to the public. The version of Anaconda that we are using in this chapter and in this book can be downloaded from `https://repo.continuum.io/archive/Anaconda3-4.4.0-Linux-x86.sh`

8. Once the Anaconda installation is complete, restart the **Terminal** application to confirm that Python 3 is now the default Python environment through Anaconda by executing `python --version` in the terminal:

```
$ python --version
Python 3.6.1 :: Anaconda 4.4.0 (64-bit)
```

9. The Python 2 version is still available under Linux, but will require an explicit call when executing a script, as seen in the following command:

```
~$ python2 --version
Python 2.7.12
```

10. Visit the following website to begin the Spark download and installation process:

    ```
    https://spark.apache.org/downloads.html
    ```

11. Select the download link. The following file will be downloaded to the Downloads folder in Ubuntu:

    ```
    spark-2.2.0-bin-hadoop2.7.tgz
    ```

12. View the file at the terminal level by executing the following commands:

    ```
    $ cd Downloads/
    ~/Downloads$ ls
    spark-2.2.0-bin-hadoop2.7.tgz
    ```

13. Extract the tgz file by executing the following command:

    ```
    ~/Downloads$ tar -zxvf spark-2.2.0-bin-hadoop2.7.tgz
    ```

14. Another look at the **Downloads** directory using ls shows both the tgz file and the extracted folder:

    ```
    ~/Downloads$ ls
    spark-2.2.0-bin-hadoop2.7 spark-2.2.0-bin-hadoop2.7.tgz
    ```

15. Move the extracted folder from the Downloads folder to the Home folder by executing the following command:

    ```
    ~/Downloads$ mv spark-2.2.0-bin-hadoop2.7 ~/
    ~/Downloads$ ls
    spark-2.2.0-bin-hadoop2.7.tgz
    ~/Downloads$ cd
    ~$ ls
    anaconda3 Downloads Pictures Templates
    Desktop examples.desktop Public Videos
    Documents Music spark-2.2.0-bin-hadoop2.7
    ```

16. Now, the `spark-2.2.0-bin-hadoop2.7` folder has been moved to the **Home** folder, which can be viewed when selecting the **Files** icon on the left-hand side toolbar, as seen in the following screenshot:

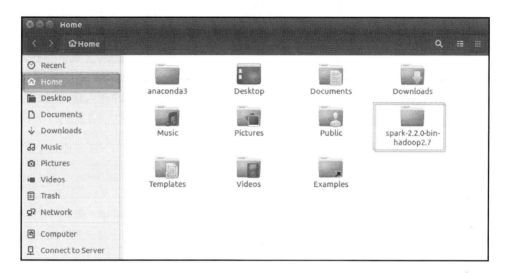

17. Spark is now installed. Initiate Spark from the terminal by executing the following script at the terminal level:

```
~$ cd ~/spark-2.2.0-bin-hadoop2.7/
~/spark-2.2.0-bin-hadoop2.7$ ./bin/pyspark
```

18. Perform a final test to ensure Spark is up and running at the terminal by executing the following command to ensure that the `SparkContext` is driving the cluster in the local environment:

```
>>> sc
<SparkContext master=local[*] appName=PySparkShell>
```

How it works...

This section explains the reasoning behind the installation process for Python, Anaconda, and Spark.

1. Spark runs on the **Java virtual machine (JVM)**, the Java **Software Development Kit (SDK)** is a prerequisite installation for Spark to run on an Ubuntu virtual machine.

    In order for Spark to run on a local machine or in a cluster, a minimum version of Java 6 is required for installation.

2. Ubuntu recommends the `sudo apt install` method for Java as it ensures that packages downloaded are up to date.

3. Please note that if Java is not currently installed, the output in the terminal will show the following message:

   ```
   The program 'java' can be found in the following packages:
   * default-jre
   * gcj-5-jre-headless
   * openjdk-8-jre-headless
   * gcj-4.8-jre-headless
   * gcj-4.9-jre-headless
   * openjdk-9-jre-headless
   Try: sudo apt install <selected package>
   ```

4. While Python 2 is fine, it is considered legacy Python. Python 2 is facing an end of life date in 2020; therefore, it is recommended that all new Python development be performed with Python 3, as will be the case in this publication. Up until recently, Spark was only available with Python 2. That is no longer the case. Spark works with both Python 2 and 3. A convenient way to install Python 3, as well as many dependencies and libraries, is through Anaconda. Anaconda is a free and open source distribution of Python, as well as R. Anaconda manages the installation and maintenance of many of the most common packages used in Python for data science-related tasks.

5. During the installation process for Anaconda, it is important to confirm the following conditions:

   - Anaconda is installed in the `/home/username/Anaconda3` location
   - The Anaconda installer prepends the Anaconda3 install location to a `PATH` in `/home/username/.bashrc`

6. After Anaconda has been installed, download Spark. Unlike Python, Spark does not come preinstalled on Ubuntu and therefore, will need to be downloaded and installed.

7. For the purposes of development with deep learning, the following preferences will be selected for Spark:

   - **Spark release**: **2.2.0** (Jul 11 2017)
   - **Package type**: Prebuilt for Apache Hadoop 2.7 and later
   - **Download type**: Direct download

8. Once Spark has been successfully installed, the output from executing Spark at the command line should look something similar to that shown in the following screenshot:

```
asherif844@ubuntu: ~/spark-2.2.0-bin-hadoop2.7
asherif844@ubuntu:~/spark-2.2.0-bin-hadoop2.7$ ./bin/pyspark
Python 3.6.1 |Anaconda 4.4.0 (64-bit)| (default, May 11 2017, 13:09:58)
[GCC 4.4.7 20120313 (Red Hat 4.4.7-1)] on linux
Type "help", "copyright", "credits" or "license" for more information.
Using Spark's default log4j profile: org/apache/spark/log4j-defaults.properties
Setting default log level to "WARN".
To adjust logging level use sc.setLogLevel(newLevel). For SparkR, use setLogLeve
l(newLevel).
17/09/18 21:48:58 WARN NativeCodeLoader: Unable to load native-hadoop library fo
r your platform... using builtin-java classes where applicable
17/09/18 21:48:58 WARN Utils: Your hostname, ubuntu resolves to a loopback addre
ss: 127.0.1.1; using 172.16.88.133 instead (on interface ens33)
17/09/18 21:48:58 WARN Utils: Set SPARK_LOCAL_IP if you need to bind to another
address
17/09/18 21:49:07 WARN ObjectStore: Version information not found in metastore.
hive.metastore.schema.verification is not enabled so recording the schema versio
n 1.2.0
17/09/18 21:49:07 WARN ObjectStore: Failed to get database default, returning No
SuchObjectException
17/09/18 21:49:08 WARN ObjectStore: Failed to get database global_temp, returnin
g NoSuchObjectException
Welcome to
      ____              __
     / __/__  ___ _____/ /__
    _\ \/ _ \/ _ `/ __/  '_/
   /__ / .__/\_,_/_/ /_/\_\   version 2.2.0
      /_/

Using Python version 3.6.1 (default, May 11 2017 13:09:58)
SparkSession available as 'spark'.
>>>
```

9. Two important features to note when initializing Spark are that it is under the `Python 3.6.1 | Anaconda 4.4.0 (64-bit) |` framework and that the Spark logo is version 2.2.0.

10. Congratulations! Spark is successfully installed on the local Ubuntu virtual machine. But, not everything is complete. Spark development is best when Spark code can be executed within a Jupyter notebook, especially for deep learning. Thankfully, Jupyter has been installed with the Anaconda distribution performed earlier in this section.

There's more...

You may be asking why we did not just use `pip install pyspark` to use Spark in Python. Previous versions of Spark required going through the installation process that we did in this section. Future versions of Spark, starting with 2.2.0 will begin to allow installation directly through the `pip` approach. We used the full installation method in this section to ensure that you will be able to get Spark installed and fully-integrated, in case you are using an earlier version of Spark.

See also

To learn more about Jupyter notebooks and their integration with Python, visit the following website:

`http://jupyter.org`

To learn more about Anaconda and download a version for Linux, visit the following website:

`https://www.anaconda.com/download/.`

Integrating Jupyter notebooks with Spark

When learning Python for the first time, it is useful to use Jupyter notebooks as an **interactive developing environment** (**IDE**). This is one of the main reasons why Anaconda is so powerful. It fully integrates all of the dependencies between Python and Jupyter notebooks. The same can be done with PySpark and Jupyter notebooks. While Spark is written in Scala, PySpark allows for the translation of code to occur within Python instead.

Getting ready

Most of the work in this section will just require accessing the `.bashrc` script from the terminal.

How to do it...

PySpark is not configured to work within Jupyter notebooks by default, but a slight tweak of the `.bashrc` script can remedy this issue. We will walk through these steps in this section:

1. Access the `.bashrc` script by executing the following command:

    ```
    $ nano .bashrc
    ```

2. Scrolling all the way to the end of the script should reveal the last command modified, which should be the `PATH` set by Anaconda during the installation earlier in the previous section. The `PATH` should appear as seen in the following:

    ```
    # added by Anaconda3 4.4.0 installer
    export PATH="/home/asherif844/anaconda3/bin:$PATH"
    ```

3. Underneath, the `PATH` added by the Anaconda installer can include a custom function that helps communicate the Spark installation with the Jupyter notebook installation from Anaconda3. For the purposes of this chapter and remaining chapters, we will name that function `sparknotebook`. The configuration should appear as the following for `sparknotebook()`:

    ```
    function sparknotebook()
    {
    export SPARK_HOME=/home/asherif844/spark-2.2.0-bin-hadoop2.7
    export PYSPARK_PYTHON=python3
    export PYSPARK_DRIVER_PYTHON=jupyter
    export PYSPARK_DRIVER_PYTHON_OPTS="notebook"
    $SPARK_HOME/bin/pyspark
    }
    ```

4. The updated `.bashrc` script should look like the following once saved:

```
asherif844@ubuntu: ~
GNU nano 2.5.3                      File: .bashrc                      Modified

if ! shopt -oq posix; then
  if [ -f /usr/share/bash-completion/bash_completion ]; then
    . /usr/share/bash-completion/bash_completion
  elif [ -f /etc/bash_completion ]; then
    . /etc/bash_completion
  fi
fi

# added by Anaconda3 4.4.0 installer
export PATH="/home/asherif844/anaconda3/bin:$PATH"

function sparknotebook()
{
export SPARK_HOME=/home/asherif844/spark-2.2.0-bin-hadoop2.7
export PYSPARK_PYTHON=python3
export PYSPARK_DRIVER_PYTHON=jupyter
export PYSPARK_DRIVER_PYTHON_OPTS="notebook"
$SPARK_HOME/bin/pyspark
}

^G Get Help   ^O Write Out  ^W Where Is   ^K Cut Text   ^J Justify    ^C Cur Pos
^X Exit       ^R Read File  ^\ Replace    ^U Uncut Text ^T To Spell   ^_ Go To Line
```

5. Save and exit from the `.bashrc` file. It is recommended to communicate that the `.bashrc` file has been updated by executing the following command and restarting the terminal application:

```
$ source .bashrc
```

How it works...

Our goal in this section is to integrate Spark directly into a Jupyter notebook so that we are not doing our development at the terminal and instead utilizing the benefits of developing within a notebook. This section explains how the Spark integration within a Jupyter notebook takes place.

1. We will create a command function, `sparknotebook`, that we can call from the terminal to open up a Spark session through Jupyter notebooks from the Anaconda installation. This requires two settings to be set in the `.bashrc` file:
   1. PySpark Python be set to python 3

> 2. PySpark driver for python to be set to Jupyter

2. The `sparknotebook` function can now be accessed directly from the terminal by executing the following command:

    ```
    $ sparknotebook
    ```

3. The function should then initiate a brand new Jupyter notebook session through the default web browser. A new Python script within Jupyter notebooks with a `.ipynb` extension can be created by clicking on the **New** button on the right-hand side and by selecting **Python 3** under **Notebook:** as seen in the following screenshot:

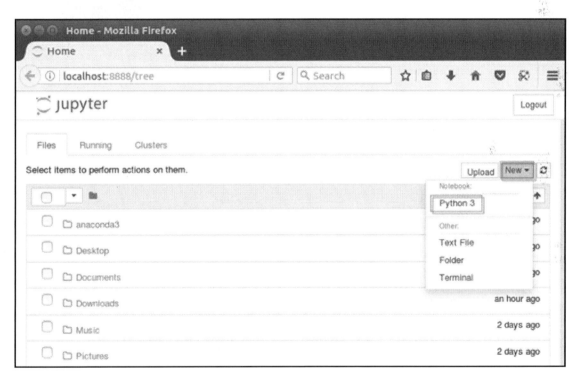

4. Once again, just as was done at the terminal level for Spark, a simple script of `sc` will be executed within the notebook to confirm that Spark is up and running through Jupyter:

```
In [1]:  sc

Out[1]:  SparkContext

         Spark UI
         Version
         v2.2.0
         Master
         local[*]
         AppName
         PySparkShell
```

5. Ideally, the **Version**, **Master**, and **AppName** should be identical to the earlier output when `sc` was executed at the terminal. If this is the case, then PySpark has been successfully installed and configured to work with Jupyter notebooks.

There's more...

It is important to note that if we were to call a Jupyter notebook through the terminal without specifying `sparknotebook`, our Spark session will never be initiated and we will receive an error when executing the `SparkContext` script.

We can access a traditional Jupyter notebook by executing the following at the terminal:

```
jupyter-notebook
```

Once we start the notebook, we can try and execute the same script for `sc.master` as we did previously, but this time we will receive the following error:

```
In [1]:  sc.master

         NameError                                 Traceback (most recent call last)
         <ipython-input-1-67f48183a30b> in <module>()
         ----> 1 sc.master

         NameError: name 'sc' is not defined
```

See also

There are many managed offerings online of companies offering Spark through a notebook interface where the installation and configuration of Spark with a notebook have already been managed for you. These are the following:

- Hortonworks (`https://hortonworks.com/`)
- Cloudera (`https://www.cloudera.com/`)
- MapR (`https://mapr.com/`)
- DataBricks (`https://databricks.com/`)

Starting and configuring a Spark cluster

For most chapters, one of the first things that we will do is to initialize and configure our Spark cluster.

Getting ready

Import the following before initializing cluster.

- `from pyspark.sql import SparkSession`

How to do it...

This section walks through the steps to initialize and configure a Spark cluster.

1. Import `SparkSession` using the following script:

```
from pyspark.sql import SparkSession
```

2. Configure `SparkSession` with a variable named `spark` using the following script:

```
spark = SparkSession.builder \
    .master("local[*]") \
    .appName("GenericAppName") \
    .config("spark.executor.memory", "6gb") \
.getOrCreate()
```

How it works...

This section explains how the `SparkSession` works as an entry point to develop within Spark.

1. Staring with Spark 2.0, it is no longer necessary to create a `SparkConf` and `SparkContext` to begin development in Spark. Those steps are no longer needed as importing `SparkSession` will handle initializing a cluster. Additionally, it is important to note that `SparkSession` is part of the `sql` module from `pyspark`.
2. We can assign properties to our `SparkSession`:
    1. `master`: assigns the Spark master URL to run on our `local` machine with the maximum available number of cores.
    2. `appName`: assign a name for the application
    3. `config`: assign `6gb` to the `spark.executor.memory`
    4. `getOrCreate`: ensures that a `SparkSession` is created if one is not available and retrieves an existing one if it is available

There's more...

For development purposes, while we are building an application on smaller datasets, we can just use `master("local")`. If we were to deploy on a production environment, we would want to specify `master("local[*]")` to ensure we are using the maximum cores available and get optimal performance.

See also

To learn more about `SparkSession.builder`, visit the following website:

```
https://spark.apache.org/docs/2.2.0/api/java/org/apache/spark/sql/SparkSession.
Builder.html
```

Stopping a Spark cluster

Once we are done developing on our cluster, it is ideal to shut it down and preserve resources.

How to do it...

This section walks through the steps to stop the `SparkSession`.

1. Execute the following script:

```
spark.stop()
```

2. Confirm that the session has closed by executing the following script:

```
sc.master
```

How it works...

This section explains how to confirm that a Spark cluster has been shut down.

1. If the cluster has been shut down, you will receive the error message seen in the following screenshot when executing another Spark command in the notebook:

```
In [1]: from pyspark.sql import SparkSession

In [2]: spark = SparkSession.builder \
            .master("local[*]") \
            .appName("GenericAppName") \
            .config("spark.executor.memory", "6gb") \
            .getOrCreate()

In [3]: sc.master
Out[3]: 'local[*]'

In [4]: spark.stop()

In [5]: sc.master()

TypeError                                 Traceback (most recent call last)
<ipython-input-5-df5a2b0a746a> in <module>()
----> 1 sc.master()

TypeError: 'str' object is not callable
```

There's more...

Shutting down Spark clusters may not be as critical when working in a local environment; however, it will prove costly when Spark is deployed in a cloud environment where you are charged for compute power.

Creating a Neural Network in 2 Spark

In this chapter, the following recipes will be covered:

- Creating a dataframe in PySpark
- Manipulating columns in a PySpark dataframe
- Converting a PySpark dataframe into an array
- Visualizing the array in a scatterplot
- Setting up weights and biases for input into the neural network
- Normalizing the input data for the neural network
- Validating array for optimal neural network performance
- Setting up the activation function with sigmoid
- Creating the sigmoid derivative function
- Calculating the cost function in a neural network
- Predicting gender based on height and weight
- Visualizing prediction scores

Introduction

Much of this book will focus on building deep learning algorithms with libraries in Python, such as TensorFlow and Keras. While these libraries are helpful to build deep neural networks without getting deep into the calculus and linear algebra of deep learning, this chapter will do a deep dive into building a simple neural network in PySpark to make a gender prediction based on height and weight. One of the best ways to understand the foundation of neural networks is to build a model from scratch, without any of the popular deep learning libraries. Once the foundation for a neural network framework is established, understanding and utilizing some of the more popular deep neural network libraries will become much simpler.

Creating a dataframe in PySpark

dataframes will serve as the framework for any and all data that will be used in building deep learning models. Similar to the `pandas` library with Python, PySpark has its own built-in functionality to create a dataframe.

Getting ready

There are several ways to create a dataframe in Spark. One common way is by importing a `.txt`, `.csv`, or `.json` file. Another method is to manually enter fields and rows of data into the PySpark dataframe, and while the process can be a bit tedious, it is helpful, especially when dealing with a small dataset. To predict gender based on height and weight, this chapter will build a dataframe manually in PySpark. The dataset used is as follows:

```
 1  Gender  Height (inches)  Weight (lbs)
 2  Female  67  150
 3  Female  65  135
 4  Female  68  130
 5  Male    70  160
 6  Female  70  130
 7  Male    69  174
 8  Male    65  126
 9  Male    74  188
10  Female  60  110
11  Female  63  125
12  Male    70  173
13  Female  70  145
14  Male    68  175
15  Female  65  123
16  Male    71  145
17  Male    74  160
18  Female  64  135
19  Male    71  175
20  Male    67  145
21  Male    67  130
22  Male    70  162
23  Female  64  107
24  Male    70  175
25  Male    64  130
26  Male    66  163
27  Female  63  137
28  Male    65  165
29  Female  65  130
30  Female  64  109
```

While the dataset will be manually added to PySpark in this chapter, the dataset can also be viewed and downloaded from the following link:

```
https://github.com/asherif844/ApacheSparkDeepLearningCookbook/blob/master/CH02/
data/HeightAndWeight.txt
```

Finally, we will begin this chapter and future chapters by starting up a Spark environment configured with a Jupyter notebook that was created in chapter 1, *Setting up your Spark Environment for Deep Learning,* using the following terminal command:

```
sparknotebook
```

How to do it...

When working with PySpark, a `SparkSession` must first be imported and initialized before any dataframe creation can occur:

1. Import a `SparkSession` using the following script:

   ```
   from pyspark.sql import SparkSession
   ```

2. Configure a `SparkSession`:

   ```
   spark = SparkSession.builder \
           .master("local") \
           .appName("Neural Network Model") \
           .config("spark.executor.memory", "6gb") \
           .getOrCreate()
   sc = spark.sparkContext
   ```

3. In this situation, the `SparkSession` appName has been named `Neural Network Model` and `6gb` has been assigned to the session memory.

How it works...

This section explains how we create our Spark cluster and configure our first dataframe.

1. In Spark, we use `.master()` to specify whether we will run our jobs on a distributed cluster or locally. For the purposes of this chapter and the remaining chapters, we will be executing Spark locally with one worker thread as specified with `.master('local')`. This is fine for testing and development purposes as we are doing in this chapter; however, we may run into performance issues if we deployed this to production. In production, it is recommended to use `.master('local[*]')` to set Spark to run on as many worker nodes that are available locally as possible. If we had 3 cores on our machine and we wanted to set our node count to match that, we would then specify `.master('local[3]')`.

2. The `dataframe` variable, `df`, is first created by inserting the row values for each column and then by inserting the column header names using the following script:

```
df = spark.createDataFrame([('Male', 67, 150), # insert column
values
                            ('Female', 65, 135),
                            ('Female', 68, 130),
                            ('Male', 70, 160),
                            ('Female', 70, 130),
                            ('Male', 69, 174),
                            ('Female', 65, 126),
                            ('Male', 74, 188),
                            ('Female', 60, 110),
                            ('Female', 63, 125),
                            ('Male', 70, 173),
                            ('Male', 70, 145),
                            ('Male', 68, 175),
                            ('Female', 65, 123),
                            ('Male', 71, 145),
                            ('Male', 74, 160),
                            ('Female', 64, 135),
                            ('Male', 71, 175),
                            ('Male', 67, 145),
                            ('Female', 67, 130),
                            ('Male', 70, 162),
                            ('Female', 64, 107),
                            ('Male', 70, 175),
                            ('Female', 64, 130),
                            ('Male', 66, 163),
                            ('Female', 63, 137),
                            ('Male', 65, 165),
                            ('Female', 65, 130),
                            ('Female', 64, 109)],
                           ['gender', 'height','weight']) # insert
header values
```

3. In PySpark, the `show()` function gives the ability to preview the **top 20 rows**, as seen in the following screenshot when using the preceding script:

```
In [4]:  df.show()

         +------+------+------+
         |gender|height|weight|
         +------+------+------+
         |  Male|    67|   150|
         |Female|    65|   135|
         |Female|    68|   130|
         |  Male|    70|   160|
         |Female|    70|   130|
         |  Male|    69|   174|
         |Female|    65|   126|
         |  Male|    74|   188|
         |Female|    60|   110|
         |Female|    63|   125|
         |  Male|    70|   173|
         |  Male|    70|   145|
         |  Male|    68|   175|
         |Female|    65|   123|
         |  Male|    71|   145|
         |  Male|    74|   160|
         |Female|    64|   135|
         |  Male|    71|   175|
         |  Male|    67|   145|
         |Female|    67|   130|
         +------+------+------+
         only showing top 20 rows
```

There's more...

The `.show()` functionality defaults to 20 rows if not explicitly stated. If we only wanted to show the first 5 rows of a dataframe, we would need to explicitly state it as seen in the following script: `df.show(5)`.

See also

In order to learn more about SparkSQL, dataframes, functions, and data sets in PySpark, visit the following website:

`https://spark.apache.org/docs/latest/sql-programming-guide.html`

Manipulating columns in a PySpark dataframe

The dataframe is almost complete; however, there is one issue that requires addressing before building the neural network. Rather than keeping the gender value as a string, it is better to convert the value to a numeric integer for calculation purposes, which will become more evident as this chapter progresses.

Getting ready

This section will require importing the following:

- `from pyspark.sql import functions`

How to do it...

This section walks through the steps for the string conversion to a numeric value in the dataframe:

- Female --> 0
- Male --> 1

1. Convert a column value inside of a dataframe requires importing `functions`:

```
from pyspark.sql import functions
```

2. Next, modify the `gender` column to a numeric value using the following script:

```
df =
df.withColumn('gender',functions.when(df['gender']=='Female',0).oth
erwise(1))
```

3. Finally, reorder the columns so that `gender` is the last column in the dataframe using the following script:

```
df = df.select('height', 'weight', 'gender')
```

How it works...

This section explains how the manipulation of the dataframe is applied.

1. `functions from pyspark.sql` have several useful logic applications that can be used to apply if-then transformations to columns in a Spark dataframe. In our case, we are converting `Female` t0 0 and `Male` to 1.

2. The function to convert to numeric is applied to the Spark dataframe using the `.withColumn()` transformation.

3. The `.select()` feature for a Spark dataframe functions like traditional SQL by selecting the columns in the order and manner requested.

4. A final preview of the dataframe will display the updated dataset, as seen in the following screenshot:

```
In [5]: from pyspark.sql import functions

In [6]: df = df.withColumn('gender',functions.when(df['gender']=='Female',0).otherwise(1))

In [7]: df = df.select('height', 'weight', 'gender')

In [8]: df.show()
        +------+------+------+
        |height|weight|gender|
        +------+------+------+
        |    67|   150|     1|
        |    65|   135|     0|
        |    68|   130|     0|
        |    70|   160|     1|
        |    70|   130|     0|
        |    69|   174|     1|
        |    65|   126|     0|
        |    74|   188|     1|
        |    60|   110|     0|
        |    63|   125|     0|
        |    70|   173|     1|
        |    70|   145|     1|
        |    68|   175|     1|
        |    65|   123|     0|
        |    71|   145|     1|
        |    74|   160|     1|
        |    64|   135|     0|
        |    71|   175|     1|
        |    67|   145|     1|
        |    67|   130|     0|
        +------+------+------+
        only showing top 20 rows
```

There's more...

In addition to the `withColumn()` method for a dataframe, there is also the `withColumnRenamed()` method, which is used for renaming columns in a dataframe.

Converting a PySpark dataframe to an array

In order to form the building blocks of the neural network, the PySpark dataframe must be converted into an array. Python has a very powerful library, `numpy`, that makes working with arrays simple.

Getting ready

The `numpy` library should be already available with the installation of the `anaconda3` Python package. However, if for some reason the `numpy` library is not available, it can be installed using the following command at the terminal:

```
asherif844@ubuntu: ~
File  Edit  View  Search  Terminal  Help
asherif844@ubuntu:~$ pip install numpy
Requirement already satisfied: numpy in ./anaconda3/lib/python3.6/site-packages
asherif844@ubuntu:~$
```

`pip install` or `sudo pip install` will confirm whether the requirements are already satisfied by using the requested library:

```
import numpy as np
```

How to do it...

This section walks through the steps to convert the dataframe into an array:

1. View the data collected from the dataframe using the following script:

```
df.select("height", "weight", "gender").collect()
```

2. Store the values from the collection into an array called `data_array` using the following script:

```
data_array = np.array(df.select("height", "weight",
"gender").collect())
```

3. Execute the following script to access the first row of the array:

```
data_array[0]
```

4. Similarly, execute the following script to access the final row of the array:

```
data_array[28]
```

How it works...

This section explains how the dataframe is converted into an array:

1. The output of our dataframe can be collected using `collect()` and viewed as seen in the following screenshot:

```
In [9]:  import numpy as np

In [10]: df.select("height", "weight", "gender").collect()

Out[10]: [Row(height=67, weight=150, gender=1),
          Row(height=65, weight=135, gender=0),
          Row(height=68, weight=130, gender=0),
          Row(height=70, weight=160, gender=1),
          Row(height=70, weight=130, gender=0),
          Row(height=69, weight=174, gender=1),
          Row(height=65, weight=126, gender=0),
          Row(height=74, weight=188, gender=1),
          Row(height=60, weight=110, gender=0),
          Row(height=63, weight=125, gender=0),
          Row(height=70, weight=173, gender=1),
          Row(height=70, weight=145, gender=1),
          Row(height=68, weight=175, gender=1),
          Row(height=65, weight=123, gender=0),
          Row(height=71, weight=145, gender=1),
          Row(height=74, weight=160, gender=1),
          Row(height=64, weight=135, gender=0),
          Row(height=71, weight=175, gender=1),
          Row(height=67, weight=145, gender=1),
          Row(height=67, weight=130, gender=0),
          Row(height=70, weight=162, gender=1),
          Row(height=64, weight=107, gender=0),
          Row(height=70, weight=175, gender=1),
          Row(height=64, weight=130, gender=0),
          Row(height=66, weight=163, gender=1),
          Row(height=63, weight=137, gender=0),
          Row(height=65, weight=165, gender=1),
          Row(height=65, weight=130, gender=0),
          Row(height=64, weight=109, gender=0)]
```

2. The dataframe is converted into an array and the output of the array from that script can be seen in the following screenshot:

```
In [11]:  data_array =  np.array(df.select("height", "weight", "gender").collect())
          data_array #view the array

Out[11]: array([[ 67, 150,    1],
                [ 65, 135,    0],
                [ 68, 130,    0],
                [ 70, 160,    1],
                [ 70, 130,    0],
                [ 69, 174,    1],
                [ 65, 126,    0],
                [ 74, 188,    1],
                [ 60, 110,    0],
                [ 63, 125,    0],
                [ 70, 173,    1],
                [ 70, 145,    1],
                [ 68, 175,    1],
                [ 65, 123,    0],
                [ 71, 145,    1],
                [ 74, 160,    1],
                [ 64, 135,    0],
                [ 71, 175,    1],
                [ 67, 145,    1],
                [ 67, 130,    0],
                [ 70, 162,    1],
                [ 64, 107,    0],
                [ 70, 175,    1],
                [ 64, 130,    0],
                [ 66, 163,    1],
                [ 63, 137,    0],
                [ 65, 165,    1],
                [ 65, 130,    0],
                [ 64, 109,    0]]})
```

3. Any set of `height`, `weight`, and `gender` values can be accessed by referencing the index of the array. The array has a shape of **(29,3)** with a length of 29 elements, and each element is composed of three items. While the length is 29, the index starts at `[0]` and ends at `[28]`. The outputs for the shape of the array as well as the first and last rows of the array can be seen in the following screenshot:

```
In [12]:  data_array.shape

Out[12]:  (29, 3)

In [13]:  data_array[0]

Out[13]:  array([ 67, 150,    1])

In [14]:  data_array[28]

Out[14]:  array([ 64, 109,    0])
```

4. The first and last values of the array can be compared with the original dataframe to confirm that the values and order have not changed as a result of the conversion.

There's more...

In addition to viewing the data points in an array, it is also useful to retrieve the minimum and maximum points of each feature in an array:

1. To retrieve the minimum and maximum values for height, weight, and gender, the following script can be used:

```
print(data_array.max(axis=0))
print(data_array.min(axis=0))
```

2. The output from the script can be seen in the following screenshot:

```
In [15]:  print(data_array.max(axis=0))
          print(data_array.min(axis=0))

          [ 74 188    1]
          [ 60 107    0]
```

The maximum height is 74 inches and minimum height is 60 inches. The maximum weight is 188 lbs, while the minimum weight is 107 lbs. The minimum and maximum values for gender are not as relevant, as we have assigned them numeric values of 0 and 1.

See also

To learn more about numpy, visit the following website:

www.numpy.org

Visualizing an array in a scatterplot

The goal of the neural network that will be developed in this chapter is to predict the gender of an individual if the `height` and `weight` are known. A powerful method for understanding the relationship between `height`, `weight`, and `gender` is by visualizing the data points feeding the neural network. This can be done with the popular Python visualization library `matplotlib`.

Getting ready

As was the case with `numpy`, `matplotlib` should be available with the installation of the anaconda3 Python package. However, if for some reason `matplotlib` is not available, it can be installed using the following command at the terminal:

```
asherif844@ubuntu: ~
File Edit View Search Terminal Help
asherif844@ubuntu:~$ pip install matplotlib
Requirement already satisfied: matplotlib in ./anaconda3/lib/python3.6/site-pack
ages
Requirement already satisfied: numpy>=1.7.1 in ./anaconda3/lib/python3.6/site-pa
ckages (from matplotlib)
Requirement already satisfied: six>=1.10 in ./anaconda3/lib/python3.6/site-packa
ges (from matplotlib)
Requirement already satisfied: python-dateutil in ./anaconda3/lib/python3.6/site
-packages (from matplotlib)
Requirement already satisfied: pytz in ./anaconda3/lib/python3.6/site-packages (
from matplotlib)
Requirement already satisfied: cycler>=0.10 in ./anaconda3/lib/python3.6/site-pa
ckages (from matplotlib)
Requirement already satisfied: pyparsing!=2.0.4,!=2.1.2,!=2.1.6,>=1.5.6 in ./ana
conda3/lib/python3.6/site-packages (from matplotlib)
```

`pip install` or `sudo pip install` will confirm the requirements are already satisfied by using the requested library.

How to do it...

This section walks through the steps to visualize an array through a scatterplot.

1. Import the `matplotlib` library and configure the library to visualize plots inside of the Jupyter notebook using the following script:

```
import matplotlib.pyplot as plt
%matplotlib inline
```

2. Next, determine the minimum and maximum values of the *x* and y-axes of the scatterplot using the `min()` and `max()` functions from `numpy`, as seen in the following script:

```
min_x = data_array.min(axis=0)[0]-10
max_x = data_array.max(axis=0)[0]+10
min_y = data_array.min(axis=0)[1]-10
max_y = data_array.max(axis=0)[1]+10
```

3. Execute the following script to plot the `height` and `weight` for each `gender`:

```
# formatting the plot grid, scales, and figure size
plt.figure(figsize=(9, 4), dpi= 75)
plt.axis([min_x,max_x,min_y,max_y])
plt.grid()
for i in range(len(data_array)):
    value = data_array[i]
    # assign labels values to specific matrix elements
    gender = value[2]
    height = value[0]
    weight = value[1]

    # filter data points by gender
    a = plt.scatter(height[gender==0],weight[gender==0], marker
        = 'x', c= 'b', label = 'Female')
    b = plt.scatter(height[gender==1],weight[gender==1], marker
        = 'o', c= 'b', label = 'Male')

    # plot values, title, legend, x and y axis
plt.title('Weight vs Height by Gender')
plt.xlabel('Height (in)')
plt.ylabel('Weight (lbs)')
plt.legend(handles=[a,b])
```

How it works...

This section explains how an array is plotted as a scatterplot:

1. The `matplotlib` library is imported into the Jupyter notebook and the `matplotlib` library is configured to plot visualizations inline in the cells of the Jupyter notebook

2. The minimum and maximum values of the x and y-axes are determined to size up our plot and give us an optimal looking graph. The output of the script can be seen in the following screenshot:

```
In [16]:  import matplotlib.pyplot as plt
          %matplotlib inline

In [17]:  min_x = data_array.min(axis=0)[0]-10
          max_x = data_array.max(axis=0)[0]+10
          min_y = data_array.min(axis=0)[1]-10
          max_y = data_array.max(axis=0)[1]+10

          print(min_x, max_x, min_y, max_y)
          50 84 97 198
```

3. A `10`-point pixel buffer has been added to each axis to ensure all data points are captured without being cut off.

4. A loop is created to iterate through each row of values and plot the `weight` versus the `height`.

5. Additionally, a different style point is assigned to the `Female` gender, x, and the `Male` gender, o.

6. The output of the script to plot the **Weight vs Height by Gender** can be seen in the following screenshot:

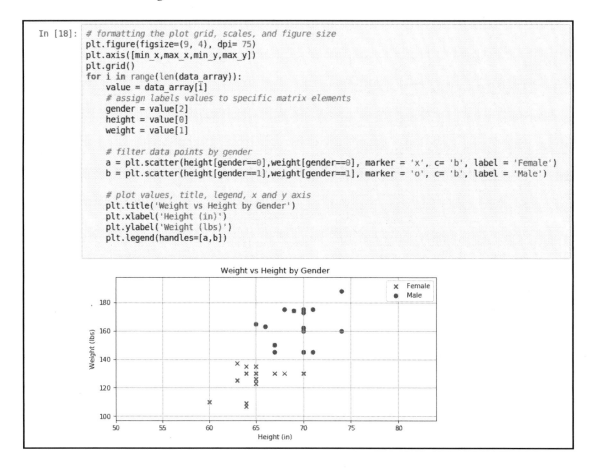

```
In [18]:  # formatting the plot grid, scales, and figure size
          plt.figure(figsize=(9, 4), dpi= 75)
          plt.axis([min_x,max_x,min_y,max_y])
          plt.grid()
          for i in range(len(data_array)):
              value = data_array[i]
              # assign labels values to specific matrix elements
              gender = value[2]
              height = value[0]
              weight = value[1]

              # filter data points by gender
              a = plt.scatter(height[gender==0],weight[gender==0], marker = 'x', c= 'b', label = 'Female')
              b = plt.scatter(height[gender==1],weight[gender==1], marker = 'o', c= 'b', label = 'Male')

              # plot values, title, legend, x and y axis
              plt.title('Weight vs Height by Gender')
              plt.xlabel('Height (in)')
              plt.ylabel('Weight (lbs)')
              plt.legend(handles=[a,b])
```

There's more...

The scatterplot gives a quick and easy visual interpretation of what is going on with the data. There is an apparent divide between the upper-right quadrant and the lower-left quadrant of the scatterplot. All of the data points above 140 lbs indicate a `Male` gender, with all of the data points below that belong to the `Female` gender, as seen in the following screenshot:

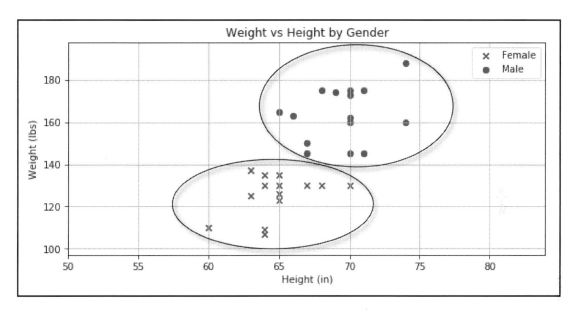

This scatterplot will help confirm what is to be expected when picking a random height and weight to predict the outcome of the gender when the neural network is created later on in this chapter.

See also

To learn more about `matplotlib`, visit the following website:

`www.matplotlib.org`

Setting up weights and biases for input into the neural network

The framework in PySpark and the data are now complete. It is time to move on to building the neural network. Regardless of the complexity of the neural network, the development follows a similar path:

1. Input data
2. Add the weights and biases
3. Sum the product of the data and weights

4. Apply an activation function
5. Evaluate the output and compare it to the desired outcome

This section will focus on setting the weights that create the input which feeds into the activation function.

Getting ready

A cursory understanding of the building blocks of a simple neural network is helpful in understanding this section and the rest of the chapter. Each neural network has inputs and outputs. In our case, the inputs are the height and weight of the individuals and the output is the gender. In order to get to the output, the inputs are multiplied with values (also known as weights: w1 and w2) and then a bias (b) is added to the end. This equation is known as the summation function, z, and is given the following equation:

$$z = (input1) \times (w1) + (input2) \times (w2) + b$$

The weights and the bias are initially just random generated values that can be performed with numpy. The weights will literally add weight to inputs by increasing or decreasing their impact on the output. The bias will serve a slightly different role in that it will shift the baseline of the summation (z) upwards or downwards, depending on what is needed to meet the prediction. Each value of z is then converted into a predicted value between 0 and 1 through an activation function. The activation function is a converter that gives us a value that we can convert into a binary output (male/female). The predicted output is then compared with the actual output. Initially, the difference between the predicted and actual output will be large as the weights will be random when first starting out. However, a process known as backpropagation is used to minimize the difference between the actual and the predicted using a technique known as gradient descent. Once we settle on a negligible difference between the actual and predicted, we store the values of w1, w2, and b for the neural network.

How to do it...

This section walks through the steps to set up the weights and bias of the neural network.

1. Set the randomness of the value generator using the following script:

```
np.random.seed(12345)
```

2. Set the weights and biases using the following script:

```
w1 = np.random.randn()
w2 = np.random.randn()
b= np.random.randn()
```

How it works...

This section explains how the weights and bias are initialized for use in later parts of this chapter:

1. The weights are generated randomly using `numpy`, and a random seed is set to ensure the same random numbers are generated each time
2. The weights will be assigned a generic variable of `w1` and `w2`
3. The bias is also generated randomly using `numpy` and a random seed is set to maintain the same random numbers is generated each time
4. The bias will be assigned a generic variable of `b`
5. The values are inserted into a summation function, `z`, which populates an initial score that will feed into another function, the activation function, to be discussed later on in this chapter
6. At the moment, all three variables are completely random. The output of `w1`, `w2`, and `b` can be seen in the following screenshot:

```
In [19]:  np.random.seed(12345)

In [20]:  w1 = np.random.randn()
          w2 = np.random.randn()
          b= np.random.randn()

In [21]:  print(w1, w2, b)

          -0.20470765948471295 0.47894333805754824 -0.5194387150567381
```

There's more...

Ultimately, the goal is to get a predicted output that matches the actual output. Summing the product of the weights and the values helps achieve part of this process. Therefore, a random input of 0.5 and 0.5 would have a summation output of the following:

```
z = 0.5 * w1 + 0.5 * w2 + b
```

Or it would have the following output with our current random values for our weights, w1 and w2:

```
z = 0.5 * (-0.2047) + 0.5 * (0.47894) + (-0.51943) = -7.557
```

The variable z is assigned as the product summation of the weights with the data points. Currently, the weights and biases are completely random. However, as mentioned earlier in the section, through a process called backpropagation, using gradient descent, the weights will be tweaked until a more desirable outcome is determined. Gradient descent is simply the process of identifying the optimal values for our weights that will give us the best prediction output with the least amount of error. The process of identifying the optimal values involves identifying the local minimum of a function. Gradient descent will be discussed later on in this chapter.

See also

In order to learn more about weights and biases in an artificial neural network, visit the following website:

```
https://en.wikipedia.org/wiki/Artificial_neuron
```

Normalizing the input data for the neural network

Neural networks work more efficiently when the inputs are normalized. This minimizes the magnitude of a particular input affecting the overall outcome over other potential inputs that have lower values of magnitude. This section will normalize the height and weight inputs of the current individuals.

Getting ready

The normalization of input values requires obtaining the mean and standard deviation of those values for the final calculation.

How to do it...

This section walks through the steps to normalize the height and weight.

1. Slice the array into inputs and outputs using the following script:

```
X = data_array[:,:2]
y = data_array[:,2]
```

2. The mean and the standard deviation can be calculated across the 29 individuals using the following script:

```
x_mean = X.mean(axis=0)
x_std = X.std(axis=0)
```

3. Create a normalization function to normalize X using the following script:

```
def normalize(X):
    x_mean = X.mean(axis=0)
    x_std = X.std(axis=0)
    X = (X - X.mean(axis=0))/X.std(axis=0)
    return X
```

How it works...

This section explains how the height and weight are normalized.

1. The data_array matrix is split into two matrices:
   1. X is composed of the height and the weight
   2. y is composed of the gender

2. The output of both arrays can be seen in the following screenshot:

```
In [22]: X = data_array[:,:2]
         y = data_array[:,2]
         print(X,y)
         [[ 67 150]
          [ 65 135]
          [ 68 130]
          [ 70 160]
          [ 70 130]
          [ 69 174]
          [ 65 126]
          [ 74 188]
          [ 60 110]
          [ 63 125]
          [ 70 173]
          [ 70 145]
          [ 68 175]
          [ 65 123]
          [ 71 145]
          [ 74 160]
          [ 64 135]
          [ 71 175]
          [ 67 145]
          [ 67 130]
          [ 70 162]
          [ 64 107]
          [ 70 175]
          [ 64 130]
          [ 66 163]
          [ 63 137]
          [ 65 165]
          [ 65 130]
          [ 64 109]] [1 0 0 1 0 1 0 1 0 0 1 1 1 0 1 1 0 1 1 0 1 0 1 0 1 0 1 0 0]
```

3. The X component is the input and is the only part that will undergo the normalization process. The *y* component, or the gender, will be disregarded for the moment. The normalization process involves extracting the mean and standard deviation of both inputs for all 29 individuals. The output of the mean and standard deviations for the height and weight can be seen in the following screenshot:

```
In [23]: x_mean = X.mean(axis=0)
         x_std = X.std(axis=0)
         print(x_mean, x_std)
         [  67.20689655  145.24137931] [  3.35671545  22.1743175 ]
```

4. The mean of the height is ~**67** inches and the standard deviation of the height is ~**3.4** inches. The mean of the weight is ~**145** lbs and the standard deviation of the weight is ~**22** lbs.

5. Once they are extracted, the inputs are normalized using the following equation:
`X_norm = (X - X_mean)/X_std`.

6. The `X` array is normalized using the Python function `normalize()` and the `X` array is now assigned to the values of the newly minted normalized set, as seen in the following screenshot:

```
In [24]: def normalize(X):
             x_mean = X.mean(axis=0)
             x_std = X.std(axis=0)
             X = (X - X.mean(axis=0))/X.std(axis=0)
             return X

In [25]: X = normalize(X)
         print(X)

         [[-0.06163661  0.21460055]
          [-0.65745714 -0.4618577 ]
          [ 0.23627366 -0.68734378]
          [ 0.8320942   0.66557271]
          [ 0.8320942  -0.68734378]
          [ 0.53418393  1.29693375]
          [-0.65745714 -0.86773265]
          [ 2.02373527  1.92829478]
          [-2.14700848 -1.58928812]
          [-1.25327768 -0.91282987]
          [ 0.8320942   1.25183653]
          [ 0.8320942  -0.01088554]
          [ 0.23627366  1.34203096]
          [-0.65745714 -1.0030243 ]
          [ 1.13000446 -0.01088554]
          [ 2.02373527  0.66557271]
          [-0.95536741 -0.4618577 ]
          [ 1.13000446  1.34203096]
          [-0.06163661 -0.01088554]
          [-0.06163661 -0.68734378]
          [ 0.8320942   0.75576715]
          [-0.95536741 -1.72457977]
          [ 0.8320942   1.34203096]
          [-0.95536741 -0.68734378]
          [-0.35954687  0.80086436]
          [-1.25327768 -0.37166327]
          [-0.65745714  0.8910588 ]
          [-0.65745714 -0.68734378]
          [-0.95536741 -1.63438533]]]
```

See also

In order to learn more about normalization in statistics, visit the following website:

`https://en.wikipedia.org/wiki/Normalization_(statistics)`

Validating array for optimal neural network performance

A little bit of validation goes a long way in ensuring that our array is normalized for optimal performance within our upcoming neural network.

Getting ready

This section will require a bit of numpy magic using the numpy.stack() function.

How to do it...

The following steps walk through validating that our array has been normalized.

1. Execute the following step to print the mean and standard deviation of array inputs:

```
print('standard deviation')
print(round(X[:,0].std(axis=0),0))
print('mean')
print(round(X[:,0].mean(axis=0),0))
```

2. Execute the following script to combine height, weight, and gender into one array, data_array:

```
data_array = np.column_stack((X[:,0], X[:,1],y))
```

How it works...

This section explains how the array is validated and constructed for optimal future use within the neural network.

1. The new mean of the height should be 0 and the standard deviation should be 1. This can be seen in the following screenshot:

```
In [26]:  print('standard deviation')
          print(round(X[:,0].std(axis=0),0))
          print('mean')
          print(round(X[:,0].mean(axis=0),0))

          standard deviation
          1.0
          mean
          -0.0
```

2. This is confirmation of a normalized dataset, as it includes a mean of 0 and a standard deviation of 1.

3. The original `data_array` is no longer useful for a neural network because it contains the original, non-normalized, input values for `height`, `weight`, and `gender`.

4. Nonetheless, with a little bit of `numpy` magic, `data_array` can be restructured to include the normalized `height` and `weight`, along with `gender`. This is done with `numpy.stack()`. The output of the new array, `data_array`, can be seen in the following screenshot:

```
In [27]:  data_array = np.column_stack((X[:,0], X[:,1],y))
          print(data_array)

          [[-0.06163661  0.21460055  1.        ]
           [-0.65745714 -0.4618577   0.        ]
           [ 0.23627366 -0.68734378  0.        ]
           [ 0.8320942   0.66557271  1.        ]
           [ 0.8320942  -0.68734378  0.        ]
           [ 0.53418393  1.29693375  1.        ]
           [-0.65745714 -0.86773265  0.        ]
           [ 2.02373527  1.92829478  1.        ]
           [-2.14700848 -1.58928812  0.        ]
           [-1.25327768 -0.91282987  0.        ]
           [ 0.8320942   1.25183653  1.        ]
           [ 0.8320942  -0.01088554  1.        ]
           [ 0.23627366  1.34203096  1.        ]
           [-0.65745714 -1.0030243   0.        ]
           [ 1.13000446 -0.01088554  1.        ]
           [ 2.02373527  0.66557271  1.        ]
           [-0.95536741 -0.4618577   0.        ]
           [ 1.13000446  1.34203096  1.        ]
           [-0.06163661 -0.01088554  1.        ]
           [-0.06163661 -0.68734378  0.        ]
           [ 0.8320942   0.75576715  1.        ]
           [-0.95536741 -1.72457977  0.        ]
           [ 0.8320942   1.34203096  1.        ]
           [-0.95536741 -0.68734378  0.        ]
           [-0.35954687  0.80086436  1.        ]
           [-1.25327768 -0.37166327  0.        ]
           [-0.65745714  0.8910588   1.        ]
           [-0.65745714 -0.68734378  0.        ]
           [-0.95536741 -1.63438533  0.        ]]
```

There's more...

Our array is now all set. Our inputs for height and weight are normalized and our output for gender is labeled as 0 or 1.

See also

To learn more about `numpy.stack()`, visit the following website:

`https://docs.scipy.org/doc/numpy/reference/generated/numpy.stack.html`

Setting up the activation function with sigmoid

An activation function is used in a neural network to help determine the output, whether it is a yes or no, true or false, or in our case 0 or 1 (male/female). At this point, the inputs have been normalized and have been summed with the weights and bias: `w1`, `w2`, and `b`. However, the weights and bias are completely random at the moment and are not optimized to produce a predicted output that matches the actual output. The missing link in building the predicted outcome resides with the activation or `sigmoid` function, which is shown in the following diagram:

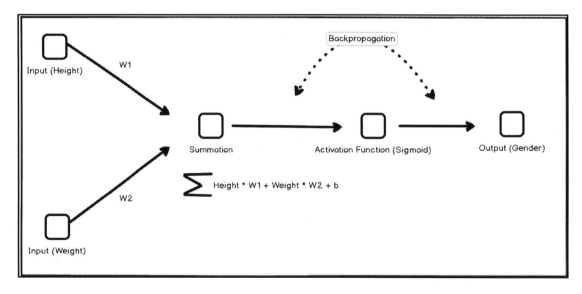

If the number that is produced out of the summation is very small, it will produce an activation of 0. Likewise, if the number produced out of the summation is quite large, it will produce an activation of 1. This function is useful because it restricts the output to a binary outcome, which is quite useful for classification. The consequences of these outputs will be discussed and clarified in the remainder of this chapter.

Getting ready

The `sigmoid` function is similar to the logistic regression function in that it computes a probabilistic outcome between 0 and 1. Additionally, it gives a range of everything in - between. Therefore, a condition could be set to associate any value greater than 0.5 to 1 and less than 0.5 to 0.

How to do it...

This section walks through the steps of creating and plotting a sigmoid function with sample data.

1. Create the `sigmoid` function using a Python function, as seen in the following script:

```
def sigmoid(input):
    return 1/(1+np.exp(-input))
```

2. Create sample x values for the `sigmoid` curve using the following script:

```
X = np.arange(-10,10,1)
```

3. Additionally, create sample y values for the `sigmoid` curve using the following script:

```
Y = sigmoid(X)
```

4. Plot the x and y values for these points using the following script:

```
plt.figure(figsize=(6, 4), dpi= 75)
plt.axis([-10,10,-0.25,1.2])
plt.grid()
plt.plot(X,Y)
plt.title('Sigmoid Function')
plt.show()
```

How it works...

This section explains the mathematics behind the sigmoid function.

1. The `sigmoid` function is a specialized version of the logistic regression used for classification. The calculation of the logistic regression is expressed with the following formula:

$$Logistic(x) = \frac{L}{1 + e^{-k(x - x_{midpoint})}}$$

2. The variables for the logistic regression function stand for the following:
   - L stands the maximum value of the function
   - k stands for the steepness of the curve
   - $x_{midpoint}$ stands for the midpoint value of the function

3. Since the `sigmoid` function has a steepness of value 1, a midpoint of 0, and a maximum value of 1, it produces the following function:

$$Sigmoid(x) = \frac{1}{1 + e^{-x}}$$

4. We can plot a general sigmoid function with x-values ranging from -5 to 5, and y-values ranging from 0 to 1 as seen in the following screenshot:

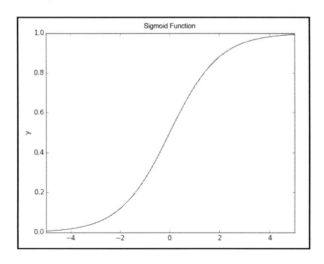

5. We created our own `sigmoid` function with Python and plotted it using sample data between -10 and 10. Our plot looks very similar to the previous general sigmoid plot. The output of our `sigmoid` function can be seen in the following screenshot:

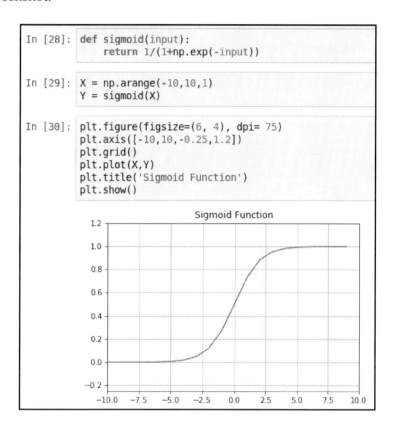

See also

In order to learn more about the origin of the `sigmoid` function, visit the following website:

`https://en.wikipedia.org/wiki/Sigmoid_function`

Creating the sigmoid derivative function

The sigmoid function is a unique function where the value of the derivative of the sigmoid function includes the value of the sigmoid function. You may be asking what's the big deal. However, since the sigmoid function is already calculated it allows for simpler and more efficient processing when performing backpropagation over many layers. Additionally, it is the derivative of the sigmoid function that is used in the calculation to derive the optimal w1, w2, and b values to derive the most accurate predicted output.

Getting ready

A cursory understanding of derivatives from calculus will assist in understanding the sigmoid derivative function.

How to do it...

This section walks through the steps to create a sigmoid derivative function.

1. Just like the sigmoid function, create the derivative of the sigmoid function can with Python using the following script:

```
def sigmoid_derivative(x):
    return sigmoid(x) * (1-sigmoid(x))
```

2. Plot the derivative of the sigmoid function alongside the original sigmoid function using the following script:

```
plt.figure(figsize=(6, 4), dpi= 75)
plt.axis([-10,10,-0.25,1.2])
plt.grid()
X = np.arange(-10,10,1)
Y = sigmoid(X)
Y_Prime = sigmoid_derivative(X)
c=plt.plot(X, Y, label="Sigmoid",c='b')
d=plt.plot(X, Y_Prime, marker=".", label="Sigmoid Derivative",
c='b')
plt.title('Sigmoid vs Sigmoid Derivative')
plt.xlabel('X')
plt.ylabel('Y')
plt.legend()
plt.show()
```

How it works...

This section explains the math behind the derivative of the sigmoid function along with the logic to create the derivative of the sigmoid function with Python.

1. The neural network will require the derivative of the `sigmoid` function to predict an accurate output for `gender`. The derivative of the `sigmoid` function is calculated using the following formula:

$$\frac{\mathrm{d}Sigmoid(x)}{\mathrm{d}x} = (\frac{1}{1+e^{-x}})^2 * \frac{\partial}{\partial x}(1+e^{-x}) = Sigmoid(x) * (1 - Sigmoid(x))$$

2. We can then create the derivative of the sigmoid function, `sigmoid_derivate()`, using the original sigmoid function, `sigmoid()`, in Python. We can plot both functions side by side as seen in the following screenshot:

```
In [31]: def sigmoid_derivative(x):
             return sigmoid(x) * (1-sigmoid(x))

In [32]: plt.figure(figsize=(6, 4), dpi= 75)
         plt.axis([-10,10,-0.25,1.2])
         plt.grid()
         X = np.arange(-10,10,1)
         Y = sigmoid(X)
         Y_Prime = sigmoid_derivative(X)
         plt.plot(X, Y, label="Sigmoid",c='b')
         plt.plot(X, Y_Prime, marker=".", label="Sigmoid Derivative", c='b')
         plt.title('Sigmoid vs Sigmoid Derivative')
         plt.xlabel('X')
         plt.ylabel('Y')
         plt.legend()
         plt.show()
```

3. **Sigmoid Derivative** tracks the slope of the original **Sigmoid** function. Early on in the plot, when the slope of the **Sigmoid** is completely horizontal, the **Sigmoid Derivative** is also **0.0**. The same holds true for **Sigmoid** when the value is approaching 1 as the slope is also almost completely horizontal. The peak value of the slope of **Sigmoid** is at the midpoint of the x-axis. Consequently, this is also the peak value of **Sigmoid Derivative**.

See also

To get a deeper dive into derivatives, visit the following website:

`https://www.khanacademy.org/math/calculus-home/taking-derivatives-calc`

Calculating the cost function in a neural network

At this point, it is time to bring together all of the parts highlighted earlier on in the chapter to calculate the cost function, which will be used by the neural network to determine how well the predicted outcome matched the original or actual outcome, given the 29 individual data points that are currently available. The purpose of the cost function is to identify the difference between the actual value and the predicted value. Gradient descent is then used to either increase or decrease the values for `w1`, `w2`, and `b` to decrease the value of the cost function and ultimately achieve our goal of deriving a predicted value that matches the actual value.

Getting ready

The formula for the cost function is the following:

$$cost(x) = (predicted - actual)^2$$

If the cost function looks familiar, it's because it is really just another way of minimizing the squared difference between the actual output and the prediction. The purpose of gradient descent or backpropagation in a neural network is to minimize the cost function until the value is close to 0. At that point, the weights and bias (`w1`, `w2`, and `b`) will no longer be random insignificant values generated by `numpy`, but actual significant weights contributing to a neural network model.

How to do it...

This section walks through the steps to calculate the cost function.

1. Set a learning rate value of `0.1` to incrementally change the weights and bias until a final output is selected using the following script:

   ```
   learningRate = 0.1
   ```

2. Initiate a Python list called `allCosts` using the following script.

   ```
   allCosts = []
   ```

3. Create a `for` loop that will iterate through 100,000 scenarios using the following script:

```
In [36]: learning_rate = 0.1

all_costs = []

for i in range(100000):
    # set the random data points that will be used to calculate the summation
    random_number = np.random.randint(len(data_array))
    random_person = data_array[random_number]

    # the height and weight from the random individual are selected
    height = random_person[0]
    weight = random_person[1]

    z = w1*height+w2*weight+b
    predictedGender = sigmoid(z)

    actualGender = random_person[2]

    cost = (predictedGender-actualGender)**2

    # the cost value is appended to the list
    all_costs.append(cost)

    # partial derivatives of the cost function and summation are calculated
    dcost_predictedGender = 2 * (predictedGender-actualGender)
    dpredictedGenger_dz = sigmoid_derivative(z)
    dz_dw1 = height
    dz_dw2 = weight
    dz_db = 1

    dcost_dw1 = dcost_predictedGender * dpredictedGenger_dz * dz_dw1
    dcost_dw2 = dcost_predictedGender * dpredictedGenger_dz * dz_dw2
    dcost_db  = dcost_predictedGender * dpredictedGenger_dz * dz_db

    # gradient descent calculation
    w1 = w1 - learning_rate * dcost_dw1
    w2 = w2 - learning_rate * dcost_dw2
    b  = b  - learning_rate * dcost_db
```

4. Plot the cost values collected over the 100,000 iterations using the following script:

```
plt.plot(all_costs)
plt.title('Cost Value over 100,000 iterations')
plt.xlabel('Iteration')
plt.ylabel('Cost Value')
plt.show()
```

5. The final values of the weights and bias can be viewed using the following script:

```
print('The final values of w1, w2, and b')
print('-------------------------------')
print('w1 = {}'.format(w1))
print('w2 = {}'.format(w2))
print('b = {}'.format(b))
```

How it works...

This section explains how the cost function is used to generate weights and bias.

1. A `for` loop will be implemented that will perform gradient descent on the weights and bias to tweak the values until the cost function gets close to 0.
2. The loop will iterate over the cost function 100,000 times. Each time, a random value for `height` and `weight` from the 29 individuals is selected.
3. A summation value, z, is calculated from the random `height` and `weight`, and the input is used to calculate a `predictedGender` score with the `sigmoid` function.
4. The cost function is calculated and added to a list that tracks all cost functions through the 100,000 iterations, `allCosts`.
5. A series of partial derivatives is calculated with respect to the summation value (z) as well as the `cost` function (`cost`).
6. These calculations are ultimately used to update the weights and bias with respect to the cost function until they (`w1`, `w2`, and `b`) return a value that is close to 0 for the cost function over the 100,000 iterations.
7. Ultimately, the goal is for the values to be decreasing for the cost function as the iterations increase. The output of the cost function values over the 100,000 iterations can be seen in the following screenshot:

```
In [37]:  plt.plot(all_costs)
          plt.title('Cost Value over 100,000 iterations')
          plt.xlabel('Iteration')
          plt.ylabel('Cost Value')
          plt.show()
```

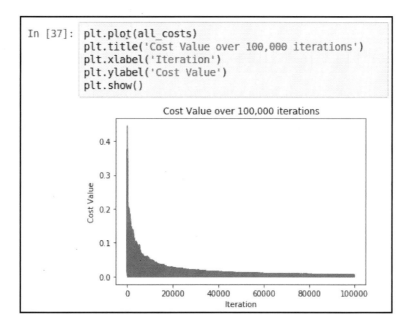

8. Over the course of the iterations, the cost value dropped from ~0.45 to ~0.01.
9. Additionally, we can view the final output for the values of w1, w2, and b that produced the lowest value of the cost function as seen in the following screenshot:

```
In [38]:  print('The final values of w1, w2, and b')
          print('----------------------------------')
          print('w1 = {}'.format(w1))
          print('w2 = {}'.format(w2))
          print('b  = {}'.format(b))

          The final values of w1, w2, and b
          ----------------------------------
          w1 = 1.8209212481467743
          w2 = 10.501412686537124
          b  = 2.6922206902934818
```

There's more...

The ability to test the final values of the weights and bias is now available to compute how well the cost function worked to compute a predicted and how it compared to the actual score.

The following script will create a loop through each individual and calculate a predicted gender score based on the weights (`w1`, `w2`) and the bias (`b`):

```
for i in range(len(data_array)):
    random_individual = data_array[i]
    height = random_individual[0]
    weight = random_individual[1]
    z = height*w1 + weight*w2 + b
    predictedGender=sigmoid(z)
    print("Individual #{} actual score: {} predicted score:
{}".format(i+1,random_individual[2],predictedGender))
```

The output of the script can be seen in the following screenshot:

```
In [39]:  for i in range(len(data_array)):
              random_individual = data_array[i]
              height = random_individual[0]
              weight = random_individual[1]
              z = height*w1 + weight*w2 + b
              predictedGender=sigmoid(z)
              print("Individual #{} actual score: {} predicted score: {}"
                  .format(i+1,random_individual[2],predictedGender))

          Individual #1 actual score: 1.0 predicted score: 0.9921049600550155
          Individual #2 actual score: 0.0 predicted score: 0.03372805542036423
          Individual #3 actual score: 0.0 predicted score: 0.016372819700798374
          Individual #4 actual score: 1.0 predicted score: 0.9999862828839244
          Individual #5 actual score: 0.0 predicted score: 0.0469456203497416
          Individual #6 actual score: 1.0 predicted score: 0.9999999688535043
          Individual #7 actual score: 0.0 predicted score: 0.0004915890916453382
          Individual #8 actual score: 1.0 predicted score: 0.9999999999972711
          Individual #9 actual score: 0.0 predicted score: 1.6712931344961645e-08
          Individual #10 actual score: 0.0 predicted score: 0.00010349306890725019
          Individual #11 actual score: 1.0 predicted score: 0.9999999709268494
          Individual #12 actual score: 1.0 predicted score: 0.9835862381176147
          Individual #13 actual score: 1.0 predicted score: 0.999999966632299
          Individual #14 actual score: 0.0 predicted score: 0.00011877876719320243
          Individual #15 actual score: 1.0 predicted score: 0.9903924909384766
          Individual #16 actual score: 1.0 predicted score: 0.9999984336125107
          Individual #17 actual score: 0.0 predicted score: 0.019887295647811554
          Individual #18 actual score: 1.0 predicted score: 0.9999999934453481
          Individual #19 actual score: 1.0 predicted score: 0.9216999710497804
          Individual #20 actual score: 0.0 predicted score: 0.009583378854204839
          Individual #21 actual score: 1.0 predicted score: 0.9999946799439814
          Individual #22 actual score: 0.0 predicted score: 3.535054577059945e-08
          Individual #23 actual score: 1.0 predicted score: 0.999999988724343
          Individual #24 actual score: 0.0 predicted score: 0.001897139967360123
          Individual #25 actual score: 1.0 predicted score: 0.9999709865300538
          Individual #26 actual score: 0.0 predicted score: 0.029515249648309982
          Individual #27 actual score: 1.0 predicted score: 0.999980642653134
          Individual #28 actual score: 0.0 predicted score: 0.003259106640364197
          Individual #29 actual score: 0.0 predicted score: 9.114783430185142e-08
```

All 29 of the actual scores approximately match the predicted scores when rounded. While this is good for confirming the model produced matching results on the training data, ultimately, the test will be to determine whether the model can make accurate gender predictions on new individuals introduced to it.

See also

In order to learn more about minimizing cost functions or squared (difference) error functions using gradient descent, visit the following site:

```
https://en.wikipedia.org/wiki/Gradient_descent
```

Predicting gender based on height and weight

A predictive model is only useful if it can actually predict based on new information. This is the case with a simple logistic or linear regression, or a more complex neural network model.

Getting ready

This is where the fun begins. The only requirements for this section are to pull sample data points for both male and female individuals and use their height and weight values to measure the accuracy of the model created in the previous section.

How to do it...

This section walks through the steps to predict gender based on height and weight.

1. Create a Python function called `input_normalize` to input new values for `height` and `weight` and output a normalized height and weight, as seen in the following script:

```
def input_normalize(height, weight):
    inputHeight = (height - x_mean[0])/x_std[0]
    inputWeight = (weight - x_mean[1])/x_std[1]
    return inputHeight, inputWeight
```

2. Assign a variable called `score` to the function for the values of `70` inches for the `height` and `180` lbs for the `weight`, as seen in the following script:

```
score = input_normalize(70, 180)
```

3. Create another Python function, called `predict_gender`, to output a probability score, `gender_score`, between 0 and 1, as well as a gender description, by applying the summation with `w1`, `w2`, and `b` as well as the `sigmoid` function, as seen in the following script:

```
def predict_gender(raw_score):
    gender_summation = raw_score[0]*w1 + raw_score[1]*w2 + b
    gender_score = sigmoid(gender_summation)
    if gender_score <= 0.5:
        gender = 'Female'
    else:
        gender = 'Male'
    return gender, gender_score
```

How it works...

This section explains how new inputs for height and weight are used to generate a prediction score for gender.

1. A function is created to input new height and weight values and convert the actual values to normalized height and weight values called `inputHeight` and `inputWeight`

2. A variable, `score`, is used to store the normalized values and another function, `predictGender`, is created to input the score values and output a gender score and description based on the values of `w1`, `w2`, and `b` that were created in the previous section. These values have already been pre-adjusted using gradient descent to tweak the values and minimize the `cost` function.

3. Applying the `score` value to the `predict_gender` function should reveal the **gender** description and **score**, as seen in the following screenshot:

```
In [40]: def input_normalize(height, weight):
             inputHeight = (height - x_mean[0])/x_std[0]
             inputWeight =  weight - x_mean[1] /x_std[1]
             return inputHeight, inputWeight

In [41]: score = input_normalize(70, 180)

In [42]: def predict_gender(raw_score):
             gender_summation = raw_score[0]*w1 + raw_score[1]*w2 + b
             gender_score = sigmoid(gender_summation)
             if gender_score <= 0.5:
                 gender = 'Female'
             else:
                 gender = 'Male'
             return gender, gender_score

In [43]: predict_gender(score)

Out[43]: ('Male', 0.99999999894375113)
```

4. It appears that the specifications of 70 inches in height and 180 lbs in weight is a high predictor (99.999%) for **Male**.

5. Another test for 50 inches in height and 150 lbs in weight will likely reveal a different gender, as seen in the following screenshot:

```
In [44]: score = input_normalize(50,120)

In [45]: predict_gender(score)

Out[45]: ('Female', 8.3923134541706229e-09)
```

6. Similarly, this input produces a very low score from the sigmoid function (0.00000000839) indicating that these features are closely associated with the Female gender.

See also

In order to learn more about testing, training, and validation data sets, visit the following website:

```
https://en.wikipedia.org/wiki/Training,_test,_and_validation_sets
```

Visualizing prediction scores

While we can individually predict the gender based on an individual with a certain height and weight, the entire dataset can be graphed and scored using every data point to determine whether the output is going to score a female or a male.

Getting ready

There are no dependencies required for this section.

How to do it...

This section walks through the steps to visualize all of the predicted points in a graph.

1. Compute the minimum and maximum points of the graph using the following script:

```
x_min = min(data_array[:,0])-0.1
x_max = max(data_array[:,0])+0.1
y_min = min(data_array[:,1])-0.1
y_max = max(data_array[:,1])+0.1
increment= 0.05

print(x_min, x_max, y_min, y_max)
```

2. Generate *x* and *y* values in increments of 0.05 units and then create an array called xy_data, as seen in the following script:

```
x_data= np.arange(x_min, x_max, increment)
y_data= np.arange(y_min, y_max, increment)
xy_data = [[x_all, y_all] for x_all in x_data for y_all in y_data]
```

3. Finally, a similar script to that used earlier in the chapter is used to generate a gender score and populate a graph, as seen in the following script:

```
for i in range(len(xy_data)):
    data = (xy_data[i])
    height = data[0]
    weight = data[1]
    z_new = height*w1 + weight*w2 + b
    predictedGender_new=sigmoid(z_new)
    # print(height, weight, predictedGender_new)
    ax = plt.scatter(height[predictedGender_new<=0.5],
            weight[predictedGender_new<=0.5],
            marker = 'o', c= 'r', label = 'Female')
    bx = plt.scatter(height[predictedGender_new > 0.5],
            weight[predictedGender_new>0.5],
            marker = 'o', c= 'b', label = 'Male')
    # plot values, title, legend, x and y axis
    plt.title('Weight vs Height by Gender')
    plt.xlabel('Height (in)')
    plt.ylabel('Weight (lbs)')
    plt.legend(handles=[ax,bx])
```

How it works...

This section explains how the data points are created to generate prediction values that will be graphed.

1. The minimum and maximum values of the graph are computed based on the array values. The output of the script can be seen in the following screenshot:

```
In [46]: x_min = min(data_array[:,0])-0.1
         x_max = max(data_array[:,0])+0.1
         y_min = min(data_array[:,1])-0.1
         y_max = max(data_array[:,1])+0.1
         increment= 0.05
         print(x_min, x_max, y_min, y_max)

         -2.24700848159 2.12373526733 -1.8245797669 2.02829477995
```

2. We generate x and y values for each data point within the minimum and maximum values within 0.05 increments and then run each (x,y) point into the prediction score to plot the values. The **Female** gender score is assigned a red color and the **Male** gender score is assigned a blue color as seen in the following screenshot:

```
In [50]: for i in range(len(xy_data)):
             data = (xy_data[i])
             height = data[0]
             weight = data[1]
             z_new = height*w1 + weight*w2 + b
             predictedGender_new=sigmoid(z_new)
             # print(height, weight, predictedGender_new)
             ax = plt.scatter(height[predictedGender_new<=0.5],
                              weight[predictedGender_new<=0.5],
                              marker = 'o', c= 'r', label = 'Female')
             bx = plt.scatter(height[predictedGender_new > 0.5],
                              weight[predictedGender_new>0.5],
                              marker = 'o', c= 'b', label = 'Male')
             # plot values, title, legend, x and y axis
             plt.title('Weight vs Height by Gender')
             plt.xlabel('Height (in)')
             plt.ylabel('Weight (lbs)')
             plt.legend(handles=[ax,bx])
```

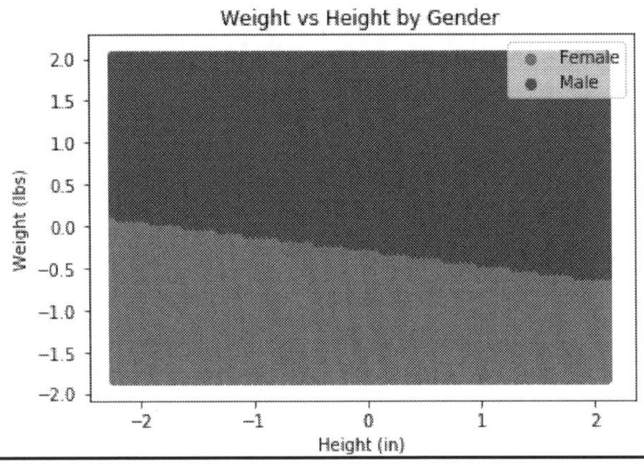

3. The graph shows the cutoff between the gender scores depending on the `height` and `weight` selected.

3
Pain Points of Convolutional Neural Networks

In this chapter, the following recipes will be covered:

- Pain Point #1: Importing MNIST images
- Pain Point #2: Visualizing MNIST images
- Pain Point #3: Exporting MNIST images as files
- Pain Point #4: Augmenting MNIST images
- Pain Point #5: Utilizing alternate sources for trained images
- Pain Point #6: Prioritizing high-level libraries for CNNs

Introduction

Convolutional neural networks (CNNs) have been enjoying a bit of resurgence in the last couple of years. They have shown great success when it comes to image recognition. This is quite relevant these days with the advent of modern smartphones as anyone now has the ability to take large volumes of pictures of objects and post them on social media sites. Just due to this phenomenon, convolutional neural networks are in high demand these days.

There are several features that make a CNN optimally perform. They require the following features:

- A high volume of training data
- Visual and spatial data
- An emphasis on filtering (pooling), activation, and convoluting as opposed to a fully connected layer that is more apparent in a traditional neural network

While CNNs have gained great popularity, there are some limitations in working with them primarily due to their computational needs as well as the volume of training data required to get a well-performing model. We will focus on techniques that can be applied to the data that will ultimately assist with the development of a convolutional neural network while addressing these limitations. In later chapters, we will apply some of these techniques when we develop models for image classification.

Pain Point #1: Importing MNIST images

One of the most common datasets used for image classification is the `MNIST` dataset, which is composed of thousands of samples of handwritten digits. The **Modified National Institute of Standards and Technology** (**MNIST**) is, according to Yann LeCun, Corinna Cortes, and Christopher J.C. Burges, useful for the following reasons:

It is a good database for people who want to try learning techniques and pattern recognition methods on real-world data while spending minimal efforts on preprocessing and formatting.

There are several methods to import the MNIST images into our Jupyter notebook. We will cover the following two methods in this chapter:

1. Directly through the TensorFlow library
2. Manually through the MNIST website

One thing to note is that we will be primarily using MNIST images as our example of how to improve performance within a convolutional neural network. All of these techniques that will be applied on MNIST images can be applied to any image that will be used to train a CNN.

Getting ready

The only requirement needed is to install `TensorFlow`. It will likely not come pre-installed with the **anaconda3** packages; therefore, a simple `pip` install will either confirm the availability of `TensorFlow` or install it if not currently available. `TensorFlow` can be easily installed in the Terminal, as seen in the following screenshot:

```
asherif844@ubuntu: ~
asherif844@ubuntu:~$ pip install tensorflow
Requirement already satisfied: tensorflow in ./anaconda3/lib/python3.6/site-pack
ages
Requirement already satisfied: numpy>=1.11.0 in ./anaconda3/lib/python3.6/site-p
ackages (from tensorflow)
Requirement already satisfied: protobuf>=3.3.0 in ./anaconda3/lib/python3.6/site
-packages (from tensorflow)
Requirement already satisfied: six>=1.10.0 in ./anaconda3/lib/python3.6/site-pac
kages (from tensorflow)
Requirement already satisfied: tensorflow-tensorboard<0.2.0,>=0.1.0 in ./anacond
a3/lib/python3.6/site-packages (from tensorflow)
Requirement already satisfied: wheel>=0.26 in ./anaconda3/lib/python3.6/site-pac
kages (from tensorflow)
Requirement already satisfied: setuptools in ./anaconda3/lib/python3.6/site-pack
ages/setuptools-27.2.0-py3.6.egg (from protobuf>=3.3.0->tensorflow)
Requirement already satisfied: html5lib==0.9999999 in ./anaconda3/lib/python3.6/
site-packages (from tensorflow-tensorboard<0.2.0,>=0.1.0->tensorflow)
Requirement already satisfied: markdown>=2.6.8 in ./anaconda3/lib/python3.6/site
-packages (from tensorflow-tensorboard<0.2.0,>=0.1.0->tensorflow)
Requirement already satisfied: bleach==1.5.0 in ./anaconda3/lib/python3.6/site-p
ackages (from tensorflow-tensorboard<0.2.0,>=0.1.0->tensorflow)
Requirement already satisfied: werkzeug>=0.11.10 in ./anaconda3/lib/python3.6/si
te-packages (from tensorflow-tensorboard<0.2.0,>=0.1.0->tensorflow)
asherif844@ubuntu:~$
```

How to do it...

The TensorFlow library has a conveniently built-in set of examples that can be used directly. One of those example datasets is MNIST. This section will walk through the steps of accessing those images.

1. Import TensorFlow into the library with an alias of tf using the following script:

    ```
    import tensorflow as tf
    ```

2. Download and extract images from the library and save to a local folder using the following script:

    ```
    from tensorflow.examples.tutorials.mnist import input_data
    data = input_data.read_data_sets('MNIST/', one_hot=True)
    ```

3. Retrieve a final count of the training and testing datasets that will be used to evaluate the accuracy of the image classification using the following script:

```
print('Image Inventory')
print('----------')
print('Training: ' + str(len(data.train.labels)))
print('Testing: '+ str(len(data.test.labels)))
print('----------')
```

How it works...

This section explains the process used to access the MNIST datasets:

1. Once we receive a confirmation that the TensorFlow library has been properly installed, it is imported into the notebook.
2. We can confirm the version of TensorFlow as well as extract the images to our local folder of MNIST/. The extraction process is visible in the output of the notebook, as seen in the following screenshot:

```
In [1]:  import tensorflow as tf



In [2]:  print(tf.__version__)

         1.4.1

In [3]:  from tensorflow.examples.tutorials.mnist import input_data
         data = input_data.read_data_sets('MNIST/', one_hot=True)

         Extracting MNIST/train-images-idx3-ubyte.gz
         Extracting MNIST/train-labels-idx1-ubyte.gz
         Extracting MNIST/t10k-images-idx3-ubyte.gz
         Extracting MNIST/t10k-labels-idx1-ubyte.gz
```

3. The four extracted files are named the following:
    1. t10k-images-idx3-ubyte.gz
    2. t10k-labels-idx1-ubyte.gz
    3. train-images-idx3-ubyte.gz
    4. train-labels-idx1-ubyte.gz

4. They have been downloaded to the `MNIST/` subfolder as seen in the following screenshot:

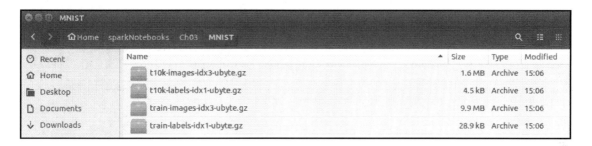

5. In addition, the four files can be viewed in our notebook, as seen in the following screenshot:

```
In [4]:  import os
         os.listdir('MNIST/')

Out[4]:  ['t10k-images-idx3-ubyte.gz',
          't10k-labels-idx1-ubyte.gz',
          'train-labels-idx1-ubyte.gz',
          'train-images-idx3-ubyte.gz']
```

6. The four files are the testing and training images along with the accompanying testing and training labels identifying each image in the testing and training datasets. Additionally, the `one_hot = True` feature is explicitly defined. This indicates that one-hot encoding is active with the labels, which assists with feature selection within modeling as each column value will be either 0 or 1.

7. A subclass of the library is also imported that stores the handwritten images of MNIST to the specified local folder. The folder containing all of the images should be approximately 12 MB in size for **55,000** training images and **10,000** testing images, as seen in the following screenshot:

```
In [5]:  print('Image Inventory')
         print('----------')
         print('Training: {}'.format(len(data.train.labels)))
         print('Testing:  {}'.format(len(data.test.labels)))
         print('----------')

         Image Inventory
         ----------
         Training: 55000
         Testing:  10000
         ----------
```

8. The 10,000 images will be used to test the accuracy of our model that will be trained on the 55,000 images.

There's more...

Occasionally, there may be errors or warnings when trying to access the MNIST datasets directly through `TensorFlow`. As was seen earlier on in the section, we received the following warning when importing MNIST:

WARNING:tensorflow:From <ipython-input-3-ceaef6f48460>:2: read_data_sets (from tensorflow.contrib.learn.python.learn.datasets.mnist) is deprecated and will be removed in a future version.
Instructions for updating:
Please use alternatives such as official/mnist/dataset.py from tensorflow/models.

The dataset may become deprecated in a future release of `TensorFlow` and therefore, no longer be directly accessible. Sometimes we may just encounter a typical *HTTP 403 error* when extracting the MNIST images through `TensorFlow`. This may be due to the website being temporarily unavailable. Have no fear in either case, there is a manual approach to downloading the four `.gz` files using the following link:

http://yann.lecun.com/exdb/mnist/

The files are located on the website, as seen in the following screenshot:

Download the files and save them to an accessible local folder similar to what was done with the files that came directly from `TensorFlow`.

See also

To learn more about the `MNIST` database of handwritten digits, visit the following website: `http://yann.lecun.com/exdb/mnist/`.

To learn more about one-hot encoding, visit the following website: `https://hackernoon.com/what-is-one-hot-encoding-why-and-when-do-you-have-to-use-it-e3c6186d008f`.

Pain Point #2: Visualizing MNIST images

Plotting images is often a major pain point when dealing with graphics within a Jupyter notebook. Displaying the handwritten images from the training dataset is critical, especially when comparing the actual value of the label that is associated with the handwritten image.

Getting ready

The only Python libraries that will be imported to visualize the handwritten images are `numpy` and `matplotlib`. Both should already be available through the packages in Anaconda. If for some reason they are not available, they can both be `pip` installed at the Terminal using the following commands:

- `pip install matplotlib`
- `pip install numpy`

How to do it...

This section will walk through the steps to visualize the MNIST handwritten images in a Jupyter notebook:

1. Import the following libraries, numpy and matplotlib, and configure matplotlib to plot inline using the following script:

```
import numpy as np
import matplotlib.pyplot as plt
%matplotlib inline
```

2. Plot the first two sample images using the following script:

```
for i in range(2):
    image = data.train.images[i]
    image = np.array(image, dtype='float')
    label = data.train.labels[i]
    pixels = image.reshape((28, 28))
    plt.imshow(pixels, cmap='gray')
    print('-----------------')
    print(label)
    plt.show()
```

How it works...

This section will walk through the process of how the MNIST handwritten images are viewed in a Jupyter notebook:

1. A loop is generated in Python that will sample two images from the training dataset.

2. Initially, the images are just a series of values in float format between 0 and 1 that are stored in a `numpy` array. The value of the array is a labeled image called `image`. The `image` array is then reshaped into a 28 x 28 matrix called `pixels` that has a black color for any value at 0 and a gray shade color for any color that is not 0. The higher the value, the lighter the gray shade of color. An example can be seen in the following screenshot for the digit **8**:

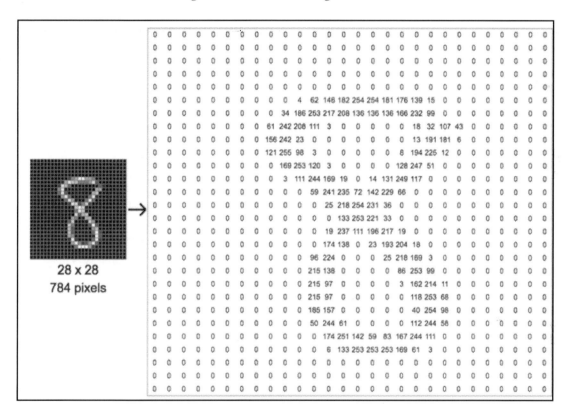

3. The output of the loop produces two handwritten images for the numbers **7** and **3** along with their labels, as seen in the following screenshot:

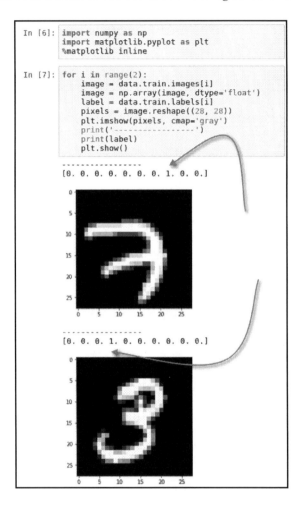

4. In addition to the images being plotted, the label from the training dataset is also printed above the image. The label is an array of length 10, with values of 0 or 1 only for all 10 digits. For digit 7, the 8th element in the array is of value 1 and for digit 3, the 4th element in the array is of value 1. All other values are 0.

There's more...

It may not be immediately obvious what the numeric value of the image is. While most will be able to identify that the first image is a 7 and the second image is a 3, it would be helpful to have confirmation from the label array.

There are 10 elements in the array, each referencing a value for labels 0 through 9 in numeric order. Since the first array has a positive or 1 value in the 8th slot, that is an indication that the value of the image is a 7, as 7 in the 8th index in the array. All other values should be 0. Additionally, the second image has a value of 1 in the 4th spot, indicating a positive value for 3.

See also

Leun, Cortes, and Burges discuss why the image pixelations were set at 28 x 28 in the following statement:

> he original black and white (bilevel) images from NIST were size normalized to fit in a 20x20 pixel box while preserving their aspect ratio. The resulting images contain grey levels as a result of the anti-aliasing technique used by the normalization algorithm. The images were centered in a 28x28 image by computing the center of mass of the pixels, and translating the image so as to position this point at the center of the 28x28 field.

> --*Leun, Cortes, and Burges from* `http://yann.lecun.com/exdb/mnist/`.

Pain Point #3: Exporting MNIST images as files

We often need to work within the image directly and not as an array vector. This section will guide us through converting our arrays to `.png` images.

Getting ready

Exporting the vectors to images requires importing the following library:

- `import image from matplotlib`

How to do it...

This section walks through the steps to convert a sample of MNIST arrays to files in a local folder.

1. Create a subfolder to save our images to our main folder of `MNIST/` using the following script:

   ```
   if not os.path.exists('MNIST/images'):
       os.makedirs('MNIST/images/')
   os.chdir('MNIST/images/')
   ```

2. Loop through the first 10 samples of MNIST arrays and convert them to `.png` files using the following script:

   ```
   from matplotlib import image
   for i in range(1,10):
       png = data.train.images[i]
       png = np.array(png, dtype='float')
       pixels = png.reshape((28, 28))
       image.imsave('image_no_{}.png'.format(i), pixels, cmap =
   'gray')
   ```

3. Execute the following script to see the list of images from `image_no_1.png` to `image_no_9.png`:

   ```
   print(os.listdir())
   ```

How it works...

This section explains how the MNIST arrays are converted to images and saved to a local folder.

1. We create a subfolder called `MNIST/images` to help us store our temporary `.png` images and separate them from the MNIST arrays and labels.

2. Once again we loop through `data.train` images and obtain nine arrays that can be used for sampling. The images are then saved as `.png` files to our local directory with the following format: `'image_no_{}.png'.format(i), pixels, cmap = 'gray'`

3. The output of the nine images can be seen in our local directory, as seen in the following screenshot:

```
In [8]: if not os.path.exists('MNIST/images'):
            os.makedirs('MNIST/images/')
        os.chdir('MNIST/images/')

In [9]: from matplotlib import image
        for i in range(1,10):
            png = data.train.images[i]
            png = np.array(png, dtype='float')
            pixels = png.reshape((28, 28))
            image.imsave('image_no_{}.png'.format(i), pixels, cmap = 'gray')

In [10]: print(os.listdir())

['image_no_9.png', 'image_no_3.png', 'image_no_4.png', 'image_no_7.png', 'image_no_2.png', 'image_no_5.png',
'image_no_8.png', 'image_no_1.png', 'image_no_6.png']
```

There's more...

In addition to seeing the list of images in our directory, we can also view the image in our directory within Linux, as seen in the following screenshot:

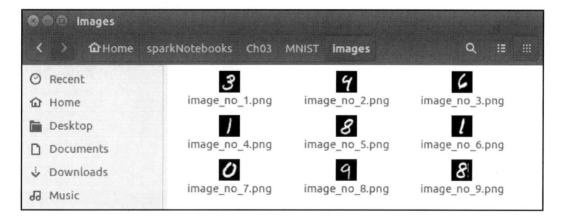

See also

To learn more about `image.imsave` from `matplotlib` visit the following website:

`https://matplotlib.org/api/_as_gen/matplotlib.pyplot.imsave.html`

Pain Point #4: Augmenting MNIST images

One of the main drawbacks of working with image recognition is the lack of variety in some of the images available. This may cause the convolutional neural network to not operate as optimally as we would like, and return less than ideal results due to the lack of variety in the training data. There are techniques available to bypass that shortcoming and we discuss one of them in this section.

Getting ready

Once again much of the heavy lifting is already done for us. We will use a popular Python package, `augmentor`, that is frequently used with machine learning and deep learning modeling to generate additional versions of existing images distorted and augmented for variety.

The package will first have to be `pip` installed using the following script: `pip install augmentor`

We should then have confirmation that the package is installed, as seen in the following screenshot:

```
asherif844@ubuntu: ~
asherif844@ubuntu:~$ pip install augmentor
Collecting augmentor
  Downloading https://files.pythonhosted.org/packages/37/c0/7baedf49229173a4fe621ca158fb18cc
88ec22fa4fac51e6cd09988fd900/Augmentor-0.2.2-py2.py3-none-any.whl
Collecting future>=0.16.0 (from augmentor)
  Downloading https://files.pythonhosted.org/packages/00/2b/8d082ddfed935f3608cc61140df6dcbf
0edea1bc3ab52fb6c29ae3e81e85/future-0.16.0.tar.gz (824kB)
    100% |                               | 829kB 1.6MB/s
Requirement already satisfied: numpy>=1.11.0 in ./anaconda3/lib/python3.6/site-packages (fro
m augmentor)
Collecting tqdm>=4.9.0 (from augmentor)
  Downloading https://files.pythonhosted.org/packages/93/24/6ab1df969db228aed36a648a8959d102
7099ce45fad67532b9673d533318/tqdm-4.23.4-py2.py3-none-any.whl (42kB)
    100% |                               | 51kB 5.7MB/s
Requirement already satisfied: Pillow>=4.0.0 in ./anaconda3/lib/python3.6/site-packages (fro
m augmentor)
Requirement already satisfied: olefile in ./anaconda3/lib/python3.6/site-packages (from Pill
ow>=4.0.0->augmentor)
Building wheels for collected packages: future
  Running setup.py bdist_wheel for future ... done
  Stored in directory: /home/asherif844/.cache/pip/wheels/bf/c9/a3/c538d90ef17cf7823fa51fc70
1a7a7a910a80f6a405bf15b1a
Successfully built future
Installing collected packages: future, tqdm, augmentor
Successfully installed augmentor-0.2.2 future-0.16.0 tqdm-4.23.4
```

We will then need to import the pipeline class from augmentor:

- `from Augmentor import Pipeline`

How to do it...

This section walks through the steps to increase the frequency and augmentation of our nine sample images.

1. Initialize the `augmentor` function using the following script:

   ```
   from Augmentor import Pipeline
   augmentor =
   Pipeline('/home/asherif844/sparkNotebooks/Ch03/MNIST/images')
   ```

2. Execute the following script so that the `augmentor` function can `rotate` our images with the following specifications:

   ```
   augmentor.rotate(probability=0.9, max_left_rotation=25,
   max_right_rotation=25)
   ```

3. Execute the following script so that each image is augmented through two iterations 10 times each:

```
for i in range(1,3):
    augmentor.sample(10)
```

How it works...

This section explains how our nine images are used to create additional images that are distorted.

1. We need to create a `Pipeline` for our image transformation and specify the location of the images that will be used. This ensures the following:
   1. The source location of the images
   2. The number of images that will be transformed
   3. The destination location of the images

2. We can see that our destination location is created with a subfolder called `/output/` as seen in the following screenshot:

```
In [11]: from Augmentor import Pipeline

In [12]: augmentor = Pipeline('/home/asherif844/sparkNotebooks/Ch03/MNIST/images')
         Initialised with 9 image(s) found.
         Output directory set to /home/asherif844/sparkNotebooks/Ch03/MNIST/images/output.
```

3. The `augmentor` function is configured to rotate each image up to 25 degrees to the right or 25 degrees to the left with a 90 percent probability. Basically, the probability configuration determines how often an augmentation takes place.

4. A loop is created to go through each image twice and apply two transformations to each image; however, since we did add a probability to each transformation some images may not get transformed and others may get transformed more than twice. Once the transformations are complete, we should get a message indicating so, as seen in the following screenshot:

```
In [14]: for i in range(1,3):
             augmentor.sample 10
         Processing <PIL.Image.Image image mode=RGBA size=28x28 at 0x7FAA10DA6358>: 100%|███████| 10/10 [00:00<00:0
         0, 214.06 Samples/s]
         Processing <PIL.Image.Image image mode=RGBA size=28x28 at 0x7FAA10DA6208>: 100%|███████| 10/10 [00:00<00:0
         0, 194.51 Samples/s]
```

5. Once we have the augmentations complete, we can visit the `/output/` subdirectory and see how each digit is slightly altered, as seen in the following screenshot:

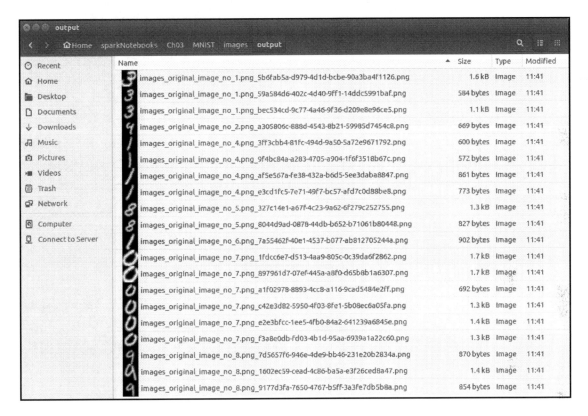

6. We can see that we have several variations of the digits **3**, **1**, **8**, **0**, and **9** all with varying degrees of rotation. We now have tripled our sample data set and added more variety without having to go out and extract more images for training and testing purposes.

There's more...

We only applied the `rotate` transformation; however, there are several transformation and augmentation features available to apply to images:

- Perspective skewing
- Elastic distortions
- Shearing
- Cropping
- Mirroring

While not all of these transformations will be necessary when looking to increase frequency and variety of a training dataset, it may be beneficial to use some combination of features and evaluate model performance.

See also

To learn more about `augmentor` visit the following website:

`https://augmentor.readthedocs.io/en/master/`

Pain Point #5: Utilizing alternate sources for trained images

Sometimes there are just not enough resources available to perform a convolutional neural network. The resources could be limited from a computational perspective or a data collection perspective. In situations like these, we rely on other sources to help us with classifying our images.

Getting ready

The technique for utilizing pre-trained models as the source for testing outcomes on other datasets is referred to as transfer learning. The advantage here is that much of the CPU resources allotted for training images is outsourced to a pre-trained model. Transfer learning has become a common extension of deep learning more recently.

How to do it...

This section explains how the process of transfer learning works.

1. Collect a series of datasets or images that you are interested in classifying, just as you would with traditional machine learning or deep learning.
2. Split the dataset into a training and testing split such as 75/25 or 80/20.
3. Identify a pre-trained model that will be used to identify the patterns and recognition of the images you are looking to classify.
4. Build a deep learning pipeline that connects the training data to the pre-trained model and develops the weights and parameters needed to identify the test data.
5. Finally, evaluate the model performance on the test data.

How it works...

This section explains the process of transfer learning when applied to the MNIST dataset.

1. We are definitely taking a shortcut approach with transfer learning as we are either limited in resources, time, or both as we are taking prior work that has already been done and hoping that it will help us solve something new.
2. Since we are dealing with an image classification problem, we should use a pre-trained model that has worked with classifying common images in the past. There are many common ones out there but two that stand out are:
   1. The ResNet model developed at Microsoft.
   2. The Inception model developed at Google.
3. Both models are useful for image classification because both Microsoft and Google have a wide spectrum of images that are available to them to train a robust model that can extract features at a more detailed level.
4. Directly within Spark, there is the ability to build a deep learning pipeline and to call about a class called `DeepImageFeaturizer` and apply the `InceptionV3` model to a set of features collected from training data. The trained dataset is then evaluated on the testing data using some type of binary or multiclassification evaluator.
5. A pipeline within deep learning or machine learning is simply the workflow process used to get from an initial environment of data collection to a final evaluation or classification environment on the collected data by applying a model.

There's more...

As with everything, there are pros and cons to using transfer learning. As we discussed earlier on in the section, transfer learning is ideal when you are limited in resources to perform your own modeling on a large dataset. There is always the chance that the source data at hand does not exhibit many of the features unique to it in the pre-trained models leading to poor model performance. There is always the option to switch from one pre-trained model to another and evaluate model performance. Again, transfer learning is a fail fast approach that can be taken when other options are not available.

See also

To learn more about ResNet at Microsoft, visit the following website:

https://resnet.microsoft.com/

To learn more about Inception at Google, visit the following website:

https://www.tensorflow.org/tutorials/image_recognition

To learn more specifically about InceptionV3, you can read the following paper titled *Rethinking the Inception Architecture for Computer Vision* at Cornell University:

https://arxiv.org/abs/1512.00567

Pain Point #6: Prioritizing high-level libraries for CNNs

There are many libraries available to perform convolutional neural networks. Some of them are considered low-level such as TensorFlow, where much of the configuration and setup requires extensive coding. This can be considered a major pain point for an inexperienced developer. There are other libraries, such as Keras, that are high-level frameworks built on top of libraries such as TensorFlow. These libraries require much less code to get up and running with building a convolutional neural network. Often times developers getting started with building a neural network will try and implement a model with TensorFlow and run into several issues along the way. This section will propose initially building a convolutional neural network with Keras instead to predict the hand-written images from the MNIST dataset.

Getting ready

In this section, we will be working with Keras to train a model for recognizing handwritten images from MNIST. You can install Keras by executing the following command at the terminal:

```
pip install keras
```

How to do it...

This section walks through the steps to build a model to recognize handwritten images from MNIST.

1. Create testing and training images and labels based on the MNIST dataset from the following variables using the following script:

```
xtrain = data.train.images
ytrain = np.asarray(data.train.labels)
xtest = data.test.images
ytest = np.asarray(data.test.labels)
```

2. Reshape the testing and training arrays using the following script:

```
xtrain = xtrain.reshape( xtrain.shape[0],28,28,1)
xtest = xtest.reshape(xtest.shape[0],28,28,1)
ytest= ytest.reshape(ytest.shape[0],10)
ytrain = ytrain.reshape(ytrain.shape[0],10)
```

3. Import the following from keras to build the convolutional neural network model:

```
import keras
import keras.backend as K
from keras.models import Sequential
from keras.layers import Dense, Flatten, Conv2D
```

4. Set the image ordering using the following script:

```
K.set_image_dim_ordering('th')
```

5. Initialize the Sequential model using the following script:

```
model = Sequential()
```

6. Add layers to the `model` using the following script:

```
model.add(Conv2D(32, kernel_size=(3, 3),activation='relu',
          input_shape=(1,28,28)))
model.add(Flatten())
model.add(Dense(128, activation='relu'))
model.add(Dense(10, activation='sigmoid'))
```

7. Compile the `model` using the following script:

```
model.compile(optimizer='adam',loss='binary_crossentropy',
          metrics=['accuracy'])
```

8. Train the `model` using the following script:

```
model.fit(xtrain,ytrain,batch_size=512,epochs=5,
          validation_data=(xtest, ytest))
```

9. Test the `model` performance using the following script:

```
stats = model.evaluate(xtest, ytest)
print('The accuracy rate is {}%'.format(round(stats[1],3)*100))
print('The loss rate is {}%'.format(round(stats[0],3)*100))
```

How it works...

This section explains how the convolutional neural network is built on Keras to identify handwritten images from MNIST.

1. For any model development, we need to identify our testing and training datasets as well as the features and the labels. In our case, it is pretty straightforward as the MNIST data from TensorFlow is already broken up into `data.train.images` for the features and `data.train.labels` for the labels. Additionally, we want to convert the labels into arrays, so we utilize `np.asarray()` for `ytest` and `ytrain`.

2. The arrays for `xtrain`, `xtest`, `ytrain`, and `ytest` are currently not in the proper shape to be used for a convolutional neural network within Keras. As we identified early on in the chapter, the features for the MNIST images represent 28 x 28-pixel images and the labels indicate one of ten values from 0 through 9. The x-arrays will be reshaped to **(,28,28,1)** and the y-arrays will be reshaped to **(,10)**. The `shape` of the new arrays can be seen in the following screenshot:

```
In [15]: xtrain = data.train.images
         ytrain = np.asarray(data.train.labels)
         xtest = data.test.images
         ytest = np.asarray(data.test.labels)

In [16]: xtrain = xtrain.reshape( xtrain.shape[0],28,28,1)
         xtest = xtest.reshape(xtest.shape[0],28,28,1)
         ytest= ytest.reshape(ytest.shape[0],10)
         ytrain = ytrain.reshape(ytrain.shape[0],10)

In [17]: print(xtrain.shape)
         print(ytrain.shape)
         print(xtest.shape)
         print(ytest.shape)

         (55000, 28, 28, 1)
         (55000, 10)
         (10000, 28, 28, 1)
         (10000, 10)
```

3. As mentioned previously, Keras is a high-level library; therefore, it does not perform tensor or convolutional operations without the assistance of a lower level library such as TensorFlow. In order to configure these operations, we set the `backend` to be K for `Keras` with the image dimensional ordering, `image_dim_ordering`, set to `tf` for TensorFlow.

Please note that the backend could also be set to other low-level libraries, such as `Theano`. Instead of `tf`, we would set the dimensional ordering to `th`. Additionally, we would need to reconstruct the shaping of the features. However, in the past few years, `Theano` has not garnered the same adoption rate `TensorFlow` has.

4. Once we import the necessary libraries to build the CNN model, we can begin constructing the sequences or layers, `Sequential()`, of the model. For demonstration purposes, we will keep this model as simple as possible with only 4 layers to prove that we can still gain a high accuracy with minimal complexity. Each layer is added using the `.add()` method.

   1. The first layer is set to build a 2-Dimensional (`Conv2D`) convolution layer, which is common for spatial images such as the MNIST data. Since it is the first layer, we must explicitly define the `input_shape` of the incoming data. Additionally, we specify a `kernel_size` that is used to set the height and width of the window filter used for convolution. Usually, this is either a 3x3 window or 5x5 window for the 32 filters. Additionally, we have to set an activation function for this layer and rectified linear units, `relu`, are a good option here for efficiency purposes, especially early on in the neural network.

   2. Next, the second layer flattens the first layer inputs to retrieve a classification that we can use to determine whether the image is one of a possible 10 digits.

   3. Third, we pass the outputs from the second layer into a `dense` layer that has 128 hidden layers with another `relu` activation function. The function within a densely connected layer incorporates the `input_shape` and `kernel_size` as well as the bias to create the output for each of the 128 hidden layers.

   4. The final layer is the output that will determine what the predicted value will be for the MNIST image. We add another `dense` layer with a `sigmoid` function to output probabilities for each of the 10 possible scenarios our MNIST image could be. Sigmoid functions are useful for binary or multiclass classification outcomes.

5. The next step is to compile the model using `adam` for the `optimizer` and evaluating `accuracy` for the `metrics`. The `adam` optimizer is common for CNN models as is using `categorical_crossentropy` as a loss function when dealing with multiclassification scenarios for 10 possible outcomes as is our case.

6. We train the model using a `batch_size` of `512` images at a time over `5` runs or `epochs`. The loss and accuracy of each epoch are captured and can be seen in the following screenshot:

```
In [18]: import keras
         import keras.backend as K
         from keras.models import Sequential
         from keras.layers import Dense, Flatten, Conv2D

         K.set_image_dim_ordering('tf')

         model = Sequential()

         model.add(Conv2D(32, kernel_size=(5, 5),activation='relu', input_shape=(28,28,1)))
         model.add(Flatten())
         model.add(Dense(128, activation='relu'))
         model.add(Dense(10, activation='sigmoid'))

         Using TensorFlow backend.

In [19]: model.compile(optimizer='adam',loss='categorical_crossentropy',
                       metrics=['accuracy'])

In [20]: model.fit(xtrain,ytrain,batch_size=512,
                   epochs=5,
                   validation_data=(xtest, ytest))

         Train on 55000 samples, validate on 10000 samples
         Epoch 1/5
         55000/55000 [==============================] - 46s 832us/step - loss: 0.3617 - acc: 0.9032 - val_loss: 0.1214
         - val_acc: 0.9651
         Epoch 2/5
         55000/55000 [==============================] - 44s 797us/step - loss: 0.0928 - acc: 0.9731 - val_loss: 0.0809
         - val_acc: 0.9770
         Epoch 3/5
         55000/55000 [==============================] - 44s 796us/step - loss: 0.0555 - acc: 0.9837 - val_loss: 0.0521
         - val_acc: 0.9839
         Epoch 4/5
         55000/55000 [==============================] - 42s 756us/step - loss: 0.0410 - acc: 0.9881 - val_loss: 0.0521
         - val_acc: 0.9823
         Epoch 5/5
         55000/55000 [==============================] - 43s 782us/step - loss: 0.0309 - acc: 0.9909 - val_loss: 0.0457
         - val_acc: 0.9861
Out[20]: <keras.callbacks.History at 0x7fe18d115c88>
```

7. We calculate the **accuracy** and the **loss rate** by evaluating the trained model on the test dataset as seen in the following screenshot:

```
In [21]: stats = model.evaluate(xtest, ytest)
         print('The accuracy rate is {}%'.format(round(stats[1],3)*100))
         print('The loss rate is {}%'.format(round(stats[0],2)*100)

         10000/10000 [==============================] - 3s 324us/step
         The accuracy rate is 98.6%
         The loss rate is 5.0%
```

8. Our model seems to be performing well with a **98.6% accuracy rate** and a **5% loss rate**.

9. We built a simple convolutional neural network in Keras using five lines of code for the actual model design. Keras is a great way to get a model up and running in little time and code. Once you are ready to move onto more sophisticated model development and control, it may make more sense to build a convolutional neural network in TensorFlow.

There's more...

In addition to retrieving the accuracy of the model we can also produce the shapes within each layer of the CNN modeling process by executing the following script:

```
model.summary()
```

The output of the `model.summary()` can be seen in the following screenshot:

```
In [22]: model.summary()

         Layer (type)                 Output Shape              Param #
         =================================================================
         conv2d_1 (Conv2D)            (None, 24, 24, 32)        832

         flatten_1 (Flatten)          (None, 18432)             0

         dense_1 (Dense)              (None, 128)               2359424

         dense_2 (Dense)              (None, 10)                1290
         =================================================================
         Total params: 2,361,546
         Trainable params: 2,361,546
         Non-trainable params: 0
```

We see that the output shape of the first layer **(None, 24, 24, 32)** was flattened out into a shape of **(None, 18432)** by multiplying 24 x 24 x 32 within the second layer. Additionally, we see our third and fourth layers have the shape that we assigned them using the **Dense** layer function

See also

To learn more about 2D convolutional layer development in Keras, visit the following website:

```
https://keras.io/layers/convolutional/#conv2d
```

To learn how to build a convolutional neural network in TensorFlow with MNIST images, visit the following website:

```
https://www.tensorflow.org/versions/r1.4/get_started/mnist/pros
```

Pain Points of Recurrent Neural Networks

4

In this chapter, we will cover the following recipes:

- Introduction to feedforward networks
- Sequential workings of RNNs
- Paint point #1 – the vanishing gradient problem
- Pain point #2 – the exploding gradient problem
- Sequential workings of LSTMs

Introduction

Recurrent neural networks have proven to be incredibly efficient at tasks involving the learning and prediction of sequential data. However, when it comes to natural language, the question of long-term dependencies comes into play, which is basically remembering the context of a particular conversation, paragraph, or sentence in order to make better predictions in the future. For example, consider a sentence that says:

Last year, I happened to visit China. Not only was Chinese food different from the Chinese food available everywhere else in the world, but the people were extremely warm and hospitable too. In my three years of stay in this beautiful country, I managed to pick up and speak very good....

If the preceding sentence were fed into a recurrent neural network to predict the next word in the sentence (such as Chinese), the network would find it difficult since it has no memory of the context of the sentence. This is what we mean by long-term dependencies. In order to predict the word Chinese correctly, the network needs to know the context of the sentence as well as remember the fact that I happened to visit China last year. Recurrent neural networks therefore become inefficient at performing such tasks. However, this problem is overcome by **Long Short-Term Memory Units (LSTMs)**, which are capable of remembering long-term dependencies and storing information in the cell state. LSTMs will be discussed later on, but the bulk of this chapter will focus on a basic introduction to Neural Networks, activation functions, Recurrent Networks, some of the main pain points or drawbacks of Recurrent Networks, and finally how these drawbacks may be overcome by the use of LSTMs.

Introduction to feedforward networks

To understand recurrent networks, first you have to understand the basics of feedforward networks. Both of these networks are named after the way they move information through a series of mathematical operations performed at the nodes of the network. One feeds information in only one direction through every node (never touching a given node twice), while the other cycles it through a loop and feeds it back to the same node (kind of like a feedback loop). It is easily understood how the first kind is called a **feedforward network,** while the latter is recurrent.

Getting ready

The most important concept while understanding any neural network diagram is the concept of computational graphs. Computational graphs are nothing but the nodes of the neural network connected to each other, and each node performs a particular mathematical function.

How to do it...

Feedforward neural networks channel the inputs (to the input layer) through a set of computational nodes which are nothing but mathematical operators and activation functions arranged in layers to calculate the network outputs. The output layer is the final layer of the neural network and usually contains linear functions. The layers between the input layer and the output layer are called **hidden layers** and usually contain nonlinear elements or functions:

1. The following diagram **(a)** shows how nodes are interconnected in feedforward neural networks with many layers:

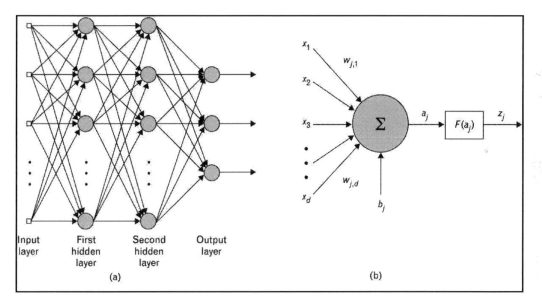

FeedForward Neural Network

1. Feedforward neural networks mainly differ from each other by the type of functions (activation functions) that are used in the hidden-layer nodes. They also differ from each other by the algorithms that are used to optimize the other parameters of the network during training.

2. The relationships between nodes shown in the preceding diagram need not be fully populated for every node; optimization strategies usually start with a large number of hidden nodes and tune the network by eliminating connections, and possibly nodes, as training progresses. It may not be necessary to utilize every node during the training process.

How it works...

The neuron is the basic structural element of any neural network. A neuron can be thought of as a simple mathematical function or operator that operates on the input flowing through it to produce an output flowing out of it. The inputs to a neuron are multiplied by the node's weight matrix, summed over all the inputs, translated, and passed through an activation function. These are basically matrix operations in mathematics as described here:

1. The computational graph representation of a neuron is shown in the preceding diagram **(b)**.

2. The transfer function for a single neuron or node is written as follows:

$$y = f(\sum_{i=1}^{n} w_i x_i + b)$$

   Here, x_i is the input to the ith node, w_i is the weight term associated with the ith node, b is the bias which is generally added to prevent overfitting, $f(\cdot)$ is the activation function operating over the inputs flowing into the node, and y is the output from the node.

3. Neurons with sigmoidal activation functions are commonly used in the hidden layer(s) of the neural network, and the identity function is usually used in the output layer.

4. The activation functions are generally chosen in a manner to ensure the outputs from the node are strictly increasing, smooth (continuous first derivative), or asymptotic.

5. The following logistic function is used as a sigmoidal activation function:

$$f(x) = \frac{1}{1 + e^{-x}}$$

6. A neural trained using backpropagation algorithm may learn faster if the activation function is antisymmetric, that is, $f(-x) = -f(x)$ as in the case of the sigmoidal activation function. The backpropagation algorithm will be discussed in detail in the following sections of this chapter.

7. The logistic function, however, is not antisymmetric, but can be made antisymmetric by a simple scaling and shift, resulting in the hyperbolic tangent function which has a first derivative described by $f'(x) = 1 - f^2(x)$, as shown in the following mathematical function:

$$f(x) = tanhx = \frac{e^x - e^{-x}}{e^x + e^{-x}}$$

8. The simple form of the sigmoidal function and its derivative allows for the quick and accurate calculation of the gradients needed to optimize the selection of the weights and biases and carry out second-order error analysis.

There's more...

At every neuron/node in the layers of a neural network, a series of matrix operations are performed. A more mathematical way of visualizing the feedforward network is given in the following diagram, which will help you to better understand the operations at each node/neuron:

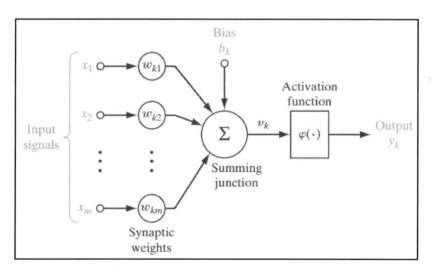

1. Intuitively, we can see that the inputs (which are vectors or matrices) are first multiplied by weight matrices. A bias is added to this term and then activated using an activation function (such as ReLU, tanh, sigmoid, threshold, and so on) to produce the output. Activation functions are key in ensuring that the network is able to learn linear as well as non-linear functions.

2. This output then flows into the next neuron as its input, and the same set of operations are performed all over again. A number of such neurons combine together to form a layer (which performs a certain function or learns a certain feature of the input vector), and many such layers combine together to form a feedforward neural network that can learn to recognize inputs completely, as shown in the following diagram:

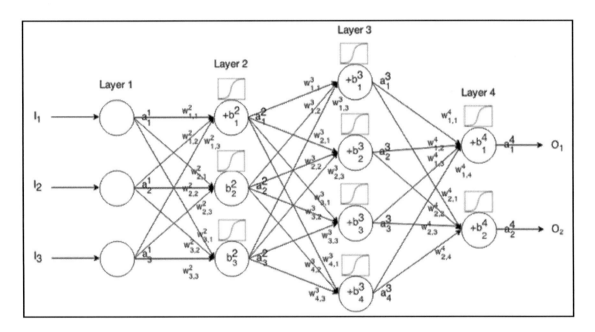

3. Let's suppose our feedforward network has been trained to classify images of dogs and images of cats. Once the network is trained, as shown in the following diagram, it will learn to label images as dog or cat when presented with new images:

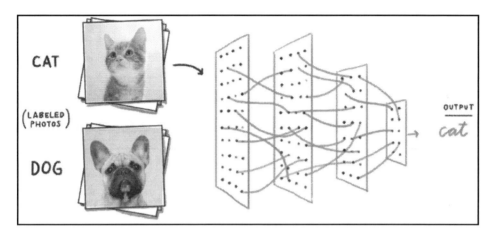

4. In such networks, there is no relation between the present output and the previous or future outputs.

5. This means the feedforward network can basically be exposed to any random collection of images and the first image it is exposed to will not necessarily alter how it classifies the second or third images. Therefore, we can say that the output at time step t is independent of the output at time step $t - 1$.

6. Feedforward networks work well in such cases as image classification, where the data is not sequential. Feedforward networks also perform well when used on two related variables such as temperature and location, height and weight, car speed and brand, and so on.

7. However, there may be cases where the current output is dependent on the outputs at previous time steps (the ordering of data is important).

8. Consider the scenario of reading a book. Your understanding of the sentences in the book is based on your understanding of all the words in the sentence. It wouldn't be possible to use a feedforward network to predict the next word in a sentence, as the output in such a case would depend on the previous outputs.

9. Similarly, there are many cases where the output requires the previous output or some information from the previous outputs (for example, stock market data, NLP, voice recognition, and so on). The feedforward network may be modified as in the following diagram to capture information from previous outputs:

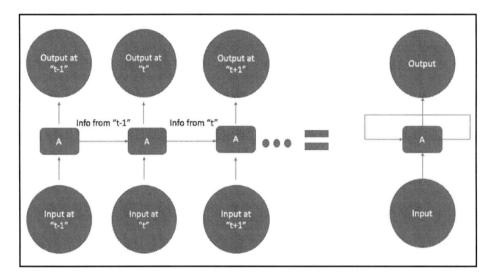

10. At time step *t*, the input at *t* as well as the information from *t-1* is both provided to the network to obtain the output at time *t*.
11. Similarly, the information from *t* as well as the new input is fed into the network at time step *t+1* to produce the output at *t+1*. The right-hand side of the preceding diagram is a generalized way of representing such a network where the output of the network flows back in as input for future time steps. Such a network is called a **recurrent neural network (RNN)**.

See also

Activation Function: In artificial neural networks, the activation function of a node decides the kind of output that node produces, given an input or set of inputs. The output y_k is given by the input u_k and bias b_k, which are passed through the activation function $\varphi(.)$ as shown in the following expression:

$$y_k = \varphi(u_k + b_k)$$

There are various types of activation functions. The following are the commonly used ones:

1. **Threshold function**:

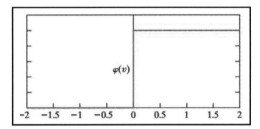

It is clear from the preceding diagram that this kind of function restricts the output values of neurons to between 0 and 1. This may be useful in many cases. However, this function is non-differentiable, which means it cannot be used to learn non-linearities, which is vital when using the backpropagation algorithm.

2. **Sigmoid function**:

$$\varphi(v) = \frac{1}{1 + exp^{(-av)}}$$

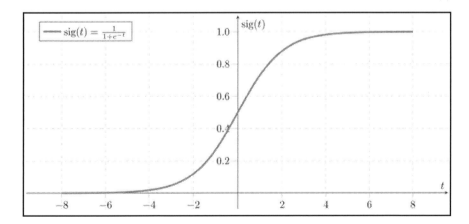

The sigmoid function is a logistic function with a lower limit of 0 and an upper limit of 1, as with the threshold function. This activation function is continuous and therefore, also differentiable. In the sigmoid function, the slope parameter of the preceding function is given by α. The function is nonlinear in nature, which is critical in increasing the performance since it is able to accommodate non linearities in the input data unlike regular linear functions. Having non linear capabilities ensure that small changes in the weights and bias causes significant changes in the output of the neuron.

3. **Hyperbolic Tangent function (tanh)**:

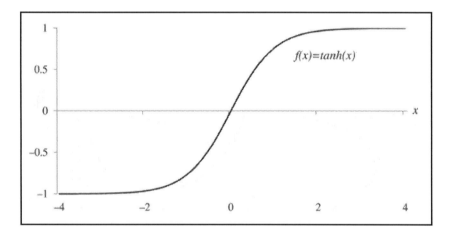

This function enables activation functions to range from -1 to +1 instead of between 0 and 1 as in the previous cases.

4. **Rectified Linear Unit (ReLU) function**: ReLUs are the smooth approximation to the sum of many logistic units, and produce sparse activity vectors. The following is the equation of the function:

$$y = max\left\{0, b + \sum_{i=1}^{k} x_i * w_i\right\}$$

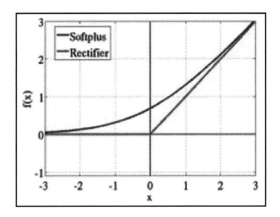

ReLU function graph

In the preceding diagram, softplus $f(x) = \log(1 + e^x)$ is the smooth approximation to the rectifier.

5. **Maxout function**: This function utilizes a technique known as **"dropout"** and improves the accuracy of the dropout technique's fast approximate model averaging in order to facilitate optimization.

   Maxout networks learn not just the relationship between hidden units, but also the activation function of each hidden unit. By actively dropping out hidden units, the network is forced to find other paths to get to the output from a given input during the training process. The following diagram is the graphical depiction of how this works:

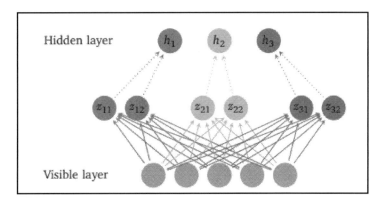

Maxout Network

The preceding diagram shows the Maxout network with five visible units, three hidden units, and two neurons for each hidden unit. The Maxout function is given by the following equations:

$$h_i = max_{j\in[1,k]} Z_{ij}$$

$$Z_{ij} = \sum_m x_m W_{mij} + b_{ij} = xW_{mij} + b_{ij}$$

Here $W_{..ij}$ is the mean vector of the size of the input obtained by accessing the matrix $W \in \mathbb{R}^{m*n*k}$ at the second coordinate i and third coordinate j. The number of intermediate units (k) is called the number of pieces used by the Maxout nets. The following diagram shows how the Maxout function compares to the ReLU and **Parametric Rectified Linear Unit (PReLU)** functions:

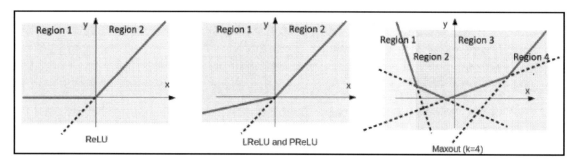

Graphical comparison of Maxout. ReLU and PReLU function

Sequential workings of RNNs

Recurrent neural networks are a type of artificial neural network designed to recognize and learn patterns in sequences of data. Some of the examples of such sequential data are:

- Handwriting
- Text such as customer reviews, books, source code, and so on
- Spoken word / Natural Language
- Numerical time series / sensor data
- Stock price variation data

Getting ready

In recurrent neural networks, the hidden state from the previous time step is fed back into the network at the next time step, as shown in the following diagram:

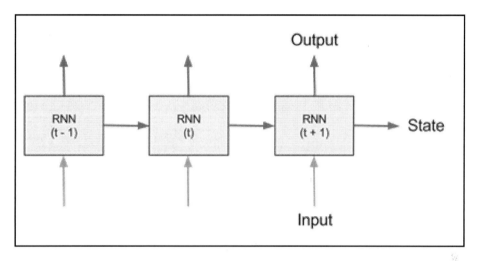

Basically, the upward facing arrows going into the network represent the inputs (matrices/vectors) to the RNN at each time step, while the upward-facing arrows coming out of the network represent the output of each RNN unit. The horizontal arrows indicate the transfer of information learned in a particular time step (by a particular neuron) onto the next time step.

 More information about using RNNs can be found at :
`https://deeplearning4j.org/usingrnns`

How to do it...

At every node/neuron of a recurrent network, a series of matrix multiplication steps are carried out. The input vector/matrix is multiplied by a weight vector/matrix first, a bias is added to this term, and this is finally passed through an activation function to produce the output (just as in the case of feedforward networks):

1. The following diagram shows an intuitive and mathematical way of visualizing RNNs in the form of a computational graph:

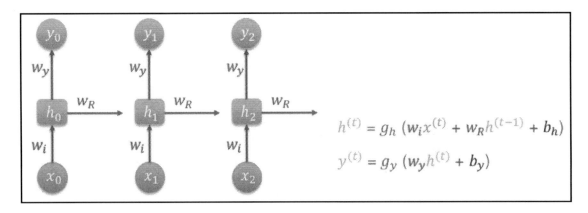

$$h^{(t)} = g_h \left(w_i x^{(t)} + w_R h^{(t-1)} + b_h \right)$$

$$y^{(t)} = g_y \left(w_y h^{(t)} + b_y \right)$$

2. At the first time step (which is *t=0*), h_0 is calculated using the first formula on the right-hand side of the preceding diagram. Since h^{-1} does not exist, the middle term becomes zero.
3. The input matrix x_0 is multiplied by the weight matrix w_i and a bias b_h is added to this term.
4. The two preceding matrices are added and then passed through an activation function g_h to obtain h_0.
5. Similarly, y_0 is calculated using the second equation on the right-hand side of the preceding diagram by multiplying h_0 with the weight matrix w_y, adding a bias b_y to it, and passing it through an activation function g_y.

6. At the next time step (which is *t=1*), $h^{(t-1)}$ does exist. It is nothing but h_0. This term, multiplied with the weight matrix w_R, is also provided as the input to the network along with the new input matrix x_1.

7. This process is repeated over a number of time steps, and the weights, matrices, and biases flow through the entire network over different time steps.

8. This entire process is executed over one single iteration, which constitutes the forward pass of the network.

How it works...

To train feedforward neural networks the most commonly used technique is backpropagation through time. It is a supervised learning method used to reduce the loss function by updating weights and biases in the network after every time step. A number of training cycles (also known as epochs) are executed where the error determined by the loss function is backward propagated by a technique called gradient descent. At the end of each training cycle, the network updates its weights and biases to produce an output which is closer to the desired output, until a sufficiently small error is achieved :

1. The backpropagation algorithm basically implements the following three fundamental steps during every iteration:
   - The forward pass of the input data and calculating the loss function
   - The computation of gradients and errors
   - Backpropagation through time and adjustment of weights and biases accordingly

2. After the weighted sum of inputs (passed through an activation function after adding a bias) is fed into the network and an output is obtained, the network immediately compares how different the predicted output is from the actual case (correct output).

3. Next, the error is calculated by the network. This is nothing but the network output subtracted from the actual/correct output.

4. The next step involves backpropagation through the entire network based on the calculated error. The weights and biases are then updated to notice whether the error increases or decreases.

5. The network also remembers whether the error increases by increasing the weights and biases or by decreasing the weights and biases.

6. Based on the preceding inferences, the network continues to update the weights and biases during every iteration in a manner such that the error becomes minimal. The following example will make things clearer.

7. Consider a simple case of teaching a machine how to double a number, as shown in the following table:

Input	Correct Output	Model Output (W = 3)	Absolute error	Square error
0	0	0	0	0
1	2	3	1	1
2	4	6	2	4
3	6	9	3	9

8. As you can see, by initializing the weights randomly ($W = 3$), we obtain outputs of 0, 3, 6, and 9.

9. The error is calculated by subtracting the column of correct outputs from the column of model outputs. The square error is nothing but each error term multiplied by itself. It is usually a better practice to use square error as it eliminates negative values from error terms.

10. The model then realizes that in order to minimize the error, the weight needs to be updated.

11. Let's suppose the model updates its weight to $W = 4$ during the next iteration. This would result in the following output:

Input	Correct Output	Model Output (W = 3)	Absolute error	Square error
0	0	0	0	0
1	2	4	2	4
2	4	8	4	16
3	6	12	6	36

12. The model now realizes that the error actually increased by increasing the weight to $W = 4$. Therefore, the model updates its weight by reducing it to $W = 2$ in its next iteration, which results in the actual/correct output.

13. Note that, in this simple case, the error increases when the weight is increased and reduces when the weight is decreased, as follows:

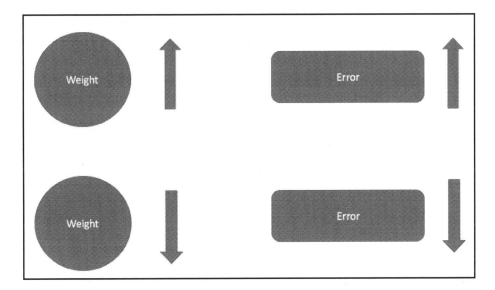

14. In an actual neural network, a number of such weight updates are performed during every iteration until the model converges with the actual/correct output.

There's more...

As seen in the preceding case, the error increased when the weight was increased but decreased when the weight was decreased. But this may not always be the case. The network uses the following graph to determine how to update weights and when to stop updating them:

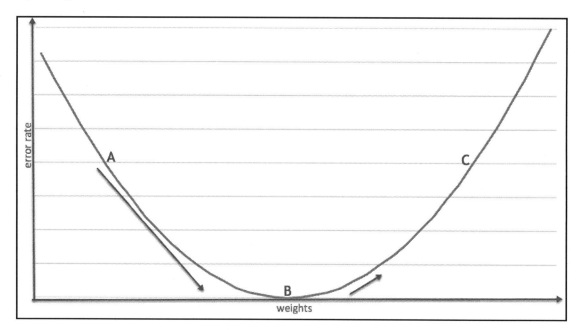

- Let the weights be initialized to zero at the beginning of the first iteration. As the network updates its weights by increasing them from point **A** to **B**, the error rate begins to decrease.
- Once the weights reach point **B**, the error rate becomes minimal. The network constantly keeps track of the error rate.
- On further increasing the weights from point **B** towards point **C**, the network realizes that the error rate begins to increase again. Thus, the network stops updating its weights and reverts back to the weights at point **B**, as they are optimal.

- In the next scenario, consider a case where the weights are randomly initialized to some value (let's say, point **C**), as shown in the following graph:

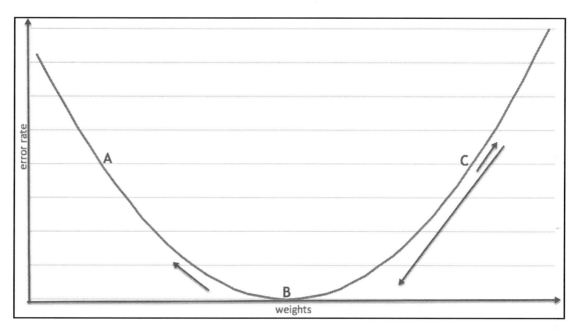

- On further increasing these random weights, the error also increases (starting at point **C** and moving away from point **B**, indicated by the small arrow in the graph).
- The network realizes that the error increased and begins to decrease the weights from point **C** so that the error decreases (indicated by the long arrow from point **C** moving towards point B in the graph). This decrease of weights happens until the error reaches a minimal value (point **B** on the graph).
- The network continues to further update its weights even after reaching point **B** (indicated by the arrow moving away from point **B** and towards point **A** on the graph). It then realizes that the error is again increasing. As a result, it stops the weight update and reverts back to the weights that gave the minimal error value (which are the weights at point **B**).

- This is how neural networks perform weight updates after backpropagation. This kind of weight update is momentum-based. It relies on the computed gradients at each neuron of the network during every iteration, as shown in the following diagram:

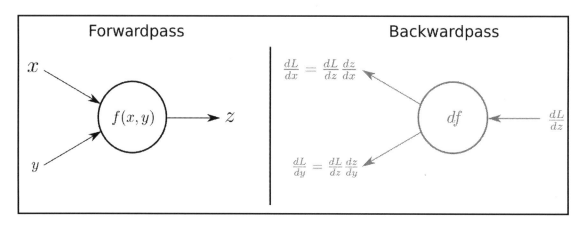

Basically, the gradients are computed for each input with respect to the output every time an input flows into a neuron. The chain rule is used to compute the gradients during the backward pass of backpropagation.

See also

A detailed explanation of the math behind backpropagation can be found at the following links:

- `https://mattmazur.com/2015/03/17/a-step-by-step-backpropagation-example/`
- `https://becominghuman.ai/back-propagation-is-very-simple-who-made-it-complicated-97b794c97e5`

Andrej Karpathy's blog has tons of useful information about recurrent neural networks. Here is a link explaining their unreasonable effectiveness:

- `http://karpathy.github.io/2015/05/21/rnn-effectiveness/`

Pain point #1 – The vanishing gradient problem

Recurrent neural networks are great for tasks involving sequential data. However, they do come with their drawbacks. This section will highlight and discuss one such drawback, known as the **vanishing gradient problem**.

Getting ready

The name vanishing gradient problem stems from the fact that, during the backpropagation step, some of the gradients vanish or become zero. Technically, this means that there is no error term being propagated backward during the backward pass of the network. This becomes a problem when the network gets deeper and more complex.

How to do it...

This section will describe how the vanishing gradient problem occurs in recurrent neural networks:

- While using backpropagation, the network first calculates the error, which is nothing but the model output subtracted from the actual output squared (such as the square error).
- Using this error, the model then computes the change in error with respect to the change in weights (de/dw).
- The computed derivative multiplied by the learning rate n gives $\triangle$w, which is nothing but the change in weights. The term $\triangle$w is added to the original weights to update them to the new weights.
- Suppose the value of de/dw (the gradient or rate of change of error with respect to weights) is much less than 1, then that term multiplied by the learning rate (which is always much less than 1) gives a very small, negligible, number which is negligible.
- This happens because the weight updates during backpropagation are only accurate for the most recent time step, and this accuracy reduces while backpropagating through the previous time steps and becomes almost insignificant when the weight updates flow through many steps back in time.

- There may be certain cases where sentences may be extremely long and the neural network is trying to predict the next word in a sentence. It does so based on the context of the sentence, for which it needs information from many previous time steps (these are called **long-term dependencies**). The number of previous times steps the network needs to backpropagate through increases with the increasing length of sentences. In such cases, the recurrent networks become incapable of remembering information from many time steps in the past and therefore are unable to make accurate predictions.
- When such a scenario occurs, the network requires many more complex calculations, as a result of which the number of iterations increases substantially and during which the change in error term vanishes (by reducing over time) and changes in weight ($\triangle$w) become negligibly small. As a result, the new or updated weight is almost equal to the previous weight.
- Since there is no weight update occurring, the network stops learning or being able to update its weights, which is a problem as this will cause the model to overfit the data.
- This entire process is illustrated in the following diagram:

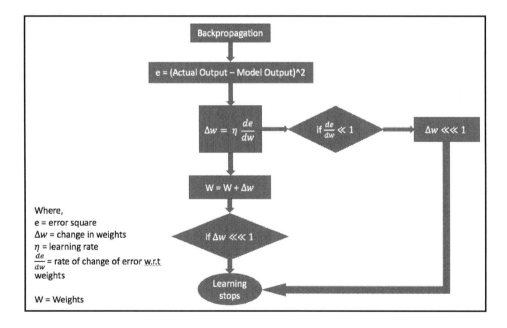

How it works...

This section will describe some of the repercussions of the vanishing gradient problem:

1. This problem occurs when we train a neural network model using some sort of optimization techniques which are gradient based.
2. Generally, adding more hidden layers tends to make the network able to learn more complex arbitrary functions, and thus do a better job in predicting future outcomes. Deep Learning makes a big difference due to the large number of hidden layers it has, ranging from 10 to 200. It is now possible to make sense of complicated sequential data, and perform tasks such as Speech Recognition, Image Classification, Image Captioning, and more.
3. The problem caused by the preceding steps is that, in some cases, the gradients become so small that they almost vanish, which in turn prevents the weights from updating their values during future time steps.
4. In the worst case, it could result in the training process of the network being stopped, which means that the network stops learning the different features it was intended to learn through the training steps.
5. The main idea behind backpropagation is that it allows us, as researchers, to monitor and understand how machine learning algorithms process and learn various features. When the gradients vanish, it becomes impossible to interpret what is going on with the network, and hence identifying and debugging errors becomes even more of a challenge.

There's more...

The following are some of the ways in which the problem of vanishing gradients can be solved:

- One method to overcome this problem to some extent by using the ReLU activation function. It computes the function $f(x)=max(0,x)$ (i.e., the activation function simply thresholds the lower level of outputs at zero) and prevents the network from producing negative gradients.

- Another way to overcome this problem is to perform unsupervised training on each layer separately and then fine-tune the entire network through backpropagation, as done by Jürgen Schmidhuber in his study of multi-level hierarchy in neural networks. The link to this paper is provided in the following section.
- A third solution to this problem is the use of **LSTM (Long Short-Term Memory)** units or **GRUs (Gated Recurrent Units)**, which are special types of RNNs.

See also

The following links provide a more in-depth description of the vanishing gradient problem and also some ways to tackle the issue:

- `https://ayearofai.com/rohan-4-the-vanishing-gradient-problem-ec68f76ffb9b`
- `http://www.cs.toronto.edu/~rgrosse/courses/csc321_2017/readings/L15%20Exploding%20and%20Vanishing%20Gradients.pdf`
- `http://people.idsia.ch/~juergen/cvpr2012.pdf`

Pain point #2 – The exploding gradient problem

Another drawback of recurrent neural networks is the problem of exploding gradients. This is similar to the vanishing gradient problem but the exact opposite. Sometimes, during backpropagation, the gradients explode to extraordinarily large values. As with the vanishing gradient problem, the problem of exploding gradients occurs when network architectures get deeper.

Getting ready

The name exploding gradient problem stems from the fact that, during the backpropagation step, some of the gradients vanish or become zero. Technically, this means that there is no error term being propagated backward during the backward pass of the network. This becomes a problem when the network gets deeper and more complex.

How to do it...

This section will describe the exploding gradient problem in recurrent neural networks:

- The exploding gradient problem is very similar to the vanishing gradient problem, but just the opposite.
- When long-term dependencies arise in recurrent neural networks, the error term is propagated backward through the network sometimes explodes or becomes very large.
- This error term multiplied by the learning rate results in an extremely large $\triangle$w. This gives rise to new weights that look very different from the previous weights. It is called the exploding gradient problem because the value of the gradient becomes too large.
- The problem of exploding gradients is illustrated in an algorithmic fashion, in the following diagram:

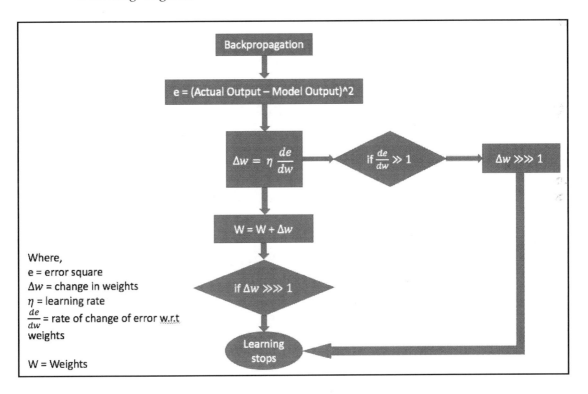

Where,
e = error square
Δw = change in weights
η = learning rate
$\frac{de}{dw}$ = rate of change of error w.r.t weights

W = Weights

How it works...

Since neural networks use a gradient-based optimization technique to learn features present in data, it is essential that these gradients are preserved in order for the network to calculate an error based on the change in gradients. This section will describe how the exploding gradient problem occurs in recurrent neural networks:

- While using backpropagation, the network first calculates the error, which is nothing but the model output subtracted from the actual output squared (such as the square error).
- Using this error, the model then computes the change in error with respect to the change in weights (de/dw).
- The computed derivative multiplied by the learning rate n gives $\triangle$w, which is nothing but the change in weights. The term $\triangle$w is added to the original weights to update them to the new weights.
- Suppose the value of de/dw (the gradient or rate of change of error with respect to weights) is greater than 1, then that term multiplied by the learning rate gives a very, very large number that is of no use to the network while trying to optimize weights further, since the weights are no longer in the same range.
- This happens because the weight updates during backpropagation are only accurate for the most recent time step, and this accuracy reduces while backpropagating through the previous time steps and becomes almost insignificant when the weight updates flow through many steps back in time.
- The number of previous times steps the network needs to backpropagate through increases with the increase in the number of sequences in the input data. In such cases, the recurrent networks become incapable of remembering information from many time steps in the past and therefore are unable to make accurate predictions of future time steps.
- When such a scenario occurs, the network requires many more complex calculations, as a result of which the number of iterations increases substantially and during which the change in error term increases beyond 1 and changes in weight ($\triangle$w) explode. As a result, the new or updated weight is completely out of range when compared to the previous weight.

- Since there is no weight update occurring, the network stops learning or being able to update its weights within a specified range, which is a problem as this will cause the model to overfit the data.

There's more...

The following are some of the ways in which the problem of exploding gradients can be solved:

- Certain gradient clipping techniques can be applied to solve this issue of exploding gradients.
- Another way to prevent this is by using truncated Backpropagation Through Time, where instead of starting the backpropagation at the last time step (or output layer), we can choose a smaller time step (say, 15) to start backpropagating. This means that the network will backpropagate through only the last 15 time steps at one instance and learn information related to those 15-time steps only. This is similar to feeding in mini batches of data to the network as it would become far too computationally expensive to compute the gradient over every single element of the dataset in the case of very large datasets.
- The final option to prevent the explosion of gradients is by monitoring them and adjusting the learning rate accordingly.

See also

A more detailed explanation of the vanishing and exploding gradient problems can be found at the following links:

- http://neuralnetworksanddeeplearning.com/chap5.html
- https://www.dlology.com/blog/how-to-deal-with-vanishingexploding-gradients-in-keras/
- https://machinelearningmastery.com/exploding-gradients-in-neural-networks/

Sequential working of LSTMs

Long Short-Term Memory Unit (LSTM) cells are nothing but slightly more advanced architectures compared to Recurrent Networks. LSTMs can be thought of as a special kind of Recurrent Neural Networks with the capabilities of learning long-term dependencies that exist in sequential data. The main reason behind this is the fact that LSTMs contain memory and are able to store and update information within their cells unlike Recurrent Neural Networks.

Getting ready

The main components of a Long Short-Term Memory unit are as follows:

- The input gate
- The forget gate
- The update gate

Each of these gates is made up of a sigmoid layer followed by a pointwise multiplication operation. The sigmoid layer outputs numbers between zero and one. These values describe how much information of each component is allowed to pass through the respective gate. A value of zero means the gate will allow nothing to pass through it, while a value of one means the gate allows all the information to pass through.

The best way to understand LSTM cells is through computational graphs, just like in the case of recurrent neural networks.

LSTMs were originally developed by Sepp Hochreiter and Jurgen Schmidhuber in 1997. The following is, link to their published paper:

- `http://www.bioinf.jku.at/publications/older/2604.pdf`

How to do it...

This section will describe the inner components of a single LSTM cell, primarily, the three different gates present inside the cell. A number of such cells stacked together form an LSTM network:

1. LSTMs also have a chain-like structure like RNNs. Standard RNNs are basically modules of repeating units like a simple function (for example, tanh).
2. LSTMs have the capability to retain information for long periods of time as

compared to RNNs owing to the presence of memory in each unit. This allows them to learn important information during the early stages in a sequence of inputs and also gives it the ability to have a significant impact on the decisions made by the model at the end of each time step.

3. By being able to store information right from the early stages of an input sequence, LSTMs are actively able to preserve the error that can be backpropagated through time and layers instead of letting that error vanish or explode.

4. LSTMs are capable of learning information over many time steps and thus have denser layer architectures by preserving the error which is backpropagated through those layers.

5. The cell structures called "**gates**" give the LSTM the ability to retain information, add information or remove information from the **cell state**.

6. The following diagram illustrates the structure of an LSTM. The key feature while trying to understand LSTMs is in understanding the LSTM network architecture and cell state, which can be visualized here:

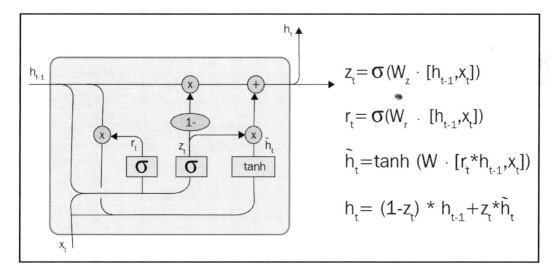

$$z_t = \sigma (W_z \cdot [h_{t-1}, x_t])$$

$$r_t = \sigma (W_r \cdot [h_{t-1}, x_t])$$

$$\tilde{h}_t = \tanh (W \cdot [r_t * h_{t-1}, x_t])$$

$$h_t = (1 - z_t) * h_{t-1} + z_t * \tilde{h}_t$$

7. In the preceding diagram, x_t and h_{t-1} are the two inputs to the cell. x_t is the input from the current time step, while h_{t-1} is the input from the previous time step (which is the output of the preceding cell during the previous time step). Besides these two inputs, we also have h which is the current output (i.e., time step t) from the LSTM cell after performing its operations on the two inputs through its gates.

8. In the preceding diagram, r_t represents the output emerging from the input gate, which takes in inputs h_{t-1} and x_t, performs multiplication of these inputs with its weight matrix W_z, and passes them through a sigmoid activation function.

9. Similarly, the term z_t represents the output emerging from the forget gate. This gate has a set of weight matrices (represented by W_r) which are specific to this particular gate and govern how the gate functions.

10. Finally, there is $\tilde{h}_t$, which is the output emerging from the update gate. In this case, there are two parts. The first part is a sigmoid layer which is also called the **input gate layer**, and its primary function is deciding which values to update. The next layer is a tanh layer . The primary function of this layer is to create a vector or array containing new values that could be added to the cell state.

How it works...

A combination of a number of LSTM cells/units forms an LSTM network. The architecture of such a network is shown in the following diagram:

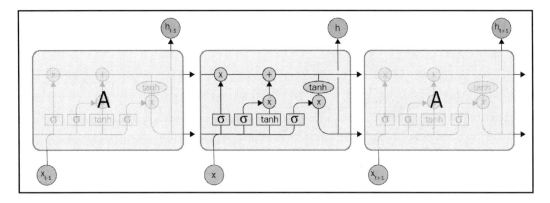

1. In the preceding diagram, the full LSTM cell is represented by "*A*". The cell takes the current input (x_i) of a sequence of inputs, and produces (h_i) which is nothing but the output of the current hidden state. This output is then sent to the next LSTM cell as its input.

2. An LSTM cell is slightly more complicated than an RNN cell. While the RNN cell has just one function/layer acting on a current input, the LSTM cell has three layers which are the three gates controlling the information flowing through the cell at any given instance in time.

3. The cell behaves a lot like the hard disk memory in a computer. The cell, therefore, has the capability to allow the writing, reading and storing of information within its cell state. The cell also makes decisions about what information to store, and when to allow reading, writing, and erasing information. This is facilitated by the gates that open or close accordingly.

4. The gates present in LSTM cells are analog in contrast to the digital storage systems in today's computers. This means that the gates can only be controlled through an element-wise multiplication through sigmoids, yielding probability values between 0 and 1. A high value will cause the gate to remain open while a low value will cause the gate to remain shut.

5. Analog systems have an edge over digital systems when it comes to neural network operations since they are differentiable. This makes analog systems more suitable for tasks like backpropagation which primarily rely on the gradients.

6. The gates pass on information or block information or let only a part of the information flow through them based on its strength and importance. The information is filtered at every time step through the sets of weight matrices specific to each gate. Therefore, each gate has complete control over how to act on the information it receives.

7. The weight matrices associated with each gate, like the weights that modulate input and hidden states, are adjusted based on the recurrent network's learning process and gradient descent.

8. The first gate is called the **forget gate** and it controls what information is maintained from the previous state. This gate takes the previous cell output (h_t - 1) as its input along with the current input (x_t), and applies a sigmoid activation (σ) in order to produce and output value between 0 and 1 for each hidden unit. This is followed by the element-wise multiplication with the current state (illustrated by the first operation in the preceding diagram).

9. The second gate is called the **update gate** and its primary function is to update the cell state based on the current input. This gate passes the same input as the forget gate's inputs (h_{t-1} and x_t) into a sigmoid activation layer (σ) followed by a tanh activation layer and then performs an element-wise multiplication between these two results. Next, element-wise addition is performed with the result and the current state (illustrated by the second operation in the preceding diagram).

10. Finally, there is an output gate which controls what information and how much information gets transferred to the adjoining cell to act as its inputs during the next time step. The current cell state is passed through a tanh activation layer and multiplied element-wise with the cell input (h_{t-1} and x_t) after being passed through a sigmoid layer (σ) for this operation.

11. The update gate behaves as the filter on what the cell decides to output to the next cell. This output, h_t, is then passed on to the next LSTM cell as its input, and also to the above layers if many LSTM cells are stacked on top of each other.

There's more...

LSTMs were a big leap forward when compared to what could be accomplished with feedforward networks and Recurrent Neural Networks. One might wonder what the next big step in the near future is, or even what that step might be. A lot researchers do believe "attention" is the next big step when it comes to the field of artificial intelligence. With the amount of data growing vastly with each day it becomes impossible to process every single bit of that data. This is where attention could be a potential game-changer, causing the networks to give their attention only to data or areas which are of high priority or interest and disregard useless information. For example, if an RNN is being used to create an image captioning engine, it will only pick a part of the image to to give its attention to for every word it outputs.

The recent (2015) paper by Xu, et al. does exactly this. They explore adding attention to LSTM cells. Reading this paper can be a good place to start learning about the use of attention in neural networks. There have been some good results with using attention for various tasks, and more research is currently being conducted on the subject. The paper by Xu, et al. can be found using the following link:
`https://arxiv.org/pdf/1502.03044v2.pdf`

Attention isn't the only variant to LSTMs. Some of the other active research is based on the utilization of grid LSTMs, as used in the paper by Kalchbrenner, et al., for which the link is at: `https://arxiv.org/pdf/1507.01526v1.pdf.`

See also

Some other useful information and papers related to RNNs and LSTMs in generative networks can be found by visiting the following links:

- `http://www.deeplearningbook.org/contents/rnn.html`
- `https://arxiv.org/pdf/1502.04623.pdf`
- `https://arxiv.org/pdf/1411.7610v3.pdf`
- `https://arxiv.org/pdf/1506.02216v3.pdf`

5
Predicting Fire Department Calls with Spark ML

In this chapter, the following recipes will be covered:

- Downloading the San Francisco fire department calls dataset
- Identifying the target variable of the logistic regression model
- Preparing feature variables for the logistic regression model
- Applying the logistic regression model
- Evaluating the accuracy of the logistic regression model

Introduction

Classification models are a popular way to predict a defined categorical outcome. We use outputs from classification models all the time. Anytime we go to see a movie in a theatre, we are interested to know whether the film is considered correct? One of the most popular classification models in the data science community is a logistic regression. The logistic regression model produces a response that is activated by a sigmoid function. The sigmoid function uses the inputs from the model and produces an output that is between 0 and 1. That output is usually in a form of a probability score. Many deep learning models are also used for classification purposes. It is common to find logistic regression models performed in conjunction with deep learning models to help establish a baseline in which deep learning models are measured against. The sigmoid activation function is one of many activation functions that are also used in deep neural networks within deep learning to produce a probability output. We will utilize the built-in machine learning libraries within Spark to build a logistic regression model that will predict whether an incoming call to the San Francisco Fire department is actually related to a fire, rather than another incident.

Downloading the San Francisco fire department calls dataset

The City of San Francisco does a great job of collecting fire department calls for services across their area. As it states on their website, each record includes the call number, incident number, address, unit identifier, call type, and disposition. The official website containing San Francisco fire department call data can be found at the following link:

```
https://data.sfgov.org/Public-Safety/Fire-Department-Calls-for-Service/nuek-
vuh3
```

There is some general information regarding the dataset with regards to the number of columns and rows, seen in the following screenshot:

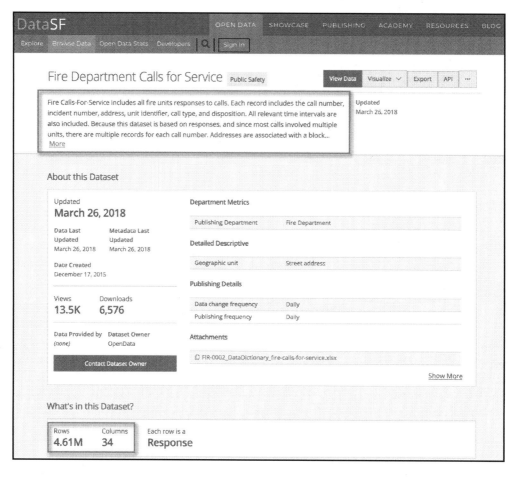

This current dataset, updated on 3/26/2018, has roughly **4.61 M** rows and **34** columns.

Getting ready

The dataset is available in a .csv file and can be downloaded locally on to your machine, where it can then be imported into Spark.

How to do it...

This section will walk through the steps to download and import the .csv file to our Jupyter notebook.

1. Download the dataset from the website by selecting **Export** and then **CSV**, as seen in the following screenshot:

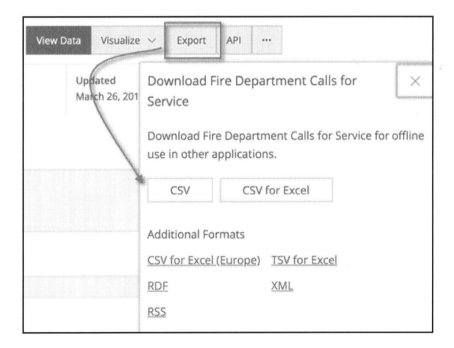

2. If not already the case, name the downloaded dataset Fire_Department_Calls_for_Service.csv

3. Save the dataset to any local directory, although ideally it should be saved to the same folder that contains the Spark notebook that will be used in this chapter, as seen in the following screenshot:

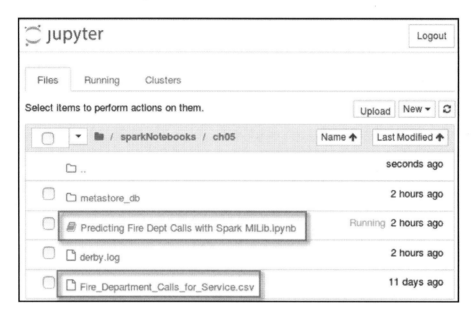

4. Once the dataset has been saved to the same directory as the notebook, execute the following `pyspark` script to import the dataset into Spark and create a dataframe called `df`:

```
from pyspark.sql import SparkSession
spark = SparkSession.builder \
                    .master("local") \
                    .appName("Predicting Fire Dept Calls") \
                    .config("spark.executor.memory", "6gb") \
                    .getOrCreate()

df = spark.read.format('com.databricks.spark.csv')\
                    .options(header='true', inferschema='true')\
                    .load('Fire_Department_Calls_for_Service.csv')
df.show(2)
```

How it works...

The dataset is saved to the same directory that houses the Jupyter notebook for ease of import into the Spark session.

1. A local `pyspark` session is initialized by importing `SparkSession` from `pyspark.sql`.

2. A dataframe, `df`, is created by reading in the CSV file with the options `header = 'true'` and `inferschema = 'true'`.

3. Finally, it is always ideal to run a script to show the data that has been imported into Spark through the dataframe to confirm that the data has made its way through. The outcome of the script, showing the first two rows of the dataset from the San Francisco fire department calls, can be seen in the following screenshot:

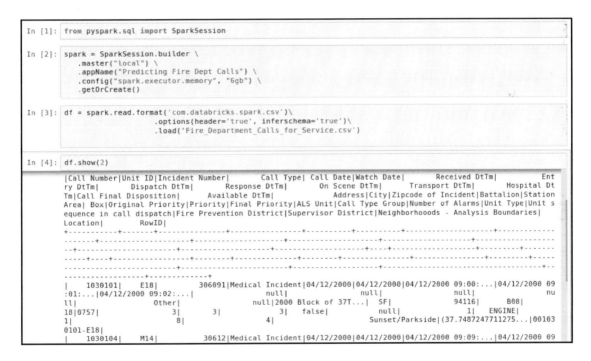

 Please note that as we read the file into spark, we are using `.load()` to pull the `.csv` file into the Jupyter notebook. This is fine for our purposes as we are using a local cluster, but would not work if we were leveraging a cluster from Hadoop.

There's more...

The dataset is accompanied by a data dictionary that defines the headers for each of the 34 columns. This data dictionary can be accessed from the same website through the following link:

```
https://data.sfgov.org/api/views/nuek-vuh3/files/ddb7f3a9-0160-4f07-bb1e-
2af744909294?download=truefilename=FIR-0002_DataDictionary_fire-calls-for-
service.xlsx
```

See also

The San Francisco government website allows for online visualization of the data, which can be used to do some quick data profiling. The visualization application can be accessed on the website by selecting the **Visualize** dropdown, as seen in the following screenshot:

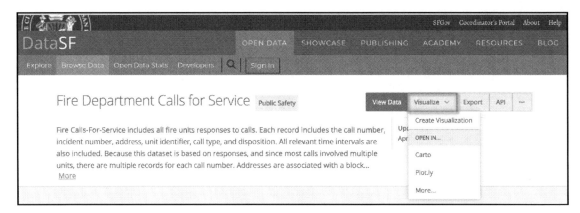

Identifying the target variable of the logistic regression model

A logistic regression model operates as a classification algorithm aiming to predict a binary outcome. In this section, we will specify the best column within the dataset to predict whether an incoming call to the operator is related to fire or non-fire incidents.

Getting ready

We will visualize many of the data points in this section, which will require the following:

1. Ensuring that `matplotlib` is installed by executing `pip install matplotlib` at the command line.
2. Running `import matplotlib.pyplot as plt` as well as ensuring graphs are viewed within cells by running `%matplotlib inline`.

Additionally, there will be some manipulation of functions within `pyspark.sql` that requires `importing functions as F`.

How to do it...

This section will walk through visualizing the data from the San Francisco Fire Department.

1. Execute the following script to get a cursory identification of the unique values in the `Call Type Group` column:

```
df.select('Call Type Group').distinct().show()
```

2. There are five main categories:
    1. `Alarm`.
    2. `Potentially Life-threatening`.
    3. `Non Life-threatening`.
    4. `Fire`.
    5. `null`.

3. Unfortunately, one of those categories is `null` values. It would be useful to get a row count of each unique value to identify how many null values there are in the dataset. Execute the following script to generate a row count of each unique value for the column `Call Type Group`:

```
df.groupBy('Call Type Group').count().show()
```

4. Unfortunately, there are over 2.8 M rows of data that do not have a `Call Type Group` associated with them. That is over 60 percent of the available rows of 4.6 M. Execute the following script to view the imbalance of null values in a bar chart:

```
df2 = df.groupBy('Call Type Group').count()
graphDF = df2.toPandas()
graphDF = graphDF.sort_values('count', ascending=False)

import matplotlib.pyplot as plt
%matplotlib inline

graphDF.plot(x='Call Type Group', y = 'count', kind='bar')
plt.title('Call Type Group by Count')
plt.show()
```

5. Another indicator may need to be chosen to determine a target variable. Instead, we can profile `Call Type` to identify calls associated with fire versus all other calls. Execute the following script to profile `Call Type`:

```
df.groupBy('Call Type').count().orderBy('count',
ascending=False).show(100)
```

6. There do not appear to be any `null` values, as there were with `Call Type Group`. There are 32 unique categories for `Call Type`; therefore, it will be used as the target variable for fire incidents. Execute the following script to tag the columns containing `Fire` in `Call Type`:

```
from pyspark.sql import functions as F
fireIndicator = df.select(df["Call Type"],F.when(df["Call
Type"].like("%Fire%"),1)\
                         .otherwise(0).alias('Fire Indicator'))
fireIndicator.show()
```

7. Execute the following script to retrieve the distinct counts of `Fire Indicator`:

```
fireIndicator.groupBy('Fire Indicator').count().show()
```

8. Execute the following script to add the `Fire Indicator` column to the original dataframe, `df`:

```
df = df.withColumn("fireIndicator",\
F.when(df["Call Type"].like("%Fire%"),1).otherwise(0))
```

9. Finally, add the `fireIndicator` column has to the dataframe, `df`, and confirm by executing the following script:

```
df.printSchema()
```

How it works...

One of the key steps to building a successful logistic regression model is establishing a binary target variable that will be used as the prediction outcome. This section walks through the logic behind selecting our target variable:

1. Data profiling of potential target columns is performed by identifying the unique column values of `Call Type Group`. We can view the unique values of the `Call Type Group` column, as seen in the following screenshot:

```
In [5]: df.select('Call Type Group').distinct().show()

+--------------------+
|     Call Type Group|
+--------------------+
|               Alarm|
|                null|
|Potentially Life-...|
|Non Life-threatening|
|                Fire|
+--------------------+
```

2. The goal is to identify whether there are any missing values within the `Call Type Group` column and what can be done with those missing values. Sometimes, the missing values in the columns can just be dropped, and other times they are manipulated to populate values.

3. The following screenshot shows how many null values are present:

```
In [6]:  df.groupBy('Call Type Group').count().show()

         +--------------------+-------+
         |     Call Type Group|  count|
         +--------------------+-------+
         |               Alarm| 429831|
         |                null|2804459|
         |Potentially Life-...| 874195|
         |Non Life-threatening| 414806|
         |                Fire|  75797|
         +--------------------+-------+
```

4. Additionally, we can also plot how many `null` values are present to get a better visual sense of the abundance of values, as seen in the following screenshot:

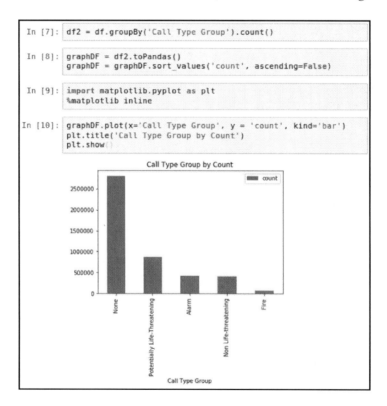

5. Since there are over 2.8 M rows that are missing from `Call Type Group`, as seen in the `df.groupBy` script as well as the bar chart, it doesn't make sense to drop all of those values, as that is over 60 percent of the total row count from the dataset. Therefore, another column will need to be chosen as the target indicator.

6. While profiling the `Call Type` column, we find that there aren't any **null** rows in the 32 unique possible values. This makes `Call Type` a better candidate for the target variable for the logistic regression model. The following is a screenshot of the `Call Type` column profiled:

```
In [11]:  df.groupBy('Call Type').count().orderBy('count', ascending=False).show(100)

          +--------------------+-------+
          |           Call Type|  count|
          +--------------------+-------+
          |    Medical Incident|2979993|
          |      Structure Fire| 609473|
          |              Alarms| 491741|
          |   Traffic Collision| 188097|
          |               Other|  74038|
          |Citizen Assist / ...|  69549|
          |        Outside Fire|  53682|
          |        Vehicle Fire|  22492|
          |        Water Rescue|  21861|
          |Gas Leak (Natural...|  17147|
          |   Electrical Hazard|  12845|
          |Odor (Strange / U...|  12339|
          |Elevator / Escala...|  12028|
          |Smoke Investigati...|  10118|
          |          Fuel Spill|   5386|
          |              HazMat|   3839|
          |Industrial Accidents|   2803|
          |           Explosion|   2530|
          |   Aircraft Emergency|   1511|
          |       Assist Police|   1318|
          |Train / Rail Inci...|   1224|
          |   High Angle Rescue|   1154|
          |Watercraft in Dis...|    884|
          |Extrication / Ent...|    672|
          |           Oil Spill|    516|
          |Confined Space / ...|    467|
          |Mutual Aid / Assi...|    423|
          |         Marine Fire|    359|
          |  Suspicious Package|    314|
          |      Administrative|    266|
          |    Train / Rail Fire|     10|
          |Lightning Strike ...|      9|
          +--------------------+-------+
```

7. Since logistic regression works best when there is a binary outcome, a new column is created using the `withColumn()` operator in the `df` dataframe to capture an indicator (0 or 1) as to whether a call is affiliated with a fire-related incident or a non-fire-related incident. The new column is called `fireIndicator` and can be seen in the following screenshot:

```
In [12]: from pyspark.sql import functions as F
         fireIndicator = df.select(df["Call Type"],F.when(df["Call Type"].like("%Fire%"),1)\
                                    .otherwise(0).alias('Fire Indicator'))
         fireIndicator.show()
```

```
+--------------------+--------------+
|           Call Type|Fire Indicator|
+--------------------+--------------+
|    Medical Incident|             0|
|    Medical Incident|             0|
|    Medical Incident|             0|
|              Alarms|             0|
|    Medical Incident|             0|
|Citizen Assist / ...|             0|
|   Electrical Hazard|             0|
|Odor (Strange / U...|             0|
|    Medical Incident|             0|
|    Medical Incident|             0|
|              Alarms|             0|
|    Medical Incident|             0|
|    Medical Incident|             0|
|    Medical Incident|             0|
|              Alarms|             0|
|              Alarms|             0|
|    Medical Incident|             0|
|               Other|             0|
|    Medical Incident|             0|
|       Structure Fire|            1|
+--------------------+--------------+
only showing top 20 rows
```

8. We can identify how prevalent fire calls are compared to the rest of the calls by doing a `groupBy().count()`, as seen in the following screenshot:

```
In [13]: fireIndicator.groupBy('Fire Indicator').count().show()
```

```
+--------------+-------+
|Fire Indicator|  count|
+--------------+-------+
|             1| 686016|
|             0|3913072|
+--------------+-------+
```

9. It is best practice to confirm that the new column has been attached to the existing dataframe by executing the `printSchema()` script of the newly modified dataframe. The output of the new schema can be seen in the following screenshot:

```
In [15]: df.printSchema()

root
 |-- Call Number: integer (nullable = true)
 |-- Unit ID: string (nullable = true)
 |-- Incident Number: integer (nullable = true)
 |-- Call Type: string (nullable = true)
 |-- Call Date: string (nullable = true)
 |-- Watch Date: string (nullable = true)
 |-- Received DtTm: string (nullable = true)
 |-- Entry DtTm: string (nullable = true)
 |-- Dispatch DtTm: string (nullable = true)
 |-- Response DtTm: string (nullable = true)
 |-- On Scene DtTm: string (nullable = true)
 |-- Transport DtTm: string (nullable = true)
 |-- Hospital DtTm: string (nullable = true)
 |-- Call Final Disposition: string (nullable = true)
 |-- Available DtTm: string (nullable = true)
 |-- Address: string (nullable = true)
 |-- City: string (nullable = true)
 |-- Zipcode of Incident: integer (nullable = true)
 |-- Battalion: string (nullable = true)
 |-- Station Area: string (nullable = true)
 |-- Box: string (nullable = true)
 |-- Original Priority: string (nullable = true)
 |-- Priority: string (nullable = true)
 |-- Final Priority: integer (nullable = true)
 |-- ALS Unit: boolean (nullable = true)
 |-- Call Type Group: string (nullable = true)
 |-- Number of Alarms: integer (nullable = true)
 |-- Unit Type: string (nullable = true)
 |-- Unit sequence in call dispatch: integer (nullable = true)
 |-- Fire Prevention District: string (nullable = true)
 |-- Supervisor District: string (nullable = true)
 |-- Neighborhooods - Analysis Boundaries: string (nullable = true)
 |-- Location: string (nullable = true)
 |-- RowID: string (nullable = true)
 |-- fireIndicator: integer (nullable = false)  <------------
```

There's more...

There were a couple of column manipulations done with the `pyspark.sql` module in this section. The `withColumn()` operator returns a new dataframe or modifies an existing dataframe by adding a new column or modifies an existing column of the same name. This is not to be confused with the `withColumnRenamed()` operator, which also returns a new dataframe, but by modifying the name of an existing column to a new column. Finally, we needed to perform some logical operations to convert values associated with `Fire` to 0 and without `Fire` to 1. This required using the `pyspark.sql.functions` module and incorporating the `where` function as an equivalent to a case statement used in SQL. The function created a case statement equation using the following syntax:

```
CASE WHEN Call Type LIKE %Fire% THEN 1 ELSE 0 END
```

The outcome of the new dataset for both columns, `Call Type` and `fireIndicator`, appear as the following:

```
In [16]: df.select('Call Type', 'fireIndicator').show(20)

+--------------------+-------------+
|           Call Type|fireIndicator|
+--------------------+-------------+
|    Medical Incident|            0|
|    Medical Incident|            0|
|    Medical Incident|            0|
|              Alarms|            0|
|    Medical Incident|            0|
|Citizen Assist / ...|            0|
|   Electrical Hazard|            0|
|Odor (Strange / U...|            0|
|    Medical Incident|            0|
|    Medical Incident|            0|
|              Alarms|            0|
|    Medical Incident|            0|
|    Medical Incident|            0|
|    Medical Incident|            0|
|              Alarms|            0|
|              Alarms|            0|
|    Medical Incident|            0|
|               Other|            0|
|    Medical Incident|            0|
|      Structure Fire|            1|
+--------------------+-------------+
only showing top 20 rows
```

See also

In order to learn more about the `pyspark.sql` module available within Spark, visit the following website:

```
http://spark.apache.org/docs/2.2.0/api/python/pyspark.sql.html
```

Preparing feature variables for the logistic regression model

In the previous section, we identified our target variable that will be used as our predictor for fire calls in our logistic regression model. This section will focus on identifying all of the features that will best help the model identify what the target should be. This is known as **feature selection**.

Getting ready

This section will require importing `StringIndexer` from `pyspark.ml.feature`. In order to ensure proper feature selection, we will need to map string columns to columns of indices. This will help generate distinct numeric values for categorical variables that will provide ease of computation for the machine learning model to ingest the independent variables used to predict the target outcome.

How to do it...

This section will walk through the steps to prepare the feature variables for our model.

1. Execute the following script to update the dataframe, `df`, by only selecting the fields that are independent of any fire indicators:

```
df = df.select('fireIndicator',
    'Zipcode of Incident',
    'Battalion',
    'Station Area',
    'Box',
    'Number of Alarms',
    'Unit sequence in call dispatch',
    'Neighborhooods - Analysis Boundaries',
    'Fire Prevention District',
```

```
        'Supervisor District')
df.show(5)
```

2. The next step is to identify any null values within the dataframe and remove them if they exist. Execute the following script to identify the row count with any null values:

```
print('Total Rows')
df.count()
print('Rows without Null values')
df.dropna().count()
print('Row with Null Values')
df.count()-df.dropna().count()
```

3. There are **16,551** rows with missing values. Execute the following script to update the dataframe to remove all rows with null values:

```
df = df.dropna()
```

4. Execute the following script to retrieve the updated target count of `fireIndicator`:

```
df.groupBy('fireIndicator').count().orderBy('count', ascending = False).show()
```

5. Import the `StringIndexer` class from `pyspark.ml.feature` to assign numeric values to each categorical variable for the features, as seen in the following script:

```
from pyspark.ml.feature import StringIndexer
```

6. Create a Python list for all the feature variables that will be used in the model using the following script:

```
column_names = df.columns[1:]
```

7. Execute the following script to specify the output column format, `outputcol`, that will be `stringIndexed` from the list of features from the input column, `inputcol`:

```
categoricalColumns = column_names
indexers = []
for categoricalCol in categoricalColumns:
    stringIndexer = StringIndexer(inputCol=categoricalCol,
outputCol=categoricalCol+"_Index")
    indexers += [stringIndexer]
```

8. Execute the following script to create a `model` that will be used to `fit` the input columns and produce the newly defined output columns to the existing dataframe, `df`:

```
models = []
for model in indexers:
    indexer_model = model.fit(df)
    models+=[indexer_model]

for i in models:
    df = i.transform(df)
```

9. Execute the following script to define a final selection of the features in the dataframe, `df`, that will be used for the model:

```
df = df.select(
        'fireIndicator',
        'Zipcode of Incident_Index',
        'Battalion_Index',
        'Station Area_Index',
        'Box_Index',
        'Number of Alarms_Index',
        'Unit sequence in call dispatch_Index',
        'Neighborhooods - Analysis Boundaries_Index',
        'Fire Prevention District_Index',
        'Supervisor District_Index')
```

How it works...

This section will explain the logic behind the steps in preparing the feature variables for our model.

1. Only the indicators in the dataframe that are truly independent of an indication of fire are selected to contribute to the logistic regression model that will predict the outcome. The reason this is performed is to remove any potential bias in the dataset that may already reveal the outcome of the prediction. This minimizes human interaction with the final outcome. The output of the updated dataframe can be seen in the following screenshot:

```
In [17]: df = df.select('fireIndicator',
                        'Zipcode of Incident',
                        'Battalion',
                        'Station Area',
                        'Box',
                        'Number of Alarms',
                        'Unit sequence in call dispatch',
                        'Neighborhoods - Analysis Boundaries',
                        'Fire Prevention District',
                        'Supervisor District',
                        'final priority')
         df.show()
```

fireIndicator	Zipcode of Incident	Battalion	Station Area	Box	Number of Alarms	Unit sequence in call dispatch	Neighborhoods - Analysis Boundaries	Fire Prevention District	Supervisor District	final priority
0	94116	B08	18	0757	1		Sunset/Parkside	8	4	3	1
0	94122	B08	23	7651	1		Sunset/Parkside	8	4	3	2
0	94102	B02	36	3111	1		Tenderloin	2	6	3	1
0	94102	B03	01	1456	1		Tenderloin	3	6	3	3
0	94108	B03	01	1322	1		Financial Distric...	1	3	3	2
0	94109	B01	03	1463	1		Nob Hill	1	3	3	1
0	94109	B04	38	3155	1						1

 Please note that the column Neighborhoooods – Analysis of Boundaries is originally misspelled from the data we extract. We will continue to use the misspelling for the rest of the chapter for continuity purposes. However, the column name can be renamed using the withColumnRenamed() function in Spark.

2. The final selection of columns are chosen as the following:
   - fireIndicator
   - Zipcode of Incident
   - Battalion

- Station Area
- Box
- Number of Alarms
- Unit sequence in call dispatch
- Neighborhooods – Analysis Boundaries
- Fire Prevention District
- Supervisor District

3. These columns are selected to avoid data leakage in our modeling. Data leakage is common in modeling and can lead to invalid predictive models because it can incorporate features that are directly a result of the outcome we are trying to predict. Ideally, we wish to incorporate features that are truly independent of the outcome. There are several columns that appeared to be leaky and, hence, are removed from our dataframe and model.

4. All rows with missing or null values are identified and removed in order to get the very best performance out of the model without overstating or understating key features. An inventory of the rows with missing values can be calculated and shown to be **16,551,** as seen in the following script:

```
In [18]: print('Total Rows')
         df.count()

         Total Rows
Out[18]: 4599088

In [19]: print('Rows without Null values')
         df.dropna().count()

         Rows without Null values
Out[19]: 4582537

In [20]: print('Row with Null Values')
         df.count()-df.dropna().count()

         Row with Null Values
Out[20]: 16551
```

5. We can get a look at the frequency of calls that are fire-related versus those that are not, as seen in the following screenshot:

```
In [22]: df.groupBy('fireIndicator').count().orderBy('count', ascending = False).show()

         +-------------+-------+
         |fireIndicator|  count|
         +-------------+-------+
         |            0|3897625|
         |            1| 684912|
         +-------------+-------+
```

6. `StringIndexer` is imported to help convert several of the categorical or string features into numerical values for ease of computation within the logistic regression model. The input of the features needs to be in a vector or array format, which is ideal for numeric values. A list of all the features that will be used in the model can be seen in the following screenshot:

```
In [23]: from pyspark.ml.feature import StringIndexer

In [24]: column_names = df.columns[1:]
         column_names

Out[24]: ['Zipcode of Incident',
          'Battalion',
          'Station Area',
          'Box',
          'Number of Alarms',
          'Unit sequence in call dispatch',
          'Neighborhooods - Analysis Boundaries',
          'Fire Prevention District',
          'Supervisor District']
```

7. An indexer is built for each of the categorical variables specifying the input
   (inputCol) and output (outputCol) columns that will be used in the
   model. Each column in the dataframe is adjusted or transformed to rebuild a new
   output with the updated indexing, ranging from 0 to the maximum value of the
   unique count of that specific column. The new column is appended with _Index
   at the end. While the updated column is created, the original column is still
   available in the dataframe, as seen in the following screenshot:

```
In [26]: models = []
         for model in indexers:
             indexer_model = model.fit(df)
             models+=[indexer_model]

         for i in models:
             df = i.transform(df)
```

```
In [27]: df.columns
```

```
Out[27]: ['fireIndicator',
          'Zipcode of Incident',
          'Battalion',
          'Station Area',
          'Box',
          'Number of Alarms',
          'Unit sequence in call dispatch',
          'Neighborhooods - Analysis Boundaries',
          'Fire Prevention District',
          'Supervisor District',
          'Zipcode of Incident_Index',
          'Battalion_Index',
          'Station Area_Index',
          'Box_Index',
          'Number of Alarms_Index',
          'Unit sequence in call dispatch_Index',
          'Neighborhooods - Analysis Boundaries_Index',
          'Fire Prevention District_Index',
          'Supervisor District_Index']
```

8. We can look at one of the newly created columns and compare it with the original to see how the strings have been converted to numeric categories. The following screenshot shows how `Neighborhoooods - Analysis Boundaries` compares with `Neighborhoooods - Analysis Boundaries_Index`:

```
In [28]: df.select('Neighborhoooods - Analysis Boundaries', 'Neighborhoooods - Analysis Boundaries_Index').show()

+--------------------------------------+--------------------------------------------+
|Neighborhoooods - Analysis Boundaries|Neighborhoooods - Analysis Boundaries_Index|
+--------------------------------------+--------------------------------------------+
|                     Sunset/Parkside|                                        5.0|
|                     Sunset/Parkside|                                        5.0|
|                           Tenderloin|                                        0.0|
|                           Tenderloin|                                        0.0|
|                  Financial Distric...|                                        3.0|
|                             Nob Hill|                                        7.0|
|                             Nob Hill|                                        7.0|
|                        Outer Mission|                                       22.0|
|                  Bayview Hunters P...|                                        4.0|
|                            Chinatown|                                       13.0|
|                     Sunset/Parkside|                                        5.0|
|                              Mission|                                        2.0|
|                          Mission Bay|                                       29.0|
|                      Western Addition|                                        6.0|
|                      Western Addition|                                        6.0|
|                     Sunset/Parkside|                                        5.0|
|                    West of Twin Peaks|                                       11.0|
|                     Lone Mountain/USF|                                       27.0|
|                  Oceanview/Merced/...|                                       23.0|
|                       South of Market|                                        1.0|
+--------------------------------------+--------------------------------------------+
only showing top 20 rows
```

9. The dataframe is then trimmed down to incorporate only the numerical values and remove the original categorical variables that were transformed. The non-numerical values no longer serve a purpose from a modeling perspective and are dropped from the dataframe.

10. The new columns are printed out to confirm that each value type of the dataframe is either double precision or integer, as seen in the following screenshot:

```
In [29]:  df = df.select(
              'fireIndicator',
              'Zipcode of Incident_Index',
              'Battalion_Index',
              'Station Area_Index',
              'Box_Index',
              'Number of Alarms_Index',
              'Unit sequence in call dispatch_Index',
              'Neighborhoods - Analysis Boundaries_Index',
              'Fire Prevention District_Index',
              'Supervisor District_Index')
```

```
In [30]:  df.printSchema()

          root
           |-- fireIndicator: integer (nullable = false)
           |-- Zipcode of Incident_Index: double (nullable = true)
           |-- Battalion_Index: double (nullable = true)
           |-- Station Area_Index: double (nullable = true)
           |-- Box_Index: double (nullable = true)
           |-- Number of Alarms_Index: double (nullable = true)
           |-- Unit sequence in call dispatch_Index: double (nullable = true)
           |-- Neighborhoods - Analysis Boundaries_Index: double (nullable = true)
           |-- Fire Prevention District_Index: double (nullable = true)
           |-- Supervisor District_Index: double (nullable = true)
```

There's more...

A final look at the newly modified dataframe will reveal only numerical values, as seen in the following screenshot:

```
In [31]:  df.show(5)

+------------+-------------------------+---------------+------------------+---------+----------------------+
|fireIndicator|Zipcode of Incident_Index|Battalion_Index|Station Area_Index|Box_Index|Number of Alarms_Index|
Unit sequence in call dispatch_Index|Neighborhoods - Analysis Boundaries_Index|Fire Prevention District_Inde
x|Supervisor District_Index|
+------------+-------------------------+---------------+------------------+---------+----------------------+

|           0|                     18.0|            5.0|              29.0|   1733.0|                   0.0|
0.0|                                 5.0|                                     7.0|                         10.0|
|           0|                      8.0|            5.0|              31.0|   1274.0|                   0.0|
1.0|                                 5.0|                                     7.0|                         10.0|
|           0|                      0.0|            1.0|               2.0|     61.0|                   0.0|
0.0|                                 0.0|                                     0.0|                          0.0|
|           0|                      0.0|            0.0|               0.0|      7.0|                   0.0|
2.0|                                 0.0|                                     1.0|                          0.0|
|           0|                     17.0|            0.0|               0.0|     47.0|                   0.0|
1.0|                                 3.0|                                     2.0|                          1.0|
+------------+-------------------------+---------------+------------------+---------+----------------------+

only showing top 5 rows
```

See also

In order to learn more about `StringIndexer`, visit the following website: `https://spark.apache.org/docs/2.2.0/ml-features.html#stringindexer`.

Applying the logistic regression model

The stage is now set to apply the model to the dataframe.

Getting ready

This section will focus on applying a very common classification model called **logistic regression**, which will involve importing some of the following from Spark:

```
from pyspark.ml.feature import VectorAssembler
from pyspark.ml.evaluation import BinaryClassificationEvaluator
from pyspark.ml.classification import LogisticRegression
```

How to do it...

This section will walk through the steps of applying our model and evaluating the results.

1. Execute the following script to lump all of the feature variables in the dataframe in a list called `features`:

    ```
    features = df.columns[1:]
    ```

2. Execute the following to import `VectorAssembler` and configure the fields that will be assigned to the feature vector by assigning the `inputCols` and `outputCol`:

    ```
    from pyspark.ml.feature import VectorAssembler
    feature_vectors = VectorAssembler(
        inputCols = features,
        outputCol = "features")
    ```

3. Execute the following script to apply `VectorAssembler` to the dataframe with the `transform` function:

```
df = feature_vectors.transform(df)
```

4. Modify the dataframe to remove all of the columns except for `fireIndicator` and `features`, as seen in the following script:

```
df = df.drop( 'Zipcode of Incident_Index',
              'Battalion_Index',
              'Station Area_Index',
              'Box_Index',
              'Number of Alarms_Index',
              'Unit sequence in call dispatch_Index',
              'Neighborhooods - Analysis Boundaries_Index',
              'Fire Prevention District_Index',
              'Supervisor District_Index')
```

5. Modify the dataframe to rename `fireIndicator` to `label`, as seen in the following script:

```
df = df.withColumnRenamed('fireIndicator', 'label')
```

6. Split the entire dataframe, `df`, into training and test sets in a 75:25 ratio, with a random seed set as `12345`, as seen in the following script:

```
(trainDF, testDF) = df.randomSplit([0.75, 0.25], seed = 12345)
```

7. Import the `LogisticRegression` library from `pyspark.ml.classification` and configure to incorporate the `label` and `features` from the dataframe, and then fit on the training dataset, `trainDF`, as seen in the following script:

```
from pyspark.ml.classification import LogisticRegression
logreg = LogisticRegression(labelCol="label",
featuresCol="features", maxIter=10)
LogisticRegressionModel = logreg.fit(trainDF)
```

8. Transform the test dataframe, `testDF`, to apply the logistic regression model. The new dataframe with the scores from the prediction is called `df_predicted`, as seen in the following script:

```
df_predicted = LogisticRegressionModel.transform(testDF)
```

How it works...

This section explains the logic behind the steps in applying our model and evaluating the results.

1. Classification models work best when all of the features are combined in a single vector for training purposes. Therefore, we begin the vectorization process by collecting all of the features into a single list called `features`. Since our label is the first column of the dataframe, we exclude it and pull in every column after as a feature column or feature variable.

2. The vectorization process continues by converting all of the variables from the `features` list into a single vector output to a column called `features`. This process requires importing `VectorAssembler` from `pyspark.ml.feature`.

3. Applying `VectorAssembler` transforms the dataframe by creating a newly added column called `features`, as seen in the following screenshot:

```
In [33]:  from pyspark.ml.feature import VectorAssembler

          feature_vectors = VectorAssembler(
                  inputCols = features,
                  outputCol = "features")

In [34]:  df = feature_vectors.transform(df)

In [35]:  df.columns

Out[35]:  ['fireIndicator',
           'Zipcode of Incident_Index',
           'Battalion_Index',
           'Station Area_Index',
           'Box_Index',
           'Number of Alarms_Index',
           'Unit sequence in call dispatch_Index',
           'Neighborhooods - Analysis Boundaries_Index',
           'Fire Prevention District_Index',
           'Supervisor District_Index',
           'features']
```

4. At this point, the only columns that are necessary for us to use in the model are the label column, `fireIndicator`, and the `features` column. All of the other columns can be dropped from the dataframe as they will no longer be needed for modeling purposes.

5. Additionally, to help with the logistic regression model, we will change the column called `fireIndicator` to `label`. The output of the `df.show()` script can be seen in the following screenshot with the newly renamed columns:

```
In [37]: df = df.withColumnRenamed('fireIndicator', 'label')

In [38]: df.show()
         +-----+--------------------+
         |label|            features|
         +-----+--------------------+
         |    0|[5.0,18.0,5.0,29....|
         |    0|[5.0,8.0,5.0,31.0...|
         |    0|[0.0,0.0,1.0,2.0,...|
         |    0|(10,[4,5,6,7,9],[...|
         |    0|[3.0,17.0,0.0,0.0...|
         |    0|[7.0,3.0,2.0,1.0,...|
         |    0|[7.0,3.0,3.0,17.0...|
         |    0|[22.0,5.0,6.0,18....|
         |    0|[4.0,4.0,4.0,7.0,...|
         |    0|[13.0,21.0,2.0,4....|
         |    0|[5.0,8.0,5.0,26.0...|
         |    0|[2.0,2.0,7.0,3.0,...|
         |    0|[29.0,7.0,0.0,8.0...|
         |    0|[6.0,6.0,3.0,6.0,...|
         |    0|[6.0,6.0,3.0,6.0,...|
         |    0|[5.0,18.0,5.0,29....|
         |    0|[11.0,22.0,5.0,37...|
         |    0|[27.0,11.0,8.0,12...|
         |    1|[23.0,5.0,6.0,21....|
         |    0|[1.0,1.0,1.0,2.0,...|
         +-----+--------------------+
         only showing top 20 rows
```

6. In order to minimize overfitting the model, the dataframe will be split into a testing and training dataset to fit the model on the training dataset, `trainDF`, and test it on the testing dataset, `testDF`. A random seed of `12345` is set to keep the randomness consistent each time the cell is executed. We can identify the row counts for the data split, as seen in the following screenshot:

```
In [39]:  (trainDF, testDF) = df.randomSplit([0.75, 0.25], seed = 12345)

In [40]:  print(trainDF.count())
          print(testDF.count())

          3436948
          1145589
```

7. A logistic regression model, `LogisticRegression`, is then imported from `pyspark.ml.classification` and configured to input the appropriate column names from the dataframe associated with the features and the label. Additionally, the logistic regression model is assigned to a variable called `logreg` that is then fit to train our data set, `trainDF`.

8. A new dataframe, `predicted_df`, is created based on the transformation of the test dataframe, `testDF`, once the logistic regression model is scored on it. The model creates three additional columns for `predicted_df`, based on the scoring. The three additional columns are `rawPrediction`, `probability`, and `prediction`, as seen in the following screenshot:

```
In [41]:  from pyspark.ml.classification import LogisticRegression
          logreg = LogisticRegression(labelCol="label", featuresCol="features", maxIter=10)
          LogisticRegressionModel = logreg.fit(trainDF)

In [42]:  df_predicted = LogisticRegressionModel.transform(testDF)

In [43]:  df_predicted.printSchema()

          root
           |-- label: integer (nullable = false)
           |-- features: vector (nullable = true)
           |-- rawPrediction: vector (nullable = true)
           |-- probability: vector (nullable = true)
           |-- prediction: double (nullable = true)
```

9. Finally, the new columns in `df_predicted` can be profiled, as seen in the following screenshot:

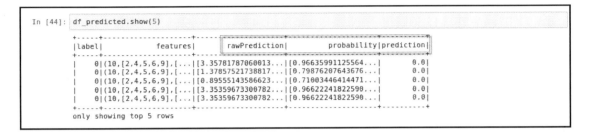

```
In [44]: df_predicted.show(5)

+-----+--------------------+--------------------+--------------------+----------+
|label|            features|       rawPrediction|         probability|prediction|
+-----+--------------------+--------------------+--------------------+----------+
|    0|(10,[2,4,5,6,9],[...|[3.35781787060013...|[0.96635991125564...|       0.0|
|    0|(10,[2,4,5,6,9],[...|[1.37857521738817...|[0.79876207643676...|       0.0|
|    0|(10,[2,4,5,6,9],[...|[0.89555143586623...|[0.71003446414471...|       0.0|
|    0|(10,[2,4,5,6,9],[...|[3.35359673300782...|[0.96622241822590...|       0.0|
|    0|(10,[2,4,5,6,9],[...|[3.35359673300782...|[0.96622241822590...|       0.0|
+-----+--------------------+--------------------+--------------------+----------+
only showing top 5 rows
```

There's more...

One important thing to keep in mind because it may initially come off as being counter-intuitive is that our **probability** threshold is set at 50 percent in our dataframe. Any call with a **probability** of 0.500 and above is given a **prediction** of **0.0** and any call with a **probability** of less than 0.500 is given a **prediction** of **1.0**. This was set during the pipeline development process and as long as we are aware of what the threshold is along with how the prediction is allocated, we are in good shape.

See also

To learn more about `VectorAssembler`, visit the following website:

`https://spark.apache.org/docs/latest/ml-features.html#vectorassembler`

Evaluating the accuracy of the logistic regression model

We are now ready to evaluate the performance of predicting whether a call was correctly classified as a fire incident.

Getting ready

We will perform the model analysis which will require importing the following:

- `from sklearn import metrics`

How to do it...

This section walks through the steps to evaluate the model performance.

1. Create a confusion matrix using the `.crosstab()` function, as seen in the following script:

   ```
   df_predicted.crosstab('label', 'prediction').show()
   ```

2. Import `metrics` from `sklearn` to help measure accuracy using the following script:

   ```
   from sklearn import metrics
   ```

3. Create two variables for the `actual` and `predicted` columns from the dataframe that will be used to measure accuracy, using the following script:

   ```
   actual = df_predicted.select('label').toPandas()
   predicted = df_predicted.select('prediction').toPandas()
   ```

4. Compute the accuracy prediction score using the following script:

   ```
   metrics.accuracy_score(actual, predicted)
   ```

How it works...

This section explains how the model performance is evaluated.

1. In order to compute the accuracy of our model, it is important to be able to identify how accurate our predictions were. Often, this is best visualized using a confusion matrix cross table that shows correct and incorrect prediction scores. We create a confusion matrix using the `crosstab()` function off the `df_predicted` dataframe that shows us we have 964,980 true negative predictions for labels that are 0 and we have 48,034 true positive predictions for labels that are 1, as seen in the following screenshot:

```
In [45]: df_predicted.crosstab('label', 'prediction').show()

+----------------+------+-----+
|label_prediction|   0.0|  1.0|
+----------------+------+-----+
|               1|123166|48034|
|               0|964980| 9409|
+----------------+------+-----+
```

2. We know from earlier in this section that there are a total of 1,145,589 rows from the `testDF` dataframe; therefore, we can calculate the accuracy of the model using the following formula: *(TP + TN) / Total*. The accuracy would then be 88.4 percent.

3. It is important to note that not all false scores are created equal. For example, it is more detrimental to classify a call as not relating to fire and ultimately have it be related to fire than vice-versa from a fire safety perspective. This is referred to as a false negative. There is a metric that accounts for a **false negative** (**FN**), known as **recall**.

4. While we can work out the accuracy manually, as seen in the last step, it is ideal to have the accuracy automatically calculated. This can be easily performed by importing `sklearn.metrics`, which is a module that is commonly used for scoring and model evaluation.

5. `sklearn.metrics` takes in two parameters, the actual results that we have for labels and the predicted values we derived from the logistic regression model. Therefore, two variables are created, `actual` and `predicted`, and an accuracy score is calculated using the `accuracy_score()` function, as seen in the following screenshot:

```
In [46]: from sklearn import metrics

In [47]: actual = df_predicted.select('label').toPandas()

In [48]: predicted = df_predicted.select('prediction').toPandas()

In [49]: metrics.accuracy_score(actual, predicted)
Out[49]: 0.88427350472115218
```

6. The accuracy score is the same as we calculated manually, 88.4 percent.

There's more...

We now know that our model was able to accurately predict whether a call coming in is related to fire or not at a rate of 88.4 percent. At first, this may sound like a strong prediction; however, it's always important to compare this to a baseline score where every call was predicted as a non-fire call. The predicted dataframe, `df_predicted`, had the following breakdown of labels `1` and `0`, as seen in the following screenshot:

```
In [50]:  df_predicted.groupBy('label').count().show()

          +-----+------+
          |label| count|
          +-----+------+
          |    1|171200|
          |    0|974389|
          +-----+------+
```

We can run some statistics on that same dataframe to get the mean of label occurrences of value 1 using the `df_predicted.describe('label').show()` script. The output of that script can be seen in the following screenshot:

```
In [51]:  df_predicted.describe('label').show()

          +-------+-------------------+
          |summary|              label|
          +-------+-------------------+
          |  count|            1145589|
          |   mean| 0.1494427757249764|
          | stddev| 0.3565245341689551|
          |    min|                  0|
          |    max|                  1|
          +-------+-------------------+
```

A base model has a prediction value of `1` at a rate of 14.94 percent, or in other words, it has a prediction rate of *100 - 14.94* percent, which is 85.06 percent for a value of **0**. Therefore, since 85.06 percent is less than the model prediction rate of 88.4 percent, this model provides an improvement over a blind guess as to whether a call is fire-related or not.

See also

To learn more about accuracy vs. precision, visit the following website:

`https://www.mathsisfun.com/accuracy-precision.html`

6
Using LSTMs in Generative Networks

After reading this chapter, you will be able to accomplish the following:

- Downloading novels/books that will be used as input text
- Preparing and cleansing data
- Tokenizing sentences
- Training and saving the LSTM model
- Generating similar text using the model

Introduction

Due to the drawbacks of **recurrent neural networks (RNNs)** when it comes to backpropagation, **Long Short-Term Memory Units (LSTMs)** and **Gated Recurrent Units (GRUs)** have been gaining popularity in recent times when it comes to learning sequential input data as they are better suited to tackle problems of vanishing and exploding gradients.

Downloading novels/books that will be used as input text

In this recipe, we will go the steps that we need to download the novels/books which we will use as input text for the execution of this recipe.

Getting ready

- Place the input data in the form of a `.txt` file in the working directory.
- The input may be any kind of text, such as song lyrics, novels, magazine articles, and source code.
- Most of the classical texts are no longer protected by copyright and may be downloaded for free and used in experiments. The best place to get access to free books is Project `Gutenberg`.
- In this chapter, we will be using *The Jungle book* by Rudyard Kipling as the input to train our model and generate statistically similar text as output. The following screenshot shows you how to download the necessary file in `.txt` format:

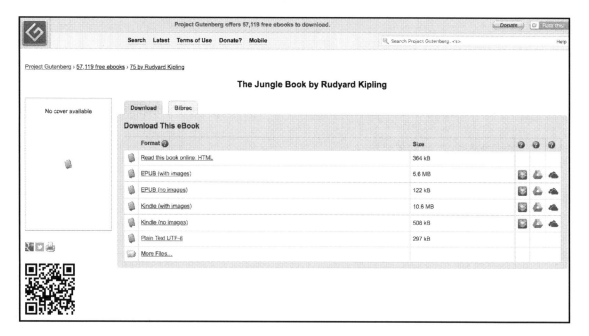

- After visiting the website and searching for the required book, click on **Plain Text UTF-8** and download it. UTF-8 basically specifies the type of encoding. The text may be copied and pasted or saved directly to the working directory by clicking on the link.

How to do it...

Before beginning, it always helps to take a look at the data and analyze it. After looking at the data, we can see that there are a lot of punctuation marks, blank spaces, quotes, and uppercase as well as lowercase letters. We need to prepare the data first before performing any kind of analysis on it or feeding it into the LSTM network. We require a number of libraries that will make handling data easier :

1. Import the necessary libraries by issuing the following commands:

```
from keras.preprocessing.text import Tokenizer
from keras.utils import to_categorical
from keras.models import Sequential
from keras.layers import Dense, lSTM, Dropout, Embedding
import numpy as np
from pickle import dump
import string
```

2. The output to the preceding commands looks like the following screenshot:

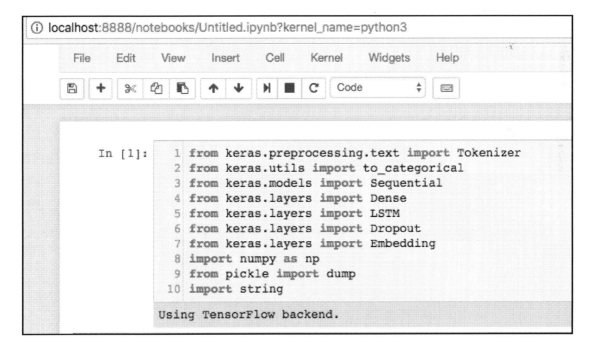

3. It is always a good idea to double check the current working directory and choose the required folder as the working directory. In our case, the `.txt` file is named `junglebook.txt` and is held in the folder named `Chapter 8`. So, we will select that folder as the working directory for the whole chapter. This may be done as shown in the following screenshot:

```
In [2]:   1 pwd

Out[2]:  '/Users/Chanti'

In [3]:     1 cd '/Users/Chanti/Desktop/Cookbook/Chapter 8'

          /Users/Chanti/Desktop/Cookbook/Chapter 8

In [4]:   1 pwd

Out[4]:  '/Users/Chanti/Desktop/Cookbook/Chapter 8'
```

4. Next, load the file into the program's memory by defining a function named `load_document`, which can be done by issuing the following commands:

```
def load_document(name):
    file = open(name, 'r')
    text = file.read()
    file.close()
    return text
```

5. Use the previously defined function to load the document into memory and print the first 2000 characters of the text file using the following script:

```
input_filename = 'junglebook.txt'
doc = load_document(input_filename)
print(doc[:2000])
```

6. Running the preceding function as well as the commands produces the output shown in the following screenshots:

```
In [5]:   1  # load doc into memory
          2  def load_document(name):
          3      file = open(name, 'r')
          4      text = file.read()
          5      file.close()
          6      return text

In [6]:   1  # load document
          2  input_filename = 'junglebook.txt'
          3  doc = load_document(input_filename)
          4  print(doc[:2000])
```

The output to the above code is shown in the screenshot here:

```
The Project Gutenberg EBook of The Jungle Book, by Rudyard Kipling

This eBook is for the use of anyone anywhere at no cost and with
almost no restrictions whatsoever.  You may copy it, give it away or
re-use it under the terms of the Project Gutenberg License included
with this eBook or online at www.gutenberg.org


Title: The Jungle Book

Author: Rudyard Kipling

Release Date: January 16, 2006 [EBook #236]
Last Updated: October 6, 2016

Language: English

Character set encoding: UTF-8

*** START OF THIS PROJECT GUTENBERG EBOOK THE JUNGLE BOOK ***




Produced by An Anonymous Volunteer and David Widger




THE JUNGLE BOOK

By Rudyard Kipling
```

The following screenshot is a continuation of the previous output:

```
Contents

    Mowgli's Brothers
    Hunting-Song of the Seeonee Pack
    Kaa's Hunting
    Road-Song of the Bandar-Log
    "Tiger! Tiger!"
     Mowgli's Song
    The White Seal
    Lukannon
    "Rikki-Tikki-Tavi"
     Darzee's Chant
    Toomai of the Elephants
    Shiv and the Grasshopper
    Her Majesty's Servants
    Parade Song of the Camp Animals




Mowgli's Brothers

    Now Rann the Kite brings home the night
        That Mang the Bat sets free--
    The herds are shut in byre and hut
        For loosed till dawn are we.
    This is the hour of pride and power,
        Talon and tush and claw.
    Oh, hear the call!--Good hunting all
        That keep the Jungle Law!
    Night-Song in the Jungle

It was seven o'clock of a very warm evening in the Seeonee hills when
Father Wolf woke up from his day's rest, scratched himself, yawned, and
spread out his paws one after the other to get rid of the sleepy feeling
in their tips. Mother Wolf lay with her big gray nose dropped across her
four tumbling, squealing cubs, and the moon shone into the mouth of the
```

7. As seen in the preceding screenshots, the first `2000` characters from the `.txt` file are printed. It is always a good idea to analyze the data by looking at it before performing any preprocessing on it. It will give a better idea of how to approach the preprocessing steps.

How it works...

1. The `array` function will be used to handle data in the form of arrays. The `numpy` library provides this function readily.
2. Since our data is only text data, we will require the string library to handle all input data as strings before encoding the words as integers, which can be fed.
3. The `tokenizer` function will be used to split all the sentences into tokens, where each token represents a word.
4. The pickle library will be required in order to save the dictionary into a pickle file by using the `dump` function.
5. The `to_categorical` function from the `keras` library converts a class vector (integers) to a binary class matrix, for example, for use with `categorical_crossentropy`, which we will require at a later stage in order to map tokens to unique integers and vice versa.
6. Some of the other Keras layers required in this chapter are the LSTM layer, dense layer, dropout layer, and the embedding layer. The model will be defined sequentially, for which we require the sequential model from the `keras` library.

There's more...

- You may also use the same model with different types of texts, such as customer reviews on websites, tweets, structured text such as source code, mathematics theories, and so on.
- The idea of this chapter to understand how LSTMs learn long-term dependencies and how they perform better at processing sequential data when compared to recurrent neural networks.
- Another good idea would be to input *Pokémon* names into the model and try to generate your own Pokémon names.

See also

More information about the different libraries used can be found at the following links:

- https://www.scipy-lectures.org/intro/numpy/array_object.html
- https://docs.python.org/2/library/string.html
- https://wiki.python.org/moin/UsingPickle

- https://keras.io/preprocessing/text/
- https://keras.io/layers/core/
- https://keras.io/layers/recurrent/

Preparing and cleansing data

This section of this chapter will discuss the various data preparation and text preprocessing steps involved before feeding it into the model as input. The specific way we prepare the data really depends on how we intend to model it, which in turn depends on how we intend to use it.

Getting ready

The language model will be based on statistics and predict the probability of each word given an input sequence of text. The predicted word will be fed in as input to the model, to, in turn, generate the next word.

A key decision is how long the input sequences should be. They need to be long enough to allow the model to learn the context for the words to predict. This input length will also define the length of the seed text used to generate new sequences when we use the model.

For the purpose of simplicity, we will arbitrarily pick a length of 50 words for the length of the input sequences.

How to do it...

Based on reviewing the text (which we did previously), the following are some operations that could be performed to clean and preprocess the text in the input file. We have presented a few options regarding text preprocessing. However, you may want to explore more cleaning operations as an exercise:

- Replace dashes – with whitespaces so you can split words better
- Split words based on whitespaces
- Remove all punctuation from the input text in order to reduce the number of unique characters in the text that is fed into the model (for example, Why? becomes Why)

- Remove all words that are not alphabetic to remove standalone punctuation tokens and emoticons
- Convert all words from uppercase to lowercase in order to reduce the size of the total number of tokens further and remove any discrepancies and data redundancy

Vocabulary size is a decisive factor in language modeling and deciding the training time for the model. A smaller vocabulary results in a more efficient model that trains faster. While it is good to have a small vocabulary in some cases, it helps to have a larger vocabulary in other cases in order to prevent overfitting. In order to preprocess the data, we are going to need a function that takes in the entire input text, splits it up based on white spaces, removes all punctuation, normalizes all cases, and returns a sequence of tokens. For this purpose, define the `clean_document` function by issuing the following commands:

```python
import string
def clean_document(doc):
    doc = doc.replace('--', ' ')
    tokens = doc.split()
    table = str.maketrans('', '', string.punctuation)
    tokens = [w.translate(table) for w in tokens]
    tokens = [word for word in tokens if word.isalpha()]
    tokens = [word.lower() for word in tokens]
    return tokens
```

1. The previously defined function will basically take the loaded document/file as its argument and return an array of clean tokens, as shown in the following screenshot:

```
In [7]:    1  import string
           2
           3  # turn a document into clean tokens
           4  def clean_document(doc):
           5      doc = doc.replace('--', ' ')
           6      tokens = doc.split()
           7      table = str.maketrans('', '', string.punctuation)
           8      tokens = [w.translate(table) for w in tokens]
           9      tokens = [word for word in tokens if word.isalpha()]
          10      tokens = [word.lower() for word in tokens]
          11      return tokens
```

2. Next, print out some of the tokens and statistics just to develop a better understanding of what the `clean_document` function is doing. This step is done by issuing the following commands:

```
tokens = clean_document(doc)
print(tokens[:200])
print('Total Tokens: %d' % len(tokens))
print('Total Unique Tokens: %d' % len(set(tokens)))
```

3. The output of the preceding set of commands prints the first two hundred tokens and is as shown in the following screenshots:

```
In [8]:    1  # clean document
           2  tokens = clean_document(doc)
           3  print(tokens[:200])
           4  print('Total Tokens: %d' % len(tokens))
           5  print('Unique Tokens: %d' % len(set(tokens)))
```

```
['project', 'gutenberg', 'ebook', 'of', 'the', 'jungle', 'book', 'by', 'rudyard', 'kipling', 'this', 'ebook', 'is',
'for', 'the', 'use', 'of', 'anyone', 'anywhere', 'at', 'no', 'cost', 'and', 'with', 'almost', 'no', 'restrictions',
'whatsoever', 'you', 'may', 'copy', 'it', 'give', 'it', 'away', 'or', 'reuse', 'it', 'under', 'the', 'terms', 'of',
'the', 'project', 'gutenberg', 'license', 'included', 'with', 'this', 'ebook', 'or', 'online', 'at', 'wwwgutenbergor
g', 'title', 'the', 'jungle', 'book', 'author', 'rudyard', 'kipling', 'release', 'date', 'january', 'ebook', 'last',
'updated', 'october', 'language', 'english', 'character', 'set', 'encoding', 'start', 'of', 'this', 'project', 'guten
berg', 'ebook', 'the', 'jungle', 'book', 'produced', 'by', 'an', 'anonymous', 'volunteer', 'and', 'david', 'widger',
'the', 'jungle', 'book', 'by', 'rudyard', 'kipling', 'contents', 'brothers', 'huntingsong', 'of', 'the', 'seeonee',
'pack', 'hunting', 'roadsong', 'of', 'the', 'bandarlog', 'song', 'the', 'white', 'seal', 'lukannon', 'chant', 'tooma
i', 'of', 'the', 'elephants', 'shiv', 'and', 'the', 'grasshopper', 'her', 'servants', 'parade', 'song', 'of', 'the',
'camp', 'animals', 'brothers', 'now', 'rann', 'the', 'kite', 'brings', 'home', 'the', 'night', 'that', 'mang', 'the',
'bat', 'sets', 'free', 'the', 'herds', 'are', 'shut', 'in', 'byre', 'and', 'hut', 'for', 'loosed', 'till', 'dawn', 'a
re', 'we', 'this', 'is', 'the', 'hour', 'of', 'pride', 'and', 'power', 'talon', 'and', 'tush', 'and', 'claw', 'oh',
'hear', 'the', 'call', 'good', 'hunting', 'all', 'that', 'keep', 'the', 'jungle', 'law', 'nightsong', 'in', 'the', 'j
ungle', 'it', 'was', 'seven', 'of', 'a', 'very', 'warm', 'evening', 'in', 'the', 'seeonee', 'hills']
Total Tokens: 51473
Unique Tokens: 5027
```

4. Next, organize all these tokens into sequences, with each sequence containing 50 words (chosen arbitrarily) using the following commands:

```
length = 50 + 1
sequences = list()
for i in range(length, len(tokens)):
    seq = tokens[i-sequence_length:i]
    line = ' '.join(seq)
    sequences.append(line)
print('Total Sequences: %d' % len(sequences))
```

The total number of sequences formed from the document may be viewed by printing them out, as shown in the following screenshot:

```
In [9]:    1  # organize into sequences (of length 50) of tokens
           2  length = 50 + 1
           3  sequences = list()
           4  for i in range(length, len(tokens)):
           5      # select sequence of tokens
           6      seq = tokens[i-length:i]
           7      # convert into a line
           8      line = ' '.join(seq)
           9      sequences.append(line)
          10  print('Total Sequences: %d' % len(sequences))

           Total Sequences: 51422
```

5. Save all the generated tokens as well as sequences into a file in the working directory by defining the `save_doc` function using the following commands:

```
def save_document(lines, name):
    data = '\n'.join(lines)
    file = open(name, 'w')
    file.write(data)
    file.close()
```

To save the sequences, use the following two commands:

```
output_filename = 'junglebook_sequences.txt'
save_document(sequences, output_filename)
```

6. This process is illustrated in the following screenshot:

```
In [10]:   1  # save tokens to file, one dialog per line
           2  def save_document(lines, name):
           3      data = '\n'.join(lines)
           4      file = open(name, 'w')
           5      file.write(data)
           6      file.close()

In [11]:   1  # save sequences to file
           2  output_filename = 'junglebook_sequences.txt'
           3  save_document(sequences, output_filename)
```

7. Next, load the saved document, which contains all the saved tokens and sequences, into the memory using the `load_document` function, which is defined as follows:

```
def load_document(name):
    file = open(name, 'r')
    text = file.read()
    file.close()
    return text

# function to load document and split based on lines
input_filename = 'junglebook_sequences.txt'
doc = load_document(input_filename)
lines = doc.split('\n')
```

```
In [12]:      1  # load document into memory
              2  def load_document(name):
              3      file = open(name, 'r')
              4      text = file.read()
              5      file.close()
              6      return text
              7
              8  # load
              9  input_filename = 'junglebook_sequences.txt'
             10  doc = load_document(input_filename)
             11  lines = doc.split('\n')
```

How it works...

1. The `clean_document` function removes all whitespaces, punctuation, uppercase text, and quotation marks, and splits the entire document into tokens, where each token is a word.
2. By printing the total number of tokens and total unique tokens in the document, we will note that the `clean_document` function generated 51,473 tokens, out of which 5,027 tokens (or words) are unique.
3. The `save_document` function then saves all of these tokens as well as unique tokens which are required to generate our sequences of 50 words each. Note how, by looping through all the generated tokens, we are able to generate a long list of 51,422 sequences. These are the same sequences that will be used as input to train the language model.

4. Before training the model on all 51,422 sequences, it is always a good practice to save the tokens as well as sequences to file. Once saved, the file can be loaded back into the memory using the defined `load_document` function.

5. The sequences are organized as 50 input tokens and one output token (which means that there are 51 tokens per sequence). For predicting each output token, the previous 50 tokens will be used as the input to the model. We can do this by iterating over the list of tokens from token 51 onwards and taking the previous 50 tokens as a sequence, then repeating this process until the end of the list of all tokens.

See also

Visit the following links for a better understanding of data preparation using various functions:

- https://docs.python.org/3/library/tokenize.html
- https://keras.io/utils/
- http://www.pythonforbeginners.com/dictionary/python-split
- https://www.tutorialspoint.com/python/string_join.htm
- https://www.tutorialspoint.com/python/string_lower.htm

Tokenizing sentences

Before defining and feeding data into an LSTM network it is important that the data is converted into a form which can be understood by the neural network. Computers understand everything in binary code (0s and 1s) and therefore, the textual or data in string format needs to be converted into one hot encoded variables.

Getting ready

For understanding how one hot encoding works, visit the following links:

- https://machinelearningmastery.com/how-to-one-hot-encode-sequence-data-in-python/
- http://scikit-learn.org/stable/modules/generated/sklearn.preprocessing.OneHotEncoder.html

- https://stackoverflow.com/questions/37292872/how-can-i-one-hot-encode-in-python
- https://www.ritchieng.com/machinelearning-one-hot-encoding/
- https://hackernoon.com/what-is-one-hot-encoding-why-and-when-do-you-have-to-use-it-e3c6186d008f

How to do it...

After the going through the previous section you should be able to clean the entire corpus and split up sentences. The next steps which involve one hot encoding and tokenizing sentences can be done in the following manner:

1. Once the tokens and sequences are saved to a file and loaded into memory, they have to be encoded as integers since the word embedding layer in the model expects input sequences to be comprised of integers and not strings.

2. This is done by mapping each word in the vocabulary to a unique integer and encoding the input sequences. Later, while making predictions, the predictions can be converted (or mapped) back to numbers to look up their associated words in the same mapping and reverse map back from integers to words.

3. To perform this encoding, utilize the `Tokenizer` class in the Keras API. Before encoding, the tokenizer must be trained on the entire dataset so it finds all the unique tokens and assigns each token a unique integer. The commands to do so as are follows:

```
tokenizer = Tokenizer()
tokenizer.fit_on_texts(lines)
sequences = tokenizer.texts_to_sequences(lines)
```

4. You also need to calculate the size of the vocabulary before defining the embedding layer later. This is determined by calculating the size of the mapping dictionary.

5. Therefore, when specifying the vocabulary size to the Embedding layer, specify it as 1 larger than the actual vocabulary. The vocabulary size is therefore defined as follows:

```
vocab_size = len(tokenizer.word_index) + 1
print('Vocabulary size : %d' % vocab_size)
```

6. Now that once the input sequences have been encoded, they need to be separated into input and output elements, which can be done by array slicing.

7. After separating, one hot encode the output word. This means converting it from an integer to an n-dimensional vector of 0 values, one for each word in the vocabulary, with a 1 to indicate the specific word at the index of the word's integer value. Keras provides the `to_categorical()` function, which can be used to one hot encode the output words for each input-output sequence pair.

8. Finally, specify to the Embedding layer how long input sequences are. We know that there are 50 words because the model was designed by specifying the sequence length as 50, but a good generic way to specify the sequence length is to use the second dimension (number of columns) of the input data's shape.

9. This can be done by issuing the following commands:

```
sequences = array(sequences)
Input, Output = sequences[:,:-1], sequences[:,-1]
Output = to_categorical(Output, num_classes=vocab_size)
sequence_length = Input.shape[1]
```

How it works...

This section will describe the outputs you must see on executing the commands in the previous section:

1. After running the commands for tokenizing the sentences and calculating vocabulary length you must see an output as shown in the following screenshot:

```
In [13]:  1  # encode sequences of words
          2  tokenizer = Tokenizer()
          3  tokenizer.fit_on_texts(lines)
          4  sequences = tokenizer.texts_to_sequences(lines)

In [14]:  1  # vocabulary size
          2  vocab_size = len(tokenizer.word_index) + 1
          3  print('Vocabulary size : %d' % vocab_size)

Vocabulary size : 5028
```

2. Words are assigned values starting from 1 up to the total number of words (for example, 5,027 in this case). The Embedding layer needs to allocate a vector representation for each word in this vocabulary from index 1 to the largest index. The index of the word at the end of the vocabulary will be 5,027; that means the array must be 5,027 + 1 in length.

3. The output after array slicing and separating sentences into sequences of 50 words per sequence must look like the following screenshot:

```
In [15]:   1  # separate into input and output
           2  sequences = array(sequences)
           3  Input, Output = sequences[:,:-1], sequences[:,-1]
           4  Output = to_categorical(Output, num_classes=vocab_size)
           5  sequence_length = Input.shape[1]
```

4. The `to_categorical()` function is used so that the model learns to predict the probability distribution for the next word.

There's more...

More information on reshaping arrays in Python can be found at the following links:

- https://docs.scipy.org/doc/numpy/reference/generated/numpy.reshape.html
- https://machinelearningmastery.com/index-slice-reshape-numpy-arrays-machine-learning-python/

Training and saving the LSTM model

You can now train a statistical language model from the prepared data.

The model that will be trained is a neural language model. It has a few unique characteristics:

- It uses a distributed representation for words so that different words with similar meanings will have a similar representation
- It learns the representation at the same time as learning the model
- It learns to predict the probability for the next word using the context of the previous 50 words

Specifically, you will use an Embedding Layer to learn the representation of words, and a **Long Short-Term Memory (LSTM)** recurrent neural network to learn to predict words based on their context.

Getting ready

The learned embedding needs to know the size of the vocabulary and the length of input sequences as previously discussed. It also has a parameter to specify how many dimensions will be used to represent each word. That is the size of the embedding vector space.

Common values are 50, 100, and 300. We will use 100 here, but consider testing smaller or larger values and evaluating metrics for those values.

The network will be comprised of the following:

- Two LSTM hidden layers with 200 memory cells each. More memory cells and a deeper network may achieve better results.

- A dropout layer with a dropout of 0.3 or 30%, which will aid the network to depend less on each neuron/unit and reduce overfitting the data.

- A dense fully connected layer with 200 neurons connects to the LSTM hidden layers to interpret the features extracted from the sequence.

- The output layer, which predicts the next word as a single vector of the size of the vocabulary with a probability for each word in the vocabulary.

- A softmax classifier is used in the second dense or fully connected layer to ensure the outputs have the characteristics of normalized probabilities (such as between 0 and 1).

How to do it...

1. The model is defined using the following commands and is also illustrated in the following screenshot:

```
model = Sequential()
model.add(Embedding(vocab_size, 100, input_length=sequence_length))
model.add(LSTM(200, return_sequences=True))
model.add(LSTM(200))
```

```
model.add(Dropout(0.3))
model.add(Dense(200, activation='relu'))
model.add(Dense(vocab_size, activation='softmax'))
print(model.summary())
```

In [16]:
```
1  # define model
2  from keras.layers import Dropout
3  model = Sequential()
4  model.add(Embedding(vocab_size, 100, input_length=sequence_length))
5  model.add(LSTM(200, return_sequences=True))
6  model.add(LSTM(200))
7  model.add(Dropout(0.3))
8  model.add(Dense(200, activation='relu'))
9  model.add(Dense(vocab_size, activation='softmax'))
10 print(model.summary())
```

```
Layer (type)                  Output Shape          Param #
=================================================================
embedding_1 (Embedding)       (None, 50, 100)       502800

lstm_1 (LSTM)                 (None, 50, 200)       240800

lstm_2 (LSTM)                 (None, 200)           320800

dropout_1 (Dropout)           (None, 200)           0

dense_1 (Dense)               (None, 200)           40200

dense_2 (Dense)               (None, 5028)          1010628
=================================================================
Total params: 2,115,228
Trainable params: 2,115,228
Non-trainable params: 0
_____
None
```

2. Print the model summary just to ensure that the model is constructed as intended.

3. Compile the model, specifying the categorical cross entropy loss needed to fit the model. The number of epochs is set to 75 and the model is trained in mini batches with a batch size of 250. This is done using the following commands:

```
model.compile(loss='categorical_crossentropy', optimizer='adam',
        metrics=['accuracy'])

model.fit(Input, Output, batch_size=250, epochs=75)
```

4. The output of the preceding commands is illustrated in the following screenshot:

```
In [17]:   1  # compile model
           2  model.compile(loss='categorical_crossentropy', optimizer='adam', metrics=['accuracy'])
           3  # fit model
           4  model.fit(Input, Output, batch_size=250, epochs=75)

Epoch 67/75
51422/51422 [==============================] - 458s 9ms/step - loss: 2.7810 - acc: 0.3441
Epoch 68/75
51422/51422 [==============================] - 516s 10ms/step - loss: 2.7346 - acc: 0.3547
Epoch 69/75
51422/51422 [==============================] - 522s 10ms/step - loss: 2.7065 - acc: 0.3570
Epoch 70/75
51422/51422 [==============================] - 458s 9ms/step - loss: 2.6710 - acc: 0.3642
Epoch 71/75
51422/51422 [==============================] - 449s 9ms/step - loss: 2.6264 - acc: 0.3716
Epoch 72/75
51422/51422 [==============================] - 450s 9ms/step - loss: 2.6027 - acc: 0.3766
Epoch 73/75
51422/51422 [==============================] - 461s 9ms/step - loss: 2.5761 - acc: 0.3784
Epoch 74/75
51422/51422 [==============================] - 454s 9ms/step - loss: 2.5370 - acc: 0.3874
Epoch 75/75
51422/51422 [==============================] - 450s 9ms/step - loss: 2.5038 - acc: 0.3938

Out[17]: <keras.callbacks.History at 0x1131338d0>
```

5. Once the model is done compiling, it is saved using the following commands:

```
model.save('junglebook_trained.h5')

dump(tokenizer, open('tokenizer.pkl', 'wb'))
```

```
In [18]:   1  # save the model to file
           2  model.save('junglebook_trained.h5')
           3  # save the tokenizer
           4  dump(tokenizer, open('tokenizer.pkl', 'wb'))
```

How it works...

1. The model is built using the `Sequential()` function in the Keras framework. The first layer in the model is an embedding layer that takes in the vocabulary size, vector dimension, and the input sequence length as its arguments.

2. The next two layers are LSTM layers with 200 memory cells each. More memory cells and a deeper network can be experimented with to check if it improves accuracy.

3. The next layer is a dropout layer with a dropout probability of 30%, which means that there is a 30% chance a certain memory unit is not used during training. This prevents overfitting of data. Again, the dropout probabilities can be played with and tuned accordingly.

4. The final two layers are two fully connected layers. The first one has a `relu` activation function and the second has a softmax classifier. The model summary is printed to check whether the model is built according to requirements.

5. Notice that in this case, the total number of trainable parameters are 2,115,228. The model summary also shows the number of parameters that will be trained by each layer in the model.

6. The model is trained in mini batches of 250 over 75 epochs, in our case, to minimize training time. Increasing the number of epochs to over 100 and utilizing smaller batches while training greatly improves the model's accuracy while simultaneously reducing loss.

7. During training, you will see a summary of performance, including the loss and accuracy evaluated from the training data at the end of each batch update. In our case, after running the model for 75 epochs, we obtained an accuracy of close to 40%.

8. The aim of the model is not to remember the text with 100% accuracy, but rather to capture the properties of the input text, such as long-term dependencies and structures that exist in natural language and sentences.

9. The model, after it is done training, is saved in the working directory named `junglebook_trained.h5`.

10. We also require the mapping of words to integers when the model is later loaded into memory to make predictions. This is present in the `Tokenizer` object, which is also saved using the `dump ()` function in the `Pickle` library.

There's more...

Jason Brownlee's blogs on Machine Learning Mastery have a lot of useful information on developing, training, and tuning machine learning models for natural language processing. They can be found at the following links:

https://machinelearningmastery.com/deep-learning-for-nlp/
https://machinelearningmastery.com/lstms-with-python/
https://machinelearningmastery.com/blog/

See also

Further information about different keras layers and other functions used in this section can be found at the following links:

- https://keras.io/models/sequential/
- https://docs.python.org/2/library/pickle.html
- https://keras.io/optimizers/
- https://keras.io/models/model/

Generating similar text using the model

Now that you have a trained language model, it can be used. In this case, you can use it to generate new sequences of text that have the same statistical properties as the source text. This is not practical, at least not for this example, but it gives a concrete example of what the language model has learned.

Getting ready

1. Begin by loading the training sequences again. You may do so by using the load_document() function, which we developed initially. This is done by using the following code:

```
def load_document(name):
    file = open(name, 'r')
    text = file.read()
    file.close()
    return text

# load sequences of cleaned text
input_filename = 'junglebook_sequences.txt'
doc = load_document(input_filename)
lines = doc.split('\n')
```

The output of the preceding code is illustrated in the following screenshot:

```
In [19]:    1  # load doc into memory
            2  def load_document(name):
            3      file = open(name, 'r')
            4      text = file.read()
            5      file.close()
            6      return text
            7
            8  # load cleaned text sequences
            9  input_filename = 'junglebook_sequences.txt'
           10  doc = load_document(input_filename)
           11  lines = doc.split('\n')
```

2. Note that the input filename is now `'junglebook_sequences.txt'`, which will load the saved training sequences into the memory. We need the text so that we can choose a source sequence as input to the model for generating a new sequence of text.

3. The model will require 50 words as input.

   Later, the expected length of input needs to be specified. This can be determined from the input sequences by calculating the length of one line of the loaded data and subtracting 1 for the expected output word that is also on the same line, as follows:

```
sequence_length = len(lines[0].split()) - 1
```

4. Next, load the trained and saved model into memory by executing the following commands:

```
from keras.models import load_model
model = load_model('junglebook.h5')
```

5. The first step in generating text is preparing a seed input. Select a random line of text from the input text for this purpose. Once selected, print it so that you have some idea of what was used. This is done as follows:

```
from random import randint
seed_text = lines[randint(0,len(lines))]
print(seed_text + '\n')
```

```
In [20]:    1  sequence_length = len(lines[0].split()) - 1

In [21]:    1  # load the model
            2  from keras.models import load_model
            3  model = load_model('junglebook_trained.h5')

In [22]:    1  # select a seed text
            2  from random import randint
            3  seed_text = lines[randint(0,len(lines))]
            4  print(seed_text + '\n')
```

to me not long ago with some rude talk that i was a naked cub and not fit to dig pignuts but i caught tabaqui by the
tail and swung him twice against a palmtree to teach him better was foolishness for though tabaqui is a mischiefmaker
he would have told

How to do it...

1. You are now ready to generate new words, one at a time. First, encode the seed
text to integers using the same tokenizer that was used when training the model,
which is done using the following code:

```
encoded = tokenizer.texts_to_sequences([seed_text])[0]
```

```
In [23]:    1  encoded = tokenizer.texts_to_sequences([seed_text])[0]
```

2. The model can predict the next word directly by
calling `model.predict_classes()`, which will return the index of the word
with the highest probability:

```
prediction = model.predict_classes(encoded, verbose=0)
```

3. Look up the index in the Tokenizers mapping to get the associated word, as
shown in the following code:

```
out_word = ''
for word, index in tokenizer.word_index.items():
        if index == prediction:
                out_word = word
                break
```

4. Append this word to the seed text and repeat the process. Importantly, the input sequence is going to get too long. We can truncate it to the desired length after the input sequence has been encoded to integers. Keras provides the `pad_sequences()` function which we can use to perform this truncation, as follows:

```
encoded = pad_sequences([encoded], maxlen=seq_length,
truncating='pre')
```

5. Wrap all of this into a function called `generate_sequence()` that takes as input the model, the tokenizer, the input sequence length, the seed text, and the number of words to generate. It then returns a sequence of words generated by the model. You may use the following code to do so:

```
from random import randint
from pickle import load
from keras.models import load_model
from keras.preprocessing.sequence import pad_sequences

def load_document(filename):
    file = open(filename, 'r')
    text = file.read()
    file.close()
    return text

def generate_sequence(model, tokenizer, sequence_length,
seed_text, n_words):
    result = list()
    input_text = seed_text
    for _ in range(n_words):
        encoded = tokenizer.texts_to_sequences([input_text])[0]
        encoded = pad_sequences([encoded], maxlen=seq_length,
truncating='pre')
        prediction = model.predict_classes(encoded, verbose=0)
        out_word = ''
        for word, index in tokenizer.word_index.items():
            if index == prediction:
                out_word = word
                break
        input_text += ' ' + out_word
        result.append(out_word)
    return ' '.join(result)
input_filename = 'junglebook_sequences.txt'
doc = load_document(input_filename)
lines = doc.split('\n')
seq_length = len(lines[0].split()) - 1
```

```
In [24]:    1  from random import randint
            2  from pickle import load
            3  from keras.models import load_model
            4  from keras.preprocessing.sequence import pad_sequences
            5
            6  # load doc into memory
            7  def load_document(name):
            8      file = open(name, 'r')
            9      text = file.read()
           10      file.close()
           11      return text
           12
           13  # generate a sequence from a language model
           14  def generate_sequence(model, tokenizer, sequence_length, seed_text, n_words):
           15      result = list()
           16      input_text = seed_text
           17      # generate a fixed number of words
           18      for _ in range(n_words):
           19          # encode the text as integer
           20          encoded = tokenizer.texts_to_sequences([input_text])[0]
           21          # truncate sequences to a fixed length
           22          encoded = pad_sequences([encoded], maxlen=seq_length, truncating='pre')
           23          # predict probabilities for each word
           24          prediction = model.predict_classes(encoded, verbose=0)
           25          # map predicted word index to word
           26          out_word = ''
           27          for word, index in tokenizer.word_index.items():
           28              if index == prediction:
           29                  out_word = word
           30                  break
           31          # append to input
           32          input_text += ' ' + out_word
           33          result.append(out_word)
           34      return ' '.join(result)
           35
           36  # load cleaned text sequences
           37  input_filename = 'junglebook_sequences.txt'
           38  doc = load_document(input_filename)
           39  lines = doc.split('\n')
           40  seq_length = len(lines[0].split()) - 1
```

How it works...

We are now ready to generate a sequence of new words, given that we have some seed text :

1. Start by loading the model into memory again using the following command:

```
model = load_model('junglebook.h5')
```

2. Next, load the tokenizer by typing the following command:

```
tokenizer = load(open('tokenizer.pkl', 'rb'))
```

3. Select a seed text randomly by using the following command:

```
seed_text = lines[randint(0,len(lines))]
print(seed_text + '\n')
```

4. Finally, a new sequence is generated by using the following command:

```
generated = generate_sequence(model, tokenizer, sequence_length,
seed_text, 50)
  print(generated)
```

5. On printing the generated sequence, you will see an output similar to the one shown in the following screenshot:

```
In [25]:    1  # load the model
            2  model = load_model('junglebook_trained.h5')
            3
            4  # load the tokenizer
            5  tokenizer = load(open('tokenizer.pkl', 'rb'))
            6
            7  # select a seed text
            8  seed_text = lines[randint(0,len(lines))]
            9  print(seed_text + '\n')
           10
           11  # generate new text
           12  generated = generate_sequence(model, tokenizer, sequence_length, seed_text, 50)
           13  print(generated)

baskets of dried grass and put grasshoppers in them or catch two praying mantises and make them fight or string a nec
klace of red and black jungle nuts or watch a lizard basking on a rock or a snake hunting a frog near the wallows the
n they sing long long songs

with odd native quavers at the end of the review and the hyaena whom he had seen the truth they feel twitched to the
noises round him for a picture of the end of the ravine and snuffing bitten and best of the bulls at the dawn is a na
tive
```

6. The model first prints 50 words of the random seed text followed by 50 words of the generated text. In this case, the random seed text is as follows:
Baskets of dried grass and put grasshoppers in them or catch two praying mantises and make them fight or string a necklace of red and black jungle nuts or watch a lizard basking on a rock or a snake hunting a frog near the wallows then they sing long long songs

The 50 words of text generated by the model, in this case, are as follows:
with odd native quavers at the end of the review and the hyaena whom he had seen the truth they feel twitched to the noises round him for a picture of the end of the ravine and snuffing bitten and best of the bulls at the dawn is a native

7. Note how the model outputs a sequence of random words it generated based on what it learned from the input text. You will also notice that the model does a reasonably good job of mimicking the input text and generating its own stories. Though the text does not make much sense, it gives valuable insight into how the model learns to place statistically similar words next to each other.

There's more...

- Upon changing the random seed that was set, the output generated by the network also changes. You may not get the exact same output text as the preceding example, but it will be very similar to the input used to train the model.
- The following are some screenshots of different results that were obtained by running the generated text piece multiple times:

```
In [26]:   1  # load the model
           2  model = load_model('junglebook_trained.h5')
           3
           4  # load the tokenizer
           5  tokenizer = load(open('tokenizer.pkl', 'rb'))
           6
           7  # select a seed text
           8  seed_text = lines[randint(0,len(lines))]
           9  print(seed_text + '\n')
          10
          11  # generate new text
          12  generated = generate_sequence(model, tokenizer, sequence_length, seed_text, 50)
          13  print(generated)
```

little toomai there was a splash and a trample and the rush of running water and kala nag strode through the bed of a river feeling his way at each step above the noise of the water as it swirled round the legs little toomai could hear more splashing and some

trumpeting both upstream and down grass and knocked him up to the jealous moon he could see bruised of dust for the p otter was rann caught him up to the plowed din of the melbourne lines where the two wolves would be forced to make th emselves rifles and the sparks

```
In [27]:   1  # load the model
           2  model = load_model('junglebook_trained.h5')
           3
           4  # load the tokenizer
           5  tokenizer = load(open('tokenizer.pkl', 'rb'))
           6
           7  # select a seed text
           8  seed_text = lines[randint(0,len(lines))]
           9  print(seed_text + '\n')
          10
          11  # generate new text
          12  generated = generate_sequence(model, tokenizer, sequence_length, seed_text, 50)
          13  print(generated)
```

is well that this nonsense ends safely next week the catching is over and we of the plains are sent back to our stati ons then we will march on smooth roads and forget all this hunting but son i am angry that thou shouldst meddle in th e business that belongs to

the shore and he had seen the emperor theodore lying speaking again and left breath of the instant in the shape of a bow and knotted he drove round his eyes starting himself to the veranda does not get them and again to get in the jun gle and the camel

```
In [29]:    1  # load the model
            2  model = load_model('junglebook_trained.h5')
            3
            4  # load the tokenizer
            5  tokenizer = load(open('tokenizer.pkl', 'rb'))
            6
            7  # select a seed text
            8  seed_text = lines[randint(0,len(lines))]
            9  print(seed_text + '\n')
           10
           11  # generate new text
           12  generated = generate_sequence(model, tokenizer, sequence_length, seed_text, 50)
           13  print(generated)
```

is in their legs and he remembered the good firm beaches of novastoshnah seven thousand miles away the games his comp
anions played the smell of the seaweed the seal roar and the fighting that very minute he turned north swimming stead
ily and as he went on he met scores of his

mates and bound like the deck of the fighters and harness under his breath and he could not be able to stop a ship an
d ducked to nag wound up with scores of marble tracery showing all the regiments went twisting his head and shoulders
and creepers very seldom shows

- The model even generates its own version of the project Gutenberg license, as can be seen in the following screenshot:

```
In [28]:    1  # load the model
            2  model = load_model('junglebook_trained.h5')
            3
            4  # load the tokenizer
            5  tokenizer = load(open('tokenizer.pkl', 'rb'))
            6
            7  # select a seed text
            8  seed_text = lines[randint(0,len(lines))]
            9  print(seed_text + '\n')
           10
           11  # generate new text
           12  generated = generate_sequence(model, tokenizer, sequence_length, seed_text, 50)
           13  print(generated)
```

prohibition against accepting unsolicited donations from donors in such states who approach us with offers to donate
international donations are gratefully accepted but we cannot make any statements concerning tax treatment of donatio
ns received from outside the united states us laws alone swamp our small staff please check the project gutenberg

literary archive foundation and michael part of electronic works if you wish to be bound at the terms of this agreeme
nt in compliance with our written explanation and the project gutenbergtm license available with below the phrase or
works donation use with project gutenbergtm electronic works in compliance with the

- The model's accuracy can be improved to about 60% by increasing the number of epochs from about 100 to 200. Another method to increase the learning is by training the model in mini batches of about 50 and 100. Try to play around with the different hyperparameters and activation functions to see what affects the results in the best possible way.
- The model may also be made denser by including more LSTM and dropout layers while defining the model. However, know that it will only increase the training time if the model is more complex and runs over more epochs.
- After much experimentation, the ideal batch size was found to be between 50 to 100, and the ideal number of epochs to train the model was determined to be between 100 and 200.

- There is no definitive way of performing the preceding task. You can also experiment with different text inputs to the model such as tweets, customer reviews, or HTML code.
- Some of the other tasks that can be performed include using a simplified vocabulary (such as with all the stopwords removed) to further enhance the unique words in the dictionary; tuning the size of the embedding layer and the number of memory cells in the hidden layers; and extending the model to use a pre-trained model such as Google's Word2Vec (pre-trained word model) to see whether it results in a better model.

See also

More information about the various functions and libraries used in the final section of the chapter can be found by visiting the following links:

- `https://keras.io/preprocessing/sequence/`
- `https://wiki.python.org/moin/UsingPickle`
- `https://docs.python.org/2/library/random.html`
- `https://www.tensorflow.org/api_docs/python/tf/keras/models/load_model`

Natural Language Processing with TF-IDF

7

In this chapter, the following recipes will be covered:

- Downloading the therapy bot session text dataset
- Analyzing the therapy bot session dataset
- Visualizing word counts in the dataset
- Calculating sentiment analysis of text
- Removing stop words from the text
- Training the TF-IDF model
- Evaluating TF-IDF model performance
- Comparing model performance to a baseline score

Introduction

Natural language processing (NLP) is all over the news lately, and if you ask five different people, you will get ten different definitions. Recently NLP has been used to help identify bots or trolls on the internet trying to spread fake news or, even worse, tactics such as cyberbullying. In fact, recently there was a case in Spain where a student at a school was getting cyberbullied through social media accounts and it was having such a serious effect on the health of the student that the teachers started to get involved. The school reached out to researchers who were able to help identify several potential sources for the trolls using NLP methods such as TF-IDF. Ultimately, the list of potential students was presented to the school and when confronted the actual suspect admitted to being the perpetrator. The story was published in a paper titled *Supervised Machine Learning for the Detection of Troll Profiles in Twitter Social Network: Application to a Real Case of Cyberbullying* by Patxi Galan-Garcia, Jose Gaviria de la Puerta, Carlos Laorden Gomez, Igor Santos, and Pablo Garcia Bringas.

This paper highlights the ability to utilize several varying methods to analyze text and develop human-like language processing. It is this methodology that incorporates NLP into machine learning, deep learning, and artificial intelligence. Having machines able to ingest text data and potentially make decisions from that same text data is the core of natural language processing. There are many algorithms that are used for NLP, such as the following:

- TF-IDF
- Word2Vec
- N-grams
- Latent Dirichlet allocation (LDA)
- Long short-term memory (LSTM)

This chapter will focus on a dataset that contains conversations between an individual and a chatbot from an online therapy website. The purpose of the chatbot is to recognize conversations that need to be flagged for immediate attention to an individual rather than continued discussion with the chatbot. Ultimately, we will focus on using a TF-IDF algorithm to perform text analysis on the dataset to determine whether the chat conversation warrants a classification that needs to be escalated to an individual or not. **TF-IDF** stands for **Term Frequency-Inverse Document Frequency**. This is a technique commonly used in algorithms to identify the importance of a word in a document. Additionally, TF-IDF is easy to compute especially when dealing with high word counts in documents and has the ability to measure the uniqueness of a word. This comes in handy when dealing with a chatbot data. The main goal is to quickly identify a unique word that would trigger escalation to an individual to provide immediate support.

Downloading the therapy bot session text dataset

This section will focus on downloading and setting up the dataset that will be used for NLP in this chapter.

Getting ready

The dataset that we will use in this chapter is based on interactions between a therapy bot and visitors to an online therapy website. It contains 100 interactions and each interaction is tagged as either `escalate` or `do_not_escalate`. If the discussion warrants a more serious conversation, the bot will tag the discussion as `escalate` to an individual. Otherwise, the bot will continue the discussion with the user.

How it works...

This section walks through the steps for downloading the chatbot data.

1. Access the dataset from the following GitHub repository: `https://github.com/asherif844/ApacheSparkDeepLearningCookbook/tree/master/CH07/data`

2. Once you arrive at the repository, right-click on the file seen in the following screenshot:

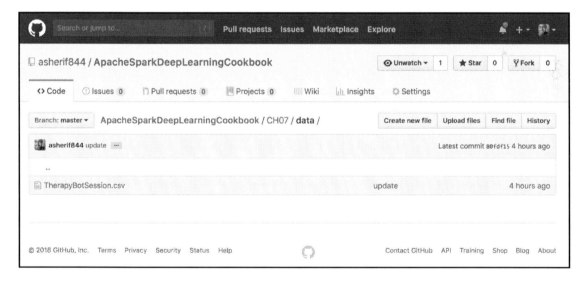

3. Download `TherapyBotSession.csv` and save to the same local directory as the Jupyter notebook `SparkSession`.

4. Access the dataset through the Jupyter notebook using the following script to build the `SparkSession` called `spark`, as well as to assign the dataset to a dataframe in Spark, called `df`:

```
spark = SparkSession.builder \
        .master("local") \
        .appName("Natural Language Processing") \
        .config("spark.executor.memory", "6gb") \
        .getOrCreate()
df = spark.read.format('com.databricks.spark.csv')\
        .options(header='true', inferschema='true')\
        .load('TherapyBotSession.csv')
```

How to do it...

This section explains how the chatbot data makes its way into our Jupyter notebook.

1. The contents of the dataset can be seen by clicking on **TherapyBotSession.csv** on the repository as seen in the following screenshot:

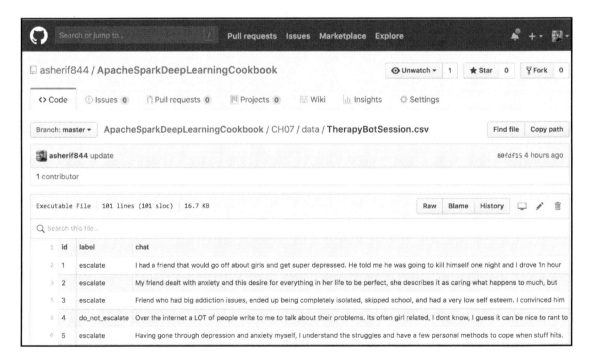

2. Once the dataset is downloaded, it can be uploaded and converted into a dataframe, df. The dataframe can be viewed by executing df.show(), as seen in the following screenshot:

```
In [1]: spark = SparkSession.builder \
            .master("local") \
            .appName("Natural Language Processing") \
            .config("spark.executor.memory", "6gb") \
            .getOrCreate()

In [2]: df = spark.read.format('com.databricks.spark.csv')\
                       .options(header='true', inferschema='true')\
                       .load('TherapyBotSession.csv')

In [3]: df.show()
+---+---------------+--------------------+----+----+----+----+
| id|          label|                chat| _c3| _c4| _c5| _c6|
+---+---------------+--------------------+----+----+----+----+
|  1|       escalate|I had a friend th...|null|null|null|null|
|  2|       escalate|"My friend dealt ...|null|null|null|null|
|  3|       escalate|Friend who had bi...|null|null|null|null|
|  4|do_not_escalate|Over the internet...|null|null|null|null|
|  5|       escalate|Having gone throu...|null|null|null|null|
|  6|       escalate|My now girlfriend...|null|null|null|null|
|  7|do_not_escalate|"Only really one ...|null|null|null|null|
|  8|do_not_escalate|Now that I've bee...|null|null|null|null|
|  9|do_not_escalate|I've always been ...|null|null|null|null|
| 10|       escalate|I feel completely...|null|null|null|null|
| 11|do_not_escalate|Took a week off w...|null|null|null|null|
| 12|       escalate|One of my best fr...|null|null|null|null|
| 13|       escalate|I've had some fri...|null|null|null|null|
| 14|do_not_escalate|Haha. In eight gr...|null|null|null|null|
| 15|do_not_escalate|Some of my friend...|null|null|null|null|
| 16|       escalate|I feel like depre...|null|null|null|null|
| 17|       escalate|i've had a couple...|null|null|null|null|
| 18|       escalate|I will always lis...|null|null|null|null|
| 19|do_not_escalate|A lot for my frie...|null|null|null|null|
| 20|do_not_escalate|When my friend ne...|null|null|null|null|
+---+---------------+--------------------+----+----+----+----+
only showing top 20 rows
```

3. There are 3 main fields that are of particular interest to us from the dataframe:

    1. id: the unique id of each transaction between a visitor to the website and the chatbot.

    2. label: since this is a supervised modeling approach where we know the outcome that we are trying to predict, each transaction has been classified as either escalate or do_not_escalate. This field will be used during the modeling process to train the text to identify words that would classify falling under one of these two scenarios.

    3. chat: lastly we have the chat text from the visitor on the website that our model will classify.

There's more...

The dataframe, `df`, has some additional columns, `_c3`, `_c4`, `_c5`, and `_c6` that will not be used in the model and therefore, can be excluded from the dataset using the following script:

```
df = df.select('id', 'label', 'chat')
df.show()
```

The output of the script can be seen in the following screenshot:

```
In [4]: df = df.select('id', 'label', 'chat')

In [5]: df.show()

+---+----------------+--------------------+
| id|           label|                chat|
+---+----------------+--------------------+
|  1|        escalate|I had a friend th...|
|  2|        escalate|"My friend dealt ...|
|  3|        escalate|Friend who had bi...|
|  4|  do_not_escalate|Over the internet...|
|  5|        escalate|Having gone throu...|
|  6|        escalate|My now girlfriend...|
|  7|  do_not_escalate|"Only really one ...|
|  8|  do_not_escalate|Now that I've bee...|
|  9|  do_not_escalate|I've always been ...|
| 10|        escalate|I feel completely...|
| 11|  do_not_escalate|Took a week off w...|
| 12|        escalate|One of my best fr...|
| 13|        escalate|I've had some fri...|
| 14|  do_not_escalate|Haha. In eight gr...|
| 15|  do_not_escalate|Some of my friend...|
| 16|        escalate|I feel like depre...|
| 17|        escalate|i've had a couple...|
| 18|        escalate|I will always lis...|
| 19|  do_not_escalate|A lot for my frie...|
| 20|  do_not_escalate|When my friend ne...|
+---+----------------+--------------------+
only showing top 20 rows
```

Analyzing the therapy bot session dataset

It is always important to first analyze any dataset before applying models on that same dataset

Getting ready

This section will require importing `functions` from `pyspark.sql` to be performed on our dataframe.

```
import pyspark.sql.functions as F
```

How to do it...

The following section walks through the steps to profile the text data.

1. Execute the following script to group the `label` column and to generate a count distribution:

```
df.groupBy("label") \
    .count() \
    .orderBy("count", ascending = False) \
    .show()
```

2. Add a new column, `word_count`, to the dataframe, `df`, using the following script:

```
import pyspark.sql.functions as F
df = df.withColumn('word_count',
F.size(F.split(F.col('response_text'),' ')))
```

3. Aggregate the average word count, `avg_word_count`, by `label` using the following script:

```
df.groupBy('label')\
    .agg(F.avg('word_count').alias('avg_word_count'))\
    .orderBy('avg_word_count', ascending = False) \
    .show()
```

How it works...

The following section explains the feedback obtained from analyzing the text data.

1. It is useful to collect data across multiple rows and group the results by a dimension. In this case, the dimension is `label`. A `df.groupby()` function is used to measure the count of 100 therapy transactions online distributed by `label`. We can see that there is a `65:35` distribution of `do_not_escalate` to `escalate` as seen in the following screenshot:

```
In [6]:  df.groupBy("label") \
             .count() \
             .orderBy("count", ascending = False) \
             .show()

         +----------------+-----+
         |           label|count|
         +----------------+-----+
         |do_not_escalate|   65|
         |        escalate|   35|
         +----------------+-----+
```

2. A new column, `word_count`, is created to calculate how many words are used in each of the 100 transactions between the chatbot and the online visitor. The newly created column, `word_count`, can be seen in the following screenshot:

```
In [7]:  import pyspark.sql.functions as F
         df = df.withColumn('word_count',F.size(F.split(F.col('chat'),' ')))

In [8]:  df.show()

         +---+----------------+--------------------+----------+
         | id|           label|                chat|word_count|
         +---+----------------+--------------------+----------+
         |  1|        escalate|I had a friend th...|       304|
         |  2|        escalate|"My friend dealt ...|       184|
         |  3|        escalate|Friend who had bi...|        90|
         |  4|do_not_escalate|Over the internet...|        88|
         |  5|        escalate|Having gone throu...|        71|
         |  6|        escalate|My now girlfriend...|        73|
         |  7|do_not_escalate|"Only really one ...|        74|
         |  8|do_not_escalate|Now that I've bee...|        62|
         |  9|do_not_escalate|I've always been ...|        60|
         | 10|        escalate|I feel completely...|        56|
         | 11|do_not_escalate|Took a week off w...|        60|
         | 12|        escalate|One of my best fr...|        59|
         | 13|        escalate|I've had some fri...|        50|
         | 14|do_not_escalate|Haha. In eight gr...|        55|
         | 15|do_not_escalate|Some of my friend...|        49|
         | 16|        escalate|I feel like depre...|        41|
         | 17|        escalate|i've had a couple...|        38|
         | 18|        escalate|I will always lis...|        41|
         | 19|do_not_escalate|A lot for my frie...|        44|
         | 20|do_not_escalate|When my friend ne...|        42|
         +---+----------------+--------------------+----------+
         only showing top 20 rows
```

3. Since the `word_count` is now added to the dataframe, it can be aggregated to calculate the average word count by `label`. Once this is performed, we can see that `escalate` conversations on average are more than twice as long as `do_not_escalate` conversations, as seen in the following screenshot:

```
In [9]: df.groupBy('label')\
            .agg(F.avg('word_count').alias('avg_word_count'))\
            .orderBy('avg_word_count', ascending = False) \
            .show()

        +---------------+-----------------+
        |          label|   avg_word_count|
        +---------------+-----------------+
        |        escalate|             44.0|
        |do_not_escalate|20.29230769230769|
        +---------------+-----------------+
```

Visualizing word counts in the dataset

A picture is worth a thousand words and this section will set out to prove that. Unfortunately, Spark does not have any inherent plotting capabilities as of version 2.2. In order to plot values in a dataframe, we must convert to `pandas`.

Getting ready

This section will require importing `matplotlib` for plotting:

```
import matplotlib.pyplot as plt
%matplotlib inline
```

How to do it...

This section walks through the steps to convert the Spark dataframe into a visualization that can be seen in the Jupyter notebook.

1. Convert Spark dataframe to a `pandas` dataframe using the following script:

```
df_plot = df.select('id', 'word_count').toPandas()
```

2. Plot the dataframe using the following script:

```
import matplotlib.pyplot as plt
%matplotlib inline

df_plot.set_index('id', inplace=True)
df_plot.plot(kind='bar', figsize=(16, 6))
plt.ylabel('Word Count')
plt.title('Word Count distribution')
plt.show()
```

How it works...

This section explains how the Spark dataframe is converted to pandas and then plotted.

1. A subset of the Spark dataframe is collected and converted to pandas using the toPandas() method in Spark.

2. That subset of data is then plotted using matplotlib setting the y-values to be word_count and the x-values to be the id as seen in the following screenshot:

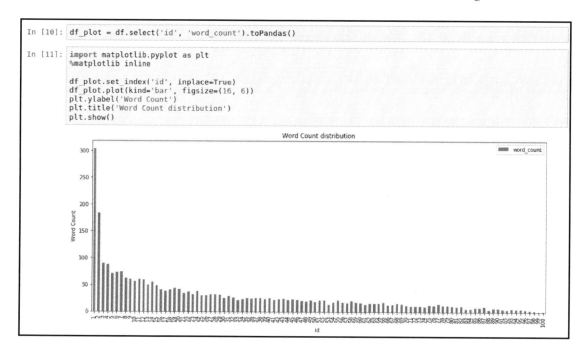

See also

There are other plotting capabilities in Python other than `matplotlib` such as `bokeh`, `plotly`, and `seaborn`.

To learn more about `bokeh`, visit the following website:

`https://bokeh.pydata.org/en/latest/`

To learn more about `plotly`, visit the following website:

`https://plot.ly/`

To learn more about `seaborn`, visit the following website:

`https://seaborn.pydata.org/`

Calculating sentiment analysis of text

Sentiment analysis is the ability to derive tone and feeling behind a word or series of words. This section will utilize techniques in python to calculate a sentiment analysis score from the 100 transactions in our dataset.

Getting ready

This section will require using functions and data types within PySpark. Additionally, we well importing the `TextBlob` library for sentiment analysis. In order to use SQL and data type functions within PySpark, the following must be imported:

```
from pyspark.sql.types import FloatType
```

Additionally, in order to use `TextBlob`, the following library must be imported:

```
from textblob import TextBlob
```

How to do it...

The following section walks through the steps to apply sentiment score to the dataset.

1. Create a sentiment score function, `sentiment_score`, using the following script:

```
from textblob import TextBlob
def sentiment_score(chat):
    return TextBlob(chat).sentiment.polarity
```

2. Apply `sentiment_score` to each conversation response in the dataframe using the following script:

3. Create a `lambda` function, called `sentiment_score_udf`, that maps `sentiment_score` into a user-defined function within Spark, `udf`, to each transaction and specifies the output type of `FloatType()` as seen in the following script:

```
from pyspark.sql.types import FloatType
sentiment_score_udf = F.udf(lambda x: sentiment_score(x),
FloatType())
```

4. Apply the function, `sentiment_score_udf`, to each `chat` column in the dataframe as seen in the following script:

```
df = df.select('id', 'label', 'chat','word_count',
sentiment_score_udf('chat').alias('sentiment_score'))
```

5. Calculate the average sentiment score, `avg_sentiment_score`, by `label` using the following script:

```
df.groupBy('label')\
    .agg(F.avg('sentiment_score').alias('avg_sentiment_score'))\
    .orderBy('avg_sentiment_score', ascending = False) \
    .show()
```

How it works...

This section explains how a Python function is converted into a user-defined function, `udf`, within Spark to apply a sentiment analysis score to each column in the dataframe.

1. `Textblob` is a sentiment analysis library in Python. It can calculate the sentiment score from a method called `sentiment.polarity` that is scored from -1 (very negative) to +1 (very positive) with 0 being neutral. Additionally, `Textblob` can measure subjectivity from 0 (very objective) to 1 (very subjective); although, we will not be measuring subjectivity in this chapter.

2. There are a couple of steps to applying a Python function to Spark dataframe:

    1. `Textblob` is imported and a function called `sentiment_score` is applied to the `chat` column to generate the sentiment polarity of each bot conversation in a new column, also called `sentiment_score`.

    2. A Python function cannot be directly applied to a Spark dataframe without first going through a user-defined function transformation, `udf`, within Spark.

    3. Additionally, the output of the function must also be explicitly stated, whether it be an integer or float data type. In our situation, we explicitly state that the output of the function will be using the `FloatType()` from `pyspark.sql.types`. Finally, the sentiment is applied across each row using a `lambda` function within the `udf` sentiment score function, called `sentiment_score_udf`.

3. The updated dataframe with the newly created field, `sentiment score`, can be seen by executing `df.show()`, as shown in the following screenshot:

```
In [12]: from textblob import TextBlob
         def sentiment_score(chat):
              return TextBlob(chat).sentiment.polarity
```

```
In [13]: from pyspark.sql.types import FloatType
         sentiment_score_udf = F.udf(lambda x: sentiment_score(x), FloatType())
```

```
In [14]: df = df.select('id', 'label', 'chat','word_count',
                      sentiment_score_udf('chat').alias('sentiment_score'))
         df.show()
```

```
+---+---------------+--------------------+----------+---------------+
| id|          label|                chat|word_count|sentiment_score|
+---+---------------+--------------------+----------+---------------+
|  1|       escalate|I had a friend th...|       304|    0.018961353|
|  2|       escalate|"My friend dealt ...|       184|     0.20601852|
|  3|       escalate|Friend who had bi...|        90|    0.008333334|
|  4|do_not_escalate|Over the internet...|        88|    0.045833334|
|  5|       escalate|Having gone throu...|        71|         0.0125|
|  6|       escalate|My now girlfriend...|        73|     0.06333333|
|  7|do_not_escalate|"Only really one ...|        74|    0.036363635|
|  8|do_not_escalate|Now that I've bee...|        62|          0.125|
|  9|do_not_escalate|I've always been ...|        60|           0.31|
| 10|       escalate|I feel completely...|        56|      -0.078125|
| 11|do_not_escalate|Took a week off w...|        60|     0.16666667|
| 12|       escalate|One of my best fr...|        59|            0.4|
| 13|       escalate|I've had some fri...|        50|           0.19|
| 14|do_not_escalate|Haha. In eight gr...|        55|     0.29666665|
| 15|do_not_escalate|Some of my friend...|        49|            0.4|
| 16|       escalate|I feel like depre...|        41|           0.05|
| 17|       escalate|i've had a couple...|        38|     0.16666667|
| 18|       escalate|I will always lis...|        41|         -0.025|
| 19|do_not_escalate|A lot for my frie...|        44|    0.035858586|
| 20|do_not_escalate|When my friend ne...|        42|   -0.094444446|
+---+---------------+--------------------+----------+---------------+
only showing top 20 rows
```

4. Now that the `sentiment_score` is calculated for each response from the chat conversation, we can denote a value range of -1 (very negative polarity) to +1 (very positive polarity) for each row. Just as we did with counts and average word count, we can compare whether `escalate` conversations are more positive or negative in sentiment than `do_not_escalate` conversations on average. We can calculate an average sentiment score, `avg_sentiment_score`, by `label` as seen in the following screenshot:

```
In [15]: df.groupBy('label')\
            .agg(F.avg('sentiment_score').alias('avg_sentiment_score'))\
            .orderBy('avg_sentiment_score', ascending = False) \
            .show()
+--------------+--------------------+
|         label| avg_sentiment_score|
+--------------+--------------------+
|      escalate| 0.06338859780558519|
|do_not_escalate|0.031975071089198955|
+--------------+--------------------+
```

5. Initially, it would make sense to assume that escalate conversations would be more negative from a polarity score than do_not_escalate. We actually find that escalate is slightly more positive in polarity than do_not_escalate; however, both are pretty neutral as they are close to 0.

See also

To learn more about the TextBlob library, visit the following website:

http://textblob.readthedocs.io/en/dev/

Removing stop words from the text

A stop word is a very common word used in the English language and is often removed from common NLP techniques because they can be distracting. Common stop word would be words such as *the* or *and*.

Getting ready

This section requires importing the following libraries:

```
from pyspark.ml.feature import StopWordsRemover
from pyspark.ml import Pipeline
```

How to do it...

This section walks through the steps to remove stop words.

1. Execute the following script to extract each word in `chat` into a string within an array:

```
df = df.withColumn('words',F.split(F.col('chat'),' '))
```

2. Assign a list of common words to a variable, `stop_words`, that will be considered stop words using the following script:

```
stop_words = ['i','me','my','myself','we','our','ours','ourselves',
'you','your','yours','yourself','yourselves','he','him',
'his','himself','she','her','hers','herself','it','its',
'itself','they','them','their','theirs','themselves',
'what','which','who','whom','this','that','these','those',
'am','is','are','was','were','be','been','being','have',
'has','had','having','do','does','did','doing','a','an',
'the','and','but','if','or','because','as','until','while',
'of','at','by','for','with','about','against','between',
'into','through','during','before','after','above','below',
'to','from','up','down','in','out','on','off','over','under',
'again','further','then','once','here','there','when','where',
'why','how','all','any','both','each','few','more','most',
'other','some','such','no','nor','not','only','own','same',
'so','than','too','very','can','will','just','don','should','now']
```

3. Execute the following script to import the `StopWordsRemover` function from PySpark and configure the input and output columns, `words` and `word without stop`:

```
from pyspark.ml.feature import StopWordsRemover

stopwordsRemovalFeature = StopWordsRemover(inputCol="words",
                    outputCol="words without
stop").setStopWords(stop_words)
```

4. Execute the following script to import Pipeline and define the `stages` for the stop word transformation process that will be applied to the dataframe:

```
from pyspark.ml import Pipeline

stopWordRemovalPipeline =
Pipeline(stages=[stopwordsRemovalFeature])
pipelineFitRemoveStopWords = stopWordRemovalPipeline.fit(df)
```

5. Finally, apply the stop word removal transformation, `pipelineFitRemoveStopWords`, to the dataframe, `df`, using the following script:

```
df = pipelineFitRemoveStopWords.transform(df)
```

How it works...

This section explains how to remove stop words from the text.

1. Just as we did by applying some analysis when profiling and exploring the `chat` data, we can also tweak the text of the `chat` conversation and break up each word into a separate array. This will be used to isolate stop words and remove them.

2. The new column with each word extracted as a string is called `words` and can be seen in the following screenshot:

```
In [16]: df = df.withColumn('words',F.split(F.col('chat'),' '))
         df.show()
+---+----------------+--------------------+----------+---------------+--------------------+
| id|           label|                chat|word_count|sentiment_score|               words|
+---+----------------+--------------------+----------+---------------+--------------------+
|  1|        escalate|I had a friend th...|       304|    0.018961353|[I, had, a, frien...|
|  2|        escalate|"My friend dealt ...|       184|     0.20601852|["My, friend, dea...|
|  3|        escalate|Friend who had bi...|        90|   0.008333334|[Friend, who, had...|
|  4|  do_not_escalate|Over the internet...|        88|    0.045833334|[Over, the, inter...|
|  5|        escalate|Having gone throu...|        71|         0.0125|[Having, gone, th...|
|  6|        escalate|My now girlfriend...|        73|    0.06333333|[My, now, girlfri...|
|  7|  do_not_escalate|"Only really one ...|        74|    0.036363635|["Only, really, o...|
|  8|  do_not_escalate|Now that I've bee...|        62|          0.125|[Now, that, I've,...|
|  9|  do_not_escalate|I've always been ...|        60|           0.31|[I've, always, be...|
| 10|        escalate|I feel completely...|        56|      -0.078125|[I, feel, complet...|
| 11|  do_not_escalate|Took a week off w...|        60|     0.16666667|[Took, a, week, o...|
| 12|        escalate|One of my best fr...|        59|            0.4|[One, of, my, bes...|
| 13|        escalate|I've had some fri...|        50|           0.19|[I've, had, some,...|
| 14|  do_not_escalate|Haha. In eight gr...|        55|     0.29666665|[Haha., In, eight...|
| 15|  do_not_escalate|Some of my friend...|        49|            0.4|[Some, of, my, fr...|
| 16|        escalate|I feel like depre...|        41|           0.05|[I, feel, like, d...|
| 17|        escalate|i've had a couple...|        38|     0.16666667|[i've, had, a, co...|
| 18|        escalate|I will always lis...|        41|         -0.025|[I, will, always,...|
| 19|  do_not_escalate|A lot for my frie...|        44|    0.035858586|[A, lot, for, my,...|
| 20|  do_not_escalate|When my friend ne...|        42|   -0.094444446|[When, my, friend...|
+---+----------------+--------------------+----------+---------------+--------------------+
only showing top 20 rows
```

3. There are many ways to assign a group of words to a stop word list. Some of these words can be automatically downloaded and updated using a proper Python library called `nltk`, which stands for natural language toolkit. For our purposes, we will utilize a common list of 124 stop words to generate our own list. Additional words can be easily added or removed from the list manually.

4. Stop words do not add any value to the text and will be removed from the newly created column by specifying `outputCol="words without stop"`. Additionally, the column that will serve as the source for the transformation is set by specifying `inputCol = "words"`.

5. We create a pipeline, `stopWordRemovalPipeline`, to define the sequence of steps or `stages` that will transform the data. In this situation, the only stage that will be used to transform the data is the feature, `stopwordsRemover`.

6. Each stage in a pipeline can have a transforming role and an estimator role. The estimator role, `pipeline.fit(df)`, is called on to produce a transformer function called `pipelineFitRemoveStopWords`. Finally, the `transform(df)` function is called on the dataframe to produce an updated dataframe with a new column called `words without stop`. We can compare both columns side by side to examine the differences as seen in the following screenshot:

```
In [17]: stop_words = ['i','me','my','myself','we','our','ours','ourselves',
                        'you','your','yours','yourself','yourselves','he','him',
                        'his','himself','she','her','hers','herself','it','its',
                        'itself','they','them','their','theirs','themselves',
                        'what','which','who','whom','this','that','these','those',
                        'am','is','are','was','were','be','been','being','have',
                        'has','had','having','do','does','did','doing','a','an',
                        'the','and','but','if','or','because','as','until','while',
                        'of','at','by','for','with','about','against','between',
                        'into','through','during','before','after','above','below',
                        'to','from','up','down','in','out','on','off','over','under',
                        'again','further','then','once','here','there','when','where',
                        'why','how','all','any','both','each','few','more','most',
                        'other','some','such','no','nor','not','only','own','same',
                        'so','than','too','very','can','will','just','don','should','now']

In [18]: from pyspark.ml.feature import StopWordsRemover

In [19]: stopwordsRemovalFeature = StopWordsRemover(inputCol="words",
                                      outputCol="words without stop").setStopWords(stop_words)

In [20]: from pyspark.ml import Pipeline
         stopWordRemovalPipeline = Pipeline(stages=[stopwordsRemovalFeature])
         pipelineFitRemoveStopWords = stopWordRemovalPipeline.fit(df)

In [21]: df = pipelineFitRemoveStopWords.transform(df)
         df.select('words', 'words without stop').show(5)

         +--------------------+--------------------+
         |               words|  words without stop|
         +--------------------+--------------------+
         |[I, had, a, frien...|[friend, would, g...|
         |["My, friend, dea...|["My, friend, dea...|
         |[Friend, who, had...|[Friend, big, add...|
         |[Over, the, inter...|[internet, LOT, p...|
         |[Having, gone, th...|[gone, depression...|
         +--------------------+--------------------+
         only showing top 5 rows
```

7. The new column, `words without stop`, contains none of the strings that are considered stop words from the original column, `words`.

See also

To learn more about stop words from `nltk`, visit the following website:

`https://www.nltk.org/data.html`

To learn more about Spark machine learning pipelines, visit the following website:

`https://spark.apache.org/docs/2.2.0/ml-pipeline.html`

To learn more about the `StopWordsRemover` feature in PySpark, visit the following website:

`https://spark.apache.org/docs/2.2.0/api/python/pyspark.ml.html#pyspark.ml.feature.StopWordsRemover`

Training the TF-IDF model

We are now ready to train our TF-IDF NLP model and see if we can classify these transactions as either `escalate` or `do_not_escalate`.

Getting ready

This section will require importing from `spark.ml.feature` and `spark.ml.classification`.

How to do it...

The following section walks through the steps to train the TF-IDF model.

1. Create a new user-defined function, `udf`, to define numerical values for the `label` column using the following script:

```
label = F.udf(lambda x: 1.0 if x == 'escalate' else 0.0,
FloatType())
df = df.withColumn('label', label('label'))
```

2. Execute the following script to set the TF and IDF columns for the vectorization of the words:

```
import pyspark.ml.feature as feat
TF_ = feat.HashingTF(inputCol="words without stop",
                    outputCol="rawFeatures", numFeatures=100000)
IDF_ = feat.IDF(inputCol="rawFeatures", outputCol="features")
```

3. Set up a pipeline, `pipelineTFIDF`, to set the sequence of stages for `TF_` and `IDF_` using the following script:

```
pipelineTFIDF = Pipeline(stages=[TF_, IDF_])
```

4. Fit and transform the IDF estimator onto the dataframe, `df`, using the following script:

```
pipelineFit = pipelineTFIDF.fit(df)
df = pipelineFit.transform(df)
```

5. Split the dataframe into a 75:25 split for model evaluation purposes using the following script:

```
(trainingDF, testDF) = df.randomSplit([0.75, 0.25], seed = 1234)
```

6. Import and configure a classification model, `LogisticRegression`, using the following script:

```
from pyspark.ml.classification import LogisticRegression
logreg = LogisticRegression(regParam=0.25)
```

7. Fit the logistic regression model, `logreg`, onto the training dataframe, `trainingDF`. A new dataframe, `predictionDF`, is created based on the `transform()` method from the logistic regression model, as seen in the following script:

```
logregModel = logreg.fit(trainingDF)
predictionDF = logregModel.transform(testDF)
```

How it works...

The following section explains to effectively train a TF-IDF NLP model.

1. It is ideal to have labels in a numerical format rather than a categorical form as the model is able to interpret numerical values while classifying outputs between 0 and 1. Therefore, all labels under the `label` column are converted to a numerical `label` of **0.0** or **1.0**, as seen in the following screenshot:

```
In [22]:  label = F.udf(lambda x: 1.0 if x == 'escalate' else 0.0, FloatType())
          df = df.withColumn('label', label('label'))

In [23]:  df.select('label').show()
          +-----+
          |label|
          +-----+
          |  1.0|
          |  1.0|
          |  1.0|
          |  0.0|
          |  1.0|
          |  1.0|
          |  0.0|
          |  0.0|
          |  0.0|
          |  1.0|
          |  0.0|
          |  1.0|
          |  1.0|
          |  0.0|
          |  0.0|
          |  1.0|
          |  1.0|
          |  1.0|
          |  0.0|
          |  0.0|
          +-----+
          only showing top 20 rows
```

2. TF-IDF models require a two-step approach by importing both `HashingTF` and `IDF` from `pyspark.ml.feature` to handle separate tasks. The first task merely involves importing both `HashingTF` and `IDF` and assigning values for the input and subsequent output columns. The `numfeatures` parameter is set to 100,000 to ensure that it is larger than the distinct number of words in the dataframe. If `numfeatures` were to be than the distinct word count, the model would be inaccurate.

3. As stated earlier, each step of the pipeline contains a transformation process and an estimator process. The pipeline, `pipelineTFIDF`, is configured to order the sequence of steps where `IDF` will follow `HashingTF`.

4. `HashingTF` is used to transform the `words without stop` into vectors within a new column called `rawFeatures`. Subsequently, `rawFeatures` will then be consumed by `IDF` to estimate the size and fit the dataframe to produce a new column called `features`, as seen in the following screenshot:

```
In [24]: import pyspark.ml.feature as feat
         TF_ = feat.HashingTF(inputCol="words without stop",
                              outputCol="rawFeatures", numFeatures=100000)
         IDF_ = feat.IDF(inputCol="rawFeatures", outputCol="features")

In [25]: pipelineTFIDF = Pipeline(stages=[TF_, IDF_])

In [26]: pipelineFit = pipelineTFIDF.fit(df)
         df = pipelineFit.transform(df)

In [27]: df.select('label', 'rawFeatures','features').show()

+-----+--------------------+--------------------+
|label|         rawFeatures|            features|
+-----+--------------------+--------------------+
|  1.0|(100000,[76,1583,...|(100000,[76,1583,...|
|  1.0|(100000,[5319,105...|(100000,[5319,105...|
|  1.0|(100000,[618,7515...|(100000,[618,7515...|
|  0.0|(100000,[3370,444...|(100000,[3370,444...|
|  1.0|(100000,[4442,101...|(100000,[4442,101...|
|  1.0|(100000,[7369,775...|(100000,[7369,775...|
|  0.0|(100000,[232,6124...|(100000,[232,6124...|
|  0.0|(100000,[2732,335...|(100000,[2732,335...|
|  0.0|(100000,[4047,425...|(100000,[4047,425...|
|  1.0|(100000,[6531,135...|(100000,[6531,135...|
|  0.0|(100000,[5330,120...|(100000,[5330,120...|
|  1.0|(100000,[1197,444...|(100000,[1197,444...|
|  1.0|(100000,[4442,107...|(100000,[4442,107...|
|  0.0|(100000,[232,4441...|(100000,[232,4441...|
|  0.0|(100000,[781,3526...|(100000,[781,3526...|
|  1.0|(100000,[13806,14...|(100000,[13806,14...|
|  1.0|(100000,[4442,108...|(100000,[4442,108...|
|  1.0|(100000,[76,11034...|(100000,[76,11034...|
|  0.0|(100000,[10001,27...|(100000,[10001,27...|
|  0.0|(100000,[29385,39...|(100000,[29385,39...|
+-----+--------------------+--------------------+
only showing top 20 rows
```

5. For training purposes, our dataframe will be conservatively split into a 75:25 ratio with a random seed set at 1234.

6. Since our main goal is to classify each conversation as either `escalate` for escalation or `do_not_escalate` for continued bot chat, we can use a traditional classification algorithm such as a logistic regression model from the PySpark library. The logistic regression model is configured with a regularization parameter, `regParam`, of 0.025. We use the parameter to slightly improve the model by minimizing overfitting at the expense of a little bias.

7. The logistic regression model is trained and fitted on `trainingDF`, and then a new dataframe, `predictionDF`, is created with the newly transformed field, `prediction`, as seen in the following screenshot:

```
In [28]: (trainingDF, testDF) = df.randomSplit([0.75, 0.25], seed = 1234)

In [29]: from pyspark.ml.classification import LogisticRegression
         logreg = LogisticRegression(regParam=0.025)

In [30]: logregModel = logreg.fit(trainingDF)

In [31]: predictionDF = logregModel.transform(testDF)

In [32]: predictionDF.select('label', 'probability', 'prediction').show()
         +-----+--------------------+----------+
         |label|         probability|prediction|
         +-----+--------------------+----------+
         |  1.0|[0.00339966489826...|       1.0|
         |  1.0|[0.55815635574642...|       0.0|
         |  1.0|[0.03557500295368...|       1.0|
         |  0.0|[0.52714451276392...|       0.0|
         |  0.0|[0.64630042307877...|       0.0|
         |  0.0|[0.69042286406135...|       0.0|
         |  1.0|[0.44672236248681...|       1.0|
         |  0.0|[0.67209249316671...|       0.0|
         |  0.0|[0.96010780703860...|       0.0|
         |  1.0|[0.75210799156076...|       0.0|
         |  0.0|[0.90904812079420...|       0.0|
         |  0.0|[0.97354469378068...|       0.0|
         |  0.0|[0.96576753489686...|       0.0|
         |  0.0|[0.89685928798301...|       0.0|
         |  0.0|[0.92552854921657...|       0.0|
         |  0.0|[0.94649994610325...|       0.0|
         |  0.0|[0.89486269398390...|       0.0|
         |  0.0|[0.65225541621797...|       0.0|
         |  0.0|[0.95636713428689...|       0.0|
         |  0.0|[0.95927102608436...|       0.0|
         +-----+--------------------+----------+
         only showing top 20 rows
```

There's more...

While we did use the user-defined function, `udf`, to manually create a numerical label column, we also could have used a built-in feature from PySpark called `StringIndexer` to assign numerical values to categorical labels. To see `StringIndexer` in action, visit `Chapter 5`, *Predicting Fire Department Calls with Spark ML.*

See also

To learn more about the TF-IDF model within PySpark, visit the following website:

`https://spark.apache.org/docs/latest/mllib-feature-extraction.html#tf-idf`

Evaluating TF-IDF model performance

At this point, we are ready to evaluate our model's performance

Getting ready

This section will require importing the following libraries:

- `metrics` from `sklearn`
- `BinaryClassificationEvaluator` from `pyspark.ml.evaluation`

How to do it...

This section walks through the steps to evaluate the TF-IDF NLP model.

1. Create a confusion matrix using the following script:

```
predictionDF.crosstab('label', 'prediction').show()
```

2. Evaluate the model using `metrics` from sklearn with the following script:

```
from sklearn import metrics

actual = predictionDF.select('label').toPandas()
predicted = predictionDF.select('prediction').toPandas()
print('accuracy score:
{}%'.format(round(metrics.accuracy_score(actual,
predicted),3)*100))
```

3. Calculate the ROC score using the following script:

```
from pyspark.ml.evaluation import BinaryClassificationEvaluator

scores = predictionDF.select('label', 'rawPrediction')
evaluator = BinaryClassificationEvaluator()
print('The ROC score is
{}%'.format(round(evaluator.evaluate(scores),3)*100))
```

How it works...

This section explains how we use the evaluation calculations to determine the accuracy of our model.

1. A confusion matrix is helpful to quickly summarize the accuracy numbers between actual results and predicted results. Since we had a 75:25 split, we should see 25 predictions from our training dataset. We can build a build a confusion matric using the following script: `predictionDF.crosstab('label', 'prediction').show()`. The output of the script can be seen in the following screenshot:

```
In [33]: predictionDF.crosstab('label', 'prediction').show()

+---------------+---+---+
|label_prediction|0.0|1.0|
+---------------+---+---+
|            1.0|  2|  3|
|            0.0| 19|  0|
+---------------+---+---+
```

2. We are now at the stage of evaluating the accuracy of the model by comparing the `prediction` values against the actual `label` values. `sklearn.metrics` intakes two parameters, the `actual` values tied to the `label` column, as well as the `predicted` values derived from the logistic regression model.

Please note that once again we are converting the column values from Spark dataframes to pandas dataframes using the `toPandas()` method.

3. Two variables are created, `actual` and `predicted`, and an accuracy score of **91.7%** is calculated using the `metrics.accuracy_score()` function, as seen in the following screenshot:

```
In [34]: from sklearn import metrics
         actual = predictionDF.select('label').toPandas()
         predicted = predictionDF.select('prediction').toPandas()

In [35]: print('accuracy score: {}%'.format(round(metrics.accuracy_score(actual, predicted),3)*100))
         accuracy score: 91.7%
```

4. The ROC (Receiver Operating Characteristic) is often associated with a curve measuring the true positive rate against the false positive rate. The greater the area under the curve, the better. The ROC score associated with the curve is another indicator that can be used to measure the performance of the model. We can calculate the `ROC` using the `BinaryClassificationEvaluator` as seen in the following screenshot:

```
In [36]: from pyspark.ml.evaluation import BinaryClassificationEvaluator

         scores = predictionDF.select('label', 'rawPrediction')
         evaluator = BinaryClassificationEvaluator()
         print('The ROC score is {}%'.format(round(evaluator.evaluate(scores),3)*100))
         The ROC score is 93.7%
```

See also

To learn more about the `BinaryClassificationEvaluator` from PySpark, visit the following website:

```
https://spark.apache.org/docs/2.2.0/api/java/index.html?org/apache/spark/ml/
evaluation/BinaryClassificationEvaluator.html
```

Comparing model performance to a baseline score

While it is great that we have a high accuracy score from our model of 91.7 percent, it is also important to compare this to a baseline score. We dig deeper into this concept in this section.

How to do it...

This section walks through the steps to calculate the baseline accuracy.

1. Execute the following script to retrieve the mean value from the `describe()` method:

   ```
   predictionDF.describe('label').show()
   ```

2. Subtract `1- mean value score` to calculate baseline accuracy.

How it works...

This section explains the concept behind the baseline accuracy and how we can use it to understand the effectiveness of our model.

1. What if every `chat` conversation was flagged for `do_not_escalate` or vice versa. Would we have a baseline accuracy higher than 91.7 percent? The easiest way to figure this out is to run the `describe()` method on the `label` column from `predictionDF` using the following script: `predictionDF.describe('label').show()`

2. The output of the script can be seen in the following screenshot:

```
In [37]:  predictionDF.describe('label').show()

+-------+-------------------+
|summary|              label|
+-------+-------------------+
|  count|                 24|
|   mean|0.208333333333333334|
| stddev|0.414851116999905336|
|    min|                0.0|
|    max|                1.0|
+-------+-------------------+
```

3. The mean of `label` is at 0.2083 or ~21%, which means that a `label` of **1** occurs only 21% of the time. Therefore, if we labeled each conversation as `do_not_escalate`, we would be correct ~79% of the time, which is less than our model accuracy of 91.7%.

4. Therefore, we can say that our model performs better than a blind baseline performance model.

See also

To learn more about the `describe()` method in a PySpark dataframe, visit the following website:

http://spark.apache.org/docs/2.2.0/api/python/pyspark.sql.html#pyspark.sql.DataFrame.describe

8
Real Estate Value Prediction Using XGBoost

The real estate market is one of the most competitive markets when it comes to pricing. This tends to vary significantly based on a number of factors such as the location, age of the property, size, and so on. Therefore, it has become a modern-day challenge to accurately predict the prices of properties (especially those in the housing market) in order to make better investment decisions. This chapter will deal with precisely that.

After going through this chapter, you will be able to:

- Downloading the King County Housing sales dataset
- Performing exploratory analysis and visualization
- Plotting correlation between price and other features
- Predicting the price of a house

Downloading the King County House sales dataset

We can't build a model without a dataset. We will download our data in this section.

Getting ready

Kaggle (`https://www.kaggle.com/`) is a platform for predictive modeling and analytics competitions in which statisticians and data miners compete to produce the best models for predicting and describing the datasets uploaded by companies and users. The King County House Sales dataset contains records of 21,613 houses sold in King County, New York between 1900 and 2015. The dataset also contains 21 different variables such as location, zip code, number of bedrooms, area of the living space, and so on, for each house.

How to do it...

1. The dataset can be accessed from the following website: `https://www.kaggle.com/harlfoxem/housesalesprediction`. The dataset is from the public records of King County and is freely available to download and use in any analysis.

2. Once you arrive at the website, you can click on the **Download** button, as shown in the following screenshot:

King County House Sales Dataset

3. One file named `kc_house_data.csv` appears from the zipped, downloaded file, `housesalesprediction.zip`.

4. Save the file named `kc_house_data.csv` in the current working directory as this will be our dataset. This will be loaded into the IPython notebook for analysis and predictions.

How it works...

1. Install the necessary libraries for this chapter using the following code:

```
import numpy as np
import pandas as pd
import matplotlib.pyplot as plt
import seaborn as sns
import mpl_toolkits
from sklearn import preprocessing
from sklearn.preprocessing import LabelEncoder, OneHotEncoder
from sklearn.feature_selection import RFE
from sklearn import linear_model
from sklearn.cross_validation import train_test_split %matplotlib
inline
```

2. The preceding step should result in an output, as shown in the following screenshot:

```
In [1]:    1  import numpy as np
           2  import pandas as pd
           3  import matplotlib.pyplot as plt
           4  import seaborn as sns
           5  import mpl_toolkits
           6  from sklearn import preprocessing
           7  from sklearn.preprocessing import LabelEncoder, OneHotEncoder
           8  from sklearn.feature_selection import RFE
           9  from sklearn import linear_model
          10  from sklearn.cross_validation import train_test_split
          11  %matplotlib inline

/Users/Chanti/anaconda3/lib/python3.6/site-packages/sklearn/cross_validation.py:41: DeprecationWarning: This module w
as deprecated in version 0.18 in favor of the model_selection module into which all the refactored classes and functi
ons are moved. Also note that the interface of the new CV iterators are different from that of this module. This modu
le will be removed in 0.20.
  "This module will be removed in 0.20.", DeprecationWarning)
```

3. It is always a good idea to check the current working directory and set it to the directory in which the dataset is stored. This is shown in the following screenshot:

```
In [2]:     1  pwd

Out[2]:  '/Users/Chanti'

In [3]:     1  cd '/Users/Chanti/Desktop/Cookbook/Chapter 10'

            /Users/Chanti/Desktop/Cookbook/Chapter 10

In [4]:     1  pwd

Out[4]:  '/Users/Chanti/Desktop/Cookbook/Chapter 10'
```

In our case, the folder named `Chapter 10` is set as the current working directory.

4. The data in the file is read into a Pandas dataframe named `dataframe` using the `read_csv()` function and the features/headers are listed out using the `list(dataframe)` command, as shown in the following screenshot:

```
In [5]:     1  dataframe = pd.read_csv("kc_house_data.csv", header='infer')

In [6]:     1  list(dataframe)

Out[6]:  ['id',
          'date',
          'price',
          'bedrooms',
          'bathrooms',
          'sqft_living',
          'sqft_lot',
          'floors',
          'waterfront',
          'view',
          'condition',
          'grade',
          'sqft_above',
          'sqft_basement',
          'yr_built',
          'yr_renovated',
          'zipcode',
          'lat',
          'long',
          'sqft_living15',
          'sqft_lot15']
```

As you may have noticed, the dataset contains 21 different variables such as **id**, **date**, **price**, **bedrooms**, **bathrooms**, and so on.

There's more...

The libraries used as well as their functions in this chapter are as follows:

- `Numpy`, which is used to wrangle data in the form of arrays as well as store lists of names in the form of arrays
- `Pandas`, which is used for all data wrangling and managing data in the form of dataframes
- `Seaborn`, which is a visualization library required for exploratory analysis and plots
- `MPL_Toolkits`, which contains a number of functions and dependencies required by `Matplotlib`
- Functions from the `Scikit Learn` library, which is the primary scientific and statistical library required in this chapter
- We will also require some other libraries such as `XGBoost`, but those will be imported as required while building the model

See also

Further documentation about the different libraries can be found by visiting the following links:

- `http://scikit-learn.org/stable/modules/preprocessing.html`
- `http://scikit-learn.org/stable/modules/generated/sklearn.feature_selection.RFE.html`
- `https://seaborn.pydata.org/`
- `https://matplotlib.org/mpl_toolkits/index.html`

Performing exploratory analysis and visualization

In situations where the goal is to predict a variable such as `price`, it helps to visualize the data and figure out how the dependent variable is being influenced by other variables. The exploratory analysis gives a lot of insight which is not readily available by looking at the data. This section of the chapter will describe how to visualize and draw insights from big data.

Getting ready

- The head of the `dataframe` can be printed using the `dataframe.head()` function which produces an output, as shown in the following screenshot:

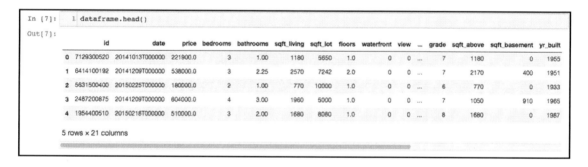

- Similarly, the tail of the `dataframe` can be printed using the `dataframe.tail()` function, which produces an output, as shown in the following screenshot:

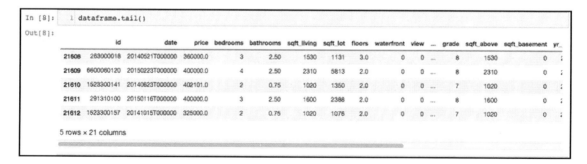

- The `dataframe.describe()` function is used to obtain some basic statistics such as the maximum, minimum, and mean values under each column. This is illustrated in the following screenshot:

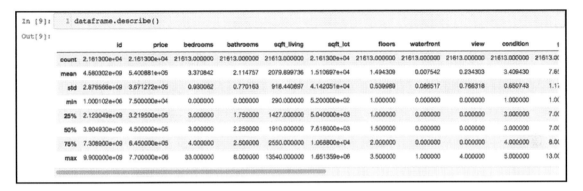

dataframe.describe() function output

- As you can observe, the dataset has 21,613 records of houses sold between 1900 and 2015.
- On taking a closer look at the statistics, we realize that most houses sold have about three bedrooms on average. We can also see that the minimum number of bedrooms in a house is 0 and the largest house has 33 bedrooms and a living area of 13,540 square feet.

How to do it...

1. Let's plot the count of bedrooms in the whole dataset to see how three bedroom houses stand compared to houses with two or one bedrooms. This is done using the following code:

```
dataframe['bedrooms'].value_counts().plot(kind='bar')
plt.title('No. of bedrooms')
plt.xlabel('Bedrooms')
plt.ylabel('Count')
sns.despine
```

2. We can also plot a pie chart of the same data using the following commands:

```
dataframe['bedrooms'].value_counts().plot(kind='pie')
plt.title('No. of bedrooms')
```

3. Next, let's try to see the number of floors in houses that are sold most frequently in King County. This may be done by plotting a bar graph using the following commands:

```
dataframe['floors'].value_counts().plot(kind='bar')
plt.title('Number of floors')
plt.xlabel('No. of floors')
plt.ylabel('Count')
sns.despine
```

4. Next, we need to have an idea of what locations have the highest number of houses sold. We can do this by using the latitude and longitude variables from the dataset, as shown in the following code:

```
plt.figure(figsize=(20,20))
sns.jointplot(x=dataframe.lat.values, y=dataframe.long.values,
size=9)
plt.xlabel('Longitude', fontsize=10)
plt.ylabel('Latitude', fontsize=10)
plt.show()
sns.despine()
```

5. Let's also take a look at how the prices compare for houses with different numbers of bedrooms by executing the following commands:

```
 plt.figure(figsize=(20,20))
sns.jointplot(x=dataframe.lat.values, y=dataframe.long.values,
size=9)
plt.xlabel('Longitude', fontsize=10)
plt.ylabel('Latitude', fontsize=10)
plt.show()
sns.despine()
```

6. A plot of the price of houses versus the number of bedrooms is obtained using the following commands:

```
plt.figure(figsize=(20,20))
sns.jointplot(x=dataframe.lat.values, y=dataframe.long.values,
size=9)
plt.xlabel('Longitude', fontsize=10)
plt.ylabel('Latitude', fontsize=10)
plt.show()
sns.despine()
```

7. Similarly, let's see how the price compares to the living area of all the houses sold. This may be done by using the following commands:

```
plt.figure(figsize=(8,8))
plt.scatter(dataframe.price, dataframe.sqft_living)
plt.xlabel('Price')
plt.ylabel('Square feet')
plt.show()
```

8. The condition of houses sold gives us some important information as well. Let's plot this against the prices to get a better idea of the general trends. This is done using the following commands:

```
plt.figure(figsize=(5,5))
plt.bar(dataframe.condition, dataframe.price)
plt.xlabel('Condition')
plt.ylabel('Price')
plt.show()
```

9. We can see which zip codes have the most house sales in King County by using the following commands:

```
plt.figure(figsize=(8,8))
plt.scatter(dataframe.zipcode, dataframe.price)
plt.xlabel('Zipcode')
plt.ylabel('Price')
plt.show()
```

10. Finally, plot the grade of each house versus the price to figure out the trends in house sales based on the grade given to each house using the following commands:

```
plt.figure(figsize=(10,10))
plt.scatter(dataframe.grade, dataframe.price)
plt.xlabel('Grade')
plt.ylabel('Price')
plt.show()
```

How it works...

1. The plot of bedroom counts must give an output, as shown in the following screenshot:

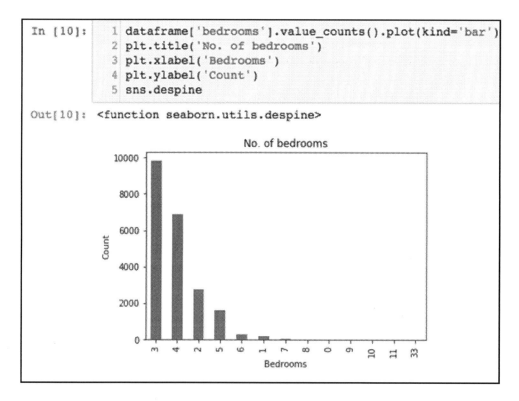

```
In [10]:    1 dataframe['bedrooms'].value_counts().plot(kind='bar')
            2 plt.title('No. of bedrooms')
            3 plt.xlabel('Bedrooms')
            4 plt.ylabel('Count')
            5 sns.despine

Out[10]: <function seaborn.utils.despine>
```

2. It is evident that three bedroom houses are sold the most, followed by four bedroom houses, then by two bedroom houses, and then surprisingly by five bedroom and six bedroom houses.

3. The pie chart of the number of bedrooms gives an output that looks like the following screenshot:

```
In [11]:    1 dataframe['bedrooms'].value_counts().plot(kind='pie')
            2 plt.title('No. of bedrooms')
```

Out[11]: Text(0.5,1,'No. of bedrooms')

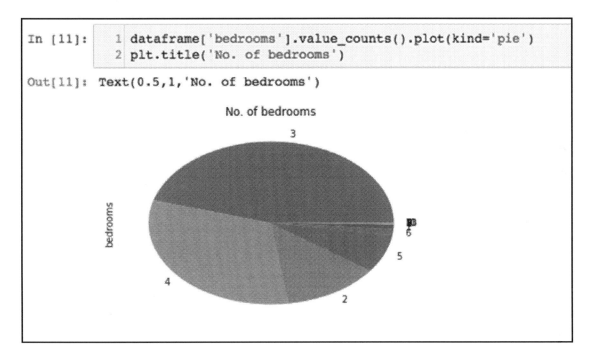

4. You will notice that three bedroom houses account for roughly 50% of all houses sold in King County. It looks like about 25% are four bedroom houses and the remaining 25% is made up of houses with two, five, six bedrooms, and so on.

5. On running the script for most houses sold categorized by the number of floors, we notice the following output:

```
In [12]:    1 dataframe['floors'].value_counts().plot(kind='bar')
            2 plt.title('Number of floors')
            3 plt.xlabel('No. of floors')
            4 plt.ylabel('Count')
            5 sns.despine

Out[12]: <function seaborn.utils.despine>
```

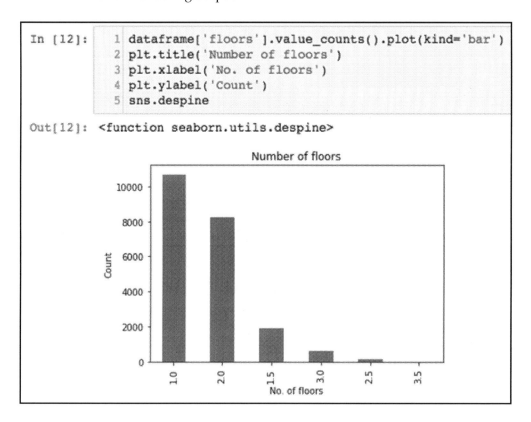

6. It is quite clear that single floor houses sell the most, followed by two-story houses. The count of houses with more than two stories is rather low, which is perhaps an indication of family sizes and the income of residents living in King County.

7. On inspecting the density of houses sold at different locations, we obtain an output, as shown in the following screenshots. It is pretty clear that some locations see a higher density of house sales compared to others:

```
In [13]:    1 plt.figure(figsize=(20,20))
            2 sns.jointplot(x=dataframe.lat.values, y=dataframe.long.values, size=9)
            3 plt.xlabel('Longitude', fontsize=10)
            4 plt.ylabel('Latitude', fontsize=10)
            5 plt.show()
            6 sns.despine()
```

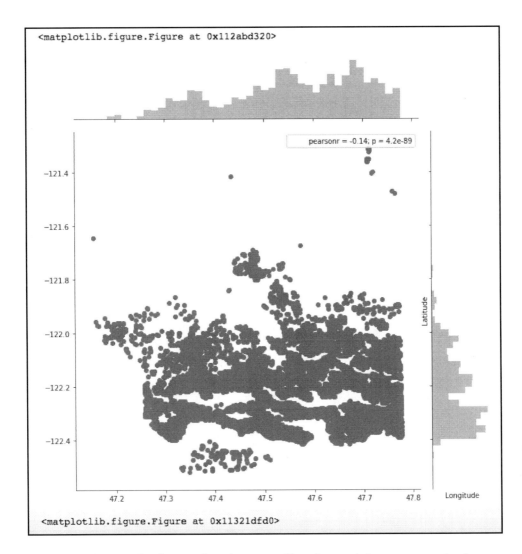

```
<matplotlib.figure.Figure at 0x112abd320>
```

```
<matplotlib.figure.Figure at 0x11321dfd0>
```

8. From the trends observed in the preceding figure, it is easy to notice how a greater number of houses are sold between latitudes -122.2 and -122.4. Similarly, the density of houses sold between longitudes 47.5 and 47.8 is higher compared to other longitudes. This could perhaps be an indication of safer and better-living communities compared to the other communities.

9. On plotting the prices of houses versus the number of bedrooms in the house, we realize that the trends regarding the number of bedrooms in a house are directly proportional to the price up to six bedrooms, and then it becomes inversely proportional, as shown in the following screenshot:

In [14]:
```
1 plt.figure(figsize=(10,5))
2 plt.bar(dataframe.bedrooms, dataframe.price)
3 plt.ylabel('Price')
4 plt.xlabel('No. of bedrooms')
5 plt.show()
```

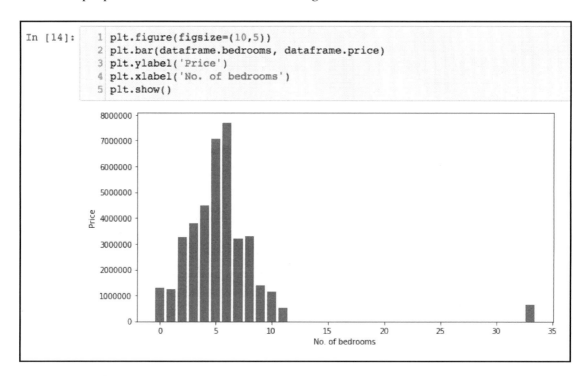

10. Plotting the living area of each house against the price gives us an expected trend of increasing prices with the increasing size of the house. The most expensive house seems to have a living area of 12,000 square feet, as shown in the following screenshot:

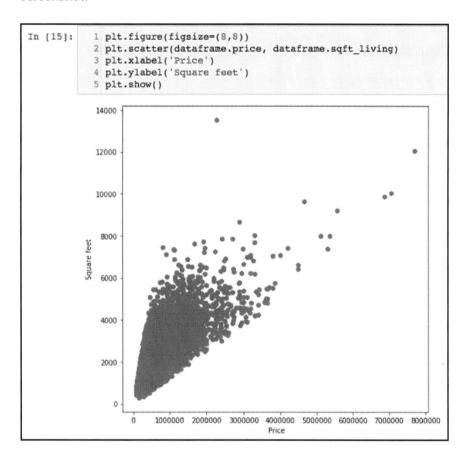

There's more...

1. On plotting the condition of houses versus price, we again notice an expected trend of increasing prices with higher condition ratings, as shown in the following screenshot. Interestingly, five bedroom prices have a lower mean price compared to four bedroom houses, which is possibly due to lesser buyers for such a big house:

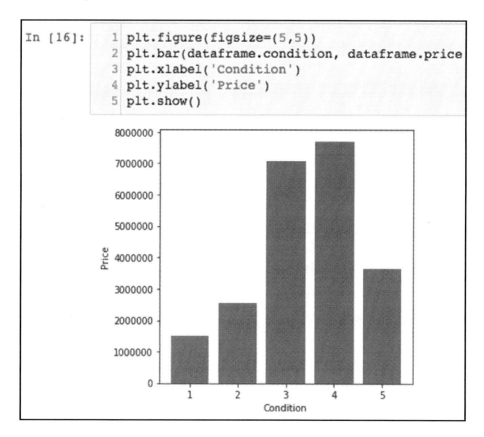

```
In [16]:    1  plt.figure(figsize=(5,5))
            2  plt.bar(dataframe.condition, dataframe.price
            3  plt.xlabel('Condition')
            4  plt.ylabel('Price')
            5  plt.show()
```

2. A plot of the **Zipcode** of the house versus price shows trends in the prices of houses in different zip codes. You may have noticed that certain zip codes, like the ones between 98100 and 98125, have a higher density of houses sold compared to other areas, while the prices of houses in zip codes like 98040 are higher than the average price, perhaps indicating a richer neighborhood, as shown in the following screenshot:

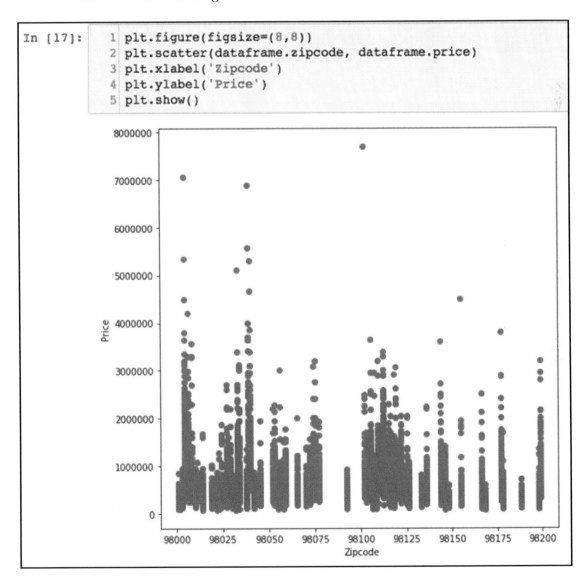

```
In [17]:    1 plt.figure(figsize=(8,8))
            2 plt.scatter(dataframe.zipcode, dataframe.price)
            3 plt.xlabel('Zipcode')
            4 plt.ylabel('Price')
            5 plt.show()
```

3. A plot of the grade of the house versus price shows a consistent increase in price with increasing grade. There seems to be a clear linear relationship between the two, as observed in the output of the following screenshots:

```
In [18]:   1  plt.figure(figsize=(10,10))
           2  plt.scatter(dataframe.grade, dataframe.price)
           3  plt.xlabel('Grade')
           4  plt.ylabel('Price')
           5  plt.show()
```

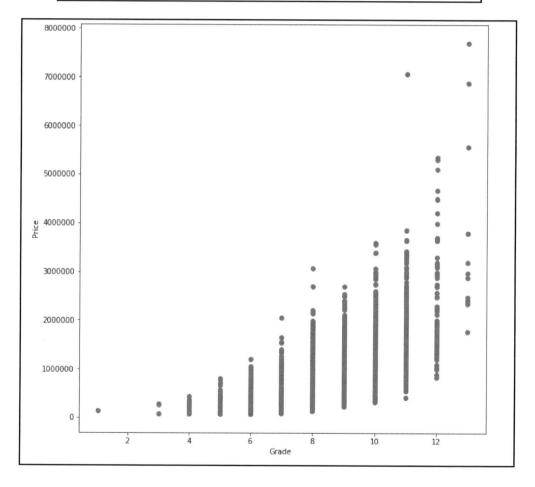

See also

The following links give a good explanation of why data visualization is so important before running any model on the data:

- https://www.slideshare.net/Centerline_Digital/the-importance-of-data-visualization
- https://data-visualization.cioreview.com/cxoinsight/what-is-data-visualization-and-why-is-it-important-nid-11806-cid-163.html
- https://www.techchange.org/2015/05/19/data-visualization-analysis-international-development/

Plotting correlation between price and other features

Now that the initial exploratory analysis is done, we have a better idea of how the different variables are contributing to the price of each house. However, we have no idea of the importance of each variable when it comes to predicting prices. Since we have 21 variables, it becomes difficult to build models by incorporating all variables in one single model. Therefore, some variables may need to be discarded or neglected if they have lesser significance than other variables.

Getting ready

Correlation coefficients are used in statistics to measure how strong the relationship is between two variables. In particular, Pearson's correlation coefficient is the most commonly used coefficient while performing linear regression. The correlation coefficient usually takes on a value between -1 and +1:

- A correlation coefficient of 1 means that for every positive increase in one variable, there is a positive increase of a fixed proportion in the other. For example, shoe sizes go up in (almost) perfect correlation with foot length.

- A correlation coefficient of -1 means that for every positive increase in one variable, there is a negative decrease of a fixed proportion in the other. For example, the amount of gas in a tank decreases in (almost) perfect correlation with acceleration or the gear mechanism (more gas is used up by traveling for longer periods in first gear compared to fourth gear).
- Zero means that for every increase, there isn't a positive or negative increase. The two just aren't related.

How to do it...

1. Begin by dropping the `id` and `date` features from the dataset using the following commands. We will not be using them in our predictions as the ID variables are all unique and have no values in our analysis while the dates require a different function to handle them correctly. This is left as an exercise for the reader to do:

```
x_df = dataframe.drop(['id','date',], axis = 1)
x_df
```

2. Copy the dependent variable (house prices, in this case) into a new `dataframe` using the following commands:

```
y = dataframe[['price']].copy()
y_df = pd.DataFrame(y)
y_df
```

3. The correlation between price and every other variable can be manually found using the following script:

```
print('Price Vs Bedrooms: %s' %
x_df['price'].corr(x_df['bedrooms']))
print('Price Vs Bathrooms: %s' %
x_df['price'].corr(x_df['bathrooms']))
print('Price Vs Living Area: %s' %
x_df['price'].corr(x_df['sqft_living']))
print('Price Vs Plot Area: %s' %
x_df['price'].corr(x_df['sqft_lot']))
print('Price Vs No. of floors: %s' %
x_df['price'].corr(x_df['floors']))
print('Price Vs Waterfront property: %s' %
x_df['price'].corr(x_df['waterfront']))
print('Price Vs View: %s' % x_df['price'].corr(x_df['view']))
print('Price Vs Grade: %s' % x_df['price'].corr(x_df['grade']))
print('Price Vs Condition: %s' %
```

```
x_df['price'].corr(x_df['condition']))
 print('Price Vs Sqft Above: %s' %
x_df['price'].corr(x_df['sqft_above']))
 print('Price Vs Basement Area: %s' %
x_df['price'].corr(x_df['sqft_basement']))
 print('Price Vs Year Built: %s' %
x_df['price'].corr(x_df['yr_built']))
 print('Price Vs Year Renovated: %s' %
x_df['price'].corr(x_df['yr_renovated']))
 print('Price Vs Zipcode: %s' %
x_df['price'].corr(x_df['zipcode']))
 print('Price Vs Latitude: %s' % x_df['price'].corr(x_df['lat']))
 print('Price Vs Longitude: %s' % x_df['price'].corr(x_df['long']))
```

4. Besides the preceding method, an easier way to find the correlation between one variable and all other variables (or columns) in a `dataframe` is done by using just one line in the following manner:
```
x_df.corr().iloc[:,-19]
```

5. The correlated variables may be plotted using the `seaborn` library and the following script:

```
sns.pairplot(data=x_df,
x_vars=['price'],
y_vars=['bedrooms', 'bathrooms', 'sqft_living',
'sqft_lot', 'floors', 'waterfront','view',
'grade','condition','sqft_above','sqft_basement',
'yr_built','yr_renovated','zipcode','lat','long'],
size = 5)
```

How it works...

1. After dropping the `id` and `date` variables, the new `dataframe`, which is named `x_df`, contains 19 variables or columns, as shown in the following screenshots. For the purposes of this book, only the first ten entries are printed out:

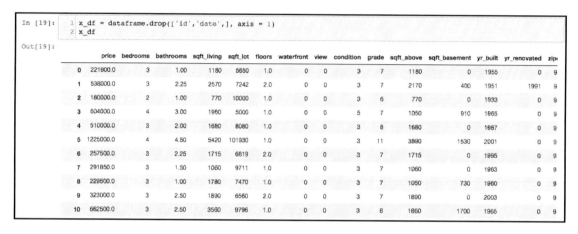

In [19]:	`1 x_df = dataframe.drop(['id','date',], axis = 1)`
	`2 x_df`

Out[19]:

	price	bedrooms	bathrooms	sqft_living	sqft_lot	floors	waterfront	view	condition	grade	sqft_above	sqft_basement	yr_built	yr_renovated	zip
0	221900.0	3	1.00	1180	5650	1.0	0	0	3	7	1180	0	1955	0	9
1	538000.0	3	2.25	2570	7242	2.0	0	0	3	7	2170	400	1951	1991	9
2	180000.0	2	1.00	770	10000	1.0	0	0	3	6	770	0	1933	0	9
3	604000.0	4	3.00	1960	5000	1.0	0	0	5	7	1050	910	1965	0	9
4	510000.0	3	2.00	1680	8080	1.0	0	0	3	8	1680	0	1987	0	9
5	1225000.0	4	4.50	5420	101930	1.0	0	0	3	11	3890	1530	2001	0	9
6	257500.0	3	2.25	1715	6819	2.0	0	0	3	7	1715	0	1995	0	9
7	291850.0	3	1.50	1060	9711	1.0	0	0	3	7	1060	0	1963	0	9
8	229500.0	3	1.00	1780	7470	1.0	0	0	3	7	1050	730	1960	0	9
9	323000.0	3	2.50	1890	6560	2.0	0	0	3	7	1890	0	2003	0	9
10	662500.0	3	2.50	3560	9796	1.0	0	0	3	8	1860	1700	1965	0	9

First 10 entries of output

21611	400000.0	3	2.50	1600
21612	325000.0	2	0.75	1020

21613 rows × 19 columns

2. On creating a new dataframe with only the dependent variable (price), you will see an output as follows. This new dataframe is named y_df. Again, only the first ten entries of the price column are printed for illustration purposes:

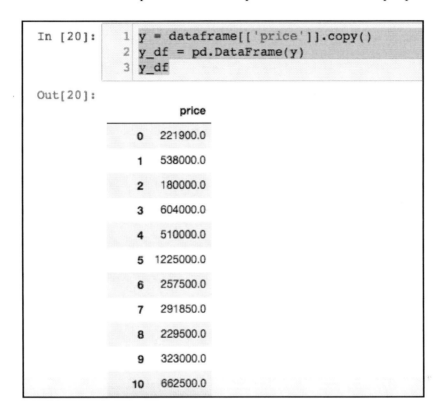

```
In [20]:    1  y = dataframe[['price']].copy()
            2  y_df = pd.DataFrame(y)
            3  y_df
```

Out[20]:

	price
0	221900.0
1	538000.0
2	180000.0
3	604000.0
4	510000.0
5	1225000.0
6	257500.0
7	291850.0
8	229500.0
9	323000.0
10	662500.0

3. The correlation between price and other variables is shown in the following screenshot:

```
In [21]:   1  print('Price Vs Bedrooms: %s' % x_df['price'].corr(x_df['bedrooms']))
           2  print('Price Vs Bathrooms: %s' % x_df['price'].corr(x_df['bathrooms']))
           3  print('Price Vs Living Area: %s' % x_df['price'].corr(x_df['sqft_living']))
           4  print('Price Vs Plot Area: %s' % x_df['price'].corr(x_df['sqft_lot']))
           5  print('Price Vs No. of floors: %s' % x_df['price'].corr(x_df['floors']))
           6  print('Price Vs Waterfront property: %s' % x_df['price'].corr(x_df['waterfront']))
           7  print('Price Vs View: %s' % x_df['price'].corr(x_df['view']))
           8  print('Price Vs Grade: %s' % x_df['price'].corr(x_df['grade']))
           9  print('Price Vs Condition: %s' % x_df['price'].corr(x_df['condition']))
          10  print('Price Vs Sqft Above: %s' % x_df['price'].corr(x_df['sqft_above']))
          11  print('Price Vs Basement Area: %s' % x_df['price'].corr(x_df['sqft_basement']))
          12  print('Price Vs Year Built: %s' % x_df['price'].corr(x_df['yr_built']))
          13  print('Price Vs Year Renovated: %s' % x_df['price'].corr(x_df['yr_renovated']))
          14  print('Price Vs Zipcode: %s' % x_df['price'].corr(x_df['zipcode']))
          15  print('Price Vs Latitude: %s' % x_df['price'].corr(x_df['lat']))
          16  print('Price Vs Longitude: %s' % x_df['price'].corr(x_df['long']))

          Price Vs Bedrooms: 0.308349598146
          Price Vs Bathrooms: 0.525137505414
          Price Vs Living Area: 0.702035054612
          Price Vs Plot Area: 0.0896608605871
          Price Vs No. of floors: 0.256793887551
          Price Vs Waterfront property: 0.266369434031
          Price Vs View: 0.397293488295
          Price Vs Grade: 0.66743425602
          Price Vs Condition: 0.036361789129
          Price Vs Sqft Above: 0.605567298356
          Price Vs Basement Area: 0.323816020712
          Price Vs Year Built: 0.0540115314948
          Price Vs Year Renovated: 0.126433793441
          Price Vs Zipcode: -0.0532028542983
          Price Vs Latitude: 0.307003479995
          Price Vs Longitude: 0.0216262410393
```

4. You may have noticed that the sqft_living variable is most highly correlated with the price and has a correlation coefficient of 0.702035. The next most highly correlated variable is grade, with a correlation coefficient of 0.667434 followed by sqft_above, which has a correlation coefficient of 0.605567. Zipcode is the least correlated variable with price and has a correlation coefficient of -0.053202.

There's more...

- The correlation coefficients found using the simplified code gives the exact same values but also gives the correlation of price with itself, which turns out to be a value of 1.0000, as expected. This is illustrated in the following screenshot:

```
In [22]:    1  x_df.corr().iloc[:,-19]

Out[22]: price                1.000000
         bedrooms             0.308350
         bathrooms            0.525138
         sqft_living          0.702035
         sqft_lot             0.089661
         floors               0.256794
         waterfront           0.266369
         view                 0.397293
         condition            0.036362
         grade                0.667434
         sqft_above           0.605567
         sqft_basement        0.323816
         yr_built             0.054012
         yr_renovated         0.126434
         zipcode             -0.053203
         lat                  0.307003
         long                 0.021626
         sqft_living15        0.585379
         sqft_lot15           0.082447
         Name: price, dtype: float64
```

- The coefficients of correlation plotted using the `seaborn` library are presented in the following screenshots. Note that price is on the x-axis for each plot:

```
In [23]:    1  sns.pairplot(data=x_df,
            2                   x_vars=['price'],
            3                   y_vars=['bedrooms', 'bathrooms', 'sqft_living',
            4                           'sqft_lot', 'floors', 'waterfront','view',
            5                           'grade','condition','sqft_above','sqft_basement',
            6                           'yr_built','yr_renovated','zipcode','lat','long'],
            7               size = 5)
            8
```

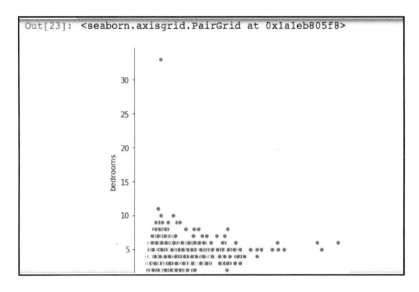

Plotting of coefficients of correlation

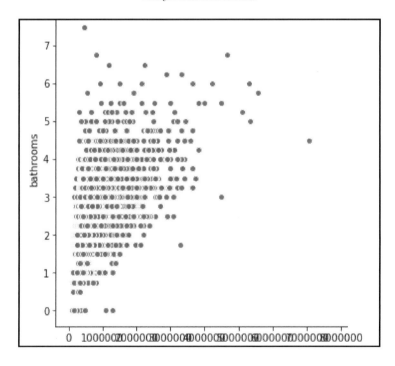

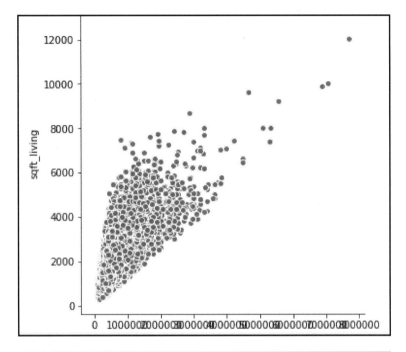

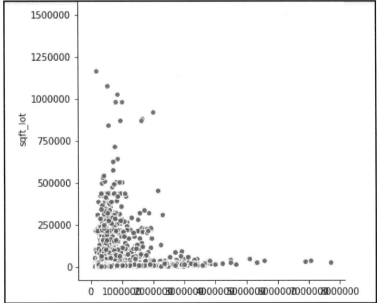

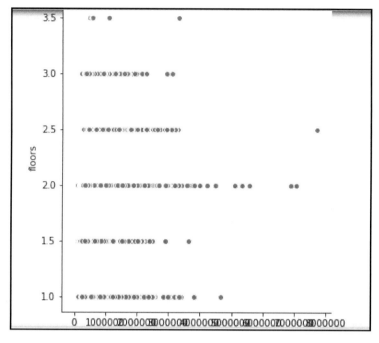

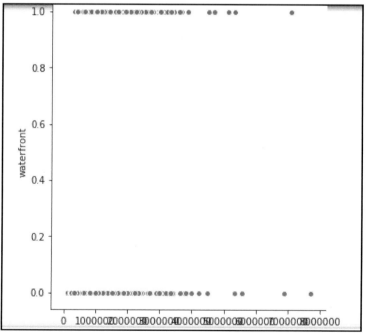

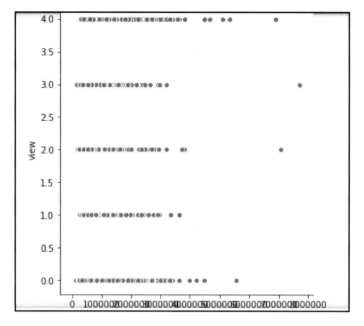

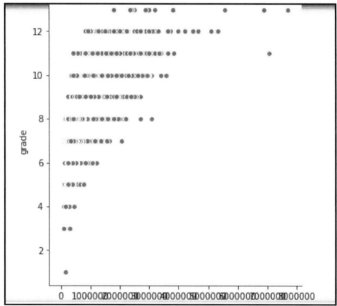

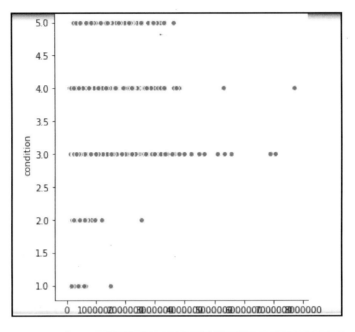

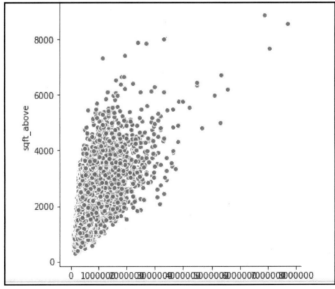

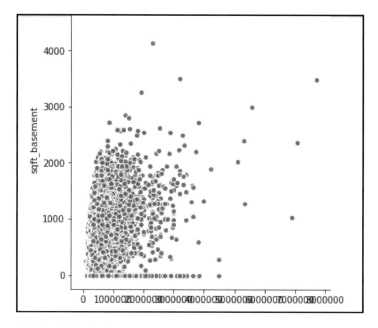

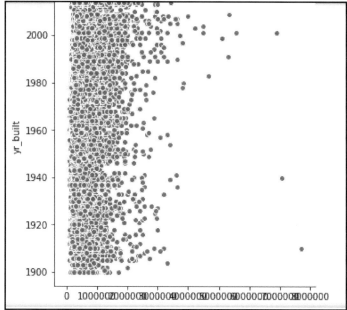

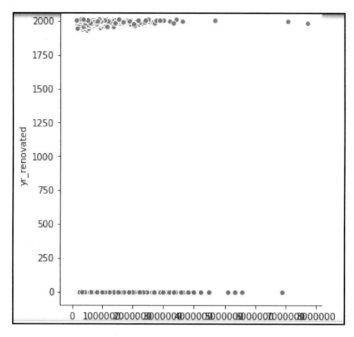

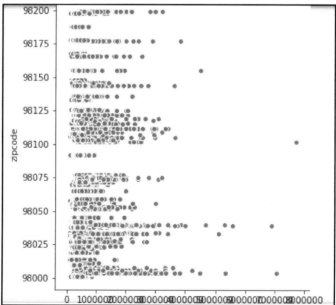

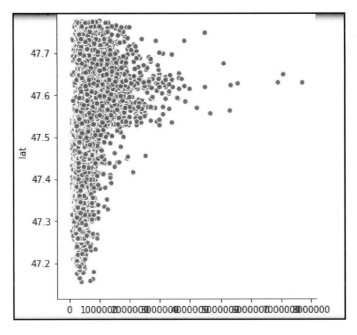

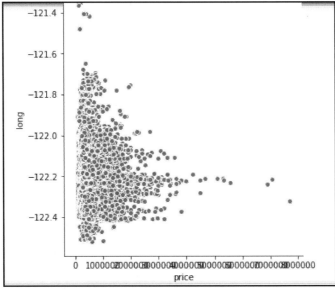

See also

The following links give an excellent explanation of Pearson's correlation coefficient and how it is manually calculated:
```
https://en.wikipedia.org/wiki/Pearson_correlation_coefficient
http://www.statisticshowto.com/probability-and-statistics/correlation-
coefficient-formula/
```

Predicting the price of a house

This section will deal with building a simple linear model to predict house prices using all the features in the current `dataframe`. We will then evaluate the model and try to improve the accuracy by using a more complex model in the latter half of the section.

Getting ready

Visit the following links to understand how linear regression works and how to use the linear regression model in the Scikit Learn library:
```
https://en.wikipedia.org/wiki/Linear_regression
```
```
http://www.stat.yale.edu/Courses/1997-98/101/linreg.htm
```
```
https://newonlinecourses.science.psu.edu/stat501/node/251/
```
```
http://scikit-learn.org/stable/modules/generated/sklearn.linear_model.
LinearRegression.html
```
```
http://scikit-learn.org/stable/modules/linear_model.html
```

How to do it...

1. Drop the `Price` column from the `x_df` dataframe and save it into a new `dataframe` named `x_df2` using the following script:

    ```
    x_df2 = x_df.drop(['price'], axis = 1)
    ```

2. Declare a variable named `reg` and equate it to the `LinearRegression()` function from the Scikit Learn library using the following script:

```
reg=linear_model.LinearRegression()
```

3. Split the dataset into test and train using the following script:

```
x_train,x_test,y_train,y_test =
train_test_split(x_df2,y_df,test_size=0.4,random_state=4)
```

4. Fit the model over the training set using the following script:

```
reg.fit(x_train,y_train)
```

5. Print the coefficients generated from applying linear regression to the training and test sets by using the `reg.coef_` command.

6. Take a look at the column of predictions generated by the model using the following script:

```
predictions=reg.predict(x_test)
predictions
```

7. Print the accuracy of the model using the following command:

```
reg.score(x_test,y_test)
```

How it works...

1. The output after fitting the regression model to the training sets must look like the following screenshot:

```
In [24]:    1 x_df2 = x_df.drop(['price'], axis = 1)

In [25]:    1 reg=linear_model.LinearRegression()

In [26]:    1 x_train,x_test,y_train,y_test = train_test_split(x_df2,y_df,test_size=0.4,random_state=4)

In [27]:    1 reg.fit(x_train,y_train)
Out[27]: LinearRegression(copy_X=True, fit_intercept=True, n_jobs=1, normalize=False)
```

2. The `reg.coeff_` command generates 18 coefficients, one for each variable in the dataset, as shown in the following screenshot:

```
In [28]:    1 reg.coef_

Out[28]:  array([[ -3.51758560e+04,    4.15668761e+04,    1.09783333e+02,
                    1.29887801e-01,    5.45361908e+03,    5.82967182e+05,
                    5.25440940e+04,    2.73530896e+04,    9.41210868e+04,
                    7.32738904e+01,    3.65094422e+01,   -2.57413912e+03,
                    2.41934076e+01,   -5.41779815e+02,    6.05771594e+05,
                   -2.15365692e+05,    1.99717345e+01,   -3.58271235e-01]])
```

3. The coefficients of features/variables with the most positive values have a higher significance on price predictions when compared to the coefficients of features/variables which have negative values. This is the main importance of the regression coefficients.

4. On printing the predictions, you must see an output which is an array of values from 1 to 21,612, one value for each row in the dataset, as shown in the following screenshot:

```
In [29]:    1 predictions=reg.predict(x_test)
            2 predictions

Out[29]:  array([[ 383196.16164229],
                 [ 625423.865746   ],
                 [ 217225.69818279],
                 ...,
                 [ 315480.46820472],
                 [ 551087.68524263],
                 [ 453070.91474855]])
```

5. Finally, on printing the accuracy of the model, we obtained an accuracy of 70.37%, which is not bad for a linear model. This is illustrated in the following screenshot:

```
In [30]:    1 reg.score(x_test,y_test)

Out[30]:  0.70372837536686927
```

There's more...

The linear model does alright at its first attempt, but if we want our model to be more accurate, we will have to use a more complex model with some non-linearities in order to fit well to all the data points. XGBoost is the model we will be using in this section in order to try and improve the accuracy obtained through linear regression. This is done in the following manner:

1. Import the XGBoost library using the import xgboost command.

2. In case this produces an error, you will have to do a pip install of the library through the terminal. This can be done by opening up a new terminal window and issuing the following command:

   ```
   /usr/bin/ruby -e "$(curl -fsSL
   https://raw.githubusercontent.com/Homebrew/install/master/install)"
   ```

3. At this stage, you must see an output which looks like the one shown in the following screenshot:

```
Last login: Wed Jun  6 20:13:34 on ttys002
[Amriths-MacBook-Air:~ Chanti$ /usr/bin/ruby -e "$(curl -fsSL https://raw.githubu]
sercontent.com/Homebrew/install/master/install)"
==> This script will install:
/usr/local/bin/brew
/usr/local/share/doc/homebrew
/usr/local/share/man/man1/brew.1
/usr/local/share/zsh/site-functions/_brew
/usr/local/etc/bash_completion.d/brew
/usr/local/Homebrew

Press RETURN to continue or any other key to abort
==> /usr/bin/sudo /bin/mkdir -p /Library/Caches/Homebrew
Password:
```

4. At this stage, you will be prompted to enter your password. After homebrew is installed, you will see an output like the one shown in the following screenshot:

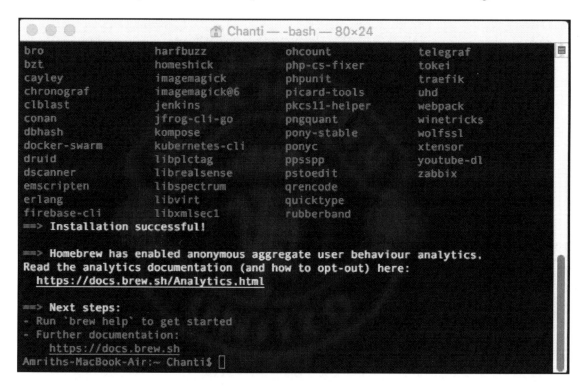

5. Next, install Python using the following command:
   ```
   brew install python
   ```
6. Check your installation using the `brew doctor` command and follow homebrew's suggestions.
7. Once `Homebrew` is installed, do a pip install of XGBoost using the following command:
   ```
   pip install xgboost
   ```
8. Once it finishes installing, you should be able to import XGBoost into the IPython environment.

Once XGBoost is imported successfully into the Jupyter environment, you will be able to use the functions within the library to declare and store the model. This can be done in the following steps:

9. Declare a variable named `new_model` to store the model and declare all its hyperparameters using the following command:

```
new_model = xgboost.XGBRegressor(n_estimators=750,
learning_rate=0.09,           gamma=0, subsample=0.65,
colsample_bytree=1, max_depth=7)
```

10. The output of the preceding command must look like the one in the following screenshot:

```
In [31]:   1 import xgboost

In [32]:   1 new_model = xgboost.XGBRegressor(n_estimators=750, learning_rate=0.09, gamma=0, subsample=0.65,
           2                     colsample_bytree=1, max_depth=7)
```

11. Split the data into test and training sets and fit the new model to the split data using the following commands:

```
from sklearn.model_selection import train_test_split
traindf, testdf = train_test_split(x_train, test_size = 0.2)
new_model.fit(x_train,y_train)
```

12. At this point, you will see an output like the one shown in the following screenshot:

```
In [33]:   1 from sklearn.model_selection import train_test_split

In [34]:   1 traindf, testdf = train_test_split(x_train, test_size = 0.2)
           2 new_model.fit(x_train,y_train)

Out[34]: XGBRegressor(base_score=0.5, booster='gbtree', colsample_bylevel=1,
            colsample_bytree=1, gamma=0, learning_rate=0.09, max_delta_step=0,
            max_depth=7, min_child_weight=1, missing=None, n_estimators=750,
            n_jobs=1, nthread=None, objective='reg:linear', random_state=0,
            reg_alpha=0, reg_lambda=1, scale_pos_weight=1, seed=None,
            silent=True, subsample=0.65)
```

13. Finally, use the newly fitted model to predict the house prices and evaluate the new model using the following commands:

```
from sklearn.metrics import explained_variance_score
predictions = new_model.predict(x_test)
print(explained_variance_score(predictions,y_test))
```

14. On executing the preceding commands, you must see an output like the one shown in the following screenshot:

```
In [35]:   1  from sklearn.metrics import explained_variance_score
           2  predictions = new_model.predict(x_test)
           3  print(explained_variance_score(predictions,y_test))

0.877998269295
```

15. Notice that the new model's accuracy is now 87.79 %, which is approximately 88%. This is considered optimal.

16. In this case, the `number of estimators` is set to 750. After experimenting between 100 to 1,000, it was determined that 750 estimators gave the most optimal accuracy. The `learning rate` is set to 0.09. `Subsample rate` is set at 65%. `Max_depth` is set at 7. There didn't seem to be too much influence of `max_depth` over the model's accuracy. However, the accuracy did show improvement in using slower learning rates. By experimenting with various hyperparameters, we were able to further improve accuracy to 89%.

17. Future steps involve one hot encoding variables such as bedrooms, bathrooms, floors, zipcodes, and so on, and normalizing all the variables before model fitting. Try to tune the hyperparameters such as learning rate, number of estimators in the XGBoost model, subsampling rates, and so on to see how they influence model accuracy. This is left as an exercise for the reader.

18. Also, you may want to try and use cross-validation along with XGBoost in order to figure out the optimal number of trees in the model, which would further improve accuracy.

19. Another exercise that can be done is using different sizes of test and train datasets as well as incorporating the `date` variable during training. In our case, we have split it into a ratio of 80% training data and 20% test data. Try to increase the test set to 40% and see how the model accuracy changes.

See also

Visit the following links to understand how to tune the hyperparameters in the XGBoost model as well as how to implement cross-validation with XGBoost:

```
https://xgboost.readthedocs.io/en/latest/python/index.html
```

```
http://xgboost.readthedocs.io/en/latest/get_started/
```

```
https://www.kaggle.com/cast42/xg-cv
```

Predicting Apple Stock Market Cost with LSTM

9

Stock market predictions have been going on for many years and it has spawned an entire industry of prognosticators. It shouldn't come as a surprise since it can turn a significant profit if predicted properly. Understanding when is a good time to buy or sell a stock is key to getting the upper hand on Wall Street. This chapter will focus on creating a deep learning model using LSTM on Keras to predict the stock market quote of AAPL.

The following recipes will be covered in this chapter:

- Downloading stock market data for Apple
- Exploring and visualizing stock market data for Apple
- Preparing stock data for model performance
- Building the LSTM model
- Evaluating the LSTM model

Downloading stock market data for Apple

There are many resources for downloading stock market data for Apple. For our purposes, we will be using the Yahoo! Finance website.

Getting ready

This section will require initializing a Spark cluster that will be used for all recipes in this chapter. A Spark notebook can be initialized in the terminal using `sparknotebook`, as seen in the following screenshot:

A `SparkSession` can be initialized in a Jupyter notebook using the following script:

```
spark = SparkSession.builder \
    .master("local") \
    .appName("StockMarket") \
    .config("spark.executor.memory", "6gb") \
    .getOrCreate()
```

How to do it...

The following section walks through the steps for downloading historical stock market data for Apple.

1. Visit the following website to track the daily historical adjusted closing stock value for Apple, which has a stock ticker value of AAPL: `https://finance.yahoo.com/quote/AAPL/history`

2. Set and apply the following parameters to the **Historical Data** tab:
    1. **Time Period: Jan 01, 2000 - Apr 30, 2018.**
    2. **Show: Historical prices.**
    3. **Frequency: Daily.**

3. Download the dataset with the specified parameter to a `.csv` file by clicking on the **Download Data** link, as seen in the following screenshot:

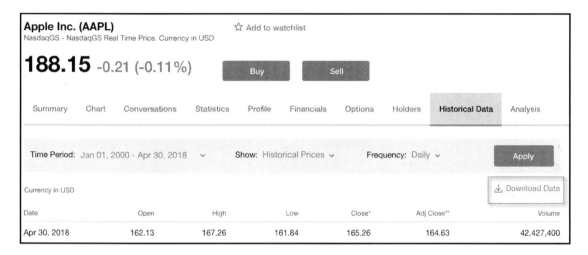

4. Download the file, `AAPL.csv`, and then upload the same dataset to a Spark dataframe using the following script:

```
df =spark.read.format('com.databricks.spark.csv')\
    .options(header='true', inferschema='true')\
    .load('AAPL.csv')
```

How it works...

The following section explains how the stock market data is incorporated into a Jupyter notebook.

1. Yahoo! Finance is a great source for stock market quotes for publicly traded companies. The stock quote for Apple, AAPL, is traded on NASDAQ and the historical quotes can be captured for model development and analysis purposes. Yahoo! Finance gives you the option to capture stock quotes on a daily, weekly, or monthly snapshot.

2. The purpose of this chapter is to forecast stock at a daily level, as that would pull in the most amount of data into our training model. We can do this by tracing data back to January 1, 2000, all the way to April 30, 2018.

3. Once our parameters are set for download, we receive a nicely formatted comma-separated value file from Yahoo! Finance that can be easily converted into a Spark dataframe with minimal issues.

4. The dataframe will allow us to view the **Date, Open, High, Low, Close, Adj Close**, and **Volume** of the stock on a daily basis. The columns in the dataframe track the opening and closing stock values as well as the highest and lowest values traded during that day. The number of shares traded during the day is also captured. The output of the Spark dataframe, `df`, can be shown by executing `df.show()`, as you can see in the following screenshot:

```
In [1]: spark = SparkSession.builder \
        .master("local") \
        .appName("StockMarket") \
        .config("spark.executor.memory", "6gb") \
        .getOrCreate()

In [2]: df =spark.read.format('com.databricks.spark.csv')\
                    .options(header='true', inferschema='true')\
                    .load('AAPL.csv')

In [3]: df.show()

        +-------------------+--------+--------+--------+--------+---------+---------+
        |               Date|    Open|    High|     Low|   Close|Adj Close|   Volume|
        +-------------------+--------+--------+--------+--------+---------+---------+
        |2000-01-03 00:00:00|3.745536|4.017857|3.631696|3.997768|  2.69592|133949200|
        |2000-01-04 00:00:00|3.866071|3.950893|3.613839|3.660714| 2.468626|128094400|
        |2000-01-05 00:00:00|3.705357|3.948661|3.678571|3.714286| 2.504751|194580400|
        |2000-01-06 00:00:00|3.790179|3.821429|3.392857|3.392857| 2.287994|191993200|
        |2000-01-07 00:00:00|3.446429|3.607143|3.410714|3.553571| 2.396373|115183600|
        |2000-01-10 00:00:00|3.642857|3.651786|3.383929|3.491071| 2.354226|126266000|
        |2000-01-11 00:00:00|3.426339|3.549107|3.232143|  3.3125| 2.233805|110387200|
        |2000-01-12 00:00:00|3.392857|3.410714|3.089286|3.113839| 2.099837|244017200|
        |2000-01-13 00:00:00|3.374439|3.526786|3.303571|3.455357| 2.330141|258171200|
        |2000-01-14 00:00:00|3.571429|3.651786|3.549107|3.587054| 2.418951| 97594000|
        |2000-01-18 00:00:00|3.607143|3.785714|3.587054|3.712054| 2.503246|114794400|
        |2000-01-19 00:00:00|3.772321|3.883929|3.691964|3.805804| 2.566468|149410800|
        |2000-01-20 00:00:00|   4.125|4.339286|4.053571|4.053571| 2.733551|457783200|
        |2000-01-21 00:00:00|4.080357|4.080357|3.935268|3.975446| 2.680867|123981200|
        |2000-01-24 00:00:00|3.872768|4.026786|3.754464|3.794643| 2.558941|110219200|
        |2000-01-25 00:00:00|    3.75|4.040179| 3.65625|4.008929| 2.703446|124286400|
        |2000-01-26 00:00:00|3.928571|4.078125|3.919643|3.935268| 2.653772| 91789600|
        |2000-01-27 00:00:00|3.886161|4.035714|3.821429|3.928571| 2.649256| 85036000|
        |2000-01-28 00:00:00|3.863839|3.959821| 3.59375|3.629464| 2.447552|105837200|
        |2000-01-31 00:00:00|3.607143|3.709821|   3.375|3.705357| 2.498731|175420000|
        +-------------------+--------+--------+--------+--------+---------+---------+
        only showing top 20 rows
```

There's more...

Python had stock market APIs that allowed you to automatically connect and pull back stock market quotes for publicly traded companies such as Apple. You would be required to input parameters and retrieve the data that can be stored in a dataframe. However, as of April 2018, the *Yahoo! Finance* API is no longer operational and therefore not a reliable solution for extracting data for this chapter.

See also

`Pandas_datareader` is a very powerful library for extracting data from websites such as Yahoo! Finance. To learn more about the library and how it may connect back to Yahoo! Finance once it is back online, visit the following website:

`https://github.com/pydata/pandas-datareader`

Exploring and visualizing stock market data for Apple

Before any modeling and predictions are performed on the data, it is important to first explore and visualize the data at hand for any hidden gems.

Getting ready

We will perform transformations and visualizations on the dataframe in this section. This will require importing the following libraries in Python:

- `pyspark.sql.functions`
- `matplotlib`

How to do it...

The following section walks through the steps to explore and visualize the stock market data.

1. Transform the `Date` column in the dataframe by removing the timestamp using the following script:

```
import pyspark.sql.functions as f
df = df.withColumn('date', f.to_date('Date'))
```

2. Create a for-cycle to add three additional columns to the dataframe. The loop breaks apart the `date` field into `year`, `month`, and `day`, as seen in the following script:

```
date_breakdown = ['year', 'month', 'day']
for i in enumerate(date_breakdown):
    index = i[0]
    name = i[1]
    df = df.withColumn(name, f.split('date', '-')[index])
```

3. Save a subset of the Spark dataframe to a `pandas` dataframe called `df_plot` using the following script: `df_plot = df.select('year', 'Adj Close').toPandas()`.

4. Graph and visualize the `pandas` dataframe, `df_plot`, inside of the notebook using the following script:

```
from matplotlib import pyplot as plt
%matplotlib inline

df_plot.set_index('year', inplace=True)
df_plot.plot(figsize=(16, 6), grid=True)
plt.title('Apple stock')
plt.ylabel('Stock Quote ($)')
plt.show()
```

5. Calculate the row and column count of our Spark dataframe using the following script: `df.toPandas().shape`.

6. Execute the following script to determine null values in the dataframe: `df.dropna().count()`.

7. Execute the following script to pull back statistics on `Open`, `High`, `Low`, `Close`, and `Adj Close`:

```
df.select('Open', 'High', 'Low', 'Close', 'Adj
Close').describe().show()
```

How it works...

The following section explains the techniques used and insights gained from exploratory data analysis.

1. The **date** column in the dataframe is more of a date-time column with the time values all ending in **00:00:00**. This is unnecessary for what we will need during our modeling and therefore can be removed from the dataset. Luckily for us, PySpark has a `to_date` function that can do this quite easily. The dataframe, `df`, is transformed using the `withColumn()` function and now only shows the date column without the timestamp, as seen in the following screenshot:

```
In [4]: import pyspark.sql.functions as f
        df = df.withColumn('date', f.to_date('Date'))

In [5]: df.show(n=5)

        +----------+--------+--------+--------+--------+---------+---------+
        |      date|    Open|    High|     Low|   Close|Adj Close|   Volume|
        +----------+--------+--------+--------+--------+---------+---------+
        |2000-01-03|3.745536|4.017857|3.631696|3.997768|  2.69592|133949200|
        |2000-01-04|3.866071|3.950893|3.613839|3.660714| 2.468626|128094400|
        |2000-01-05|3.705357|3.948661|3.678571|3.714286| 2.504751|194580400|
        |2000-01-06|3.790179|3.821429|3.392857|3.392857| 2.287994|191993200|
        |2000-01-07|3.446429|3.607143|3.410714|3.553571| 2.396373|115183600|
        +----------+--------+--------+--------+--------+---------+---------+
        only showing top 5 rows
```

2. For analysis purposes, we want to extract the `day`, `month`, and `year` from the `date` column. We can do this by enumerating through a custom list, `date_breakdown`, to split the date by a – and then adding a new column for **the year**, **month**, and **day** using the `withColumn()` function. The updated dataframe with the newly added columns can be seen in the following screenshot:

```
In [6]:  date_breakdown = ['year', 'month', 'day']
         for i in enumerate(date_breakdown):
             index = i[0]
             name = i[1]
             df = df.withColumn(name, f.split('date', '-')[index])

In [7]:  df.show(n=10)
```

```
+----------+--------+--------+--------+--------+---------+---------+----+-----+---+
|      date|    Open|    High|     Low|   Close|Adj Close|   Volume|year|month|day|
+----------+--------+--------+--------+--------+---------+---------+----+-----+---+
|2000-01-03|3.745536|4.017857|3.631696|3.997768|  2.69592|133949200|2000|   01| 03|
|2000-01-04|3.866071|3.950893|3.613839|3.660714| 2.468626|128094400|2000|   01| 04|
|2000-01-05|3.705357|3.948661|3.678571|3.714286| 2.504751|194580400|2000|   01| 05|
|2000-01-06|3.790179|3.821429|3.392857|3.392857| 2.287994|191993200|2000|   01| 06|
|2000-01-07|3.446429|3.607143|3.410714|3.553571| 2.396373|115183600|2000|   01| 07|
|2000-01-10|3.642857|3.651786|3.383929|3.491071| 2.354226|126266000|2000|   01| 10|
|2000-01-11|3.426339|3.549107|3.232143|  3.3125| 2.233805|110387200|2000|   01| 11|
|2000-01-12|3.392857|3.410714|3.089286|3.113839| 2.099837|244017200|2000|   01| 12|
|2000-01-13|3.374439|3.526786|3.303571|3.455357| 2.330141|258171200|2000|   01| 13|
|2000-01-14|3.571429|3.651786|3.549107|3.587054| 2.418951| 97594000|2000|   01| 14|
+----------+--------+--------+--------+--------+---------+---------+----+-----+---+
only showing top 10 rows
```

One important takeaway is that `PySpark` also has a SQL function for dates that can extract the day, month, or year from a date timestamp. For example, if we were to add a month column to our dataframe, we would use the following script: `df.withColumn("month",f.month("date")).show()`. This is to highlight the fact that there are multiple ways to transform data within Spark.

3. Spark dataframes are more limited in visualization features than `pandas` dataframes. Therefore, we will subset two columns from the Spark dataframe, `df`, and convert them into a `pandas` dataframe for plotting a line or time-series chart. The y-axis will be the adjusted close of the stock and the x-axis will be the year of the date.

4. The pandas dataframe, df_plot, is ready to be plotted using matplotlib once some formatting features are set, such as the grid visibility, the figure size of the plot, and the labels for the title and axes. Additionally, we explicitly state that the index of the dataframe needs to point to the year column. Otherwise, the default index will appear on the x-axis and not the year. The final time-series plot can be seen in the following screenshot:

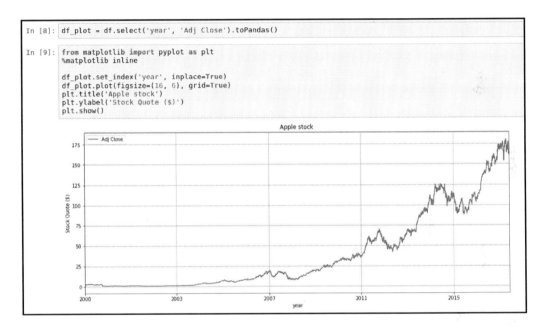

```
In [8]: df_plot = df.select('year', 'Adj Close').toPandas()

In [9]: from matplotlib import pyplot as plt
        %matplotlib inline

        df_plot.set_index('year', inplace=True)
        df_plot.plot(figsize=(16, 6), grid=True)
        plt.title('Apple stock')
        plt.ylabel('Stock Quote ($)')
        plt.show()
```

5. Apple has experienced extensive growth over the last 18 years. While a few years saw some downward dips, the overall trend has been a steady upward move with the last couple of year's stock quotes hovering between $150 and $175.

6. We have made some changes to our dataframe so far, so it is important to get an inventory count of the rows and columns total as this will affect how the dataset is broken up for testing and training purposes later on in the chapter. As can be seen in the following screenshot, we have a total of 10 columns and 4,610 rows:

```
In [10]: df.toPandas().shape
Out[10]: (4610, 10)
```

7. When executing `df.dropna().count()`, we can see that the row count is still 4,610, which is identical to the row count from the previous step, indicating that none of the rows have any null values.

8. Finally, we can get a good read on the row count, mean, standard deviation, minimum, and maximum values of each of the columns that will be used in the model. This can help to identify whether there are anomalies in the data. One important thing to note is that each of the five fields that will be used in the model has a standard deviation higher than the mean value, indicating that the data is more spread out and not so clustered around the mean. The statistics for **Open**, **High**, **Low**, **Close**, and **Adj Close** can be seen in the following screenshot:

```
In [10]: df.toPandas().shape
Out[10]: (4610, 10)

In [11]: df.dropna().count()
Out[11]: 4610

In [12]: df.select('Open', 'High', 'Low', 'Close', 'Adj Close').describe().show()
```

summary	Open	High	Low	Close	Adj Close
count	4610	4610	4610	4610	4610
mean	46.319638522993586	46.75264737505422	45.853888678091	46.31249455574832	39.94770416811271
stddev	49.20256362250941	49.5813980430415	48.81455218501357	49.203718795182205	47.79307553718152
min	0.927857	0.942143	0.908571	0.937143	0.631968
max	182.589996	183.5	180.210007	181.720001	181.021957

There's more...

While dataframes in Spark do not have the same native visualization features that are found in `pandas` dataframes, there are companies that manage Spark for enterprise solutions that allow for advanced visualization capabilities through notebooks without having to use libraries such as `matplotlib`. Databricks is one such company that offers this feature.

The following is an example of a visualization using the built-in features available in notebooks from Databricks:

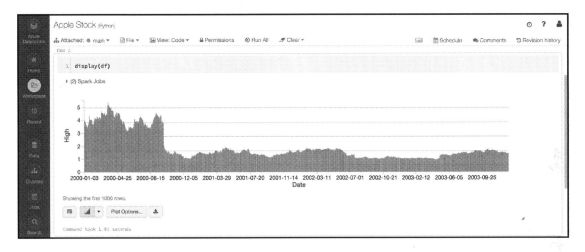

See also

To learn more about Databricks in general, visit the following website: `https://databricks.com/`.

To learn more about visualizations in Databricks notebooks, visit the following website: `https://docs.databricks.com/user-guide/visualizations/index.html`.

To learn more about accessing Databricks through a Microsoft Azure subscription, visit the following website:

`https://azure.microsoft.com/en-us/services/databricks/`

Preparing stock data for model performance

We are almost ready to build a prediction algorithm for the stock value performance of Apple. The remaining task at hand is to prepare the data in a manner that ensures the best possible predictive outcome.

Getting ready

We will perform transformations and visualizations on the dataframe in this section. This will require importing the following libraries in Python:

- `numpy`
- `MinMaxScaler()`

How to do it...

This section walks through the steps for preparing the stock market data for our model.

1. Execute the following script to group the year column by the `Adj Close` count:

```
df.groupBy(['year']).agg({'Adj Close':'count'})\
    .withColumnRenamed('count(Adj Close)', 'Row Count')\
    .orderBy(["year"],ascending=False)\
    .show()
```

2. Execute the following script to create two new dataframes for training and testing purposes:

```
trainDF = df[df.year < 2017]
testDF = df[df.year > 2016]
```

3. Convert the two new dataframes to `pandas` dataframes to get row and column counts with `toPandas()` using the following script:

```
trainDF.toPandas().shape
testDF.toPandas().shape
```

4. As we did previously with `df`, we visualize `trainDF` and `testDF` using the following script:

```
trainDF_plot = trainDF.select('year', 'Adj Close').toPandas()
trainDF_plot.set_index('year', inplace=True)
trainDF_plot.plot(figsize=(16, 6), grid=True)
plt.title('Apple Stock 2000-2016')
plt.ylabel('Stock Quote ($)')
plt.show()

testDF_plot = testDF.select('year', 'Adj Close').toPandas()
testDF_plot.set_index('year', inplace=True)
testDF_plot.plot(figsize=(16, 6), grid=True)
```

```
plt.title('Apple Stock 2017-2018')
plt.ylabel('Stock Quote ($)')
plt.show()
```

5. We create two new arrays, `trainArray` and `testArray`, based on the dataframes with the exception of the date columns using the following script:

```
import numpy as np
trainArray = np.array(trainDF.select('Open', 'High', 'Low',
'Close','Volume', 'Adj Close' ).collect())
testArray = np.array(testDF.select('Open', 'High', 'Low',
'Close','Volume',      'Adj Close' ).collect())
```

6. In order to scale the arrays between 0 and 1, import `MinMaxScaler` from `sklearn` and create a function call, `MinMaxScale`, using the following script:

```
from sklearn.preprocessing import MinMaxScaler
minMaxScale = MinMaxScaler()
```

7. `MinMaxScaler` is then fit on the `trainArray` and used to create two new arrays that are scaled to fit using the following script:

```
minMaxScale.fit(trainArray)

testingArray = minMaxScale.transform(testArray)
trainingArray = minMaxScale.transform(trainArray)
```

8. Split both `testingArray` and `trainingArray` into features, x, and label, y, using the following script:

```
xtrain = trainingArray[:, 0:-1]
xtest = testingArray[:, 0:-1]
ytrain = trainingArray[:, -1:]
ytest = testingArray[:, -1:]
```

9. Execute the following script to retrieve a final inventory of the shape of all four arrays:

```
print('xtrain shape = {}'.format(xtrain.shape))
print('xtest shape = {}'.format(xtest.shape))
print('ytrain shape = {}'.format(ytrain.shape))
print('ytest shape = {}'.format(ytest.shape))
```

10. Execute the following script to plot the training array for the quotes `open`, `high`, `low`, and `close`:

```
plt.figure(figsize=(16,6))
plt.plot(xtrain[:,0],color='red', label='open')
plt.plot(xtrain[:,1],color='blue', label='high')
plt.plot(xtrain[:,2],color='green', label='low')
plt.plot(xtrain[:,3],color='purple', label='close')
plt.legend(loc = 'upper left')
plt.title('Open, High, Low, and Close by Day')
plt.xlabel('Days')
plt.ylabel('Scaled Quotes')
plt.show()
```

11. Additionally, we plot the training array for `volume` using the following script:

```
plt.figure(figsize=(16,6))
plt.plot(xtrain[:,4],color='black', label='volume')
plt.legend(loc = 'upper right')
plt.title('Volume by Day')
plt.xlabel('Days')
plt.ylabel('Scaled Volume')
plt.show()
```

How it works...

This section explains the transformations needed on the data to be used in the model.

1. One of the first steps to building a model is splitting the data into a training and test dataset for model evaluation purposes. Our goal is to use all of the stock quotes from 2000 through 2016 to predict stock trends in 2017-2018. We know from previous sections that we have a total of 4,610 days of stock quotes, but we don't know exactly how many fall in each year. We can use the `groupBy()` function within the dataframe to get a unique count of stock quotes per year, as can be seen in the following screenshot:

```
In [13]: df.groupBy(['year']).agg({'Adj Close':'count'})\
                .withColumnRenamed('count(Adj Close)', 'Row Count')\
                .orderBy ["year"],ascending=False \
                .show()
```

```
+----+---------+
|year|Row Count|
+----+---------+
|2018|       82|
|2017|      251|
|2016|      252|
|2015|      252|
|2014|      252|
|2013|      252|
|2012|      250|
|2011|      252|
|2010|      252|
|2009|      252|
|2008|      253|
|2007|      251|
|2006|      251|
|2005|      252|
|2004|      252|
|2003|      252|
|2002|      252|
|2001|      248|
|2000|      252|
+----+---------+
```

2. 2016 and 2017's combined data represents approximately 7% of the total data, which is a bit small for a testing dataset. However, for the purposes of this model, it should be sufficient. The remaining 93% of the dataset will be used for training purposes between 2000 and 2016. Therefore, two dataframes are created using a filter to determine whether to include or exclude rows before or after 2016.

3. We can now see that the test dataset, testDF, contains 333 rows and that the training dataset, trainDF, contains 4,277 rows. When both are combined, we reach our total row count from our original dataframe, df, of 4,610. Finally, we see that testDF is comprised of 2017 and 2018 data only, which is 251 rows for 2017 and 82 rows for 2018 for a total of 333 rows, as can be seen in the following screenshot:

```
In [14]: trainDF = df[df.year < 2017]
         testDF = df[df.year > 2016]

In [15]: trainDF.toPandas().shape
Out[15]: (4277, 10)

In [16]: testDF.toPandas().shape
Out[16]: (333, 10)
```

Please note that anytime we are converting a Spark dataframe to a `pandas` dataframe it may not always scale for big data. While it will work for our specific example as we are using a relatively small dataset, the conversion to a `pandas` dataframe means that all of the data is loaded into the memory of the driver. Once this conversion occurs, the data is not stored in the Spark worker nodes but is instead to the main driver node. This is not optimal and may produce an out of memory error. If you find that you need to convert to a `pandas` dataframe from Spark to visualize data it is recommended to pull a random sample from Spark or to aggregate the spark data to a more manageable dataset and then visualize in `pandas`.

4. Both testing and training dataframes can be visualized using `matplotlib` once a subset of the data is converted using `toPandas()` to leverage the built-in graphing capabilities of `pandas`. Visualizing the dataframes side by side showcases how the graphs appear to be similar when the y-axis for adjusted close is not scaled. In reality, we can see that `trainDF_plot` starts close to 0, but `testDF_plot` starts closer to 110, as seen in the following two screenshots:

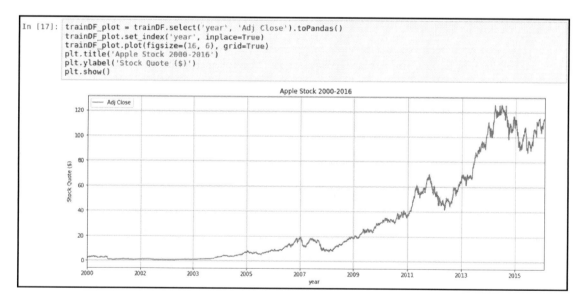

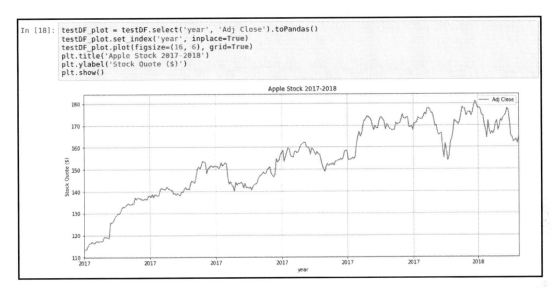

```
In [18]: testDF_plot = testDF.select('year', 'Adj Close').toPandas()
         testDF_plot.set_index('year', inplace=True)
         testDF_plot.plot(figsize=(16, 6), grid=True)
         plt.title('Apple Stock 2017-2018')
         plt.ylabel('Stock Quote ($)')
         plt.show()
```

5. Our stock values, as they stand, don't lend themselves well to deep learning modeling because there isn't a baseline for normalization or standardization. When working with neural networks, it is best to keep the values between 0 and 1 to match outcomes found in sigmoid or step functions that are used for activation. In order for us to accomplish this, we must first convert our `pyspark` dataframes, `trainDF` and `testDF`, into `numpy` arrays, these being `trainArray` and `testArray`. As these are now arrays and not dataframes, we will not be using the date column as the neural network is only interested in numerical values. The first values in each can be seen in the following screenshot:

```
In [19]: import numpy as np
         trainArray = np.array(trainDF.select('Open', 'High', 'Low', 'Close','Volume', 'Adj Close' ).collect())
         testArray = np.array(testDF.select('Open', 'High', 'Low', 'Close','Volume', 'Adj Close' ).collect())

In [20]: print(trainArray[0])
         print('--------------')
         print(testArray[0])

         [  3.74553600e+00    4.01785700e+00    3.63169600e+00    3.99776800e+00
            1.33949200e+08    2.69592000e+00]
         --------------
         [  1.15800003e+02    1.16330002e+02    1.14760002e+02    1.16150002e+02
            2.87819000e+07    1.13410263e+02]
```

6. There are many ways to scale array values to a range between 0 and 1. It involves using the following formula: `scaled array value = (array value - min array value) / (max array value - min array value)`. Fortunately, we do not need to manually make this calculation on arrays. We can leverage the `MinMaxScaler()` function from `sklearn` to scale down both arrays.

7. The `MinMaxScaler()` function is fit on the training array, `trainArray`, and is then applied to create two brand new arrays, `trainingArray` and `testingArray`, that are scaled to values between 0 and 1. The first row for each array can be seen in the following screenshot:

```
In [21]: from sklearn.preprocessing import MinMaxScaler
         minMaxScale = MinMaxScaler()

In [22]: minMaxScale.fit(trainArray)

Out[22]: MinMaxScaler(copy=True, feature_range=(0, 1))

In [23]: testingArray = minMaxScale.transform(testArray)
         trainingArray = minMaxScale.transform(trainArray)

In [24]: print(testingArray[0])
         print('---------------')
         print(trainingArray[0])

         [ 0.86025834  0.86369548  0.8724821   0.87240926  0.01026612  0.90325687]
         ---------------
         [ 0.02110113  0.02302218  0.02086823  0.02317552  0.0672496   0.01653048]
```

8. We are now ready to set our label and feature variables by slicing up the array into x and y for both testing and training purposes. The first five elements in the array are the features or the x values and the last element is the label or y value. The features are composed of the values from **Open**, **High**, **Low**, **Close**, and **Volume**. The label is composed of **Adj Close**. The breakout of the first row for `trainingArray` can be seen in the following screenshot:

```
In [25]: xtrain = trainingArray[:, 0:-1]
         xtest = testingArray[:, 0:-1]
         ytrain = trainingArray[:, -1:]
         ytest = testingArray[:, -1:]

In [26]: trainingArray[0]

Out[26]: array([ 0.02110113,  0.02302218,  0.02086823,  0.02317552,  0.0672496 ,
                 0.01653048])

In [27]: xtrain[0]

Out[27]: array([ 0.02110113,  0.02302218,  0.02086823,  0.02317552,  0.0672496 ])

In [28]: ytrain[0]

Out[28]: array([ 0.01653048])
```

9. A final look at the shape of the four arrays that we will be using in the model can be used to confirm that we have **4,227** matrix rows of training data, **333** matrix rows of test data, **5** elements for features (x), and **1** element for the label (y), as can be seen in the following screenshot:

```
In [29]: print('xtrain shape = {}'.format(xtrain.shape))
         print('xtest shape = {}'.format(xtest.shape))
         print('ytrain shape = {}'.format(ytrain.shape))
         print('ytest shape = {}'.format(ytest.shape))

         xtrain shape = (4277, 5)
         xtest shape = (333, 5)
         ytrain shape = (4277, 1)
         ytest shape = (333, 1)
```

10. The values for the training array, xtrain, for **open**, **low**, **high**, and **close** can be plotted using the newly adjusted scales between 0 and 1 for the quotes, as shown in the following screenshot:

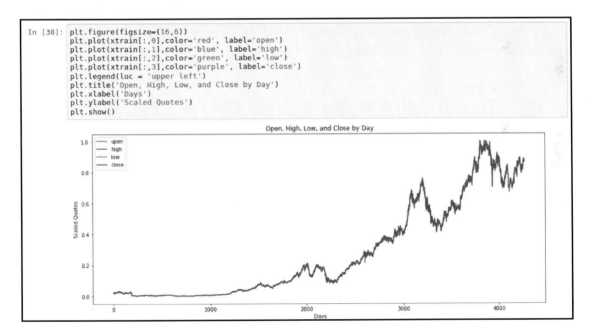

11. Additionally, to **volume** can also be plotted with the scaled volume scores between 0 and 1, as shown in the following screenshot:

```
In [31]: plt.figure(figsize=(16,6))
         plt.plot(xtrain[:,4],color='black', label='volume')
         plt.legend(loc = 'upper right')
         plt.title('Volume by Day')
         plt.xlabel('Days')
         plt.ylabel('Scaled Volume')
         plt.show()
```

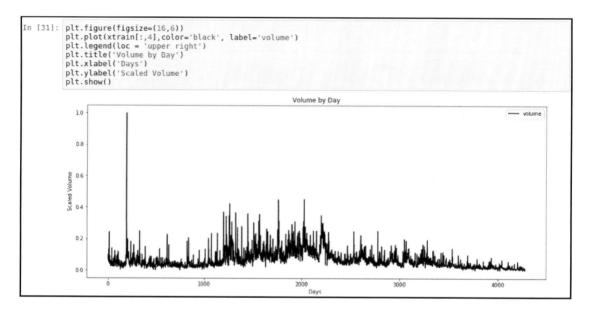

There's more...

While we did use `MinMaxScaler` from `sklearn`, it is also important to understand that there is also a `MinMaxScaler` function that is available directly through `pyspark.ml.feature`. It works exactly the same way by rescaling each feature to a value between 0 and 1. Had we used a machine learning library natively through PySpark in this chapter to make our prediction, we would have used `MinMaxScaler` from `pyspark.ml.feature`.

See also

To learn more about `MinMaxScaler` from `sklearn`, visit the following website:

http://scikit-learn.org/stable/modules/generated/sklearn.preprocessing.
MinMaxScaler.html.

To learn more about `MinMaxScaler` from `pyspark`, visit the following website:

`https://spark.apache.org/docs/2.2.0/ml-features.html#minmaxscaler`.

Building the LSTM model

The data is now in a format compatible with model development in Keras for LSTM modeling. Therefore, we will spend this section setting up and configuring the deep learning model for predicting stock quotes for Apple in 2017 and 2018.

Getting ready

We will perform model management and hyperparameter tuning of our model in this section. This will require importing the following libraries in Python:

```
from keras import models
from keras import layers
```

How to do it...

This section walks through the steps to setting up and tuning the LSTM model.

1. Import the following libraries from `keras` using the following script:

   ```
   from keras import models, layers
   ```

2. Build a `Sequential` model using the following script:

   ```
   model = models.Sequential()
   model.add(layers.LSTM(1, input_shape=(1,5)))
   model.add(layers.Dense(1))
   model.compile(loss='mean_squared_error', optimizer='adam')
   ```

3. Transform the testing and training data sets into three-dimensional arrays using the following script:

   ```
   xtrain = xtrain.reshape((xtrain.shape[0], 1, xtrain.shape[1]))
   xtest = xtest.reshape((xtest.shape[0], 1, xtest.shape[1]))
   ```

4. Fit the `model` using a variable called `loss` with the following script:

```
loss = model.fit(xtrain, ytrain, batch_size=10, epochs=100)
```

5. Create a new array, `predicted`, using the following script:

```
predicted = model.predict(xtest)
```

6. Combine the `predicted` and `ytest` arrays into a single unified array, `combined_array`, using the following script:

```
combined_array = np.concatenate((ytest, predicted), axis = 1)
```

How it works...

This section explains how the LSTM neural network model is configured to train on our dataset.

1. Most of the functionality from `keras` used to build the LSTM model will come from `models` and `layers`.

2. The `LSTM` model that has been built will be defined using a `Sequential` class that works well with time series that are sequence dependent. The LSTM model has an `input_shape = (1,5)` for one dependent variable and five independent variables in our training dataset. Only one `Dense` layer will be used to define the neural network as we are looking to keep the model simple. A loss function is required when compiling a model in keras, and since we are performing it on a recurrent neural network, a `mean_squared_error` calculation is best to determine how close the predicted value is to the actual value. Finally, an optimizer is also defined when the model is compiled to adjust the weights in the neural network. `adam` has given good results, especially when being used with recurrent neural networks.

3. Our current arrays, xtrain and xtest, are currently two-dimensional arrays; however, to incorporate them into the LSTM model, they will need to be converted to three-dimensional arrays using reshape(), as shown in the following screenshot:

```
In [32]: from keras import models, layers

         Using TensorFlow backend.

In [33]: model = models.Sequential()
         model.add(layers.LSTM(1, input_shape=(1,5)))
         model.add(layers.Dense(1))
         model.compile(loss='mean_squared_error', optimizer='adam')

In [34]: xtrain = xtrain.reshape((xtrain.shape[0], 1, xtrain.shape[1]))
         xtest  = xtest.reshape((xtest.shape[0], 1, xtest.shape[1]))

In [35]: print('The shape of xtrain is {}: '.format(xtrain.shape))
         print('The shape of xtest is {}: '.format(xtest.shape))

         The shape of xtrain is (4277, 1, 5):
         The shape of xtest is (333, 1, 5):
```

4. The LSTM model is fit with xtrain and ytrain and the batch size is set to 10 with 100 epochs. The batch size is the setting that defines the number of objects that are trained together. We can go as low or as high as we like in terms of setting the batch size, keeping in mind that the lower the number of batches, the more memory is required. Additionally, an epoch is a measurement of how often the model goes through the entire dataset. Ultimately, these parameters can be tuned based on time and memory allotment.

The **mean squared error** loss in each **epoch** is captured and visualized. After the fifth or sixth **epoch**, we can see that the **loss** tapers off, as shown in the following screenshot:

```
In [36]: loss = model.fit(xtrain, ytrain, batch_size=10, epochs=100)
         4277/4277 [==============================] - 1s 233us/step - loss: 6.8037e-04
         Epoch 92/100
         4277/4277 [==============================] - 1s 303us/step - loss: 6.8333e-04
         Epoch 93/100
         4277/4277 [==============================] - 1s 294us/step - loss: 6.7891e-04
         Epoch 94/100
         4277/4277 [==============================] - 1s 285us/step - loss: 6.7643e-04
         Epoch 95/100
         4277/4277 [==============================] - 1s 249us/step - loss: 6.8788e-04
         Epoch 96/100
         4277/4277 [==============================] - 1s 309us/step - loss: 6.8759e-04
         Epoch 97/100
         4277/4277 [==============================] - 1s 301us/step - loss: 6.7556e-04
         Epoch 98/100
         4277/4277 [==============================] - 1s 298us/step - loss: 6.7970e-04
         Epoch 99/100
         4277/4277 [==============================] - 1s 259us/step - loss: 6.7016e-04
         Epoch 100/100
         4277/4277 [==============================] - 1s 213us/step - loss: 6.8047e-04
```

```
In [37]: plt.plot(loss.history['loss'], label = 'loss')
         plt.title('mean squared error by epoch')
         plt.legend()
         plt.show()
```

5. We can now create a new array, `predicted`, based on the fitted model applied on `xtest` and then combine it with `ytest` to compare them side by side for accuracy purposes.

See also

To learn more about parameter tuning models within keras, visit the following website: https://keras.io/models/model/

Evaluating the model

Here's the moment of truth: we are going to see if our model is able to give us a good prediction for the AAPL stock in 2017 and 2018.

Getting ready

We will perform a model evaluation using the mean squared error. Therefore, we will need to import the following library:

```
import sklearn.metrics as metrics
```

How to do it...

This section walks through visualizing and calculating the predicted vs. actual stock quotes for Apple in 2017 and 2018.

1. Plot a side by side comparison of `Actual` versus `Predicted` stock to compare trends using the following script:

```
plt.figure(figsize=(16,6))
plt.plot(combined_array[:,0],color='red', label='actual')
plt.plot(combined_array[:,1],color='blue', label='predicted')
plt.legend(loc = 'lower right')
plt.title('2017 Actual vs. Predicted APPL Stock')
plt.xlabel('Days')
plt.ylabel('Scaled Quotes')
plt.show()
```

2. Calculate the mean squared error between the actual `ytest` versus `predicted` stock using the following script:

```
import sklearn.metrics as metrics
np.sqrt(metrics.mean_squared_error(ytest,predicted))
```

How it works...

This section explains the results of the LSTM model's evaluation.

1. From a graphical perspective, we can see that our predictions were close to the actual stock quotes from 2017-2018, as shown in the following screenshot:

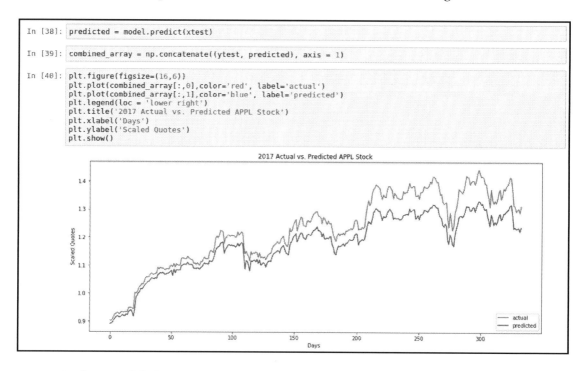

2. Our model shows that the predicted values are closer to the actual values earlier on in the days for 2017 and 2018 than later on. Overall, while it seems that our predicted and actual scores are very close, it would be best to get a mean squared error calculation to understand how much deviation is between the two. As we can see, we have a mean squared error of 0.05841 or approximately 5.8%:

```
In [41]: import sklearn.metrics as metrics
         np.sqrt(metrics.mean_squared_error(ytest,predicted))

Out[41]: 0.05841243272182954
```

See also

In order to learn more about how the mean squared error is calculated within sklearn, visit the following website:

`http://scikit-learn.org/stable/modules/generated/sklearn.metrics.mean_squared_error.html`.

10
Face Recognition Using Deep Convolutional Networks

In this chapter, we will cover the following recipes:

- Downloading and loading the MIT-CBCL dataset into the memory
- Plotting and visualizing images from the directory
- Preprocessing images
- Model building, training, and analysis

Introduction

In today's world, the need to maintain the security of information is becoming increasingly important, as well as increasingly difficult. There are various methods by which this security can be enforced (passwords, fingerprint IDs, PIN numbers, and so on). However, when it comes to ease of use, accuracy, and low intrusiveness, face recognition algorithms have been doing very well. With the availability of high-speed computing and the evolution of deep convolutional networks, it has been made possible to further increase the robustness of these algorithms. They have gotten so advanced that they are now being used as the primary security feature in many electronic devices (for example, iPhoneX) and even banking applications. The goal of this chapter is to develop a robust, pose-invariant face recognition algorithm for use in security systems. For the purposes of this chapter, we will be using the openly available `MIT-CBCL` dataset of face images of 10 different subjects.

Downloading and loading the MIT-CBCL dataset into the memory

In this recipe, we will understand how to download the MIT-CBCL dataset and load it into the memory.

With a predicted worth of $15 billion by 2025, the biometrics industry is poised to grow like never before. Some of the examples of physiological characteristics used for biometric authentication include fingerprints, DNA, face, retina or ear features, and voice. While technologies such as DNA authentication and fingerprints are quite advanced, face recognition brings its own advantages to the table.

Ease of use and robustness due to recent developments in deep learning models are some of the driving factors behind face recognition algorithms gaining so much popularity.

Getting ready

The following key points need to be considered for this recipe:

- The MIT-CBCL dataset is composed of 3,240 images (324 images per subject). In our model, we will make arrangements to augment the data in order to increase model robustness. We will employ techniques such as shifting the subject, rotation, zooming, and shearing of the subject to obtain this augmented data.
- We will use 20% of the dataset to test our model (648 images) by randomly selecting these images from the dataset. Similarly, we randomly select 80% of the images in the dataset and use this as our training dataset (2,592 images).
- The biggest challenge is cropping the images to the exact same size so that they can be fed into the neural network.
- It is a known fact that it is much easier to design a network when all the input images are of the same size. However, since some of the subjects in these images have a side profile or rotated/tilted profiles, we have to adapt our network to take input images of different sizes.

How to do it...

The steps are as follows.

1. Download the `MIT-CBCL` dataset by visiting the **FACE RECOGNITION HOMEPAGE**, which contains a number of databases for face recognition experiments. The link, as well as a screenshot of the homepage, is provided as follows:

   `http://www.face-rec.org/databases/`:

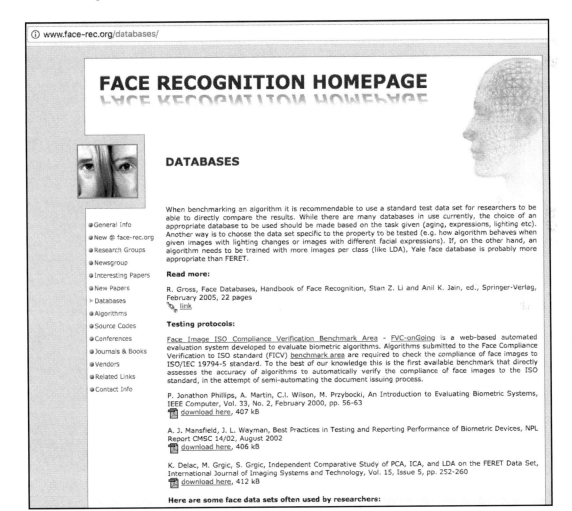

2. Navigate down to the link that is named **MIT-CBCL Face Recognition Database** and click on it, as shown in the following screenshot:

AT&T "The Database of Faces" (formerly "The ORL Database of Faces")

Ten different images of each of 40 distinct subjects. For some subjects, the images were taken at different times, varying the lighting, facial expressions (open / closed eyes, smiling / not smiling) and facial details (glasses / no glasses). All the images were taken against a dark homogeneous background with the subjects in an upright, frontal position (with tolerance for some side movement).

Cohn-Kanade AU Coded Facial Expression Database

Subjects in the released portion of the Cohn-Kanade AU-Coded Facial Expression Database are 100 university students. They ranged in age from 18 to 30 years. Sixty-five percent were female, 15 percent were African-American, and three percent were Asian or Latino. Subjects were instructed by an experimenter to perform a series of 23 facial displays that included single action units and combinations of action units. Image sequences from neutral to target display were digitized into 640 by 480 or 490 pixel arrays with 8-bit precision for grayscale values. Included with the image files are "sequence" files; these are short text files that describe the order in which images should be read.

MIT-CBCL Face Recognition Database

The MIT-CBCL face recognition database contains face images of 10 subjects. It provides two training sets: 1. High resolution pictures, including frontal, half-profile and profile view; 2. Synthetic images (324/subject) rendered from 3D head models of the 10 subjects. The head models were generated by fitting a morphable model to the high-resolution training images. The 3D models are not included in the database. The test set consists of 200 images per subject. We varied the illumination, pose (up to about 30 degrees of rotation in depth) and the background.

Image Database of Facial Actions and Expressions - Expression Image Database

24 subjects are represented in this database, yielding between about 6 to 18 examples of the 150 different requested actions. Thus, about 7,000 color images are included in the database, and each has a matching gray scale image used in the neural network analysis.

Face Recognition Data, University of Essex, UK

395 individuals (male and female), 20 images per individual. Contains images of people of various racial origins, mainly of first year undergraduate students, so the majority of indivuals are between 18-20 years old but some older individuals are also present. Some individuals are wearing glasses and beards.

NIST Mugshot Identification Database

There are images of 1573 individuals (cases) 1495 male and 78 female. The database contains both front and side (profile) views when available. Separating front views and profiles, there are 131 cases with two or more front views and 1418 with only one front view. Profiles have 89 cases with two or more profiles and 1268 with only one profile. Cases with both fronts and profiles have 89 cases with two or more of both fronts and profiles, 27 with two or more fronts and one profile, and 1217 with only one front and one profile.

---

3. Once you have clicked on it, it will take you to a license page on which you are required to accept the license agreement and proceed to the download page. Once on the download page, click on `download now`. This downloads a zip file of about 116 MB. Go ahead and extract the contents into the working directory.

How it works...

The functionality is as follows:

1. The license agreement requires the appropriate citation for the use of the database in any projects. This database was developed by the research team from the Massachusetts Institute of Technology.

2. Credit is hereby given to the Massachusetts Institute of Technology and to the center for biological and computational learning for providing the database of facial images. The license also requires the mentioning of the paper titled *Component-based Face Recognition with 3D Morphable Models, First IEEE Workshop on Face Processing in Video,* Washington, D.C., 2004, B. Weyrauch, J. Huang, B. Heisele, and V. Blanz.

3. The following screenshot describes the license agreement as well as the link to download the dataset:

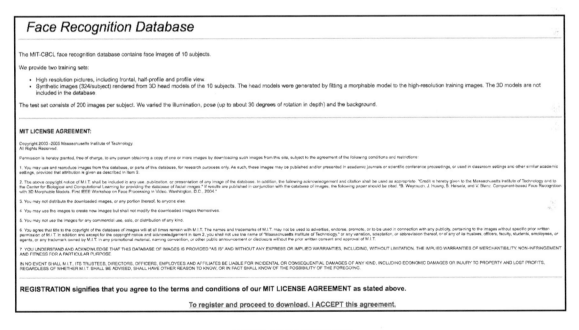

Face Recognition Database Homepage

4. Once the dataset is downloaded and extracted, you will see a folder titled **MIT-CBCL-facerec-database**.

5. For the purposes of this chapter, we will only be using the images in the `training-synthetic` folder, which contains all 3,240 images, as shown in the following screenshot:

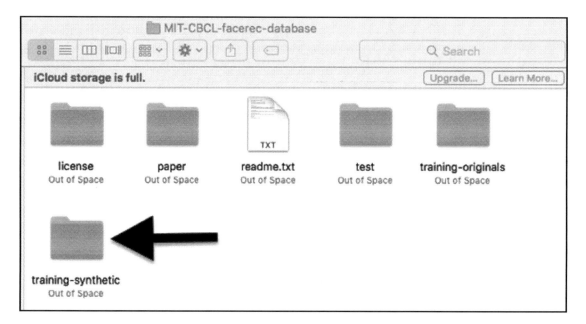

There's more...

For this chapter, you will require the following libraries to be imported by Python:

- `os`
- `matplotlib`
- `numpy`
- `keras`
- `TensorFlow`

The following section of the chapter will deal with importing the necessary libraries and preprocessing the images before building the neural network model and loading them into it.

See also

For complete information on the packages used in this chapter, visit the following links:

- `https://matplotlib.org/`
- `https://docs.python.org/2/library/os.html`
- `https://www.tensorflow.org/get_started/`
- `https://keras.io/layers/about-keras-layers/`
- `https://docs.scipy.org/doc/numpy-1.9.1/reference/`

Plotting and visualizing images from the directory

This section will describe how to read and visualize the downloaded images before they are preprocessed and fed into the neural network for training. This is an important step in this chapter because the images need to be visualized to get a better understanding of the image sizes so they can be accurately cropped to omit the background and preserve only the necessary facial features.

Getting ready

Before beginning, complete the initial setup of importing the necessary libraries and functions as well as setting the path of the working directory.

How to do it...

The steps are as follows:

1. Download the necessary libraries using the following lines of code. The output must result in a line that says `Using TensorFlow backend`, as shown in the screenshot that follows:

```
%matplotlib inline
from os import listdir
from os.path import isfile, join
import matplotlib.pyplot as plt
import matplotlib.image as mpimg
```

```
import numpy as np
from keras.models import Sequential
from keras.layers import Dense, Dropout, Activation, Flatten,
Conv2D
from keras.optimizers import Adam
from keras.layers.normalization import BatchNormalization
from keras.utils import np_utils
from keras.layers import MaxPooling2D
from keras.preprocessing.image import ImageDataGenerator
```

The importing of the libraries is as shown:

```
In [1]:    1 %matplotlib inline
           2 from os import listdir
           3 from os.path import isfile, join
           4 import matplotlib.pyplot as plt
           5 import matplotlib.image as mpimg
           6 import numpy as np
           7 from keras.models import Sequential
           8 from keras.layers import Dense, Dropout, Activation, Flatten
           9 from keras.optimizers import Adam
          10 from keras.layers.normalization import BatchNormalization
          11 from keras.utils import np_utils
          12 from keras.layers import Conv2D, MaxPooling2D
          13 from keras.preprocessing.image import ImageDataGenerator

Using TensorFlow backend.
```

2. Print and set the current working directory as shown in the following screenshot. In our case, the desktop was set as the working directory:

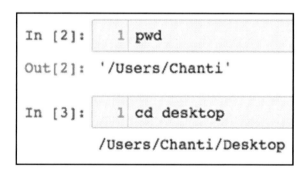

```
In [2]:    1 pwd

Out[2]:  '/Users/Chanti'


In [3]:    1 cd desktop

         /Users/Chanti/Desktop
```

3. Read all the images directly from the folder by using the commands illustrated in the following screenshot:

```
In [4]:  1  #reading images from the local drive
         2  mypath='MIT-CBCL-facerec-database//training-synthetic'
         3  onlyfiles= [ f for f in listdir(mypath) if isfile(join(mypath,f)) ]
         4  images =np.empty([3240,200,200],dtype=int)
         5  for n in range(0, len(onlyfiles)):
         6    images[n] = mpimg.imread( join(mypath,onlyfiles[n]) ).astype(np.float32)
         7
```

4. Print a few random images from the dataset using the `plt.imshow (images[])` command, as shown in the following screenshots, to get a better idea of the face profiles in the images. This will also give an idea of the size of the image, which will be required at a later stage:

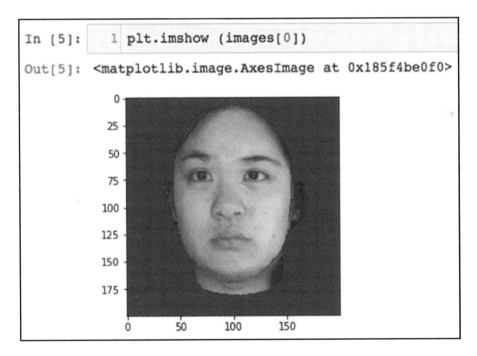

5. Shown here are the images of different test subjects from the first image.

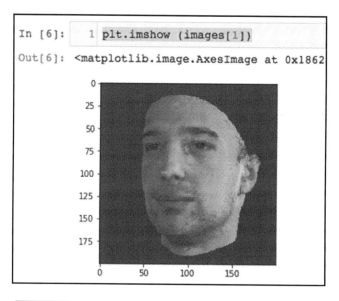

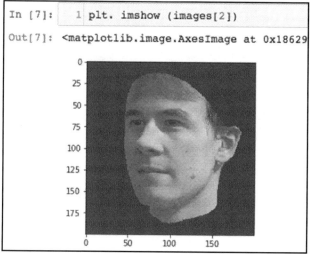

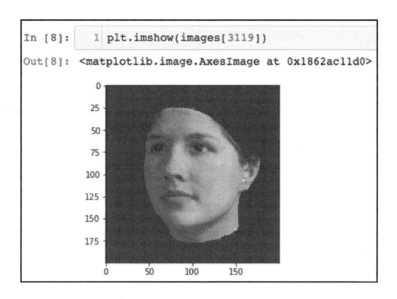

```
In [8]:    1  plt.imshow(images[3119])

Out[8]:  <matplotlib.image.AxesImage at 0x1862ac11d0>
```

How it works...

The functionality is as follows:

1. The `mypath` variable sets the path to read all the files from. The `training-synthetic` folder is specified in this step, as only the files in this folder are going to be used for this chapter.

2. The `onlyfiles` variable is used in order to count all the files under the folder whose path is provided in the previous step by looping through all the files contained in the folder. This will be required in the next step for reading and storing the images.

3. The `images` variable is used to create an empty array of size 3,240 in order to store the images, which are all 200 x 200-pixels.

4. Next, by looping through all the files using the `onlyfiles` variable as an argument in the for loop, each image contained in the folder is read and stored into the previously defined `images` array using the `matplotlib.image` function.

5. Finally, on printing randomly chosen images by specifying different indices of the images you will notice that each image is a 200 x 200-pixel array and each subject may either be facing forward or rotated between zero and fifteen degrees on either side.

There's more...

The following points are of note:

- An interesting feature of this database is that the fourth digit of each filename describes which subject is in the respective image.
- The names of the images are unique in the sense that the fourth digit represents the individual in the respective image. Two examples of image names are `0001_-4_0_0_60_45_1.pgm` and `0006_-24_0_0_0_75_15_1.pgm`. One can easily understand that the fourth digits represent the second and seventh individual respectively.
- We will need to store this information for later use while making predictions. This will help the neural network during training by knowing what subject's facial features it is learning.
- The filenames of each image can be read into an array, and each of the ten subjects can be segregated by using the following lines of code:

```
y =np.empty([3240,1],dtype=int)
for x in range(0, len(onlyfiles)):
    if onlyfiles[x][3]=='0': y[x]=0
    elif onlyfiles[x][3]=='1': y[x]=1
    elif onlyfiles[x][3]=='2': y[x]=2
    elif onlyfiles[x][3]=='3': y[x]=3
    elif onlyfiles[x][3]=='4': y[x]=4
    elif onlyfiles[x][3]=='5': y[x]=5
    elif onlyfiles[x][3]=='6': y[x]=6
    elif onlyfiles[x][3]=='7': y[x]=7
    elif onlyfiles[x][3]=='8': y[x]=8
    elif onlyfiles[x][3]=='9': y[x]=9
```

- The preceding code will initialize an empty one-dimensional `numpy` array of size 3,240 (the number of images in the `training-synthetic` folder) and store the relevant subjects in different arrays by looping through the whole set of files.
- The `if` statements are basically checking what the fourth digit is under each filename and storing that digit in the initialized `numpy` array.

- The output in the iPython notebook for the same is shown in the following screenshot:

```
In [9]:    1  y =np.empty(([3240,1],dtype=int)
           2  for x in range(0, len(onlyfiles)):
           3      if onlyfiles[x][3]=='0': y[x]=0
           4      elif onlyfiles[x][3]=='1': y[x]=1
           5      elif onlyfiles[x][3]=='2': y[x]=2
           6      elif onlyfiles[x][3]=='3': y[x]=3
           7      elif onlyfiles[x][3]=='4': y[x]=4
           8      elif onlyfiles[x][3]=='5': y[x]=5
           9      elif onlyfiles[x][3]=='6': y[x]=6
          10      elif onlyfiles[x][3]=='7': y[x]=7
          11      elif onlyfiles[x][3]=='8': y[x]=8
          12      elif onlyfiles[x][3]=='9': y[x]=9
```

See also

The following blog describes a method of cropping images in Python and can be used for image preprocessing which will be required in the following section:

- https://www.blog.pythonlibrary.org/2017/10/03/how-to-crop-a-photo-with-python/

More information about the Adam Optimizer and its use cases can be found by visiting the following links:

- https://www.tensorflow.org/api_docs/python/tf/train/AdamOptimizer
- https://arxiv.org/abs/1412.6980
- https://www.coursera.org/lecture/deep-neural-network/adam-optimization-algorithm-w9VCZ

Preprocessing images

In the previous section, you may have noticed how all the images are not a front view of the face profiles, and that there are also slightly rotated side profiles. You may also have noticed some unnecessary background areas in each image that needs to be omitted. This section will describe how to preprocess and handle the images so that they are ready to be fed into the network for training.

Getting ready

Consider the following:

- A lot of algorithms are devised to crop the significant part of an image; for example, SIFT, LBP, Haar-cascade filter, and so on.
- We will, however, tackle this problem with a very simplistic naïve code to crop the facial portion from the image. This is one of the novelties of this algorithm.
- We have found that the pixel intensity of the unnecessary background part is 28.
- Remember that each image is a three-channel matrix of 200 x 200-pixels. This means that every image contains three matrices or Tensors of red, green, and blue pixels with an intensity ranging from 0 to 255.
- Therefore, we will discard any row or column of the images that contain only 28s as the pixel intensities.
- We will also make sure that all the images have the same pixel size after the cropping action to achieve the highest parallelizability of the convolutional neural network.

How to do it...

The steps are as follows:

1. Define the `crop()` function to crop images to obtain only the significant part, as shown in the following lines of code:

```
#function for cropping images to obtain only the significant part
def crop(img):
    a=28*np.ones(len(img))
    b=np.where((img== a).all(axis=1))
    img=np.delete(img,(b),0)
    plt.imshow(img)
    img=img.transpose()
    d=28*np.ones(len(img[0]))
    e=np.where((img== d).all(axis=1))
    img=np.delete(img,e,0)
    img=img.transpose()
    print(img.shape)
    super_threshold_indices = img < 29
    img[super_threshold_indices] = 0
    plt.imshow (img)
    return img[0:150, 0:128]
```

2. Use the following lines of code to loop through every image in the folder and crop it using the preceding defined function:

```
#cropping all the images
image = np.empty([3240,150,128],dtype=int)
for n in range(0, len(images)):
    image[n]=crop(images[n])
```

3. Next, randomly choose an image and print it to check that it has been cropped from a 200 x 200 sized image to a different size. We have chosen image 23 in our case. This can be done using the following lines of code:

```
print (image[22])
print (image[22].shape)
```

4. Next, split the data into a test and train set using 80% of the images in the folder as the training set and the remaining 20% as the test set. This can be done with the following commands:

```
# Split data into 80/20 split for testing and training
test_ind=np.random.choice(range(3240), 648, replace=False)
train_ind=np.delete(range(0,len(onlyfiles)),test_ind)
```

5. Once the data has finished splitting, segregate the training and test images using the following commands:

```
# slicing the training and test images
y1_train=y[train_ind]
x_test=image[test_ind]
y1_test=y[test_ind]
```

6. Next, reshape all the cropped images into sizes of 128 x 150, since this is the size that is to be fed into the neural network. This can be done using the following commands:

```
#reshaping the input images
x_train = x_train.reshape(x_train.shape[0], 128, 150, 1)
x_test = x_test.reshape(x_test.shape[0], 128, 150, 1)
```

7. Once the data is done reshaping, convert it into `float32` type, which will make it easier to handle in the next step when it is normalized. Converting from int to float32 can be done using the following commands:

```
#converting data to float32
x_train = x_train.astype('float32')
x_test = x_test.astype('float32')
```

8. After reshaping and converting the data into the float32 type, it has to be normalized in order to adjust all the values to a similar scale. This is an important step in preventing data redundancy. Perform normalization using the following commands:

```
#normalizing data
x_train/=255
x_test/=255
#10 digits represent the 10 classes
number_of_persons = 10
```

9. The final step is to convert the reshaped, normalized images into vectors, as this is the only form of input the neural network understands. Convert the images into vectors using the following commands:

```
#convert data to vectors
y_train = np_utils.to_categorical(y1_train, number_of_persons)
y_test = np_utils.to_categorical(y1_test, number_of_persons)
```

How it works...

The functionality is as follows:

1. The `crop()` function executes the following tasks:
    1. Multiplies all pixels with an intensity of 28 with a numpy array of 1s and stores in variable a.
    2. Checks for all instances where an entire column consists of only pixel intensities of 28 and stores in variable b.
    3. Deletes all columns (or Y axes) where pixel intensities are 28 for the entire column.
    4. Plots the resulting image.

5. Transposes the image in order to perform the preceding set of operations on all the rows (or *X* axes) in a similar manner.

6. Multiplies all pixels with an intensity of 28 with a `numpy` array of 1s and stores in variable d.

7. Checks for all instances where an entire column consists of only pixel intensities of 28 and stores in variable e.

8. Deletes all columns (from the transposed image) where pixel intensities are 28 for the entire column.

9. Transposes the image to get back the original image.

10. Prints the shape of the image.

11. Wherever a pixel intensity of less than 29 is found, replaces those pixel intensities with zeros, which will result in the cropping of all those pixels by making them white.

12. Plots the resulting image.

13. Reshapes the resulting image to a size of 150 x 128 pixels.

The output for the `crop()` function, as seen on the Jupyter notebook during execution, is shown in the following screenshot:

```
In [10]:   1  #funtion for cropping images to obtain only the significant part
           2  def crop(img):
           3      a=28*np.ones(len(img)) #background has pixel intensity of 28
           4      b=np.where((img== a).all(axis=1)) #check image background
           5      img=np.delete(img,(b),0) #deleting the unwanted part from the Y axis
           6      plt.imshow(img)
           7      img=img.transpose()
           8      d=28*np.ones(len(img[0]))
           9      e=np.where((img== d).all(axis=1))
          10      img=np.delete(img,e,0) #deleting the unwanted part from the X axis
          11      img=img.transpose()
          12      super_threshold_indices = img < 29 #padding zeros instead of background data
          13      img[super_threshold_indices] = 0
          14      return img[0:150, 0:128]
```

2. Next, the defined `crop()` function is applied to all the files contained in the `training-synthetic` folder by looping through every file. This will result in an output as shown in the following screenshots:

```
In [11]:    1  #cropping all the images
            2  image = np.empty([3240,150,128],dtype=int)
            3  for n in range(0, len(images)):
            4    image[n]=crop(images[n])
```

```
(176, 139)
(179, 139)
(175, 141)
(166, 132)
(173, 140)
(154, 134)
(176, 144)
(167, 128)
(175, 138)
(167, 128)
(175, 138)
(176, 144)
(175, 138)
(166, 132)
(173, 140)
(165, 140)
(175, 141)
(175, 141)
(154, 137)
```

The output continues as follows:

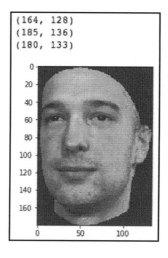

Notice that only the relevant facial features are preserved and the resulting shapes of all the cropped images are less than 200 x 200, which was the initial size.

3. On printing the image and shape of any random image, you will notice that every image is now resized to a 150 x 128-pixel array, and you will see the following output:

```
In [12]:    1 print (image[22])

            [[104    0 106 ...,    0    0    0]
             [   0    0    0 ...,    0    0    0]
             [   0    0    0 ...,    0    0    0]
             ...,
             [   0    0    0 ...,    0    0    0]
             [   0    0    0 ...,    0    0    0]
             [   0    0    0 ...,    0    0    0]]

In [13]:    1 print (image[22].shape)

            (150, 128)
```

4. Splitting the images into test and train sets as well as segregating them into variables named x_train, y1_train, x_test, and y1_test will result in the output shown in the following screenshot:

```
In [14]:    1 # randomly splitting data into training(80%) and test(20%) sets
            2 test_ind=np.random.choice(range(3240), 648, replace=False)
            3 train_ind=np.delete(range(0,len(onlyfiles)),test_ind)
```

5. Segregating the data is done as follows:

```
In [15]:    1 # segregating the training and test images
            2 x_train=image[train_ind]
            3 y1_train=y[train_ind]
            4 x_test=image[test_ind]
            5 y1_test=y[test_ind]
```

6. Reshaping the training and test images and converting the data type to float32 will result in the output seen in the following screenshot:

```
In [16]:    1  #reshaping the input images
            2  x_train = x_train.reshape(x_train.shape[0], 128, 150, 1)
            3  x_test = x_test.reshape(x_test.shape[0], 128, 150, 1)

In [17]:    1  #converting data to float32
            2  x_train = x_train.astype('float32')
            3  x_test = x_test.astype('float32')
```

There's more...

Consider the following:

- Once the images are done preprocessing they still need to be normalized and converted into vectors (in this case tensors) before being fed into the network.
- Normalization, in the simplest case, means adjusting values measured on different scales to a notionally common scale, often prior to averaging. It is always a good idea to normalize data in order to prevent gradients from exploding or vanishing as seen in the vanishing and exploding gradient problems during gradient descent. Normalization also ensures there is no data redundancy.
- Normalization of the data is done by dividing each pixel in each image by 255 since the pixel values range between 0 and 255. This will result in the output shown in the following screenshot:

```
In [18]:    1  #normalizing data
            2  x_train/=255
            3  x_test/=255
            4  #10 digits represent the 10 classes
            5  number_of_persons = 10
```

- Next, the images are converted to input vectors with ten different classes using the `to_categorical()` function from `numpy_utils`, as shown in the following screenshot:

```
In [19]:    1  #convert data to vectors
            2  y_train = np_utils.to_categorical(y1_train, number_of_persons)
            3  y_test = np_utils.to_categorical(y1_test, number_of_persons)
```

See also

Additional resources are as follows:

- For more information on data normalization, check the following link:
  https://www.quora.com/What-is-normalization-in-machine-learning
- For information on overfitting and why data is split into test and training sets, visit the following link:
  https://towardsdatascience.com/train-test-split-and-cross-validation-in-python-80b61beca4b6
- For more information on encoding variables and their importance, visit the following link:
  http://pbpython.com/categorical-encoding.html

Model building, training, and analysis

We will use a standard sequential model from the `keras` library to build the CNN. The network will consist of three convolutional layers, two maxpooling layers, and four fully connected layers. The input layer and the subsequent hidden layers have 16 neurons, while the maxpooling layers contain a pool size of (2,2). The four fully connected layers consist of two dense layers and one flattened layer and one dropout layer. Dropout 0.25 was used to reduce the overfitting problem. Another novelty of this algorithm is the use of data augmentation to fight the overfitting phenomenon. Data augmentation is carried by rotating, shifting, shearing, and zooming the images to different extents to fit the model.

The `relu` function is used as the activation function in both the input and hidden layers, while the `softmax` classifier is used in the output layer to classify the test images based on the predicted output.

Getting ready

The network which will be constructed can be visualized as shown in the following diagram:

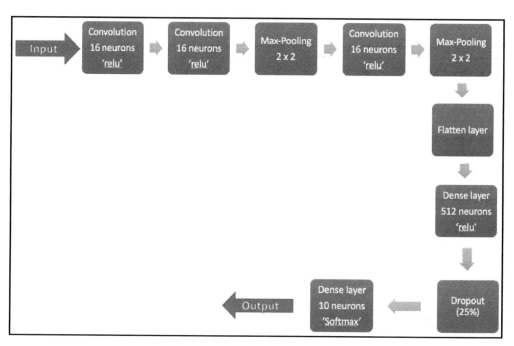

How to do it...

The steps are as follows:

1. Define the model using the `Sequential()` function in the Keras framework using the following commands:

```
model = Sequential()
model.add(Conv2D(16, (3, 3), input_shape=(128,150,1)))
model.add(Activation('relu'))
model.add(Conv2D(16, (3, 3)))
model.add(Activation('relu'))
model.add(MaxPooling2D(pool_size=(2,2)))
model.add(Conv2D(16,(3, 3)))
model.add(Activation('relu'))
```

```
model.add(MaxPooling2D(pool_size=(2,2)))
model.add(Flatten())

model.add(Dense(512))
model.add(Activation('relu'))
model.add(Dropout(0.25))
model.add(Dense(10))

model.add(Activation('softmax'))
```

2. Print the summary of the model to get a better understanding of how the model is built and to ensure that it is built as per the preceding specifications. This can be done by using the `model.summary()` command.

3. Next, compile the model using the following command:

```
model.compile(loss='categorical_crossentropy', optimizer=Adam(),
metrics=            ['accuracy'])
```

4. In order to prevent overfitting and improve model accuracy further, implement some form of data augmentation. In this step, the images will be sheared, shifted on a horizontal as well as the vertical axis, zoomed in, and rotated. The ability of the model to learn and identify these anomalies will dictate how robust the model is. Augment the data using the following commands:

```
# data augmentation to minimize overfitting
gen = ImageDataGenerator(rotation_range=8,
        width_shift_range=0.08, shear_range=0.3,
        height_shift_range=0.08,zoom_range=0.08)
test_gen = ImageDataGenerator()
train_generator = gen.flow(x_train, y_train, batch_size=16)
test_generator = test_gen.flow(x_test, y_test, batch_size=16)
```

5. Finally, fit and evaluate the model after data augmentation using the following commands:

```
model.fit_generator(train_generator, epochs=5,
validation_data=test_generator)

scores = model.evaluate(x_test, y_test, verbose=0)
print("Recognition Error: %.2f%%" % (100-scores[1]*100))
```

How it works...

The functionality is as follows:

1. By using the sequential function, a nine-layer convolutional neural network is defined with each layer performing the following functions:

    1. The first layer is a convolutional layer with 16 neurons and performs convolution on the input tensor/matrix. The size of the feature map is defined to be a 3 x 3 matrix. The input shape needs to be specified for the first layer since the neural network needs to know what type of input to expect. Since all the images have been cropped to a size of 128 x 150 pixels, this will be the input shape defined for the first layer of the network as well. The activation function used in this layer is a **rectified linear unit (relu)**.

    2. The second layer of the network (first hidden layer) is another convolution layer with 16 neurons as well. Again, a `relu` will be used as the activation function for this layer.

    3. The third layer of the network (second hidden layer) is a max pooling layer with a pool size of 2 x 2. The function of this layer is to extract all the valid features learned by performing convolution in the first two layers and reducing the size of the matrix with all the learned features. Convolution is nothing but a matrix multiplication between the feature map and the input matrix (in our case, an image). The resulting values, which form the convolution process, are stored by the network in a matrix. The maximum values from these stored values will define a certain feature in the input image. These maximum values are what will be preserved by the max pooling layer, which will omit the non-relevant features.

    4. The fourth layer of the network (third hidden layer) is another convolutional layer with a feature map of 3 x 3 again. The activation function used in this layer will again be a `relu` function.

    5. The fifth layer of the network (fourth hidden layer) is a max pooling layer with a pool size of 2 x 2.

    6. The sixth layer of the network (fifth hidden layer) is a flatten layer that will convert the matrix containing all the learned features (stored in the form of numbers) into a single row instead of a multi-dimensional matrix.

7. The seventh layer in the network (sixth hidden layer) is a dense layer with 512 neurons and a `relu` activation. Each neuron will basically process a certain weight and bias, which is nothing but a representation of all the learned features from a particular image. This is done in order to easily classify the image by using a `softmax` classifier on the dense layer.

8. The eighth layer in the network (seventh hidden layer) is a dropout layer with a dropout probability of 0.25 or 25%. This layer will randomly `dropout` 25% of the neurons during the training process and help prevent overfitting by encouraging the network to learn a given feature using many alternative paths.

9. The final layer in the network is a dense layer with just 10 neurons and the `softmax` classifier. This is the eighth hidden layer and will also serve as the output layer of the network.

2. The output after defining the model must look like the one in the following screenshot:

```
In [20]:    1  # model building
            2  model = Sequential()
            3  model.add(Conv2D(16, (3, 3), input_shape=(128,150,1))) #Input layer
            4  model.add(Activation('relu')) # 'relu' as activation function
            5  model.add(Conv2D(16, (3, 3))) #first hidden layer
            6  model.add(Activation('relu'))
            7  model.add(MaxPooling2D(pool_size=(2,2))) # Maxpooling from (2,2)
            8  model.add(Conv2D(16,(3, 3))) # second hidden layer
            9  model.add(Activation('relu'))
           10  model.add(MaxPooling2D(pool_size=(2,2))) # Maxpooling from (2,2)
           11  model.add(Flatten()) #flatten the maxpooled data
           12  # Fully connected layer
           13  model.add(Dense(512))
           14  model.add(Activation('relu'))
           15  model.add(Dropout(0.25)) #Dropout is applied to overcome overfitting
           16  model.add(Dense(10))
           17  #output layer
           18  model.add(Activation('softmax')) # 'softmax' is used for SGD
           19  model.summary()
```

3. On printing the `model.summary()` function, you must see an output like the one in the following screenshot:

Layer (type)	Output Shape	Param #
conv2d_1 (Conv2D)	(None, 126, 148, 16)	160
activation_1 (Activation)	(None, 126, 148, 16)	0
conv2d_2 (Conv2D)	(None, 124, 146, 16)	2320
activation_2 (Activation)	(None, 124, 146, 16)	0
max_pooling2d_1 (MaxPooling2	(None, 62, 73, 16)	0
conv2d_3 (Conv2D)	(None, 60, 71, 16)	2320
activation_3 (Activation)	(None, 60, 71, 16)	0
max_pooling2d_2 (MaxPooling2	(None, 30, 35, 16)	0
flatten_1 (Flatten)	(None, 16800)	0
dense_1 (Dense)	(None, 512)	8602112
activation_4 (Activation)	(None, 512)	0
dropout_1 (Dropout)	(None, 512)	0
dense_2 (Dense)	(None, 10)	5130
activation_5 (Activation)	(None, 10)	0

```
Total params: 8,612,042
Trainable params: 8,612,042
Non-trainable params: 0
```

4. The model is compiled using categorical crossentropy, which is a function to measure and compute the loss from the network while transferring information from one layer to the subsequent layers. The model will make use of the `Adam()` optimizer function from the Keras framework, which will basically dictate how the network optimizes the weights and biases while learning the features. The output of the `model.compile()` function must look like the following screenshot:

```
In [21]:   1 #model compliation
           2 model.compile(loss='categorical_crossentropy', optimizer=Adam(), metrics=['accuracy'])
```

5. Since the neural network is quite dense and the number of total images is only 3,240, we devise a method to prevent overfitting. This is done by generating more images from the training set by performing data augmentation. In this step, the images are generated through the `ImageDataGenerator()` function. This function takes the training and test sets and augments images by:

- Rotating them
- Shearing them
- Shifting the width, which is basically widening the images
- Shifting the images on a horizontal axis
- Shifting the images on a vertical axis

The output of the preceding function must look like the following screenshot:

```
In [22]:   1  # data augmentation to reduce overfitting problem
           2  gen = ImageDataGenerator(rotation_range=8, width_shift_range=0.08, shear_range=0.3,
           3                          height_shift_range=0.08,zoom_range=0.08)
           4  test_gen = ImageDataGenerator()
           5  train_generator = gen.flow(x_train, y_train, batch_size=16)
           6  test_generator = test_gen.flow(x_test, y_test, batch_size=16)
```

6. Finally, the model is fitted to the data and evaluated after training over 5 epochs. The output we obtained is shown in the following screenshot:

```
1  #model fitting
2  model.fit_generator(train_generator, epochs=5, validation_data=test_generator)
3  # Final evaluation of the model
4  scores = model.evaluate(x_test, y_test, verbose=0)
5  print("Recognition Error: %.2f%%" % (100-scores[1]*100))

Epoch 1/5
162/162 [==============================] - 257s 2s/step - loss: 2.9746 - acc: 0.3468 - val_loss: 0.7733 - val_acc: 0.
7238
Epoch 2/5
162/162 [==============================] - 338s 2s/step - loss: 0.5461 - acc: 0.8067 - val_loss: 0.0999 - val_acc: 0.
9846
Epoch 3/5
162/162 [==============================] - 259s 2s/step - loss: 0.2179 - acc: 0.9282 - val_loss: 0.0603 - val_acc: 0.
9830
Epoch 4/5
162/162 [==============================] - 277s 2s/step - loss: 0.1679 - acc: 0.9394 - val_loss: 0.0445 - val_acc: 0.
9892
Epoch 5/5
162/162 [==============================] - 347s 2s/step - loss: 0.1242 - acc: 0.9606 - val_loss: 0.0501 - val_acc: 0.
9846
Recognition Error: 1.54%
```

7. As you can see, we obtained an accuracy of 98.46%, which resulted in an error rate of 1.54%. This is pretty good, but convolutional networks have advanced so much that we can improve this error rate by tuning a few hyperparameters or using a deeper network.

There's more...

Using a deeper CNN with 12 layers (one extra convolution and one extra max pooling layer) resulted in an improvement of accuracy to 99.07%, as shown in the following screenshot:

```
In [29]:   1 #model fitting
           2 model.fit_generator(train_generator, epochs=5, validation_data=test_generator)
           3 # Final evaluation of the model
           4 scores = model.evaluate(x_test, y_test, verbose=0)
           5 print("Recognition Error: %.2f%%" % (100-scores[1]*100))

Epoch 1/5
162/162 [==============================] - 296s 2s/step - loss: 1.5980 - acc: 0.4645 - val_loss: 0.2235 - val_acc: 0.
9552
Epoch 2/5
162/162 [==============================] - 297s 2s/step - loss: 0.3713 - acc: 0.8661 - val_loss: 0.1324 - val_acc: 0.
9475
Epoch 3/5
162/162 [==============================] - 289s 2s/step - loss: 0.1413 - acc: 0.9529 - val_loss: 0.0312 - val_acc: 0.
9892
Epoch 4/5
162/162 [==============================] - 250s 2s/step - loss: 0.1083 - acc: 0.9622 - val_loss: 0.0028 - val_acc: 1.
0000
Epoch 5/5
162/162 [==============================] - 229s 1s/step - loss: 0.0455 - acc: 0.9873 - val_loss: 0.0262 - val_acc: 0.
9907
Recognition Error: 0.93%
```

Using data normalization after every two layers during model building, we were further able to improve the accuracy to 99.85%, as shown in the following screenshot:

```
In [23]:   1 #model fitting
           2 model.fit_generator(train_generator, epochs=5, validation_data=test_generator)
           3 # Final evaluation of the model
           4 scores = model.evaluate(x_test, y_test, verbose=0)
           5 print("Recognition Error: %.2f%%" % (100-scores[1]*100))

Epoch 1/5
162/162 [==============================] - 72s 444ms/step - loss: 1.9148 - acc: 0.2924 - val_loss: 0.8199 - val_acc:
0.7901
Epoch 2/5
162/162 [==============================] - 122s 751ms/step - loss: 0.6824 - acc: 0.7631 - val_loss: 0.1210 - val_acc:
0.9799
Epoch 3/5
162/162 [==============================] - 203s 1s/step - loss: 0.2766 - acc: 0.9140 - val_loss: 0.1808 - val_acc: 0.
9167
Epoch 4/5
162/162 [==============================] - 153s 948ms/step - loss: 0.1444 - acc: 0.9479 - val_loss: 0.0278 - val_acc:
1.0000
Epoch 5/5
162/162 [==============================] - 142s 879ms/step - loss: 0.0928 - acc: 0.9734 - val_loss: 0.0137 - val_acc:
0.9985
Recognition Error: 0.15%
```

You may obtain different results, but feel free to run the training step a few times. The following are some of the steps you can take to experiment with the network in the future to understand it better:

- Try to tune hyperparameters better and implement a higher dropout percentage and see how the network responds.
- The accuracy greatly reduced when we tried using different activation functions or a smaller (less dense) network.
- Also, change the size of the feature maps and max pooling layer and see how this influences training time and model accuracy.
- Try including more neurons in a less dense CNN and tune it to improve accuracy. This may also result in a faster network that trains in less time.
- Use more training data. Explore other online repositories and find larger databases to train the network. Convolutional neural networks usually perform better when the size of the training data is increased.

See also

The following published papers are good resources to obtain a better understanding of convolutional neural networks. They may be used as further reading in order to gain more understanding of various applications of convolutional neural networks:

- http://papers.nips.cc/paper/4824-imagenet-classification-with-deep-convolutional-neural-networks
- https://arxiv.org/abs/1408.5882
- https://www.cv-foundation.org/openaccess/content_cvpr_2014/papers/Karpathy_Large-scale_Video_Classification_2014_CVPR_paper.pdf
- http://www.cs.cmu.edu/~bhiksha/courses/deeplearning/Fall.2016/pdfs/Simard.pdf
- https://dl.acm.org/citation.cfm?id=2807412
- https://ieeexplore.ieee.org/abstract/document/6165309/
- http://openaccess.thecvf.com/content_cvpr_2014/papers/Oquab_Learning_and_Transferring_2014_CVPR_paper.pdf
- http://www.aaai.org/ocs/index.php/IJCAI/IJCAI11/paper/download/3098/3425
- https://ieeexplore.ieee.org/abstract/document/6288864/

Creating and Visualizing Word Vectors Using Word2Vec

11

In this chapter, we will cover the following recipes:

- Acquiring data
- Importing the necessary libraries
- Preparing the data
- Building and training the model
- Visualizing further
- Analyzing further

Introduction

Before training a neural network on text data and generating text using LSTM cells, it is important to understand how text data (such as words, sentences, customer reviews, or stories) is converted to word vectors first before it is fed into a neural network. This chapter will describe how to convert a text into a corpus and generate word vectors from the corpus, which makes it easy to group similar words using techniques such as Euclidean distance calculation or cosine distance calculation between different word vectors.

Acquiring data

The first step is to acquire some data to work with. For this chapter, we will require a lot of text data to convert it into tokens and visualize it to understand how neural networks rank word vectors based on Euclidean and Cosine distances. It is an important step in understanding how different words get associated with each other. This, in turn, can be used to design better, more efficient language and text-processing models.

Getting ready

Consider the following:

- The text data for the model needs to be in files of `.txt` format, and you must ensure that the files are placed in the current working directory. The text data can be anything from Twitter feeds, news feeds, customer reviews, computer code, or whole books saved in the `.txt` format in the working directory. In our case, we have used the *Game of Thrones* books as the input text to our model. However, any text can be substituted in place of the books, and the same model will work.
- Many classical texts are no longer protected under copyright. This means that you can download all of the text for these books for free and use them in experiments, such as creating generative models. The best place to get access to free books that are no longer protected by copyright is Project Gutenberg (`https://www.gutenberg.org/`).

How to do it...

The steps are as follows:

1. Begin by visiting the Project Gutenberg website and browsing for a book that interests you. Click on the book, and then click on **UTF-8**, which allows you to download the book in plain-text format. The link is shown in the following screenshot:

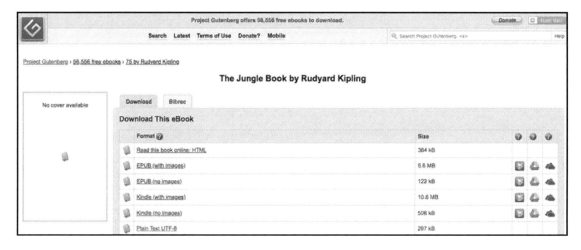

Project Gutenberg Dataset download page

2. After clicking on **Plain Text UTF-8**, you should see a page that looks like the following screenshot. Right click on the page and click on **Save As...** Next, rename the file to whatever you choose and save it in your working directory:

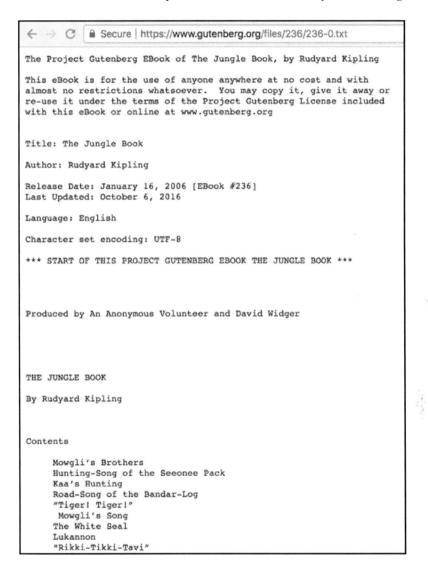

3. You should now see a .txt file with the specified filename in your current working directory.
4. Project Gutenberg adds a standard header and footer to each book; this is not part of the original text. Open the file in a text editor, and delete the header and the footer.

How it works...

The functionality is as follows:

1. Check for the current working directory using the following command: pwd.
2. The working directory can be changed using the cd command as shown in the following screenshot:

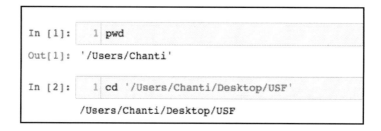

```
In [1]:    1 pwd

Out[1]:  '/Users/Chanti'

In [2]:    1 cd '/Users/Chanti/Desktop/USF'

         /Users/Chanti/Desktop/USF
```

3. Notice that, in our case, the text files are contained in a folder named USF, and, therefore, this is set as the working directory. You may similarly store one or more .txt files in the working directory for use as input to the model.
4. UTF-8 specifies the type of encoding of the characters in the text file. **UTF-8** stands for **Unicode Transformation Format**. The **8** means it uses **8-bit** blocks to represent a character.
5. UTF-8 is a compromise character encoding that can be as compact as ASCII (if the file is just plain-English text) but can also contain any Unicode characters (with some increase in file size).
6. It is not necessary for the text file to be in a UTF-8 format, as we will use the codecs library at a later stage to encode all the text into the Latin1 encoding format.

There's more...

For more information about UTF-8 and Latin1 encoding formats, visit the following links:

- `https://en.wikipedia.org/wiki/UTF-8`
- `http://www.ic.unicamp.br/~stolfi/EXPORT/www/ISO-8859-1-Encoding.html`

See also

Visit the following link to understand the need for word vectors in neural networks better:
`https://medium.com/deep-math-machine-learning-ai/chapter-9-1-nlp-word-vectors-d51bff9628c1`

Listed below are some other useful articles related to the topic of converting words to vectors:
`https://monkeylearn.com/blog/word-embeddings-transform-text-numbers/`

`https://towardsdatascience.com/word-to-vectors-natural-language-processing-b253dd0b0817`

Importing the necessary libraries

Before we begin, we require the following libraries and dependencies, which need to be imported into our Python environment. These libraries will make our tasks a lot easier, as they have readily available functions and models that can be used instead of doing that ourselves. This also makes the code more compact and readable.

Getting ready

The following libraries and dependencies will be required to create word vectors and plots and visualize the n-dimensional word vectors in a 2D space:

- `future`
- `codecs`
- `glob`
- `multiprocessing`

- os
- pprint
- re
- nltk
- Word2Vec
- sklearn
- numpy
- matplotlib
- pandas
- seaborn

How to do it...

The steps are as follows:

1. Type the following commands into your Jupyter notebook to import all the required libraries:

```
from __future__ import absolute_import, division, print_function
import codecs
import glob
import logging
import multiprocessing
import os
import pprint
import re
import nltk
import gensim.models.word2vec as w2v
import sklearn.manifold
import numpy
as np
import matplotlib.pyplot as plt
import pandas as pd
import seaborn as sns
%pylab inline
```

2. You should see an output that looks like the following screenshot:

```
In [3]:   1 from __future__ import absolute_import, division, print_function

In [4]:   1 import codecs
          2 import glob
          3 import logging
          4 import multiprocessing
          5 import os
          6 import pprint
          7 import re

In [5]:   1 import nltk
          2 import gensim.models.word2vec as w2v
          3 import sklearn.manifold
          4 import numpy as np
          5 import matplotlib.pyplot as plt
          6 import pandas as pd
          7 import seaborn as sns

In [6]:   1 %pylab inline

          Populating the interactive namespace from numpy and matplotlib
```

3. Next, import the `stopwords` and `punkt` libraries using the following commands:

```
nltk.download("punkt")
nltk.download("stopwords")
```

4. The output you see must look like the following screenshot:

```
In [7]:   1 logging.basicConfig(format='%(asctime)s : %(levelname)s : %(message)s', level=logging.INFO)

In [8]:   1 nltk.download("punkt")
          2 nltk.download("stopwords")

          [nltk_data] Downloading package punkt to /Users/Chanti/nltk_data...
          [nltk_data]   Package punkt is already up-to-date!
          [nltk_data] Downloading package stopwords to
          [nltk_data]     /Users/Chanti/nltk_data...
          [nltk_data]   Package stopwords is already up-to-date!

Out[8]: True
```

How it works...

This section will describe the purpose of each library being used for this recipe.

1. The `future` library is the missing link between Python 2 and Python 3. It acts as a bridge between the two versions and allows us to use syntax from both versions.

2. The `codecs` library will be used to perform the encoding of all words present in the text file. This constitutes our dataset.

3. Regex is the library used to look up or search for a file really quickly. The `glob` function allows quick and efficient searching through a large database for a required file.

4. The `multiprocessing` library allows us to perform concurrency, which is a way of running multiple threads and having each thread run a different process. It is a way of making programs run faster by parallelization.

5. The `os` library allows easy interaction with the operating system, such as a Mac, Windows, and so on, and performs functions such as reading a file.

6. The `pprint` library provides a capability for pretty-printing arbitrary Python data structures in a form that can be used as input to the interpreter.

7. The `re` module provides regular expression matching operations similar to those found in Perl.

8. NLTK is a natural language toolkit capable of tokenizing words in very short code. When fed in a whole sentence, the `nltk` function breaks up sentences and outputs tokens for each word. Based on these tokens, the words may be organized into different categories. NLTK does this by comparing each word with a huge database of pre-trained words called a **lexicon**.

9. `Word2Vec` is Google's model, trained on a huge dataset of word vectors. It groups semantically similar words close to one another. This will be the most important library for this section.

10. `sklearn.manifold` allows the dimensionality reduction of the dataset by employing **t-distributed Stochastic Neighbor Embedding (t-SNE)** techniques. Since each word vector is multi-dimensional, we require some form of dimensionality reduction techniques to bring the dimensionality of these words down to a lower dimensional space so it can be visualized in a 2D space.

There's more...

`Numpy` is a commonly used `math` library. `Matplotlib` is the `plotting` library we will utilize, and `pandas` provide a lot of flexibility in data handling by allowing easy reshaping, slicing, indexing, subsetting, and manipulation of data.

The `Seaborn` library is another statistical data visualization library that we require along with `matplotlib`. `Punkt` and `Stopwords` are two data-processing libraries that simplify tasks such as splitting a piece of text from a corpus into tokens (that is, via tokenization) and removing `stopwords`.

See also

For more information regarding some of the libraries utilized, visit the following links:

- `https://docs.python.org/3/library/codecs.html`
- `https://docs.python.org/2/library/pprint.html`
- `https://docs.python.org/3/library/re.html`
- `https://www.nltk.org/`
- `https://www.tensorflow.org/tutorials/word2vec`
- `http://scikit-learn.org/stable/modules/manifold.html`

Preparing the data

A number of data-preprocessing steps are to be performed before the data is fed into the model. This section will describe how to clean the data and prepare it so it can be fed into the model.

Getting ready

All the text from the .txt files is first converted into one big corpus. This is done by reading each sentence from each file and adding it to an empty corpus. A number of preprocessing steps are then executed to remove irregularities such as white spaces, spelling errors, stopwords, and so on. The cleaned text data has to then be tokenized, and the tokenized sentences are added to an empty array by running them through a loop.

How to do it...

The steps are as follows:

1. Type in the following commands to search for the .txt files within the working directory and print the names of the files found:

```
book_names = sorted(glob.glob("./*.txt"))
print("Found books:")
book_names
```

In our case, there are five books named got1, got2, got3, got4, and got5 saved in the working directory.

2. Create a corpus, read each sentence starting with the first file, encode it, and add the encoded characters to a corpus using the following commands:

```
corpus = u''
for book_name in book_names:
print("Reading '{0}'...".format(book_name))
with codecs.open(book_name,"r","Latin1") as book_file:
corpus += book_file.read()
print("Corpus is now {0} characters long".format(len(corpus)))
print()
```

3. Execute the code in the preceding steps, which should result in an output that looks like the following screenshot:

```
In [9]:    1  book_names = sorted(glob.glob("./*.txt"))

In [10]:   1  print("Found books:")
           2  book_names

           Found books:

Out[10]:  ['./got1.txt', './got2.txt', './got3.txt', './got4.txt', './got5.txt']

In [11]:   1  corpus = u''
           2  for book_name in book_names:
           3      print("Reading '{0}'...".format(book_name))
           4      with codecs.open(book_name,"r","Latin1") as book_file:
           5          corpus += book_file.read()
           6      print("Corpus is now {0} characters long".format(len(corpus)))
           7      print()

           Reading './got1.txt'...
           Corpus is now 1770660 characters long

           Reading './got2.txt'...
           Corpus is now 3172017 characters long

           Reading './got3.txt'...
           Corpus is now 4003969 characters long

           Reading './got4.txt'...
           Corpus is now 5089222 characters long

           Reading './got5.txt'...
           Corpus is now 5919089 characters long
```

4. Load the English pickle `tokenizer` from `punkt` using the following command:

```
tokenizer = nltk.data.load('tokenizers/punkt/english.pickle')
```

5. `Tokenize` the entire `corpus` into sentences using the following command:

```
raw_sentences = tokenizer.tokenize(corpus)
```

6. Define the function to split sentences into their constituent words as well as remove unnecessary characters in the following manner:

```
def sentence_to_wordlist(raw):
    clean = re.sub("[^a-zA-Z]"," ", raw)
    words = clean.split()
    return words
```

7. Add all the raw sentences where each word of the sentence is tokenized to a new array of sentences. This is done by using the following code:

```
sentences = []
for raw_sentence in raw_sentences:
    if len(raw_sentence) > 0:
        sentences.append(sentence_to_wordlist(raw_sentence))
```

8. Print a random sentence from the corpus to visually see how the `tokenizer` splits sentences and creates a word list from the result. This is done using the following commands:

```
print(raw_sentences[50])
print(sentence_to_wordlist(raw_sentences[50]))
```

9. Count the total tokens from the dataset using the following commands:

```
token_count = sum([len(sentence) for sentence in sentences])
print("The book corpus contains {0:,} tokens".format(token_count))
```

How it works...

Executing the tokenizer and tokenizing all the sentences in the corpus should result in an output that looks like the one in the following screenshot:

```
In [12]:   1  #Load the English pickle tokenizer from punkt
           2  tokenizer = nltk.data.load('tokenizers/punkt/english.pickle')

In [13]:   1  #Tokenize the corpus into sentences
           2  raw_sentences = tokenizer.tokenize(corpus)
```

Next, removing unnecessary characters, such as hyphens and special characters, are done in the following manner. Splitting up all the sentences using the user-defined `sentence_to_wordlist()` function produces an output as shown in the following screenshot:

```
In [14]:    1  #Convert sentences into list of words
            2  #remove unecessary characters, split into words, remove hyphens and special characters
            3  def sentence_to_wordlist(raw):
            4      clean = re.sub("[^a-zA-Z]"," ", raw)
            5      words = clean.split()
            6      return words
            7
```

Adding the raw sentences to a new array named `sentences[]` produces an output as shown in the following screenshot:

```
In [15]:    1  #for each sentence, sentences where each word is tokenized
            2  sentences = []
            3  for raw_sentence in raw_sentences:
            4      if len(raw_sentence) > 0:
            5          sentences.append(sentence_to_wordlist(raw_sentence))

In [16]:    1  print(raw_sentences[50])
            2  print(sentence_to_wordlist(raw_sentences[50]))

Two years past, he had fallen and shattered a hip, and it had never mended properly.
['Two', 'years', 'past', 'he', 'had', 'fallen', 'and', 'shattered', 'a', 'hip', 'and', 'it', 'had', 'never', 'mende
d', 'properly']
```

On printing the total number of tokens in the corpus, we notice that there are 1,110,288 tokens in the entire corpus. This is illustrated in the following screenshot:

```
In [17]:    1  #count tokens, each one being a sentence
            2  token_count = sum([len(sentence) for sentence in sentences])
            3  print("The book corpus contains {0:,} tokens".format(token_count))

The book corpus contains 1,110,288 tokens
```

The functionality is as follows:

1. The pre-trained `tokenizer` from NLTK is used to tokenize the entire corpus by counting each sentence as a token. Every tokenized sentence is added to the variable `raw_sentences`, which stores the tokenized sentences.
2. In the next step, common stopwords are removed, and the text is cleaned by splitting each sentence into its words.
3. A random sentence along with its wordlist is printed to understand how this works. In our case, we have chosen to print the 50th sentence in the `raw_sentences` array.
4. The total number of tokens (in our case, sentences) in the sentences array are counted and printed. In our case, we see that 1,110,288 tokens are created by the `tokenizer`.

There's more...

More information about tokenizing paragraphs and sentences can be found by visiting the following links:

- `https://textminingonline.com/dive-into-nltk-part-ii-sentence-tokenize-and-word-tokenize`
- `https://stackoverflow.com/questions/37605710/tokenize-a-paragraph-into-sentence-and-then-into-words-in-nltk`
- `https://pythonspot.com/tokenizing-words-and-sentences-with-nltk/`

See also

For more information about how regular expressions work, visit the following link:

`https://stackoverflow.com/questions/13090806/clean-line-of-punctuation-and-split-into-words-python`

Building and training the model

Once we have the text data in the form of tokens in an array, we are able to input it in the array format to the model. First, we have to define a number of hyperparameters for the model. This section will describe how to do the following:

- Declare model hyperparameters
- Build a model using `Word2Vec`
- Train the model on the prepared dataset
- Save and checkpoint the trained model

Getting ready

Some of the model hyperparameters that are to be declared include the following:

- Dimensionality of resulting word vectors
- Minimum word count threshold

- Number of parallel threads to run while training the model
- Context window length
- Downsampling (for frequently occurring words)
- Setting a seed

Once the previously mentioned hyperparameters are declared, the model can be built using the Word2Vec function from the Gensim library.

How to do it...

The steps are as follows:

1. Declare the hyperparameters for the model using the following commands:

```
num_features = 300
min_word_count = 3
num_workers = multiprocessing.cpu_count()
context_size = 7
downsampling = 1e-3
seed = 1
```

2. Build the model, using the declared hyperparameters, with the following lines of code:

```
got2vec = w2v.Word2Vec(
    sg=1,
    seed=seed,
    workers=num_workers,
    size=num_features,
    min_count=min_word_count,
    window=context_size,
    sample=downsampling
)
```

3. Build the model's vocabulary using the tokenized sentences and iterating through all the tokens. This is done using the build_vocab function in the following manner:

```
got2vec.build_vocab(sentences,progress_per=10000,
keep_raw_vocab=False, trim_rule=None)
```

4. Train the model using the following command:

```
got2vec.train(sentences, total_examples=got2vec.corpus_count,
total_words=None, epochs=got2vec.iter, start_alpha=None,
end_alpha=None, word_count=0, queue_factor=2, report_delay=1.0,
compute_loss=False)
```

5. Create a directory named trained, if it doesn't already exist. Save and checkpoint the `trained` model using the following commands:

```
if not os.path.exists("trained"):
    os.makedirs("trained")
got2vec.wv.save(os.path.join("trained", "got2vec.w2v"), ignore=[])
```

6. To load the saved model at any point, use the following command:

```
got2vec = w2v.KeyedVectors.load(os.path.join("trained",
"got2vec.w2v"))
```

How it works...

The functionality is as follows:

1. The declaration of model parameters does not produce any output. It just makes space in the memory to store variables as model parameters. The following screenshot describes this process:

```
In [18]:   1  #Define hyperparameters
           2
           3  # Dimensionality of the resulting word vectors.
           4  num_features = 300
           5
           6  # Minimum word count threshold.
           7  min_word_count = 3
           8
           9  # Number of threads to run in parallel.
          10  num_workers = multiprocessing.cpu_count()
          11
          12  # Context window length.
          13  context_size = 7
          14
          15  # Downsample setting for frequent words.
          16  downsampling = 1e-3
          17
          18  # Seed for the RNG, to make the results reproducible.
          19  seed = 1
```

2. The model is built using the preceding hyperparameters. In our case, we have named the model `got2vec` ,but the model may be named as per your liking. The model definition is illustrated in the following screenshot:

```
In [19]:   1  got2vec = w2v.Word2Vec(
           2      sg=1,
           3      seed=seed,
           4      workers=num_workers,
           5      size=num_features,
           6      min_count=min_word_count,
           7      window=context_size,
           8      sample=downsampling
           9  )
```

3. Running the `build_vocab` command on the model should produce an output as seen in the following screenshot:

```
In [20]:   1  got2vec.build_vocab(sentences,progress_per=10000, keep_raw_vocab=False, trim_rule=None)

2018-06-10 23:06:03,435 : INFO : collecting all words and their counts
2018-06-10 23:06:03,442 : INFO : PROGRESS: at sentence #0, processed 0 words, keeping 0 word types
2018-06-10 23:06:03,501 : INFO : PROGRESS: at sentence #10000, processed 141019 words, keeping 10280 word types
2018-06-10 23:06:03,547 : INFO : PROGRESS: at sentence #20000, processed 279976 words, keeping 13565 word types
2018-06-10 23:06:03,593 : INFO : PROGRESS: at sentence #30000, processed 420646 words, keeping 16602 word types
2018-06-10 23:06:03,640 : INFO : PROGRESS: at sentence #40000, processed 556994 words, keeping 18330 word types
2018-06-10 23:06:03,695 : INFO : PROGRESS: at sentence #50000, processed 699254 words, keeping 20291 word types
2018-06-10 23:06:03,747 : INFO : PROGRESS: at sentence #60000, processed 835958 words, keeping 21841 word types
2018-06-10 23:06:03,806 : INFO : PROGRESS: at sentence #70000, processed 970547 words, keeping 23057 word types
2018-06-10 23:06:03,849 : INFO : collected 23960 word types from a corpus of 1110288 raw words and 79418 sentences
2018-06-10 23:06:03,852 : INFO : Loading a fresh vocabulary
2018-06-10 23:06:03,899 : INFO : min_count=3 retains 13351 unique words (55% of original 23960, drops 10609)
2018-06-10 23:06:03,902 : INFO : min_count=3 leaves 1096572 word corpus (98% of original 1110288, drops 13716)
2018-06-10 23:06:03,958 : INFO : deleting the raw counts dictionary of 23960 items
2018-06-10 23:06:03,961 : INFO : sample=0.001 downsamples 49 most-common words
2018-06-10 23:06:03,963 : INFO : downsampling leaves estimated 851575 word corpus (77.7% of prior 1096572)
2018-06-10 23:06:03,966 : INFO : estimated required memory for 13351 words and 300 dimensions: 38717900 bytes
2018-06-10 23:06:04,029 : INFO : resetting layer weights
```

4. Training the model is done by defining the parameters as seen in the following screenshot:

```
In [21]:   1  #train model on sentences
           2  got2vec.train(sentences, total_examples=got2vec.corpus_count,
           3                total_words=None, epochs=got2vec.iter,
           4                start_alpha=None, end_alpha=None, word_count=0,
           5                queue_factor=2, report_delay=1.0, compute_loss=False)
```

5. The above command produces an output as shown in the following screenshot:

```
2018-06-10 23:06:04,319 : INFO : training model with 4 workers on 13351 vocabulary and 300 features, using sg=1 ha=0
sample=0.001 negative=5 window=7
2018-06-10 23:06:05,342 : INFO : PROGRESS: at 3.73% examples, 160036 words/s, in_qsize 7, out_qsize 0
2018-06-10 23:06:06,389 : INFO : PROGRESS: at 8.22% examples, 171593 words/s, in_qsize 7, out_qsize 0
2018-06-10 23:06:07,409 : INFO : PROGRESS: at 12.59% examples, 174664 words/s, in_qsize 7, out_qsize 0
2018-06-10 23:06:08,414 : INFO : PROGRESS: at 17.04% examples, 176645 words/s, in_qsize 7, out_qsize 0
2018-06-10 23:06:09,428 : INFO : PROGRESS: at 21.37% examples, 178994 words/s, in_qsize 7, out_qsize 0
2018-06-10 23:06:10,470 : INFO : PROGRESS: at 25.35% examples, 176095 words/s, in_qsize 7, out_qsize 0
2018-06-10 23:06:11,471 : INFO : PROGRESS: at 29.53% examples, 176031 words/s, in_qsize 7, out_qsize 0
2018-06-10 23:06:12,483 : INFO : PROGRESS: at 33.42% examples, 174908 words/s, in_qsize 8, out_qsize 0
2018-06-10 23:06:13,552 : INFO : PROGRESS: at 37.95% examples, 174545 words/s, in_qsize 7, out_qsize 0
2018-06-10 23:06:14,597 : INFO : PROGRESS: at 42.06% examples, 174654 words/s, in_qsize 7, out_qsize 0
2018-06-10 23:06:15,617 : INFO : PROGRESS: at 46.55% examples, 175824 words/s, in_qsize 7, out_qsize 0
2018-06-10 23:06:16,665 : INFO : PROGRESS: at 51.14% examples, 176453 words/s, in_qsize 7, out_qsize 0
2018-06-10 23:06:17,680 : INFO : PROGRESS: at 55.48% examples, 176822 words/s, in_qsize 7, out_qsize 0
2018-06-10 23:06:18,696 : INFO : PROGRESS: at 59.75% examples, 177108 words/s, in_qsize 7, out_qsize 0
2018-06-10 23:06:19,729 : INFO : PROGRESS: at 64.01% examples, 177182 words/s, in_qsize 8, out_qsize 0
2018-06-10 23:06:20,747 : INFO : PROGRESS: at 68.31% examples, 177407 words/s, in_qsize 7, out_qsize 0
2018-06-10 23:06:21,750 : INFO : PROGRESS: at 72.68% examples, 177766 words/s, in_qsize 6, out_qsize 1
2018-06-10 23:06:22,787 : INFO : PROGRESS: at 77.13% examples, 177748 words/s, in_qsize 6, out_qsize 1
2018-06-10 23:06:23,797 : INFO : PROGRESS: at 81.46% examples, 178328 words/s, in_qsize 7, out_qsize 0
2018-06-10 23:06:24,812 : INFO : PROGRESS: at 85.61% examples, 178113 words/s, in_qsize 6, out_qsize 1
2018-06-10 23:06:25,830 : INFO : PROGRESS: at 90.19% examples, 178609 words/s, in_qsize 7, out_qsize 0
2018-06-10 23:06:26,859 : INFO : PROGRESS: at 94.06% examples, 177939 words/s, in_qsize 7, out_qsize 0
2018-06-10 23:06:27,934 : INFO : PROGRESS: at 98.58% examples, 177623 words/s, in_qsize 7, out_qsize 0
2018-06-10 23:06:28,176 : INFO : worker thread finished; awaiting finish of 3 more threads
2018-06-10 23:06:28,205 : INFO : worker thread finished; awaiting finish of 2 more threads
2018-06-10 23:06:28,272 : INFO : worker thread finished; awaiting finish of 1 more threads
2018-06-10 23:06:28,295 : INFO : worker thread finished; awaiting finish of 0 more threads
2018-06-10 23:06:28,297 : INFO : training on 5551440 raw words (4258565 effective words) took 24.0s, 177726 effective
words/s
Out[21]: 4258565
```

6. The commands to save, checkpoint, and load the model produce the following output, as shown in the screenshot:

```
In [22]:    1 #save model
            2 if not os.path.exists("trained"):
            3     os.makedirs("trained")

In [23]:    1 got2vec.wv.save(os.path.join("trained", "got2vec.w2v"), ignore=[])

2018-06-10 23:06:28,326 : INFO : saving KeyedVectors object under trained/got2vec.w2v, separately None
2018-06-10 23:06:28,767 : INFO : saved trained/got2vec.w2v

In [24]:    1 #load model
            2 got2vec = w2v.KeyedVectors.load(os.path.join("trained", "got2vec.w2v"))

2018-06-10 23:06:28,787 : INFO : loading KeyedVectors object from trained/got2vec.w2v
2018-06-10 23:06:29,362 : INFO : loaded trained/got2vec.w2v
```

There's more...

Consider the following:

- In our case, we notice the `build_vocab` function identifies 23,960 different word types from a list of 1,110,288 words. However, this number will vary for different text corpora.
- Each word is represented by a 300-dimensional vector since we have declared the dimensionality to be 300. Increasing this number increases the training time of the model but also makes sure the model generalizes easily to new data.
- The downsampling rate of $1e-3$ is found to be a good rate. This is specified to let the model know when to downsample frequently occurring words, as they are not of much importance when it comes to analysis. Examples of such words are this, that, those, them, and so on.
- A seed is set to make results reproducible. Setting a seed also makes debugging a lot easier.
- Training the model takes about 30 seconds using regular CPU computing since the model is not very complex.
- The model, when check-pointed, is saved under the `trained` folder inside the working directory.

See also

For more information on `Word2Vec` models and the Gensim library, visit the following link:

```
https://radimrehurek.com/gensim/models/word2vec.html
```

Visualizing further

This section will describe how to squash the dimensionality of all the trained words and put it all into one giant matrix for visualization purposes. Since each word is a 300-dimensional vector, it needs to be brought down to a lower dimension for us to visualize it in a 2D space.

Getting ready

Once the model is saved and checkpointed after training, begin by loading it into memory, as you did in the previous section. The libraries and modules that will be utilized in this section are:

- tSNE
- pandas
- Seaborn
- numpy

How to do it...

The steps are as follows:

1. Squash the dimensionality of the 300-dimensional word vectors by using the following command:

```
tsne = sklearn.manifold.TSNE(n_components=2, random_state=0)
```

2. Put all the word vectors into one giant matrix (named all_word_vectors_matrix), and view it using the following commands:

```
all_word_vectors_matrix = got2vec.wv.syn0
print (all_word_vectors_matrix)
```

3. Use the tsne technique to fit all the learned representations into a two-dimensional space using the following command:

```
all_word_vectors_matrix_2d =
tsne.fit_transform(all_word_vectors_matrix)
```

4. Gather all the word vectors, as well as their associated words, using the following code:

```
points = pd.DataFrame(
    [
        (word, coords[0], coords[1])
        for word, coords in [
            (word,
all_word_vectors_matrix_2d[got2vec.vocab[word].index])
            for word in got2vec.vocab
        ]
```

```
        ],
        columns=["word", "x", "y"]
    )
```

5. The X and Y coordinates and associated words of the first ten points can be obtained using the following command:

```
points.head(10)
```

6. Plot all the points using the following commands:

```
sns.set_context("poster")
points.plot.scatter("x", "y", s=10, figsize=(15, 15))
```

7. A selected region of the plotted graph can be zoomed into for a closer inspection. Do this by slicing the original data using the following function:

```
def plot_region(x_bounds, y_bounds):
    slice = points[
        (x_bounds[0] <= points.x) &
        (points.x <= x_bounds[1]) &
        (y_bounds[0] <= points.y) &
        (points.y <= y_bounds[1])
    ]
    ax = slice.plot.scatter("x", "y", s=35, figsize=(10, 8))
        for i, point in slice.iterrows():
            ax.text(point.x + 0.005, point.y + 0.005, point.word,
    fontsize=11)
```

8. Plot the sliced data using the following command. The sliced data can be visualized as a zoomed-in region of the original plot of all data points:

```
plot_region(x_bounds=(20.0, 25.0), y_bounds=(15.5, 20.0))
```

How it works...

The functionality is as follows:

1. The t-SNE algorithm is a non-linear dimensionality reduction technique. Computers are easily able to interpret and process many dimensions during their computations. However, humans are only capable of visualizing two or three dimensions at a time. Therefore, these dimensionality reduction techniques come in very handy when trying to draw insights from data.

2. On applying t-SNE to the 300-dimensional vectors, we are able to squash it into just two dimensions to plot it and view it.

3. By specifying `n_components` as 2, we let the algorithm know that it has to squash the data into a two-dimensional space. Once this is done, we add all the squashed vectors into one giant matrix named `all_word_vectors_matrix`, which is illustrated in the following screenshot:

```
In [25]:    1 #Squash dimensionality to 2
            2 tsne = sklearn.manifold.TSNE(n_components=2, random_state=0)

In [26]:    1 #Put all the word vectors into one big matrix
            2 all_word_vectors_matrix = got2vec.wv.syn0

In [27]:    1 print (all_word_vectors_matrix)

[[ 0.09056767   0.13808218  -0.15090199 ...,  -0.0429583    0.37500036
   0.08323756]
 [ 0.21597612   0.14266475   0.10169824 ...,  -0.24987067   0.23634805
  -0.0658862 ]
 [ 0.1161018    0.00083609  -0.12968211 ...,  -0.02102427   0.14930068
   0.15946394]
 ...,
 [ 0.04589215  -0.00924069   0.12722564 ...,  -0.08988392   0.07124554
   0.0107049 ]
 [ 0.04099707   0.02326098   0.16791834 ...,  -0.11710527   0.07844222
   0.03250155]
 [ 0.00718155  -0.00764655   0.14178357 ...,  -0.06933824   0.05238995
   0.02870508]]
```

4. The t-SNE algorithm needs to be trained on all these word vectors. The training takes about five minutes on a regular CPU.

5. Once the t-SNE is finished training on all the word vectors, it outputs 2D vectors for each word. These vectors may be plotted as points by converting all of them into a data frame. This is done as shown in the following screenshot:

```
In [28]:    1 #train tsne
            2 all_word_vectors_matrix_2d = tsne.fit_transform(all_word_vectors_matrix)

In [29]:    1 #plot point in 2d space
            2 points = pd.DataFrame(
            3     [
            4         (word, coords[0], coords[1])
            5         for word, coords in [
            6             (word, all_word_vectors_matrix_2d[got2vec.vocab[word].index])
            7             for word in got2vec.vocab
            8         ]
            9     ],
           10     columns=["word", "x", "y"]
           11 )
```

6. We see that the preceding code produces a number of points where each point represents a **word** along with its **X** and **Y** coordinates. On inspection of the first twenty points of the data frame, we see an output as illustrated in the following screenshot:

```
In [30]:    1 points.head(20)
```

Out[30]:

	word	x	y
0	This	49.950523	-25.327841
1	edition	35.310001	56.534756
2	the	-1.957921	-10.210916
3	complete	14.203405	1.723180
4	of	-32.203743	38.342068
5	original	7.682618	44.520737
6	hardcover	32.301609	53.877991
7	ONE	17.199678	45.970676
8	A	4.724955	-11.747786
9	OF	37.043114	58.189484
10	KINGS	34.051868	56.641701
11	Bantam	37.084698	57.890003
12	Spectra	36.364651	56.821690
13	Book	36.035824	54.772251
14	PUBLISHING	32.160858	53.860893
15	HISTORY	32.051739	53.599449
16	published	34.316971	56.022495
17	paperback	31.942375	53.843864
18	September	31.740513	53.542671
19	and	-19.186104	27.123867

7. On plotting all the points using the `all_word_vectors_2D` variable, you should see an output that looks similar to the one in the following screenshot:

```
In [31]:    1 # Plotting using the seaborn library
            2 sns.set_context("poster")

In [32]:    1 points.plot.scatter("x", "y", s=10, figsize=(10, 10))
```

8. The above command will produce a plot of all tokens or words generated from the entire text as shown in the following screenshot:

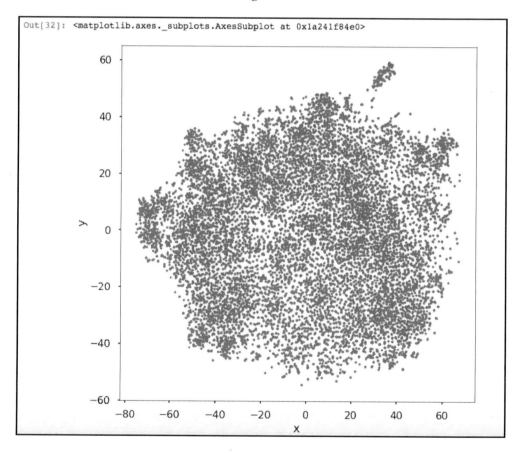

```
Out[32]: <matplotlib.axes._subplots.AxesSubplot at 0x1a241f84e0>
```

9. We can use the `plot_region` function to zoom into a certain area of the plot so that we are able to actually see the words, along with their coordinates. This step is illustrated in the following screenshot:

```
In [33]:    1  def plot_region(x_bounds, y_bounds):
            2      slice = points[
            3          (x_bounds[0] <= points.x) &
            4          (points.x <= x_bounds[1]) &
            5          (y_bounds[0] <= points.y) &
            6          (points.y <= y_bounds[1])
            7      ]
            8
            9      ax = slice.plot.scatter("x", "y", s=35, figsize=(10, 8))
           10      for i, point in slice.iterrows():
           11          ax.text(point.x + 0.005, point.y + 0.005, point.word, fontsize=11)
```

10. An enlarged or zoomed in area of the plot can be visualized by setting the `x_bounds` and `y_bounds`, values as shown in the following screenshot:

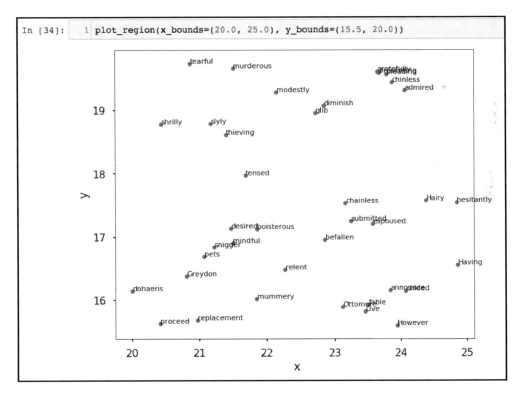

11. A different region of the same plot can be visualized by varying the `x_bounds` and `y_bounds` values as shown in the following two screenshots:

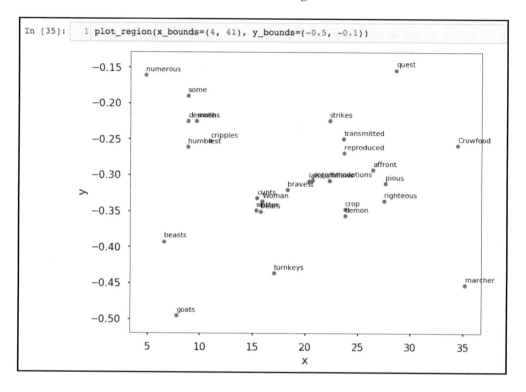

```
In [35]:    1 plot_region(x_bounds=(4, 41), y_bounds=(-0.5, -0.1))
```

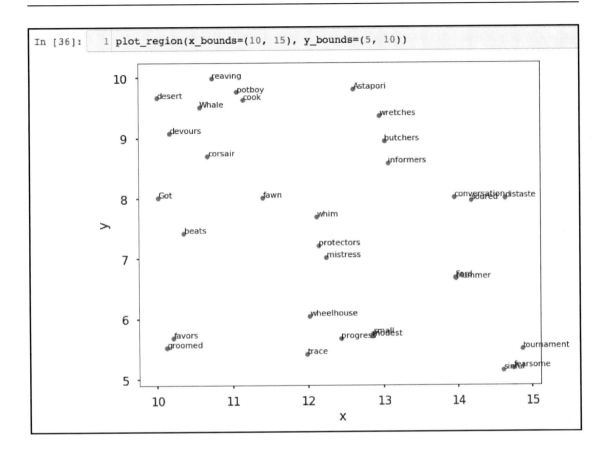

```
In [36]:    1  plot_region(x_bounds=(10, 15), y_bounds=(5, 10))
```

See also

The following additional points are of note:

- For more information on how the t-SNE algorithm works, visit the following link:
- https://www.oreilly.com/learning/an-illustrated-introduction-to-the-t-sne-algorithm
- More information about cosine distance similarity and ranking can be found by visiting the following link:
  https://code.google.com/archive/p/word2vec/
- Use the following link to explore the different functions of the Seaborn library:
  https://seaborn.pydata.org/

Analyzing further

This section will describe further analysis that can be performed on the data after visualization. For example, exploring cosine distance similarity between different word vectors.

Getting ready

The following link is a great blog on how cosine distance similarity works and also discusses some of the math involved:

http://blog.christianperone.com/2013/09/machine-learning-cosine-similarity-for-vector-space-models-part-iii/

How to do it...

Consider the following:

- Various natural-language processing tasks can be performed using the different functions of `Word2Vec`. One of them is finding the most semantically similar words given a certain word (that is, word vectors that have a high cosine similarity or a short Euclidean distance between them). This can be done by using the `most_similar` function form `Word2Vec`, as shown in the following screenshot:

```
In [37]:   1  got2vec.most_similar("Stark")

           2018-06-10 23:19:58,525 : INFO : precomputing L2-norms of word weight vectors

Out[37]: [('Eddard', 0.7668936252593994),
         ('Winterfell', 0.7056568264961243),
         ('Robb', 0.6961060762405396),
         ('ward', 0.6951630711555481),
         ('Benjen', 0.6915132403373718),
         ('beheaded', 0.691235363483429),
         ('Brandon', 0.6858698725700378),
         ('Rickard', 0.6805354952812195),
         ('Roslin', 0.6784009337425232),
         ('Tully', 0.6777351498603821)]
```

- This screenshots all the closest words related to the word `Lannister`:

```
In [38]:      1  got2vec.most_similar("Lannister")

Out[38]: [('pays', 0.7002766728401184),
          ('debts', 0.6817960143089294),
          ('Kevan', 0.6544679999351501),
          ('Kingslayer', 0.6358460783958435),
          ('lion', 0.6246482133865356),
          ('Jaime', 0.6158034205436707),
          ('scorn', 0.6151726245880127),
          ('Cersei', 0.6130942702293396),
          ('Stafford', 0.6115696430206299),
          ('Tywin', 0.6111588478088379)]
```

This screenshot shows a list of all the words related to word `Jon`:

```
In [39]:      1  got2vec.most_similar("Jon")

Out[39]: [('Snow', 0.743793249130249),
          ('Sam', 0.7024655938148499),
          ('Theon', 0.6459170579910278),
          ('Qhorin', 0.6453526616096497),
          ('Ygritte', 0.6438825130462646),
          ('Pyp', 0.6253669261932373),
          ('Ned', 0.6234972476959229),
          ('Ghost', 0.6164664626121521),
          ('Benjen', 0.6151096224784851),
          ('Reek', 0.6134048700332642)]
```

How it works...

Consider the following:

- There are various methods to measure the semantic similarity between words. The one we are using in this section is based on cosine similarity. We can also explore linear relationships between words by using the following lines of code:

```
def nearest_similarity_cosmul(start1, end1, end2):
    similarities = got2vec.most_similar_cosmul(
        positive=[end2, start1],
        negative=[end1]
```

```
)
start2 = similarities[0][0]
print("{start1} is related to {end1}, as {start2} is related to
{end2}".format(**locals()))
return start2
```

- To find the cosine similarity of nearest words to a given set of words, use the following commands:

```
nearest_similarity_cosmul("Stark", "Winterfell", "Riverrun")
nearest_similarity_cosmul("Jaime", "sword", "wine")
nearest_similarity_cosmul("Arya", "Nymeria", "dragons")
```

- The preceding process is illustrated in the following screenshot:

```
In [40]:  1  #distance, similarity, and ranking
          2  def nearest_similarity_cosmul(start1, end1, end2):
          3      similarities = got2vec.most_similar_cosmul(
          4          positive=[end2, start1],
          5          negative=[end1]
          6      )
          7      start2 = similarities[0][0]
          8      print("{start1} is related to {end1}, as {start2} is related to {end2}".format(**locals()))
          9      return start2
         10
```

- The results are as follows:

```
In [41]:  1  nearest_similarity_cosmul("Stark", "Winterfell", "Riverrun")
          2  nearest_similarity_cosmul("Jaime", "sword", "wine")
          3  nearest_similarity_cosmul("Arya", "Nymeria", "dragons")

Stark is related to Winterfell, as Tully is related to Riverrun
Jaime is related to sword, as Cersei is related to wine
Arya is related to Nymeria, as Dany is related to dragons
```

- As seen in this section, word vectors form the basis of all NLP tasks. It is important to understand them and the math that goes into building these models before diving into more complicated NLP models such as **recurrent neural networks** and **Long Short-Term Memory (LSTM)** cells.

See also

Further reading can be undertaken for a better understanding of the use of cosine distance similarity, clustering and other machine learning techniques used in ranking word vectors. Provided below are a few links to useful published papers on this topic:

- https://s3.amazonaws.com/academia.edu.documents/32952068/pg049_
  Similarity_Measures_for_Text_Document_Clustering.pdf?AWSAccessKeyId=
  AKIAIWOWYYGZ2Y53UL3AExpires=1530163881Signature=
  YG6YjvJb2z0JjmfHzaYujA2ioIo%3Dresponse-content-disposition=
  inline%3B%20filename%3DSimilarity_Measures_for_Text_Document_Cl.pdf

- http://csis.pace.edu/ctappert/dps/d861-12/session4-p2.pdf

12
Creating a Movie Recommendation Engine with Keras

The following recipes will be covered in this chapter:

- Downloading MovieLens datasets
- Manipulating and merging the MovieLens datasets
- Exploring the MovieLens datasets
- Preparing dataset for the deep learning pipeline
- Applying the deep learning pipeline with Keras
- Evaluating the recommendation engine's accuracy

Introduction

In 2006, a small DVD rental company set out to make their recommendation engine 10% better. That company was Netflix and The Netflix Prize was worth $1M. This competition attracted many engineers and scientists from some of the largest tech companies around the world. The recommendation engine for the winning participant was built with machine learning. Netflix is now one of the leading tech giants when it comes to streaming data and recommending to its customers what they should watch next.

Ratings are everywhere these days, no matter what you are doing. If you are looking for a recommendation to go out to eat at a new restaurant, to order some clothing online, to watch a new movie at your local theater, or to watch a new series on television or online, there is most likely a website or a mobile application that will give you some type of rating along with feedback on the product or service you are looking to purchase. It is because of this immediate increase in feedback that recommendation algorithms have become more in demand over the last couple of years. This chapter will focus on building a movie recommendation engine for users, using the deep learning library Keras.

Downloading MovieLens datasets

There is a great research lab center that began in 1992 in Minneapolis, MN called **GroupLens**, which focuses on recommendation engines and has graciously put together millions of rows of data over several years from the MovieLens website. We will use its dataset as our data source for training our recommendation engine model.

Getting ready

The MovieLens dataset is housed and maintained by GroupLens on the following website:

`https://grouplens.org/datasets/movielens/.`

It is important to note that the dataset we will use will come directly from their website and not from a third-party intermediary or repository. Additionally, there are two different datasets that are available for us to query:

- Recommended for new research
- Recommended for education and development

The purpose of using this dataset is purely for educational purposes, so we will download the data from the **education and development** section of the website. The educational data still contains a significant number of rows for our model, as it contains 100,000 ratings, as seen in the following screenshot:

recommended for **education** and **development**

MovieLens Latest Datasets

These datasets will change over time, and are not appropriate for reporting research results. We will keep the download links stable for automated downloads. We will not archive or make available previously released versions.

Small: 100,000 ratings and 1,300 tag applications applied to 9,000 movies by 700 users. Last updated 10/2016.

- README.html
- ml-latest-small.zip (size: 1 MB)

Full: 26,000,000 ratings and 750,000 tag applications applied to 45,000 movies by 270,000 users. Includes tag genome data with 12 million relevance scores across 1,100 tags. Last updated 8/2017.

- README.html
- ml-latest.zip (size: 224 MB)

Permalink: http://grouplens.org/datasets/movielens/latest/

Additionally, this dataset has information regarding over 600 anonymous users collected over a period of several years between 1/9/1995 and 3/31/2015. The dataset was last updated in October 2017.

F Maxwell Harper and Joseph A Konstan, 2015. *The MovieLens Datasets: History and Context*. ACM **Transactions on Interactive Intelligent Systems (TiiS)** 5, 4, Article 19 (December 2015), 19 pages. DOI: http://dx.doi.org/10.1145/2827872

How to do it...

This section will cover downloading and unzipping the MovieLens dataset:

1. Download the research version of the smaller MovieLens dataset, which is available for public download at the following website: https://grouplens.org/datasets/movielens/latest/.

2. Download the ZIP file called `ml-latest-small.zip` to one of our local folders, as seen in in the following screenshot:

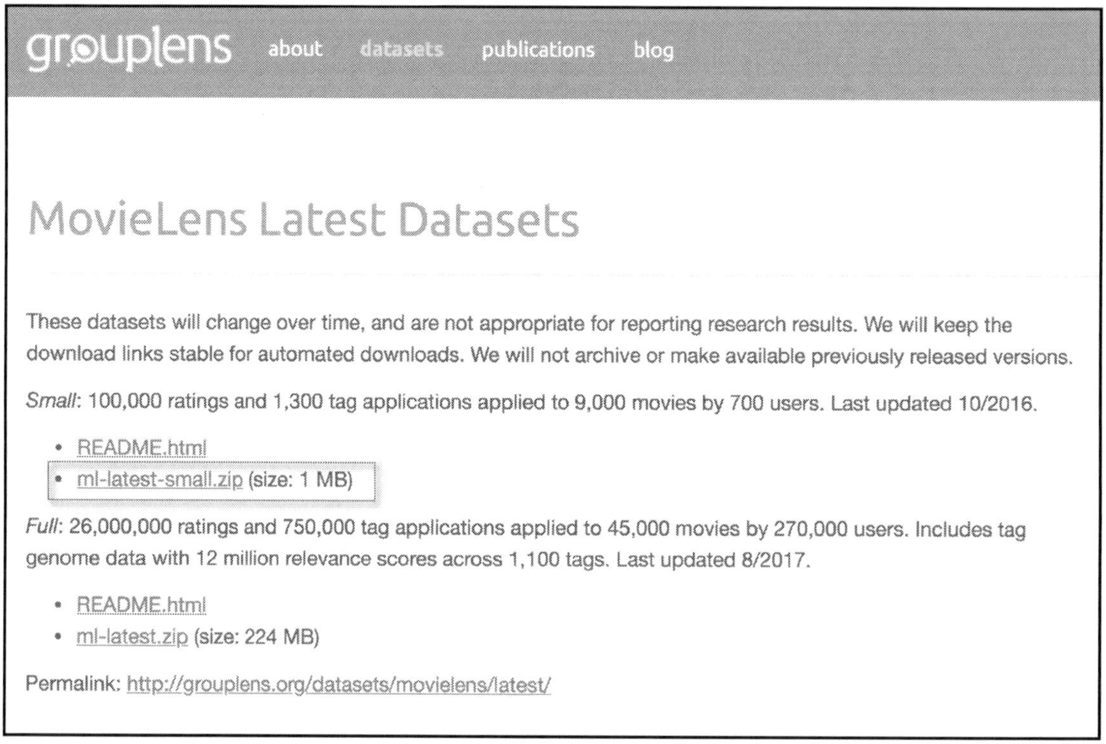

3. When `ml-latest-small.zip` is downloaded and unzipped, the following four files should be extracted:

   1. `links.csv`
   2. `movies.csv`
   3. `ratings.csv`
   4. `tags.csv`

4. Execute the following script to begin our `SparkSession`:

```
spark = SparkSession.builder \
        .master("local") \
        .appName("RecommendationEngine") \
        .config("spark.executor.memory", "6gb") \
        .getOrCreate()
```

5. Confirm the following six files are available for access by executing the following script:

```
import os
os.listdir('ml-latest-small/')
```

6. Load each dataset into a Spark dataframe using the following script:

```
movies = spark.read.format('com.databricks.spark.csv')\
            .options(header='true', inferschema='true')\
            .load('ml-latest-small/movies.csv')
tags = spark.read.format('com.databricks.spark.csv')\
            .options(header='true', inferschema='true')\
            .load('ml-latest-small/tags.csv')
links = spark.read.format('com.databricks.spark.csv')\
            .options(header='true', inferschema='true')\
            .load('ml-latest-small/links.csv')
ratings = spark.read.format('com.databricks.spark.csv')\
            .options(header='true', inferschema='true')\
            .load('ml-latest-small/ratings.csv')
```

7. Confirm the row counts for each dataset by executing the following script:

```
print('The number of rows in movies dataset is
{}'.format(movies.toPandas().shape[0]))
print('The number of rows in ratings dataset is
{}'.format(ratings.toPandas().shape[0]))
print('The number of rows in tags dataset is
{}'.format(tags.toPandas().shape[0]))
print('The number of rows in links dataset is
{}'.format(links.toPandas().shape[0]))
```

How it works...

This section will focus on explaining the fields in each of the datasets available in the MovieLens 100K dataset. Take a look at these steps:

1. The datasets are all available in the zipped file, `ml-latest-small.zip`, where the `ratings.csv` dataset will serve as the pseudo-fact table of our data, since it has transactions for each movie that is rated. The dataset, `ratings`, has the four column names shown in the following screenshot:

```
In [1]: spark = SparkSession.builder \
            .master("local") \
            .appName("RecommendationEngine") \
            .config("spark.executor.memory", "6gb") \
            .getOrCreate()

In [2]: import os
        os.listdir('ml-latest-small/')
Out[2]: ['tags.csv', 'links.csv', 'README.txt', 'ratings.csv', 'movies.csv']

In [3]: movies = spark.read.format('com.databricks.spark.csv')\
                        .options(header='true', inferschema='true')\
                        .load('ml-latest-small/movies.csv')
        tags = spark.read.format('com.databricks.spark.csv')\
                        .options(header='true', inferschema='true')\
                        .load('ml-latest-small/tags.csv')
        links = spark.read.format('com.databricks.spark.csv')\
                        .options(header='true', inferschema='true')\
                        .load('ml-latest-small/links.csv')
        ratings = spark.read.format('com.databricks.spark.csv')\
                        .options(header='true', inferschema='true')\
                        .load('ml-latest-small/ratings.csv')

In [4]: ratings.columns
Out[4]: ['userId', 'movieId', 'rating', 'timestamp']
```

2. The dataset shows the **rating** selected by each **userId** over the course of their time, from the earliest rating to the latest rating. The range of a **rating** can vary from 0.5 to 5.0 stars, as seen by `userId = 1` in the following screenshot:

```
In [5]: ratings.show(truncate=False)

+------+-------+------+----------+
|userId|movieId|rating|timestamp |
+------+-------+------+----------+
|1     |31     |2.5   |1260759144|
|1     |1029   |3.0   |1260759179|
|1     |1061   |3.0   |1260759182|
|1     |1129   |2.0   |1260759185|
|1     |1172   |4.0   |1260759205|
|1     |1263   |2.0   |1260759151|
|1     |1287   |2.0   |1260759187|
|1     |1293   |2.0   |1260759148|
|1     |1339   |3.5   |1260759125|
|1     |1343   |2.0   |1260759131|
|1     |1371   |2.5   |1260759135|
|1     |1405   |1.0   |1260759203|
|1     |1953   |4.0   |1260759191|
|1     |2105   |4.0   |1260759139|
|1     |2150   |3.0   |1260759194|
|1     |2193   |2.0   |1260759198|
|1     |2294   |2.0   |1260759108|
|1     |2455   |2.5   |1260759113|
|1     |2968   |1.0   |1260759200|
|1     |3671   |3.0   |1260759117|
+------+-------+------+----------+
only showing top 20 rows
```

3. The `tags` dataset contains a **tag** column that contains a specific word or phrase used by that user to describe a specific **movieId** at a specific **timestamp**. As can be seen in the following screenshot, **userId 15** was not particularly fond of **Sandra Bulluck** in one of her movies:

```
In [6]:  tags.show(truncate = False)

+------+-------+----------------------+----------+
|userId|movieId|tag                   |timestamp |
+------+-------+----------------------+----------+
|15    |339    |sandra 'boring' bullock|1138537770|
|15    |1955   |dentist               |1193435061|
|15    |7478   |Cambodia              |1170560997|
|15    |32892  |Russian               |1170626366|
|15    |34162  |forgettable           |1141391765|
|15    |35957  |short                 |1141391873|
|15    |37729  |dull story            |1141391806|
|15    |45950  |powerpoint            |1169616291|
|15    |100365 |activist              |1425876220|
|15    |100365 |documentary           |1425876220|
|15    |100365 |uganda                |1425876220|
|23    |150    |Ron Howard            |1148672905|
|68    |2174   |music                 |1249808064|
|68    |2174   |weird                 |1249808102|
|68    |8623   |Steve Martin          |1249808497|
|73    |107999 |action                |1430799184|
|73    |107999 |anime                 |1430799184|
|73    |107999 |kung fu               |1430799184|
|73    |111624 |drama                 |1431584497|
|73    |111624 |indie                 |1431584497|
+------+-------+----------------------+----------+
only showing top 20 rows
```

4. The `movies` dataset is primarily a lookup table for the genre of films that have ratings. There are 19 unique **genres** that can be associated with a film; however, it is important to note that a film can be affiliated with more than one genre at a time, as seen in the following screenshot:

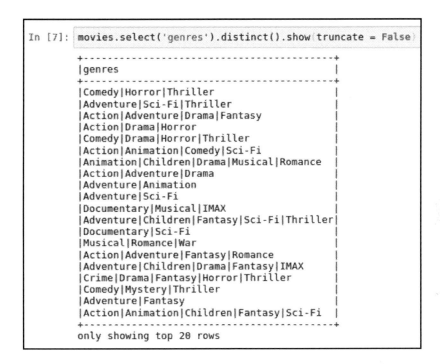

5. The final dataset is the `links` dataset, which also functions as a lookup table. It connects movies from MovieLens to data available for those same movies on popular film database sites such as `http://www.imdb.com`, as well as `https://www.themoviedb.org`. Links to IMDB are under the column called **imdbId**, and links to the MovieDB are under the column called **tmdbId**, as seen in the following screenshot:

```
In [8]:  links.show()

+--------+-------+-------+
|movieId|imdbId|tmdbId|
+--------+-------+-------+
|       1|114709|   862|
|       2|113497|  8844|
|       3|113228| 15602|
|       4|114885| 31357|
|       5|113041| 11862|
|       6|113277|   949|
|       7|114319| 11860|
|       8|112302| 45325|
|       9|114576|  9091|
|      10|113189|   710|
|      11|112346|  9087|
|      12|112896| 12110|
|      13|112453| 21032|
|      14|113987| 10858|
|      15|112760|  1408|
|      16|112641|   524|
|      17|114388|  4584|
|      18|113101|     5|
|      19|112281|  9273|
|      20|113845| 11517|
+--------+-------+-------+
only showing top 20 rows
```

6. Before we finish, it is always a good idea to confirm that we are truly experiencing the expected row counts from all of the datasets. This helps to ensure that we did not encounter any issues with uploading the files to the notebook. We should expect to see around 100k rows for the **ratings** dataset, as seen in the following screenshot:

```
In [9]:  print('The number of rows in movies dataset is {}'.format(movies.toPandas().shape[0]))
         print('The number of rows in ratings dataset is {}'.format(ratings.toPandas().shape[0]))
         print('The number of rows in tags dataset is {}'.format(tags.toPandas().shape[0]))
         print('The number of rows in links dataset is {}'.format(links.toPandas().shape[0]))

The number of rows in movies dataset is 9125
The number of rows in ratings dataset is 100004
The number of rows in tags dataset is 1296
The number of rows in links dataset is 9125
```

There's more...

While we are not going to use the 20 million-row dataset version of MovieLens for this chapter, you could elect to use it for this recommendation engine. You will still have the same four datasets, but with much more data, especially for the `ratings` dataset. If you choose to go with this approach, the full zipped dataset can be downloaded from the following website:

```
http://files.grouplens.org/datasets/movielens/ml-latest.zip
```

See also

To learn more about the metadata behind the MovieLens dataset used in this chapter, visit the following website:

```
http://files.grouplens.org/datasets/movielens/ml-latest-small-README.html
```

To learn more about the history and context of the MovieLens dataset used in this chapter, visit the following website:

```
https://www.slideshare.net/maxharp3r/the-movielens-datasets-history-and-context
```

To learn more about *The Netflix Prize*, visit the following website:

```
https://www.netflixprize.com/
```

Manipulating and merging the MovieLens datasets

We currently have four separate datasets that we are working with, but ultimately we would like to get it down to a single dataset. This chapter will focus on pairing down our datasets to one.

Getting ready

This section will not require any import of PySpark libraries but a background in SQL joins will come in handy, as we will explore multiple approaches to joining dataframes.

How to do it...

This section will walk through the following steps for joining dataframes in PySpark:

1. Execute the following script to rename all field names in `ratings`, by appending a _1 to the end of the name:

```
for i in ratings.columns:
    ratings = ratings.withColumnRenamed(i, i+'_1')
```

2. Execute the following script to `inner join` the `movies` dataset to the `ratings` dataset, creating a new table called `temp1`:

```
temp1 = ratings.join(movies, ratings.movieId_1 == movies.movieId,
how = 'inner')
```

3. Execute the following script to inner join the `temp1` dataset to the `links` dataset, creating a new table called `temp2`:

```
temp2 = temp1.join(links, temp1.movieId_1 == links.movieId, how =
'inner')
```

4. Create our final combined dataset, `mainDF`, by left-joining `temp2` to `tags` using the following script:

```
mainDF = temp2.join(tags, (temp2.userId_1 == tags.userId) &
(temp2.movieId_1 == tags.movieId), how = 'left')
```

5. Select only the columns needed for our final `mainDF` dataset by executing the following script:

```
mainDF = mainDF.select('userId_1',
                       'movieId_1',
                       'rating_1',
                       'title',
                       'genres',
                       'imdbId',
                       'tmdbId',
                       'timestamp_1').distinct()
```

How it works...

This section will walk through our design process for joining tables together as well as which final columns will be kept:

1. As was mentioned in the previous section, the **ratings** dataframe will serve as our fact table, since it contains all the main transactions of ratings for each user over time. The columns in **ratings** will be used in each subsequent join with the other three tables, and to maintain a uniqueness of the columns, we will attach a _1 to the end of each column name, as seen in the following screenshot:

```
In [10]: for i in ratings.columns:
             ratings = ratings.withColumnRenamed(i, i+'_1')

In [11]: ratings.show()
```

```
+--------+--------+--------+----------+
|userId_1|movieId_1|rating_1|timestamp_1|
+--------+--------+--------+----------+
|       1|      31|     2.5| 1260759144|
|       1|    1029|     3.0| 1260759179|
|       1|    1061|     3.0| 1260759182|
|       1|    1129|     2.0| 1260759185|
|       1|    1172|     4.0| 1260759205|
|       1|    1263|     2.0| 1260759151|
|       1|    1287|     2.0| 1260759187|
|       1|    1293|     2.0| 1260759148|
|       1|    1339|     3.5| 1260759125|
|       1|    1343|     2.0| 1260759131|
|       1|    1371|     2.5| 1260759135|
|       1|    1405|     1.0| 1260759203|
|       1|    1953|     4.0| 1260759191|
|       1|    2105|     4.0| 1260759139|
|       1|    2150|     3.0| 1260759194|
|       1|    2193|     2.0| 1260759198|
|       1|    2294|     2.0| 1260759108|
|       1|    2455|     2.5| 1260759113|
|       1|    2968|     1.0| 1260759200|
|       1|    3671|     3.0| 1260759117|
+--------+--------+--------+----------+
only showing top 20 rows
```

2. We can now join the three lookup tables to the **ratings** table. The first two joins to **ratings** are **inner** joins, as the row counts for **temp1** and **temp2** are still **100,004** rows. The third join to **ratings** from **tags** needs to be an **outer** join to avoid dropping rows. Additionally, the join needs to be applied to both **movieId** as well as **userId,** as a tag is unique to both a specific user and a specific movie at any given time. The row counts for the three tables **temp1, temp2,** and **mainDF** can be seen in the following screenshot:

```
In [12]: temp1 = ratings.join(movies, ratings.movieId_1 == movies.movieId, how = 'inner')

In [13]: temp2 = temp1.join(links, temp1.movieId_1 == links.movieId, how = 'inner')

In [14]: mainDF = temp2.join(tags, (temp2.userId_1 == tags.userId) &
                             (temp2.movieId_1 == tags.movieId), how = 'left')

In [15]: print(temp1.count())
         print(temp2.count())
         print(mainDF.count())

         100004
         100004
         100441
```

Often times when working with joins between datasets, we encounter three types of joins: inner, left, and right. An inner join will only produce a result set when both join keys are available from dataset 1 and dataset 2. A left join will produce all of the rows from dataset 1 and only the rows with matching keys from dataset 2. A right join will produce all of the rows from dataset 2 and only the rows from the matching keys from dataset 1. Later on in this section, we will explore SQL joins within Spark.

3. It is interesting to note that our newly created dataset, **mainDF**, has **100,441** rows, instead of the **100,004** rows that are in the original dataset for **ratings,** as well as **temp1** and **temp2**. There are 437 ratings that have more than one tag associated with them. Additionally, we can see that the majority of **ratings_1** have a **null tag** value affiliated with them, as seen in the following screenshot:

```
In [16]: mainDF.groupBy(['tag']).agg({'rating_1':'count'})\
             .withColumnRenamed('count(rating_1)', 'Row Count').orderBy(["Row Count"],ascending=False)\
             .show()

         +------------+---------+
         |         tag|Row Count|
         +------------+---------+
         |        null|    99502| <----
         |    toplist07|      22|
         |    toplist12|      18|
         |    toplist15|      16|
         |    toplist10|      16|
         |    toplist11|      16|
         |    toplist06|      15|
         |    toplist09|      15|
         |    toplist08|      15|
         |    toplist13|      14|
         |    toplist14|      13|
         |       funny|      13|
         |twist ending|      12|
         |       anime|      10|
         |      sci-fi|      10|
         |      comedy|      10|
         |      quirky|       8|
         |martial arts|       8|
         | dark comedy|       7|
         |  psychology|       7|
         +------------+---------+
         only showing top 20 rows
```

4. We have accumulated additional duplicative columns that will no longer be needed. There are 14 columns in total, as seen in the following screenshot:

```
In [17]:  mainDF.columns

Out[17]:  ['userId_1',
           'movieId_1',
           'rating_1',
           'timestamp_1',
           'movieId',
           'title',
           'genres',
           'movieId',
           'imdbId',
           'tmdbId',
           'userId',
           'movieId',
           'tag',
           'timestamp']
```

5. Additionally, we have determined that the **tags** field is relatively useless as it has over 99k null values. Therefore, we will use the `select()` function on the dataframe to pull in only the eight columns that we will use for our recommendation engine. We can then confirm that our final new dataframe, **mainDF**, has the correct amount of rows, **100,004**, as seen in the following screenshot:

```
In [17]: mainDF.columns

Out[17]: ['userId_1',
          'movieId_1',
          'rating_1',
          'timestamp_1',
          'movieId',
          'title',
          'genres',
          'movieId',
          'imdbId',
          'tmdbId',
          'userId',
          'movieId',
          'tag',
          'timestamp']

In [18]: mainDF = mainDF.select('userId_1','movieId_1','rating_1','title','genres', 'imdbId','tmdbId', 'timestamp_1')\
                 .distinct()

In [19]: mainDF.count()

Out[19]: 100004
```

There's more...

While we did do our joins using functions within a Spark dataframe using PySpark, we could have also done it by registering the dataframes as temporary tables and then joining them using `sqlContext.sql()`:

1. First, we would register each of our datasets as temporary views using `creatorReplaceTempView()`, as seen in the following script:

```
movies.createOrReplaceTempView('movies_')
links.createOrReplaceTempView('links_')
ratings.createOrReplaceTempView('ratings_')
```

2. Next, we would write our SQL script just as we would do with any other relational database using the `sqlContext.sql()` function, as seen in the following script:

```
mainDF_SQL = \
sqlContext.sql(
"""
```

```
select
r.userId_1
,r.movieId_1
,r.rating_1
,m.title
,m.genres
,l.imdbId
,l.tmdbId
,r.timestamp_1
from ratings_ r

inner join movies_ m on
r.movieId_1 = m.movieId
inner join links_ l on
r.movieId_1 = l.movieId
"""
)
```

3. Finally, we can profile the new dataframe, **mainDF_SQL**, and observe that it looks the same as our other dataframe, **mainDF**, while also keeping the exact same row count, as seen in the following screenshot:

```
In [20]: movies.createOrReplaceTempView('movies_')
         links.createOrReplaceTempView('links_')
         ratings.createOrReplaceTempView('ratings_')

In [21]: mainDF_SQL = \
         sqlContext.sql(
         """
         select
         r.userId_1
         ,r.movieId_1
         ,r.rating_1
         ,m.title
         ,m.genres
         ,l.imdbId
         ,l.tmdbId
         ,r.timestamp_1
         from ratings_ r
         inner join movies_ m on
         r.movieId_1 = m.movieId
         inner join links_ l on
         r.movieId_1 = l.movieId
         """
         )

In [22]: mainDF_SQL.show(n = 5)

         +--------+---------+--------+--------------------+--------------------+-------+------+-----------+
         |userId_1|movieId_1|rating_1|               title|              genres|imdbId |tmdbId|timestamp_1|
         +--------+---------+--------+--------------------+--------------------+-------+------+-----------+
         |       1|       31|     2.5|Dangerous Minds (...|               Drama|112792|  9909| 1260759144|
         |       1|     1029|     3.0|        Dumbo (1941)|Animation|Childre...| 33563| 11360| 1260759179|
         |       1|     1061|     3.0|     Sleepers (1996)|            Thriller|117665|   819| 1260759182|
         |       1|     1129|     2.0|Escape from New Y...|   Action|Adventure...| 82340|  1103| 1260759185|
         |       1|     1172|     4.0|Cinema Paradiso (...|               Drama| 95765| 11216| 1260759205|
         +--------+---------+--------+--------------------+--------------------+-------+------+-----------+
         only showing top 5 rows

In [23]: mainDF_SQL.count()
Out[23]: 100004
```

See also

To learn more about SQL programming within Spark, visit the following website:

```
https://spark.apache.org/docs/latest/sql-programming-guide.html
```

Exploring the MovieLens datasets

Before any modeling takes place, it is important to get familiar with the source dataset and perform some exploratory data analysis.

Getting ready

We will import the following library to assist with visualizing and exploring the MovieLens dataset: `matplotlib`.

How to do it...

This section will walk through the steps to analyze the movie ratings in the MovieLens database:

1. Retrieve some summary statistics on the `rating_1` column by executing the following script:

   ```
   mainDF.describe('rating_1').show
   ```

2. Build a histogram of the distribution of ratings by executing the following script:

   ```
   import matplotlib.pyplot as plt
   %matplotlib inline

   mainDF.select('rating_1').toPandas().hist(figsize=(16, 6),
   grid=True)
   plt.title('Histogram of Ratings')
   plt.show()
   ```

3. Execute the following script to view the values of the histogram in a spreadsheet dataframe:

```
mainDF.groupBy(['rating_1']).agg({'rating_1':'count'})\
  .withColumnRenamed('count(rating_1)', 'Row Count').orderBy(["Row
Count"],ascending=False)\
  .show()
```

4. A unique count of user selections of ratings can be stored as a dataframe, `userId_frequency`, by executing the following script:

```
userId_frequency =
mainDF.groupBy(['userId_1']).agg({'rating_1':'count'})\
        .withColumnRenamed('count(rating_1)', '# of
Reviews').orderBy(["# of            Reviews"],ascending=False)
```

5. Plot a histogram of `userID_frequency` using the following script:

```
userId_frequency.select('# of
Reviews').toPandas().hist(figsize=(16, 6), grid=True)
plt.title('Histogram of User Ratings')
plt.show()
```

How it works...

This section will discuss how the ratings and user activities are distributed in the MovieLens database. Take a look at these steps:

1. We can see that the average movie rating made by a user is approximately 3.5, as seen in the following screenshot:

```
In [24]: mainDF.describe('rating_1').show()

         +-------+------------------+
         |summary|          rating_1|
         +-------+------------------+
         |  count|            100004|
         |   mean| 3.543608255669773|
         | stddev|1.0580641091070384|
         |    min|               0.5|
         |    max|               5.0|
         +-------+------------------+
```

2. Even though the average rating is 3.54, we can see that the histogram shows that the median rating is 4, which indicates that the user ratings are heavily skewed towards higher ratings, as seen in the following screenshot:

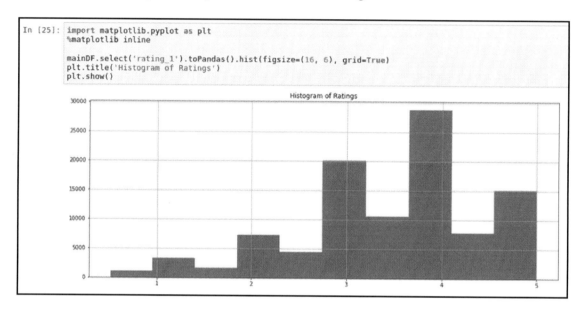

```
In [25]: import matplotlib.pyplot as plt
         %matplotlib inline

         mainDF.select('rating_1').toPandas().hist(figsize=(16, 6), grid=True)
         plt.title('Histogram of Ratings')
         plt.show()
```

3. Another look at the data behind the histogram shows that users select **4.0** most frequently, followed by **3.0,** and then **5.0**. Additionally, it is interesting to note that users are more likely to give ratings that are at the 0.0 level and not at the 0.5 level, as seen in the following screenshot:

```
In [26]: mainDF.groupBy(['rating_1']).agg({'rating_1':'count'})\
                .withColumnRenamed('count(rating_1)', 'Row Count').orderBy(["Row Count"],ascending=False)\
                .show()

         +--------+---------+
         |rating_1|Row Count|
         +--------+---------+
         |     4.0|    28750|
         |     3.0|    20064|
         |     5.0|    15095|
         |     3.5|    10538|
         |     4.5|     7723|
         |     2.0|     7271|
         |     2.5|     4449|
         |     1.0|     3326|
         |     1.5|     1687|
         |     0.5|     1101|
         +--------+---------+
```

4. We can look at the distribution of user selection of ratings and see that some users are very active in expressing their opinions on the films they've seen. This is the case with anonymous user **547** who has posted **2391** ratings, as seen in the following screenshot:

```
In [27]: userId_frequency = mainDF.groupBy(['userId_1']).agg({'rating_1':'count'})\
                .withColumnRenamed('count(rating_1)', '# of Reviews')\
                .orderBy(["# of Reviews"],ascending=False)

In [28]: userId_frequency.show()

         +--------+------------+
         |userId_1|# of Reviews|
         +--------+------------+
         |     547|        2391|
         |     564|        1868|
         |     624|        1735|
         |      15|        1700|
         |      73|        1610|
         |     452|        1340|
         |     468|        1291|
         |     380|        1063|
         |     311|        1019|
         |      30|        1011|
         |     294|         947|
         |     509|         923|
         |     580|         922|
         |     213|         910|
         |     212|         876|
         |     472|         830|
         |     388|         792|
         |      23|         726|
         |     457|         713|
         |     518|         707|
         +--------+------------+
         only showing top 20 rows
```

5. However, when we look at the distribution of users making rating selections, we do see that while there are some instances of users making over a thousand selections on their own, the overwhelming majority of users have made less than 250 selections, as seen in the following screenshot:

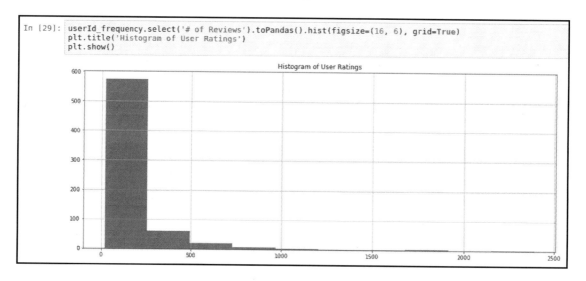

```
In [29]:  userId_frequency.select('# of Reviews').toPandas().hist(figsize=(16, 6), grid=True)
          plt.title('Histogram of User Ratings')
          plt.show()
```

6. The distribution of the histogram is the previous screenshot is in a long-tail format which indicates that the majority of the occurrences are away from the center of the histogram. This is an indication that the overwhelming majority of ratings are defined by a few users.

There's more...

There are features that the `pyspark` dataframe that are similar to those of the `pandas` dataframe and can perform some summary statistics on specific columns.

In `pandas`, we perform summary statistics using the following script:
```
dataframe['column'].describe().
```

In `pyspark`, we perform summary statistics using the following script:
```
dataframe.describe('column').show().
```

See also

To learn more about the `describe()` function in PySpark, visit the following website:
`http://spark.apache.org/docs/2.1.0/api/python/pyspark.sql.html#pyspark.sql.DataFrame.describe`

Preparing dataset for the deep learning pipeline

We are now ready to prepare our dataset to be fed into the deep learning model that we will build in Keras.

Getting ready

While preparing the dataset for `Keras` we will import the following libraries into our notebook:

- `import pyspark.sql.functions as F`
- `import numpy as np`
- `from pyspark.ml.feature import StringIndexer`
- `import keras.utils`

How to do it...

This section walks through the following steps to prepare the dataset for the deep learning pipeline:

1. Execute the following script to clean up the column names:

```
mainDF = mainDF.withColumnRenamed('userId_1', 'userid')
mainDF = mainDF.withColumnRenamed('movieId_1', 'movieid')
mainDF = mainDF.withColumnRenamed('rating_1', 'rating')
mainDF = mainDF.withColumnRenamed('timestamp_1', 'timestamp')
mainDF = mainDF.withColumnRenamed('imdbId', 'imdbid')
mainDF = mainDF.withColumnRenamed('tmdbId', 'tmdbid')
```

2. The `rating` column is currently divided into 0.5 increments. Tweak the ratings to be rounded to a whole integer using the following script:

```
import pyspark.sql.functions as F
mainDF = mainDF.withColumn("rating", F.round(mainDF["rating"], 0))
```

3. Convert the `genres` column from a string to an index with a name of `genreCount` based on the frequency of the `genres` labels as seen in the following script:

```
from pyspark.ml.feature import StringIndexer
string_indexer = StringIndexer(inputCol="genres",
outputCol="genreCount")
mainDF = string_indexer.fit(mainDF).transform(mainDF)
```

4. Pair down our dataframe using the following script:

```
mainDF = mainDF.select('rating', 'userid', 'movieid', 'imdbid',
'tmdbid', 'timestamp', 'genreCount')
```

5. Split `mainDF` into a training and testing set for model-training purposes, using the following script:

```
trainDF, testDF = mainDF.randomSplit([0.8, 0.2], seed=1234)
```

6. Convert our two Spark dataframes, `trainDF` and `testDF`, into four numpy arrays for consumption within our deep learning model using the following script:

```
import numpy as np

xtrain_array = np.array(trainDF.select('userid','movieid',
'genreCount').collect())
xtest_array = np.array(testDF.select('userid','movieid',
'genreCount').collect())

ytrain_array = np.array(trainDF.select('rating').collect())
ytest_array = np.array(testDF.select('rating').collect()
```

7. Convert both `ytrain_array` and `ytest_array` into one-hot encoded labels, `ytrain_OHE` and `ytest_OHE`, using the following script:

```
import keras.utils as u
ytrain_OHE = u.to_categorical(ytrain_array)
ytest_OHE = u.to_categorical(ytest_array)
```

How it works...

This section explains how we prepare the dataset for the deep learning pipeline:

1. For ease of use inside the deep learning pipeline, it is best to clean up the column names and the order of the columns before the pipeline receives the data. After renaming the column headers, we can view the updated columns, as seen in the following script:

```
In [30]: mainDF = mainDF.withColumnRenamed('userId_1', 'userid')
         mainDF = mainDF.withColumnRenamed('movieId_1', 'movieid')
         mainDF = mainDF.withColumnRenamed('rating_1', 'rating')
         mainDF = mainDF.withColumnRenamed('timestamp_1', 'timestamp')
         mainDF = mainDF.withColumnRenamed('imdbId', 'imdbid')
         mainDF = mainDF.withColumnRenamed('tmdbId', 'tmdbid')

In [31]: mainDF.columns

Out[31]: ['userid',
          'movieid',
          'rating',
          'title',
          'genres',
          'imdbid',
          'tmdbid',
          'timestamp']
```

2. A bit of manipulation is performed on the `ratings` column to round up values of 0.5 increments to the next-highest whole number. This will assist when we are doing our multi-class classification within Keras to group `ratings` into six categories, instead of 11 categories.

3. To consume the movie genre types into the deep learning model within, we need to convert the string values of `genres` into a numeric label. The most frequent genres type will get a value of 0, and the values increase for the next most frequent- type. In the following screenshot, we can see that **Good Will Hunting** has two **genres** associated with it (**Drama | Romance**), and that is the fourth most-frequent **genreCount,** with a value of **3.0**:

```
In [33]:  from pyspark.ml.feature import StringIndexer
          string_indexer = StringIndexer(inputCol="genres", outputCol="genreCount")
          mainDF = string_indexer.fit(mainDF).transform(mainDF)
          mainDF.show()
```

userid	movieid	rating	title	genres	imdbid	tmdbid	timestamp	genreCount
2	367	3.0	Mask, The (1994)	Action|Comedy|Cri...	110475	854	835355619	119.0
4	913	5.0	Maltese Falcon, T...	Film-Noir|Mystery	33870	963	949919247	231.0
4	1344	5.0	Cape Fear (1962)	Crime|Drama|Thriller	55824	11349	949919247	15.0
4	2454	5.0	Fly, The (1958)	Horror|Mystery|Sc...	51622	11815	949982274	448.0
4	2986	3.0	RoboCop 2 (1990)	Action|Crime|Sci-...	100502	5549	949896015	406.0
15	3755	2.0	Perfect Storm, Th...	Drama|Thriller	177971	2133	1416119541	11.0
15	3994	4.0	Unbreakable (2000)	Drama|Sci-Fi	217869	9741	997937442	65.0
15	5956	3.0	Gangs of New York...	Crime|Drama	217505	3131	1163876422	6.0
15	71282	3.0	Food, Inc. (2008)	Documentary	1286537	18570	1465793912	13.0
15	110553	1.0	The Amazing Spide...	Action|Sci-Fi|IMAX	1872181	102382	1416120149	238.0
15	152081	3.0	Zootopia (2016)	Action|Adventure|...	2948356	269149	1460076733	126.0
16	527	4.0	Schindler's List ...	Drama|War	108052	424	1178364921	12.0
19	805	3.0	Time to Kill, A (...	Drama|Thriller	117913	1645	855190199	11.0
19	1073	4.0	Willy Wonka & the...	Children|Comedy|F...	67992	252	855190128	83.0
21	21	3.0	Get Shorty (1995)	Comedy|Crime|Thri...	113161	8012	853846669	67.0
21	1321	4.0	American Werewolf...	Comedy|Horror|Thr...	82010	814	853851156	154.0
22	1645	3.0	The Devil's Advoc...	Drama|Mystery|Thr...	118971	1813	1131662268	20.0
26	2692	5.0	Run Lola Run (Lol...	Action|Crime	130827	104	1354752751	48.0
26	30810	3.0	Life Aquatic with...	Adventure|Comedy|...	362270	421	1353708965	61.0
27	1704	5.0	Good Will Hunting...	Drama|Romance	119217	489	939080090	3.0

```
only showing top 20 rows
```

4. The **genres** column is no longer needed for the deep model, as it will be replaced by the **genreCount** column, as seen in the following screenshot:

```
In [34]:  mainDF = mainDF.select('rating', 'userid', 'movieid', 'imdbid', 'tmdbid', 'timestamp', 'genreCount')

In [35]:  mainDF.show()

          +------+------+-------+-------+-------+-----------+----------+
          |rating|userid|movieid| imdbid|tmdbid|  timestamp|genreCount|
          +------+------+-------+-------+-------+-----------+----------+
          |   3.0|     2|    367| 110475|   854|  835355619|     119.0|
          |   5.0|     4|    913|  33870|   963|  949919247|     231.0|
          |   5.0|     4|   1344|  55824| 11349|  949919247|      15.0|
          |   5.0|     4|   2454|  51622| 11815|  949982274|     448.0|
          |   3.0|     4|   2986| 100502|  5549|  949896015|     406.0|
          |   2.0|    15|   3755| 177971|  2133| 1416119541|      11.0|
          |   4.0|    15|   3994| 217869|  9741|  997937442|      65.0|
          |   3.0|    15|   5956| 217505|  3131| 1163876422|       6.0|
          |   3.0|    15|  71282|1286537| 18570| 1465793912|      13.0|
          |   1.0|    15| 110553|1872181|102382| 1416120149|     238.0|
          |   3.0|    15| 152081|2948356|269149| 1460076733|     126.0|
          |   4.0|    16|    527| 108052|   424| 1178364921|      12.0|
          |   3.0|    19|    805| 117913|  1645|  855190199|      11.0|
          |   4.0|    19|   1073|  67992|   252|  855190128|      83.0|
          |   3.0|    21|     21| 113161|  8012|  853846669|      67.0|
          |   4.0|    21|   1321|  82010|   814|  853851156|     154.0|
          |   3.0|    22|   1645| 118971|  1813| 1131662268|      20.0|
          |   5.0|    26|   2692| 130827|   104| 1354752751|      48.0|
          |   3.0|    26|  30810| 362270|   421| 1353708965|      61.0|
          |   5.0|    27|   1704| 119217|   489|  939080090|       3.0|
          +------+------+-------+-------+-------+-----------+----------+
          only showing top 20 rows
```

5. Our main dataframe, **mainDF**, is split into a **trainDF** and **testDF** for modeling, training, and evaluation purposes, using an 80/20 split. The row count for all three dataframes can be seen in the following screenshot:

```
In [36]:  trainDF, testDF = mainDF.randomSplit([0.8, 0.2], seed=1234)

In [37]:  print('The number of rows in mainDF is {}'.format(mainDF.count()))
          print('The number of rows in trainDF is {}'.format(trainDF.count()))
          print('The number of rows in testDF is {}'.format(testDF.count()))

          The number of rows in mainDF is 100004
          The number of rows in trainDF is 80146
          The number of rows in testDF is 19858
```

6. Data is passed into a Keras deep learning model, using matrices instead of dataframes. Therefore, our training and testing dataframes are converted into numpy arrays and split out into *x* and *y*. The features selected for `xtrain_array` and `xtest_array` are **userid**, **movieid**, and **genreCount**. These are the only features that will we will use to determine what a potential rating will be for a user. We are dropping `imdbid` and `tmdbid`, as they are directly tied to the `movieid` and therefore will not provide any additional value. `timestamp` will be removed to filter out any bias associated with frequency of voting. Finally, `ytest_array` and `ytrain_array` will contain the label value for rating. The `shape` of all four arrays can be seen in the following screenshot:

```
In [38]: import numpy as np
         xtrain_array = np.array(trainDF.select('userid','movieid', 'genreCount').collect())
         xtest_array = np.array(testDF.select('userid','movieid', 'genreCount').collect())

In [39]: ytrain_array = np.array(trainDF.select('rating').collect())
         ytest_array = np.array(testDF.select('rating').collect())

In [40]: print(xtest_array.shape)
         print(ytest_array.shape)
         print(xtrain_array.shape)
         print(ytrain_array.shape)

         (19858, 3)
         (19858, 1)
         (80146, 3)
         (80146, 1)
```

There's more...

While `ytrain_array` and `ytest_array` are both labels in a matrix format, they are not ideally encoded for deep learning. Since this is technically a classification model that we are building we need to encode our labels in a manner for them to be understood by the model. This means that our ratings of 0 through 5 should be encoded as 0 or 1 values, based on their value elements. Therefore, if a rating received the highest value of 5, it should be encoded as [0,0,0,0,0,1]. The first position is reserved for 0, and the sixth position is reserved for 1, indicating a value of 5. We can make this conversion using `keras.utils` and convert our categorical variables to one-hot encoded variables. In doing this, the shape of our training label is converted from **(80146,1)** to **(80146,6)** as seen in the following screenshot:

```
In [40]:  print(xtest_array.shape)
          print(ytest_array.shape)
          print(xtrain_array.shape)
          print(ytrain_array.shape)

          (19858, 3)
          (19858, 1)
          (80146, 3)
          (80146, 1)

In [41]:  import keras.utils as u
          ytrain_OHE = u.to_categorical(ytrain_array)
          ytest_OHE = u.to_categorical(ytest_array)

          Using TensorFlow backend.

In [42]:  print ytrain_OHE.shape
          print(ytest_OHE.shape)

          (80146, 6)
          (19858, 6)
```

See also

To learn more about `keras.utils` visit the following website: `https://keras.io/utils/`

Applying the deep learning model with Keras

At this point, we are ready to apply Keras to our data.

Getting ready

We will be using the following from Keras:

- `from keras.models import Sequential`
- `from keras.layers import Dense, Activation`

How to do it...

This section walks through the following steps to apply a deep learning model, using Keras on our dataset:

1. Import the following libraries to build a `Sequential` model from `keras`, using the following script:

    ```
    from keras.models import Sequential
    from keras.layers import Dense, Activation
    ```

2. Configure the `Sequential` model from `keras`, using the following script:

    ```
    model = Sequential()
    model.add(Dense(32, activation='relu',
    input_dim=xtrain_array.shape[1]))
    model.add(Dense(10, activation='relu'))
    model.add(Dense(ytrain_OHE.shape[1], activation='softmax'))
    model.compile(optimizer='adam', loss='categorical_crossentropy',
    metrics=['accuracy'])
    ```

3. We `fit` and train the model and store the results to a variable called `accuracy_history`, using the following script:

    ```
    accuracy_history = model.fit(xtrain_array, ytrain_OHE, epochs=20,
    batch_size=32)
    ```

How it works...

This section explains the configuration of the Keras model that is applied to the dataset to predict a rating based on the features selected.

1. In Keras, a `Sequential` model is simply a linear combination of layers, which are the following: `Dense` is used to define the layer types to a fully-connected layer within a deep neural network. Finally, `Activation` is used to convert the inputs from the features into an output that can be used as a prediction. There are many types of activation functions that can be used in a neural network; however, for this chapter, we will go with `relu` and `softmax`.

2. The `Sequential` model is configured to include three `Dense` layers:

    1. The first layer has `input_dim` set to the number of features from `xtrain_array`. The `shape` feature pulls in the value of 3, using `xtrain_array.shape[1]`. Additionally, the first layer is set to have `32` neurons in the first layer of the neural network. Finally, the three input parameters are activated using the `relu` activation function. Only the first layer requires an explicit definition of the input dimensions. This is not required in subsequent layers, as they will be able to infer the number of dimensions from the previous layer.

    2. The second layer in the `Sequential` model has `10` neurons in the neural network along with an activation function set to `relu`. Rectified linear units are used early on in the neural network process because they are effective during the training process. This is due to the simplicity of the equation as any value less than 0 is thrown out, which is not the case with other activation functions.

    3. The third and final layer of the `Sequential` model requires six outputs based on every possible scenario of a rating from 0 to 5. This requires setting the output to the value of `ytrain_OHE.shape[1]`. The output is generated using a `softmax` function which is often the case at the end of a neural network, as it is very useful for classification purposes. At this point, we are looking to classify a value between 0 and 5.

    4. Once the layers are specified, we must `compile` the model.

    5. We optimize the model using `adam`, which stands for **Adaptive Moment Estimation**. Optimizers are great for configuring the learning rate of the gradient descent that the model uses to tweak and update the weights of the neural network. `adam` is a popular optimizer, as it is said to combine some of the best features from other common optimizers.

    6. Our loss function is set to `categorical_crossentroy`, which is often used when looking to predict a multi-class classification. The loss function evaluates the performance of the model as it is being trained.

3. We train the model using the training features, `xtrain_array`, and the training labels `ytrain_OHE`. The model is trained over 20 **epochs,** each time with a **batch_size** set to **32**. The model output for `accuracy` and `loss` over each epoch are captured in a variable called `accuracy_history` and can be viewed as seen in the following screenshot:

```
In [45]: accuracy_history = model.fit(xtrain_array, ytrain_OHE, epochs=20, batch_size=32)

Epoch 1/20
80146/80146 [==============================] - 4s 45us/step - loss: 4.4843 - acc: 0.3385
Epoch 2/20
80146/80146 [==============================] - 4s 56us/step - loss: 1.4123 - acc: 0.3939
Epoch 3/20
80146/80146 [==============================] - 4s 46us/step - loss: 1.4056 - acc: 0.3939
Epoch 4/20
80146/80146 [==============================] - 3s 43us/step - loss: 1.4037 - acc: 0.3939
Epoch 5/20
80146/80146 [==============================] - 3s 42us/step - loss: 1.4031 - acc: 0.3939
Epoch 6/20
80146/80146 [==============================] - 3s 43us/step - loss: 1.4028 - acc: 0.3939
Epoch 7/20
80146/80146 [==============================] - 3s 43us/step - loss: 1.4028 - acc: 0.3939
Epoch 8/20
80146/80146 [==============================] - 4s 45us/step - loss: 1.4028 - acc: 0.3939
Epoch 9/20
80146/80146 [==============================] - 4s 53us/step - loss: 1.4027 - acc: 0.3939
Epoch 10/20
80146/80146 [==============================] - 4s 44us/step - loss: 1.4027 - acc: 0.3939
Epoch 11/20
80146/80146 [==============================] - 4s 45us/step - loss: 1.4027 - acc: 0.3939
Epoch 12/20
80146/80146 [==============================] - 4s 44us/step - loss: 1.4027 - acc: 0.3939
Epoch 13/20
80146/80146 [==============================] - 4s 44us/step - loss: 1.4027 - acc: 0.3939
Epoch 14/20
80146/80146 [==============================] - 4s 44us/step - loss: 1.4027 - acc: 0.3939
Epoch 15/20
80146/80146 [==============================] - 4s 49us/step - loss: 1.4027 - acc: 0.3939
Epoch 16/20
80146/80146 [==============================] - 4s 45us/step - loss: 1.4027 - acc: 0.3939
Epoch 17/20
80146/80146 [==============================] - 4s 44us/step - loss: 1.4027 - acc: 0.3939
Epoch 18/20
80146/80146 [==============================] - 4s 45us/step - loss: 1.4027 - acc: 0.3939
Epoch 19/20
80146/80146 [==============================] - 4s 47us/step - loss: 1.4027 - acc: 0.3939
Epoch 20/20
80146/80146 [==============================] - 4s 46us/step - loss: 1.4027 - acc: 0.3939
```

There's more...

While we can print out the **loss** and **accuracy** scores over each epoch, it is always better to visualize both outputs over each of the 20 epochs. We can plot both by using the following script:

```
plt.plot(accuracy_history.history['acc'])
plt.title('Accuracy vs. Epoch')
plt.xlabel('Epoch')
plt.ylabel('Accuracy')
```

```
plt.show()

plt.plot(accuracy_history.history['loss'])
plt.title('Loss vs. Epoch')
plt.xlabel('Epoch')
plt.ylabel('Loss')
plt.show()
```

The output of the script can be seen in the following screenshot:

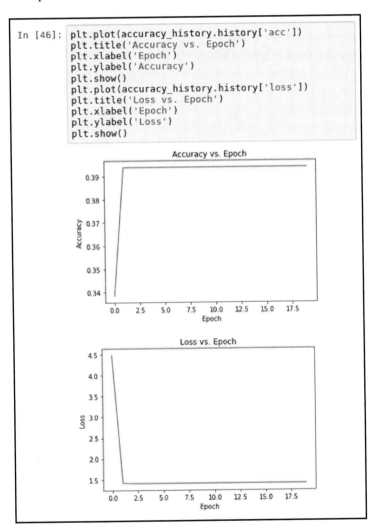

It appears that after the second epoch, both the loss and accuracy are stabilized in the model.

See also

To learn more about getting started with the `Sequential` model from `keras`, visit the following website: `https://keras.io/getting-started/sequential-model-guide/`.

Evaluating the recommendation engine's accuracy

We can now calculate the accuracy rate of our deep learning model built on Keras.

Getting ready

Evaluating a `Sequential` model for accuracy requires using the `model.evaluate()` function within Keras.

How to do it...

We can simply calculate the accuracy score, `accuracy_rate`, by executing the following script:

```
score = model.evaluate(xtest_array, ytest_OHE, batch_size=128)
accuracy_rate = score[1]*100
print('accuracy is {}%'.format(round(accuracy_rate,2)))
```

How it works...

Our model performance is based on evaluating our test features, `xtest_array`, with our test labels, `ytest_OHE`. We can use `model.evaluate()` and set the `batch_size` for evaluation at `128` elements. We can see that our accuracy is around 39%, as seen in the following screenshot:

```
In [47]:  score = model.evaluate(xtest_array, ytest_OHE, batch_size=128)
          accuracy_rate = score[1]*100
          print('accuracy is {}%'.format(round(accuracy_rate,2)))

          19858/19858 [==============================] - 0s 9us/step
          accuracy is 38.87%
```

This means that we are able to determine the rating by a user between 0 and 5 and at nearly a 39% accuracy rate.

See also

To learn more about model performance with Keras metrics, visit the following website:

https://keras.io/metrics/

13
Image Classification with TensorFlow on Spark

The following recipes will be covered in this chapter:

- Downloading 30 images each of Messi and Ronaldo
- Configuring PySpark installation with deep learning packages
- Loading images onto PySpark dataframes
- Understanding transfer learning
- Creating a pipeline for image classification training
- Evaluating model performance
- Fine-tuning model parameters

Introduction

Over the last couple of years, image recognition software has become increasingly in demand. It is not a coincidence that this demand has coincided with the advancements of big data storage. Google Photos, Facebook, and Apple all utilize image classification software to tag photos for their users. Much of the image recognition software used by these companies are powered by deep learning models built on top of popular libraries such as TensorFlow. This chapter extends the technique of deep learning by leveraging the training of one set of images to the learning or recognition of another set of images. This concept is referred to as transfer learning. In this chapter, we will focus on leveraging transfer learning to recognize the top two football players in the world:

1. Lionel Messi
2. Cristiano Ronaldo

Take a look at this photo:

Downloading 30 images each of Messi and Ronaldo

Before any classification of images can take place, we must first download images of our footballers from the web.

Getting ready

There are several add-ons to browsers that download images in bulk. Since Ubuntu comes pre-installed with Mozilla Firefox as a browser, we will use it as our browser of choice to install a bulk image downloader extension.

How to do it...

The following section explains how to download images in bulk. Take a look at these steps:

1. Visit the following website for downloading and installing Firefox add-ons:

   ```
   https://addons.mozilla.org/en-US/firefox/
   ```

2. Search for and select the **Download all Images** add-on, as seen in the following screenshot:

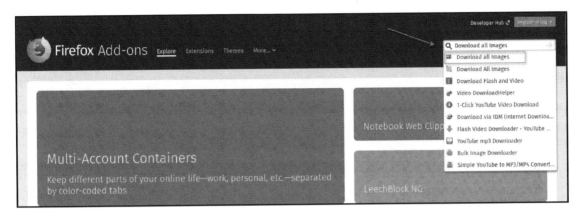

3. This will take us to the installation page. At which point, select **Add to Firefox,** as seen in the following screenshot:

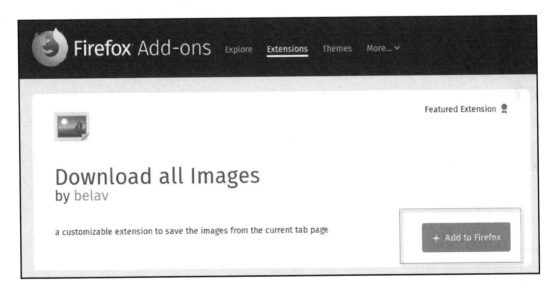

4. Confirm your installation, as this add-on will require permission to access your browser's download history, access your data for all websites, and send you notifications.

5. Once that is complete, you should see a small picture icon for **Download all Images** on the upper right-hand side of your browser, as seen in the following screenshot:

6. We are now ready to begin downloading images of our footballers, using the newly added extension for Firefox. We can visit many different websites to download images from, such as `https://www.google.com`. For the purposes of this chapter, search for Cristiano Ronaldo and download his images using `https://www.pexels.com`, as seen in the following screenshot:

7. Next, click on the **Download all Images** icon and specify the following download settings for the images as shown in the following screenshot:

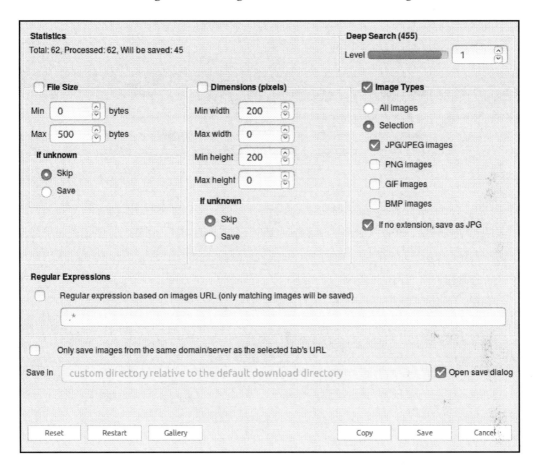

8. Click on **Save**, as you will then have the option to download all of the pictures as a `.zip` file to a local directory. You can then unzip the file into a folder and peruse through all of the images. In our example, the images have all been extracted to `/Home/sparkNotebooks/Ch13/football/ronaldo/`, as seen in the following screenshot:

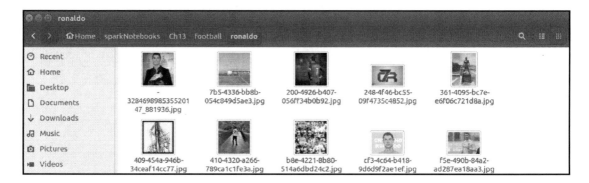

9. Of all the images that are available in the folder, choose 30 images of Ronaldo and name them `ronaldo1.jpg, ronaldo2.jpg....ronaldo30.jpg`, as shown in the following screenshot:

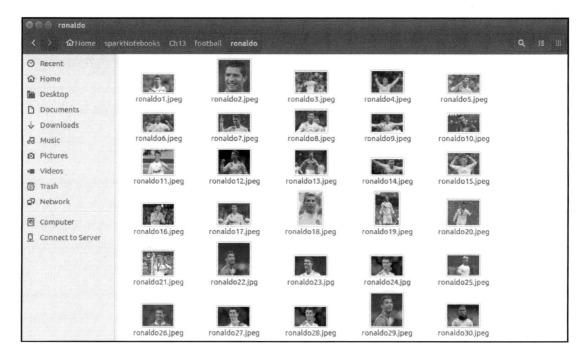

10. Repeat the steps again, this time for Messi to obtain 30 images of each. The final folder structure should look like the following:

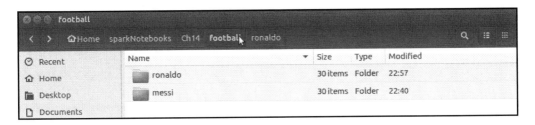

How it works...

This section explains the process of how the add-on downloads the images in bulk to our desired location:

1. Bulk image downloading software is readily available these days and integrated within browsers. We will use **Download all Images** as an add-on with Firefox to quickly download images for Messi and Ronaldo.

2. We want to specify settings in the app to download lower-quality images, so we set a minimum threshold of 0 bytes, a maximum threshold of 500 bytes, and an image type of jpg or jpeg.

3. Finally, we want to handpick only the 30 images that best represent each player, as 20 of them will serve as our training dataset, and the remaining 10 will serve as our test dataset. All other images can be deleted.

4. All of the images will be tagged or labeled for training purposes by their last name and a number between 1 and 30. For example, Messi1.jpg, Messi2.jpg, Ronaldo1.jpg, Ronaldo2.jpg, and so on.

There's more...

While you can use your own images that you have downloaded using **Download all Images**, you can download the same images for Ronaldo and Messi that will be used for training purposes in this chapter by visiting the following websites:

For Messi:

```
https://github.com/asherif844/ApacheSparkDeepLearningCookbook/tree/master/CH13/
football/messi
```

For Ronaldo:

```
https://github.com/asherif844/ApacheSparkDeepLearningCookbook/tree/master/CH13/
football/ronaldo
```

See also

There are similar add-ons and extensions for other browsers. If you are working with Google Chrome, there is a similar add-on called **Download'em All** that can be downloaded from the following website:

```
https://chrome.google.com/webstore/detail/downloadem-all/
ccdfjnniglfbpaplecpifdiglfmcebce?hl=en-US
```

Configuring PySpark installation with deep learning packages

There are some additional configurations that need to be done within PySpark to implement deep learning packages from Databricks called `spark-deep-learning`. These are configurations that were made all the way back in chapter 1, *Setting up your Spark Environment for Deep Learning*.

Getting ready

This configuration requires making changes in the terminal, using **bash**.

How to do it...

The following section walks through the steps to configure PySpark with deep learning packages:

1. Open the terminal application and type in the following command:

   ```
   nano .bashrc.
   ```

2. Scroll all the way to the bottom of the document and look for the `sparknotebook()` function we created back in chapter 1, *Setting up your Spark Environment for Deep Learning*.

3. Update the last row of the function. It should currently look like the following:

```
$SPARK_HOME/bin/pyspark.
```

Change it to the following:

```
$SPARK_HOME/bin/pyspark --packages databricks:spark-deep-
learning:0.1.0-spark2.1-s_2.11.
```

4. Once the configuration change is made, exit the document and execute the following script to confirm that all necessary changes were saved:

```
source .bashrc.
```

How it works...

The following section explains how PySpark is modified to incorporate deep learning packages take a look at these steps:

1. Accessing bash allows us to make configurations at the command line, as seen in the following screenshot:

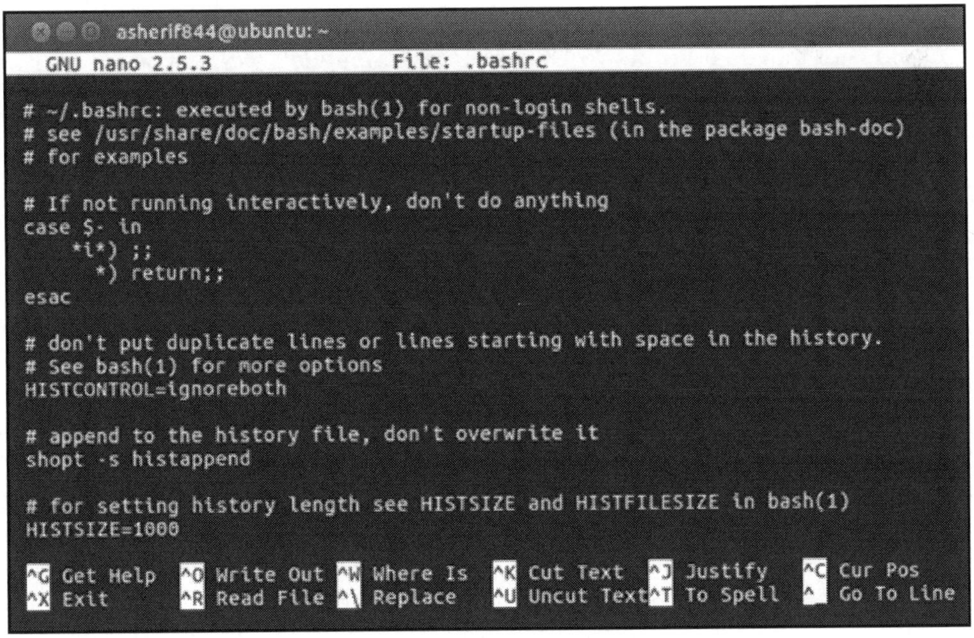

2. At the end of our document, we can see our original function, `sparknotebook()`, still intact; however, we need to modify it to incorporate the `spark-deep-learning` package.

3. Since this modification is to PySpark directly, and not to a Python library, we cannot incorporate it into our framework using a typical `pip` installation. Instead, we will modify our PySpark configuration to appear as shown in the following screenshot:

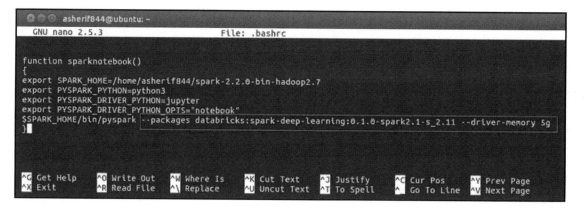

4. We have now configured our PySpark installation to incorporate deep learning libraries that incorporate APIs that help build models for all types of solutions, such as image classification.

There's more...

This package, `spark-deep-learning`, is managed by `Databricks`. Databricks was founded by one of the co-creators of Spark, Ali Ghodsi, and is used to deliver managed Spark offerings through a unified platform.

See also

To learn more about other third-party packages developed for Spark, visit the following website:

```
https://spark-packages.org/.
```

Loading images on to PySpark dataframes

We are now ready to begin importing our images into our notebook for classification.

Getting ready

We will be using several libraries and their dependencies in this section, which will require us to install the following packages through `pip install` on the terminal within Ubuntu Desktop:

```
pip install tensorflow==1.4.1
pip install keras==2.1.5
pip install sparkdl
pip install tensorframes
pip install kafka
pip install py4j
pip install tensorflowonspark
pip install jieba
```

How to do it...

The following steps will demonstrate how to decode images into a Spark dataframe:

1. Initiate a `spark` session, using the following script:

```
spark = SparkSession.builder \
        .master("local") \
        .appName("ImageClassification") \
        .config("spark.executor.memory", "6gb") \
        .getOrCreate()
```

2. Import the following libraries from PySpark to create dataframes, using the following script:

```
import pyspark.sql.functions as f
import sparkdl as dl
```

3. Execute the following script to create two dataframes for **Messi** and **Ronaldo,** using the main folder location for each player:

```
dfMessi = dl.readImages('football/messi/').withColumn('label',
f.lit(0))
dfRonaldo = dl.readImages('football/ronaldo/').withColumn('label',
f.lit(1))
```

4. Split each dataframe into a train-and-test set at a $66.7/33.3$ ratio, and set a random seed set to 12, using the following script:

```
trainDFmessi, testDFmessi = dfMessi.randomSplit([66.7, 33.3], seed
= 12)
trainDFronaldo, testDFronaldo = dfRonaldo.randomSplit([66.7, 33.3],
seed =    12)
```

5. Finally, merge both the training dataframes and the testing dataframes into one new dataframe each, `trainDF` and `testDF`, using the following script:

```
trainDF = trainDFmessi.unionAll(trainDFronaldo)
testDF = testDFmessi.unionAll(testDFronaldo)
```

How it works...

The following section explains how the images are loaded and read into a Jupyter notebook. Take a look at these steps:

1. We always begin a Spark project by initiating a Spark session to set the application name as well as to set the Spark executor memory.
2. We import both `pyspark.sql.functions` and `sparkdl` to help build dataframes based on encoded images. When `sparkdl` is imported, we see that it is using **TensorFlow** in the backend, as seen in the following screenshot:

```
In [1]:  spark = SparkSession.builder \
             .master("local") \
             .appName("ImageClassification") \
             .config("spark.executor.memory", "6gb") \
             .getOrCreate()

In [2]:  import pyspark.sql.functions as f
         import sparkdl as dl

         Using TensorFlow backend.
```

3. The dataframes are created using `sparkdl` with three columns: **filepath**, **image**, and **label**. Sparkdl is used to import each image and encode it by color and shape. Additionally, a function, `lit`, is used to tag a literal value (**0 or 1**) to each of the two dataframes under the **label** column for training purposes, as seen in the following screenshot:

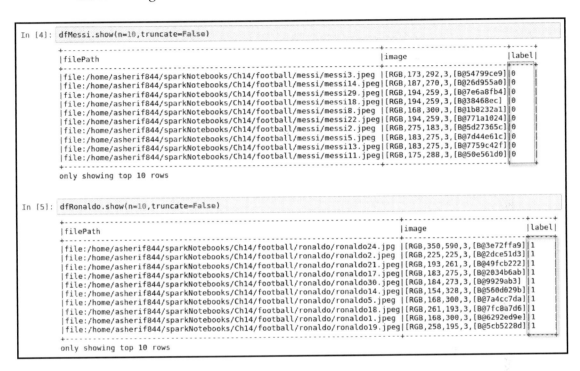

4. Since there are 30 images for each footballer, a split of 66.7/33.3 is used to create **18** training images and **12** testing images, as seen in the following screenshot:

 Please note that the more images used in the training process the better when using deep learning. However, the point we will try and prove in this chapter is that with transfer learning being implemented as an extension of deep learning, we can classify images using fewer training samples, as is the case in this chapter with only 30 images for Ronaldo and Messi each.

```
In [6]:  trainDFmessi, testDFmessi = dfMessi.randomSplit([66.7, 33.3], seed =12)
         trainDFronaldo, testDFronaldo = dfRonaldo.randomSplit([66.7, 33.3], seed=12)

In [7]:  print('The number of images in trainDFmessi is {}'.format(trainDFmessi.toPandas().shape[0]))
         print('The number of images in testDFmessi is {}'.format(testDFmessi.toPandas().shape[0]))
         print('The number of images in trainDFronaldo is {}'.format(trainDFronaldo.toPandas().shape[0]))
         print('The number of images in testDFronaldo is {}'.format(testDFronaldo.toPandas().shape[0]))

         The number of images in trainDFmessi is 18
         The number of images in testDFmessi is 12
         The number of images in trainDFronaldo is 18
         The number of images in testDFronaldo is 12
```

5. To build out our model, we are only interested in creating a single training dataframe with the **36** images, as well as a single testing dataframe with the remaining **24** images. Once we merge the dataframes we can confirm that they are the correct size, as seen in the following screenshot:

```
In [8]:  trainDF = trainDFmessi.unionAll(trainDFronaldo)
         testDF = testDFmessi.unionAll(testDFronaldo)

In [9]:  print('The number of images in the training data is {}' .format(trainDF.toPandas().shape[0]))
         print('The number of images in the testing  data is {}' .format(testDF.toPandas().shape[0]))

         The number of images in the training data is 36
         The number of images in the testing  data is 24
```

There's more...

It may be lost in the process but it is important to note that loading the images into a dataframe was easy, and only took a few lines of code using `sparkdl.readImages`. This showcases the power of the machine learning pipelines that are available with Spark.

See also

To learn more about the `sparkdl` package, visit the following repository:

`https://databricks.github.io/spark-deep-learning/site/api/python/sparkdl.html`

Understanding transfer learning

The rest of this chapter will involve transfer learning techniques; therefore, we will spend this section explaining how transfer learning works within our architecture.

Getting ready

There are no dependencies required for this section.

How to do it...

This section walks through the steps for how transfer learning works:

1. Identify a pre-trained model that will be used as the training methodology that will be transferred to our chosen task. In our case, the task will be in identifying images of Messi and Ronaldo.
2. There are several available pre-trained models that can be used. The most popular ones are the following:
    1. Xception
    2. InceptionV3
    3. ResNet50
    4. VGG16
    5. VGG19
3. The features from the pre-trained convolutional neural network are extracted and saved for a certain set of images over several layers of filtering and pooling.
4. The final layer for the pre-trained convolutional neural network is substituted with the specific features that we are looking to classify based on our dataset.

How it works...

This section explains the methodology of transfer learning:

1. In early chapters, we discuss how machine learning models, and more importantly deep learning models, work best with larger samples for training purposes. In fact, the general motto with deep learning is the more the merrier.

2. However, there are situations when a high volume of data or images is just not available to train a model. It is in these circumstances where we wish to transfer the learning of one field to predict the outcome of a different field. The heavy lifting of extracting features and filtering through layers and layers within a convolutional neural network have already been performed by institutions that have developed many pre-trained models such as InceptionV3 and ResNet50:

    1. InceptionV3 was developed over at Google and has smaller weights than ResNet50 and VGG

    2. ResNet50 uses 50 weight layers

    3. VGG16 and VGG19 have 16 and 19 weight layers respectively

3. Several higher level deep learning libraries such as Keras now come pre-built with these pre-trained networks for a more simplified application by specifying the model name.

There's more...

Determining which pre-trained model works best for the data or image set in question will depend on the image types used. It is always best to try different pre-trained sets and determine which one delivers the best accuracy.

See also

To learn more about the Inception V3 pre-trained model, read the following paper:

```
https://arxiv.org/abs/1409.4842
```

To learn more about the VGG pre-trained models, read the following paper:

```
https://arxiv.org/abs/1409.1556
```

Creating a pipeline for image classification training

We are now ready to build the deep learning pipeline for training our dataset.

Getting ready

The following libraries will be imported to assist with the pipeline development:

- `LogisticRegression`
- `Pipeline`

How to do it...

The following section walks through the following steps for creating a pipeline for image classification:

1. Execute the following script to begin the deep learning pipeline as well as to configure the classification parameters:

```
from pyspark.ml.classification import LogisticRegression
from pyspark.ml import Pipeline

vectorizer = dl.DeepImageFeaturizer(inputCol="image",
                            outputCol="features",
                            modelName="InceptionV3")
logreg = LogisticRegression(maxIter=30,
        labelCol="label")
pipeline = Pipeline(stages=[vectorizer, logreg])
pipeline_model = pipeline.fit(trainDF)
```

2. Create a new dataframe, `predictDF`, that houses the original testing labels as well as the new prediction scores, using the following script:

```
predictDF = pipeline_model.transform(testDF)
predictDF.select('prediction', 'label').show(n =
testDF.toPandas().shape[0], truncate=False)
```

How it works...

The following section explains how the pipeline for image classification is configured for optimal performance:

1. `LogisticRegression` is imported, as it will be the main classification algorithm used to distinguish between Messi and Ronaldo images. `DeepImageFeaturizer` is imported from `sparkdl` to create features based off of the images that will be used as the final input to the logistic regression algorithm.

 It is important to note that the features created from `DeepImageFeaturizer` will be using a pre-trained model based on `InceptionV3`, and assigned a variable of `vectorizer`.

The logistic regression model is tuned to run for a maximum of **30** iterations. Finally, the pipeline ingests both `vectorizer` and `LogisticRegression` variables and fits it into the training dataframe, `trainDF`. `vectorizer` is used to create numeric values out of the images. The output of the `DeepImageFeaturizer` can be seen in the following screenshot:

```
In [10]: from pyspark.ml.classification import LogisticRegression
         from pyspark.ml import Pipeline

         vectorizer = dl.DeepImageFeaturizer(inputCol="image", outputCol="features", modelName="InceptionV3")
         logreg = LogisticRegression(maxIter=30,
                                     regParam=0.05,
                                     elasticNetParam=0.25,
                                     labelCol="label")
         pipeline = Pipeline(stages=[vectorizer, logreg])
         pipeline_model = pipeline.fit(trainDF)

         INFO:tensorflow:Froze 376 variables.
         Converted 376 variables to const ops.
         INFO:tensorflow:Froze 0 variables.
         Converted 0 variables to const ops.
```

2. The test dataframe, `testDF`, is transformed into a new dataframe, `predictDF`, by applying the fitted pipeline model, `pipeline_model`, which creates a new column called **prediction**. We can then compare our **label** column with our **prediction** column, as seen in the following screenshot:

```
In [11]:  predictDF = pipeline_model.transform(testDF)
          predictDF.select('label', 'prediction').show(n = testDF.toPandas().shape[0], truncate=False)

          INFO:tensorflow:Froze 376 variables.
          Converted 376 variables to const ops.
          INFO:tensorflow:Froze 0 variables.
          Converted 0 variables to const ops.
          +-----+----------+
          |label|prediction|
          +-----+----------+
          |0    |0.0       |
          |0    |0.0       |
          |0    |0.0       |
          |0    |0.0       |
          |0    |0.0       |
          |0    |0.0       |
          |0    |0.0       |
          |0    |0.0       |
          |0    |0.0       |
          |0    |0.0       |
          |0    |0.0       |
          |0    |0.0       |
          |1    |1.0       |
          |1    |0.0       |
          |1    |1.0       |
          |1    |1.0       |
          |1    |1.0       |
          |1    |1.0       |
          |1    |1.0       |
          |1    |1.0       |
          |1    |1.0       |
          |1    |1.0       |
          |1    |1.0       |
          |1    |1.0       |
          +-----+----------+
```

There's more...

InceptionV3 is the image classifier model that we used for classifying our images; however, we could have very easily chosen other pre-trained models and compared accuracy within our pipeline.

See also

To learn more about transfer learning, read the following article from the University of Wisconsin:

http://ftp.cs.wisc.edu/machine-learning/shavlik-group/torrey.handbook09.pdf

Evaluating model performance

We are ready to evaluate our model and see how well we can distinguish between Messi and Ronaldo.

Getting ready

Since we will be doing some model evaluation, we will need to import the following library:

- `MulticlassClassificationEvaluator`

How to do it...

The following section walks through the following steps to evaluate model performance:

1. Execute the following script to create a confusion matrix from the `predictDF` dataframe:

    ```
    predictDF.crosstab('prediction', 'label').show().
    ```

2. Calculate an accuracy score based on our 24 test images of Ronaldo and Messi by executing the following script:

    ```
    from pyspark.ml.evaluation import MulticlassClassificationEvaluator

    scoring = predictDF.select("prediction", "label")
    accuracy_score =
    MulticlassClassificationEvaluator(metricName="accuracy")
    rate = accuracy_score.evaluate(scoring)*100
    print("accuracy: {}%" .format(round(rate,2))).
    ```

How it works...

The following section explains how we evaluate the model performance. Take a look at these images:

1. We can convert our dataframe, **predictDF**, into a crosstab to create a confusion matrix. This allows us to understand how many true positives, false positives, true negatives, and false negatives are in our model, as seen in the following screenshot:

```
In [12]: predictDF.crosstab('prediction', 'label').show()

         +----------------+---+---+
         |prediction_label|  0|  1|
         +----------------+---+---+
         |             1.0|  0| 11|
         |             0.0| 12|  1|
         +----------------+---+---+
```

2. At this point, we are ready to calculate how well we did with our model in using the 36 training images to accurately classify the 24 remaining test images of Ronaldo and Messi. From the previous screenshot, it shows that we had 21 accurate classifications out of 24. We had 2 images of Messi misclassified as Ronaldo and only one image of Ronaldo misclassified as Messi. This should come out to an accuracy score of 88%. We can see that the accuracy score from the **MulticlassClassificationEvaluator** also scores our accuracy at 87.5%, as seen in the following screenshot:

```
In [13]: from pyspark.ml.evaluation import MulticlassClassificationEvaluator
         scoring = predictDF.select("prediction", "label")
         accuracy_score = MulticlassClassificationEvaluator(metricName="accuracy")
         print("accuracy: {}" .format(accuracy_score.evaluate(scoring)))

         accuracy: 0.9583333333333334
```

There's more...

While we did end up using accuracy as our benchmark indicator for how well our model performed, we could have just as easily used precision or recall. Additionally, we used the MulticlassClassificationEvaluator for evaluating the accuracy of the model. Since we are dealing with a binary outcome in this specific case for only two types of images for Ronaldo or Messi, we could have also just used a BinaryClassificationEvaluator as seen in the following screenshot:

```
In [14]:  from pyspark.ml.evaluation import BinaryClassificationEvaluator

          binaryevaluator = BinaryClassificationEvaluator(rawPredictionCol="prediction")
          binary_rate = binaryevaluator.evaluate(predictDF)*100
          print("accuracy: {}%" .format(round(binary_rate,2)))

          accuracy: 87.5%
```

We still end up with the same accuracy rate of **87.5%**.

See also

To learn more about MulticlassClassificationEvaluator from the logistic regression function in PySpark, visit the following website:

https://spark.apache.org/docs/2.2.0/ml-classification-regression.html

Fine-tuning model parameters

There is always room for improvement in the accuracy of any model. In this section, we will talk about some of the parameters that can be tweaked to improve our model accuracy score of **87.5%** obtained from the previous section.

Getting ready

This section does not require any new prerequisites.

How to do it...

This section walks through the steps to fine-tune the model.

1. Define a new logistic regression model with additional parameters for `regParam` and `elasticNetParam` as seen in the following script:

```
logregFT = LogisticRegression(
 regParam=0.05,
 elasticNetParam=0.3,
 maxIter=15,labelCol = "label", featuresCol="features")
```

2. Create a new pipeline configured for the newly created model using the following script:

```
pipelineFT = Pipeline(stages=[vectorizer, logregFT])
```

3. Fit the pipeline to the trained dataset, `trainDF`, using the following script:

```
pipeline_model_FT = pipelineFT.fit(trainDF)
```

4. Apply the model transformation to the test dataset, `testDF`, to be able to compare actual versus predicted scores using the following script:

```
predictDF_FT = pipeline_model_FT.transform(testDF)
predictDF_FT.crosstab('prediction', 'label').show()
```

5. Finally, evaluate the new model accuracy rate, `binary_rate_FT`, using the following script:

```
binary_rate_FT = binaryevaluator.evaluate(predictDF_FT)*100
print("accuracy: {}%" .format(round(binary_rate_FT,2)))
```

How it works...

This section explains how the model is fine-tuned:

1. The logistic regression model, `logregFT`, is fine-tuned using both the `regParam` and the `elasticNetParam` parameters. Both parameters correspond to the γ and the α parameters of a logistic regression model. The regularization parameter or `regParam` is used to find a balance between minimizing the loss function and minimizing overfitting the model. The more complex we make the model, the more likely it will overfit and not be generalized, but we will also likely get a lower training error. Additionally, the less complex we make the model, the less likely it will overfit, but the more likely it will have a higher training error.

2. The elastic net parameter or `elasticNetParam` is another regularization technique that is used to combine multiple regularizers, L1 and L2, to minimize overfitting in a model. Additionally, we have decreased our iteration run from 20 to 15 to see if we can achieve a better accuracy score by including regularization and decreasing runs at the same time.

3. Once again, as we did previously in this chapter, we create a pipeline that incorporates our numerical features generated from our images, `vectorizer`, as well our logistic regression model, `logregFT`.

4. The model is then fit on the training data, `trainDF`, and the transformation of the model is applied to the testing data, `testDF`.

5. We can once again compare our actual versus predicted results from the outcome of the model in a crosstab as seen in the following screenshot:

```
In [15]:  logregFT = LogisticRegression(
              regParam=0.05,
              elasticNetParam=0.3,
              maxIter=15,labelCol = "label", featuresCol="features")
          pipelineFT = Pipeline(stages=[vectorizer, logregFT])

          pipeline_model_FT = pipelineFT.fit(trainDF)
```

```
INFO:tensorflow:Froze 376 variables.
Converted 376 variables to const ops.
INFO:tensorflow:Froze 0 variables.
Converted 0 variables to const ops.
```

```
In [16]:  predictDF_FT = pipeline_model_FT.transform(testDF)
          predictDF_FT.crosstab('prediction', 'label').show()
```

```
INFO:tensorflow:Froze 376 variables.
Converted 376 variables to const ops.
INFO:tensorflow:Froze 0 variables.
Converted 0 variables to const ops.
+----------------+---+---+
|prediction_label|  0|  1|
+----------------+---+---+
|             1.0|  0| 11|
|             0.0| 12|  1|
+----------------+---+---+
```

6. We have now only 1 miss-classified image compared to 3 from the previous section. We accomplished this by lowering our maxIter to 15 runs and setting regParam to 0.05 and the elasticNetParam to 0.3.

7. Our new accuracy rate is now at 95.83% as seen in the following screenshot:

```
In [17]:  binary_rate_FT = binaryevaluator.evaluate(predictDF_FT)*100
          print("accuracy: {}%" .format(round(binary_rate_FT,2)))

          accuracy: 95.83%
```

There's more...

Certainly, we have improved our rate from **87.5%** from **95.83%** simply by incorporating specific parameters into our model. Additional fine-tuning and tweaking of our parameters could take place to determine if an accuracy of 100% could be reached for our image classification model.

See also

To learn more about the regularization and elastic net parameters within a logistic regression, visit the following website:

```
https://spark.apache.org/docs/2.2.0/mllib-linear-methods.html#logistic-
regression
```

Other Books You May Enjoy

If you enjoyed this book, you may be interested in these other books by Packt:

Mastering Apache Spark 2.x - Second Edition
Romeo Kienzler

ISBN: 978-1-78646-274-9

- Examine Advanced Machine Learning and DeepLearning with MLlib, SparkML, SystemML, H2O and DeepLearning4J
- Study highly optimised unified batch and real-time data processing using SparkSQL and Structured Streaming
- Evaluate large-scale Graph Processing and Analysis using GraphX and GraphFrames
- Apply Apache Spark in Elastic deployments using Jupyter and Zeppelin Notebooks, Docker, Kubernetes and the IBM Cloud
- Understand internal details of cost based optimizers used in Catalyst, SystemML and GraphFrames
- Learn how specific parameter settings affect overall performance of an Apache Spark cluster
- Leverage Scala, R and python for your data science projects

Apache Spark 2.x Machine Learning Cookbook
Siamak Amirghodsi et al.

ISBN: 978-1-78355-160-6

- Get to know how Scala and Spark go hand-in-hand for developers when developing ML systems with Spark
- Build a recommendation engine that scales with Spark
- Find out how to build unsupervised clustering systems to classify data in Spark
- Build machine learning systems with the Decision Tree and Ensemble models in Spark
- Deal with the curse of high-dimensionality in big data using Spark
- Implement Text analytics for Search Engines in Spark
- Streaming Machine Learning System implementation using Spark

Leave a review - let other readers know what you think

Please share your thoughts on this book with others by leaving a review on the site that you bought it from. If you purchased the book from Amazon, please leave us an honest review on this book's Amazon page. This is vital so that other potential readers can see and use your unbiased opinion to make purchasing decisions, we can understand what our customers think about our products, and our authors can see your feedback on the title that they have worked with Packt to create. It will only take a few minutes of your time, but is valuable to other potential customers, our authors, and Packt. Thank you!

Index

Made in the USA
Columbia, SC
29 August 2018